NH

EUROPEAN INDUSTRY:
PUBLIC POLICY AND
CORPORATE STRATEGY

EUROPEAN INDUSTRY: PUBLIC POLICY AND CORPORATE STRATEGY

Edited by
ALEXIS JACQUEMIN

Professor of Economics,
University of Louvain-la-Neuve
and Senior Fellow at the Centre
for European Policy Studies

CLARENDON PRESS · OXFORD
1984

Oxford University Press, Walton Street, Oxford OX2 6DP

London New York Toronto
Delhi Bombay Calcutta Madras Karachi
Kuala Lumpur Singapore Hong Kong Tokyo
Nairobi Dar es Salaam Cape Town
Melbourne Auckland
and associated companies in
Beirut Berlin Ibadan Mexico City Nicosia

Oxford is a trade mark of Oxford University Press

Published in the United States
by Oxford University Press, New York

British Library Cataloguing in Publication Data
European industry
1. Industry and state—European Economic
Community countries
I. Jacquemin, Alexis
338.94   HD3616.E833
ISBN 0-19-828486-1
ISBN 0-19-828500-0 Pbk

Library of Congress Cataloging in Publication Data
Main entry under title:
European industry.
Bibliography: p.
1. Industry and state—European Economic Community
countries—Congresses.   2. Industrial promotion—
European Economic Community countries—Congresses.
3. European Economic Community countries—Commercial
policy—Congresses.   4. Corporations—European Economic
Community countries—Congresses.   5. Industrial management
—European Economic Community countries—Congresses.
I. Jacquemin, Alex.
HD3616.E833E97 1984   338.94   84-5041
ISBN 0-19-828486-1
ISBN 0-19-828500-0 Pbk

Typeset by Joshua Associates, Oxford
and printed in Great Britain
at the Alden Press, Oxford

Preface

The present book has its origins in a conference entitled 'Western European Priorities' which the Centre for European Policy Studies organized in Brussels as its inaugural event in December 1982. Oxford University Press will shortly publish two other books based on the conference: R. Masera and R. Triffin (eds.), *Europe's Money*, and Michael Emerson (ed.), *Europe's Stagflation*. We hope that together these books will constitute a significant contribution to the discussion of central questions of public policy at a European level, complementing and reinforcing the contributions that the Centre has already begun to make through the *CEPS Papers*.

Although based on the conference, essays in the present book have been updated to take account of more recent events, and some new chapters have been commissioned to fill the gaps that existed in the conference programme. All this has involved heavier editorial responsibilities than were originally envisaged when Professor Jacquemin agreed to chair the study group on industrial policies and external trade, and I should therefore like to take this opportunity to acknowledge the work that he has done in the preparation of the volume.

Neither the contributions of the authors nor the efforts of the editors would however have materialized at all, had it not been for a grant from the Ford Foundation, who in this way, as in others, provided support to a new centre when it was most needed. It is therefore, finally, a particular pleasure to thank the President of the Ford Foundation and his staff for their help.

PETER LUDLOW

Centre for European Policy Studies, Brussels

[15192]

Contents

List of Figures   ix

List of Tables   x

Notes on Contributors   xii

INTRODUCTION: WHICH POLICY FOR INDUSTRY?
Alexis Jacquemin   1

PART I. THE PRESENT PREDICAMENT OF EUROPEAN INDUSTRY AND CURRENT POLICIES

  I. THE CHANGING CONTEXT OF INDUSTRIAL POLICY:
      EXTERNAL AND INTERNAL DEVELOPMENTS
      Jacques Lesourne   13

 II. TRENDS IN INDUSTRIAL POLICY IN THE EC:
      THEORY AND PRACTICE
      Christopher Wilkinson   39

III. EMPLOYMENT AND INDUSTRIAL ASSISTANCE
      David Metcalf   84

 IV. THE LOGIC OF EC COMMERCIAL AND INDUSTRIAL
      POLICY MAKING
      Jean Waelbroeck   99

      STATISTICAL APPENDIX   126

PART II. SECTORAL PATTERNS OF ADJUSTMENT AND INTERVENTION

  V. SECTORAL DEVELOPMENT AND SECTORAL
      POLICIES IN THE EC
      Henk W. de Jong   147

VI. INTRA-INDUSTRY TRADE ADJUSTMENT AND
EUROPEAN INDUSTRIAL POLICIES
Geoff White 172

VII. INDUSTRIAL CHANGE IN EUROPEAN COUNTRIES:
THE EXPERIENCE OF SIX SECTORS
Geoffrey Shepherd 191

VIII. STEEL: A CASE STUDY IN INDUSTRIAL POLICY
Albert Kervyn de Lettenhove 215

IX. THE EUROPEAN INFORMATION TECHNOLOGY
INDUSTRY
Maurice English 227

X. FRENCH INDUSTRIAL STRATEGY IN
SUNRISE SECTORS
Christian Stoffaës 274

PART III. CORPORATE STRATEGY AND THE FUTURE OF EUROPEAN INDUSTRIAL POLICIES

XI. THE MICRO-FOUNDATIONS OF INDUSTRIAL POLICY
Gunnar Eliasson 295

XII. CORPORATE STRATEGIES IN TRANSITION
Henry Ergas 327

XIII. LARGE FIRMS IN THE EUROPEAN CORPORATE
ECONOMY AND INDUSTRIAL POLICY IN THE 1980s
Paul Geroski and Alexis Jacquemin 343

XIV. TOWARDS CONCERTED INDUSTRIAL POLICIES
IN THE EC
Pierre Defraigne 368

List of Figures

5.1 Relationship between percentage service employment and real per capita income — 153

5.2 Relationship between growth of service employment and per capita productivity growth, 1960–79 — 154

5.3 Volume of gross investment in fixed assets in EC, 1958–82 — 157

9.1 Share of market of major computer products in Europe and Japan (excluding IBM) — 230

9.2 Capital and technical co-operation in the computer industry — 232

9.3 Market strengths of major EC-IT companies — 235

9.4 Per cent change in share of world machine tool exports 1981 *vs* 1970 — 237

9.5 Robots: cross relationships—technology agreements, OEM arrangements, etc., among Japanese, American, and European firms — 238

9.6 Projected robot usage worldwide, 1985 — 239

9.7 Estimate of robot population — 239

9.8 Per cent share of West European robot installations by suppliers, 1981–6 — 240

9.9 Lead time of various IC producers *vs* Japan — 242

9.10 Production and consumption of 64-K dynamic RAMs — 243

9.11 Comparison of consumer electronics markets in EC, US, and Japan — 245

9.12 Impact of US telecom deregulation — 254

9.13 European market fragmentation: next generation digital exchange — 255

9.14 Share of world telecom exports — 256

9.15 European telecommunications companies and PTT support — 256

11.1 Activity structure of modern firm — 300

List of Tables

3.1 Spending on selected items of industrial support   85

3.2 Selected characteristics of British industry relevant to intervening to maximize social benefit   92

3.3 Employment change, elasticities of substitution and spending on the Regional Development Grant, by industry   94

A.1 Regional distribution of world gross product at current prices and exchange rates and at constant prices and exchange rates, 1970–80   128

A.2 Annual growth rates of regional gross products at constant prices, 1970–80   129

A.3 Regional distribution of world gross product at prices corresponding to purchasing power parities, 1970–80   129

A.4 Growth rates of regional manufactured value added at constant prices, 1970–8   130

A.5 Growth rates of manufacturing industries, 1960–81   130

A.6 Regional distribution of world manufactured value added at current prices and exchange rates and at constant prices and exchange rates, 1970–8   131

A.7 Regional distribution of world trade in manufactured products in 1970 at current $US (intra-regional trade included)   132

A.8 Regional distribution of world trade in manufactured products in 1970 at current $US (intra-regional trade included)   133

A.9 Regional distribution of world trade in manufactured products in 1970 at current $US (intra-regional trade excluded)   134

A.10 Regional distribution of world trade in manufactured products in 1980 at current $US (intra-regional trade excluded)   135

A.11 Evolution of trade in manufactured products by region, 1970–80 (intra-regional trade excluded)   136

A.12 Industrial value added as a percentage of GDP in the main EC countries, 1970–9   137

A.13 Structure of industrial value added in the main EC countries, 1970–9   138

A.14 Structure of industrial value added in constant prices for
the five main industrial economies, 1970–9   139

A.15 Ratios of Imports/Demand and Exports/Production for
nine sectors in the five main industrial countries, 1970   140

A.16 Ratios of Imports/Demand and Exports/Production for
nine sectors in the main EC countries, 1978   141

A.17 Surpluses and deficits by sector for the five main
economies, 1970–80   142

A.18 Impact on employment of trade in manufactured products
between developed and developing countries, 1976   143

A.19 Average annual rates of change of unit labour costs for
a sample of industrial countries, 1960–81   144

A.20 Transfers and subsidies to industry and commerce in
EC countries, 1973–5   144

A.21 Share of subsidies in gross investment for a few industrial
countries, 1960–77   144

5.1 Total employment and major sector shares in US and EC,
1960–81   150

5.2 Sectoral structures of added value, employment, and
fixed investment in the EC-6   151

5.3 Investment goods in the EC-6, 1970–9   156

5.4 Development phases of a sector: structure and process 160

5.5 The meso-economic policy matrix   165

7.1 Major industrial countries: levels of trade intensity for
selected products, 1960–80   194–5

8.1 Number of blast furnaces and oxygen converters   216

8.2 Employment in the steel industry, December 1982   221

8.3 EC net exports of steel products   224

9.1 Market potential in Western Europe for electronics   229

9.2 Development of the NC machine tool market in EC, US,
and Japan   236

9.3 Japanese VTR exports, 1982   248

9.4 System markets for telecommunications equipment   251

9.5 Comparative assessment of the strengths in information
technology   266

13.1 Country location of the largest 100 firms in the EC:
the number of firms from the largest 100 originating
from various EC countries   359

13.2 Percentage of the top 100 firms in 1980 by industry
and country   361

Notes on Contributors

Pierre Defraigne has been Chef de Cabinet to EC Vice-President Etienne Davignon, Commissioner for Industrial Affairs, Energy, and Research, since 1977. Before that he was a member of the cabinets of EC Commissioners Cheysson, Deniau, and Coppe, and was Head of the Agricultural, Regional, and Social Budgets Section of the Commission of the European Communities.

Gunnar Eliasson is President of the Industrial Institute for Economic and Social Research (IUI), Stockholm, and Associate Professor of Economics, Uppsala University. He was previously Chief Economist of the Federation of Swedish Industries. The author and editor of numerous books and articles, he is currently completing a book on the IUI micro-to-macro model.

Maurice English is at present Head of the European Commission's Information Technology Task Force Intelligence Unit. In addition, he is involved in the preparation of ESPRIT and complementary Community actions respecting telecommunications and other leading-edge IT activities. He was Economic Adviser to the head of the Progressive Conservative Party of Canada and Chief Economist of the Atlantic Provinces Economic Council, subsequent to working in UK industry.

Henry Ergas is Principal Administrator in the Planning and Evaluation Unit of the OECD in Paris, where he is mainly concerned with issues of industrial and structural adjustment. He also teaches industrial strategy at the Ecole Nationale de la Statistique et de l'Administration Economique in Paris.

Paul A. Geroski is Lecturer in Economics at the University of Southampton, Visiting Professor of Economics at the Center for Economic and Legal Studies in Industrial Organization at the Catholic University of Louvain, and Research Fellow at the Centre for European Policy Studies. He is a regular contributor to professional journals and Associate Editor of the *International Journal of Industrial Organization*.

Alexis Jacquemin, an expert on industrial and competition policy, is Professor of Economics at the University of Louvain-la-Neuve, Director of the Center for Economic and Legal Studies in Industrial Organization, and Senior Fellow at the Centre for European Policy Studies. He has published several major works on industrial economic issues and is editor of the *International Journal of Industrial Organization*.

Henk Wouter de Jong is Professor of Economics at the University of Amsterdam, a member of the Dutch Competition Commission, and has participated in several commissions of the Social and Economic Council at The Hague. He has written several books and edited others in the field of industrial organization, dealing mainly with competition, concentration, and industrial sectors.

Albert Kervyn de Lettenhove is Professor of Economics at the University of Louvain. Formerly he was Head of the Economic Planning Office of the Belgian Government (1959–65) and Chairman of the Medium-Term Working Party of the EEC (1969–81).

Jacques Lesourne is Professor of Economics at the Conservatoire National des Arts et Métiers (Paris), former Director of the Interfutures Project at the OECD, and Chairman of the French Economic Association. He is author of several books, including *Economic technique and Industrial management, Cost benefit Analysis, Theory and Applications*, and *Les mille sentiers de l'avenir*.

David Metcalf is Professor of Economics at the University of Kent. Previously he taught at the London School of Economics. He has written extensively on labour market issues, most recently on British special employment measures such as subsidies and short-time working.

Geoffrey Shepherd is Acting Director of the European Research Centre, University of Sussex, where he has been working on a programme of research on comparative Western European industrial performance and policy. He is co-editor (with Françoise Duchêne and Christopher Saunders) of *Europe's Industries: Public and Private Strategies for Change*.

Christian Stoffaës is Deputy Assistant Secretary for Electronics and Information Technology in the French Ministry of Industry and Research and Professor of Industrial Economics at the Institut d'Etudes Politiques. He is the author of various books and articles on economic matters, including *Nationalisations, La Grande Menace Industrielle*, and *The Political Economy of the United States*.

Jean Waelbroeck is Professor at the Free University of Brussels, where he is a member of its Centre for Econometrics and Mathematical Economics. He is also a member of the Catholic University of Louvain Centre for Operations Research and Econometrics and is a Senior Fellow at the Centre for European Policy Studies.

Geoff White is Senior Economic Advisor in the Department of Trade and Industry. He has served in an advisory capacity in the department since 1973, dealing with a variety of issues—from general matters of industrial policy and strategy to more specific questions concerning vehicles, information-technology, and electronics. Before 1973 he worked at the London Business School in the Department of Economic Affairs.

Christopher Wilkinson is Head of the Strategy Division in the European Commission Task Force for Information Technology and Telecommunications. He has also worked on industrial economics, regional financing, and development economics. His contribution to this book was written while he was at the Center for International Affairs, Harvard University.

Unless otherwise indicated, the views expressed in this book are attributable only to the authors in a personal capacity and not to any institution.

Introduction:
Which Policy for Industry?

ALEXIS JACQUEMIN*

I. Industrial policy as a positive response to market imperfections

Industrial policies are at the moment a topic of active debate in Europe, as well as in the United States and Japan.[1] Within the EC there is a widespread agreement on the unsatisfactory performance of our economies and the need for a new industrial policy direction. However, there is such a strong political and ideological tone to this debate that it is difficult to present an objective view of the issues involved. It is precisely the aim of this book to provide a critical and independent analysis of the main factual, methodological, and theoretical aspects of industrial policies.

A general framework for the analysis is to consider that these policies are mainly tools used to affect the speed of the process of resource allocation among and within industrial sectors. This implies that for a variety of reasons the public authorities can be unhappy with the way the market allocates resources and achieves major structural changes. According to the goals pursued by the public authorities, the process of reallocation will be retarded or accelerated, facilitated or impeded.

For example, the national security argument might justify the maintenance of otherwise uneconomical production facilities. Anti-unemployment measures may be needed because labour markets are imperfect: although in a fully employed, neo-classical world, employment subsidies reducing the marginal cost of labour would lead to a distortion of relative factor prices and to a loss of overall efficiency, a case can be made for subsidizing extra jobs in our economies, characterized by large-scale unemployment and real wage restraint.[2] Manpower policies can also reduce the costs of adjustment, hence increasing the speed of allocating human resources. Similarly, economic growth-orientated, science and technological policies can be a useful complement to private R&D programmes when externalities, information failures, and risk aversion could lead to a socially insufficient flow of resources. There is also a case for subsidizing R&D in high technology industries affected by large fixed costs: governmental intervention could enable a domestic firm to be among the 'happy few' constituting an international oligopoly in the field.

* Professor of Economics, University of Louvain-la-Neuve.

According to this approach, industrial policy should not be regarded as just a new name for protectionism, but as a possible positive response to the imperfection of modern markets. It purports to serve as a second-best tool for complementing market mechanisms that are not functioning well—be they capital markets, industrial markets, or markets for scientific and engineering manpower.[3]

But a much wider role than the one of correcting for market distortions can be suggested. A positive industrial policy could supply valuable answers to the new issues raised by various phenomena, such as the continued rise in the cost of economic adjustment and the social resistance to it; the necessities of simultaneously safeguarding social peace (in a society deeply divided by class) and shifting resources out of uncompetitive activities because of the pressure of international economic forces; and the fact that for a wide range of manufacturers, comparative advantage may be relatively malleable instead of rigidly predetermined by national endowments of resources and factors.

This last argument becomes critical today as several economic and political rationales for an industrial policy reflect the view that the government must help domestic industries to respond to the challenges of international competition. Contrasting with the traditional trade theory—treating the determinants of national factor endowments and national technological developments as exogenous, it is argued that in most sectors comparative advantage rests on relative capital endowments, and these result from accumulated investment.

Government policies can then alter the process of both physical and human accumulation over time and strategically modify in their favour the often asymmetric oligopolistic equilibria in the international markets.

Recent models[4] have explored the value of public intervention in affecting the result of international rivalry between domestic and foreign sellers in the presence of imperfect competition. They illustrate the complexity of the strategic game at policy level when instruments, like commitments and threats, play a role, and question some of the results of conventional trade theory that assumes competitive markets.

The classic illustration for this argument is the Japanese industrial policy. Vice-Minister Ojimi, of the Ministry of International Trade and Industry (MITI), twelve years ago made an often quoted statement which summarizes this perfectly:

The MITI decided to establish in Japan industries which require intensive employment of capital and technology, industries that in consideration of comparative cost of production should be the most inappropriate for Japan . . . From a short-run, static viewpoint, encouragement of such industries would seem to conflict with economic rationalism. But, from a long-range viewpoint, these are precisely the industries where income elasticity of demand is high, technological progress is rapid, and labor productivity rises fast . . . According to Napoleon and Clausewitz, the secret of a successful strategy is the concentration of fighting power on the main battle ground; fortunately, owing to good luck and wisdom spawned by necessity, Japan has been able to concentrate its scant capital in strategic industries.[5]

According to various authors,[6] such a voluntary policy, based on a national consensus and a close relationship between government and enterprises, does indeed represent successful policy implementation and a substantial contribution to the positive growth of Japan's real income.

II. The failures of industrial policy

Contrasting with the former approach, it may be argued that far from supplementing the market process, industrial policy tends to preclude it; that modern industrial structures generate enough competitive forces spontaneously to guarantee a reasonably efficient allocation of resources; that public choices for industrial redevelopment are not self-evident and that exact criteria are lacking; and that the steady expansion of government in economic affairs will lead to a 'corporatist' system with politicized economic decisions and a decline of individual intiatives. The best policy would then be to abandon any form of industrial policy and to improve directly the functioning of capital and labour markets.

For example, Victoria Curzon-Price argues that 'negative' industrial policies aiming to slow down the process of structural change or to keep declining sectors alive must be rejected: 'First, the damage to the rest of the economy is greater the longer a stricken industry is allowed to prolong the agony and secondly, it is not obvious that prolonged adjustment is really any easier to bear than quick surgery.'[7]

'Positive' industrial policies intended to accelerate structural change have also been criticized. Firstly, the government is not likely to get the mixture of industries to axe and ones to encourage quite right. Secondly, replacing government for the markets as allocator of the nation's resources raises the familiar question of the link between economic systems and individual liberty.

The Japanese experience as well as the positive role of MITI have also been questioned. According to R. Caves,[8] 'It is easy to forget that Japanese consumers have paid heavy implicit taxes to support this developmental effort, and that some short-run misallocations of resources clearly occurred.' A supplementary argument is that the differences between Japan and our industrialized countries are so great that a borrowing of social organization between them seems impossible.

The authors of this book have more or less relied on this normative debate. But instead of trying to reach general agreement on the optimal degree of public intervention, they have mainly discussed the principles that have guided current industrial policies, the instruments for carrying them out, the decision processes, the economic and political experience in Europe, and the actual priorities. Since, for good or evil, national industrial policies take place and will continue to take place in European countries, how can we limit the negative effects of such policies, which are often a substitute for intra-EC trade barriers, and how can we improve their coordination at EC level? More ambitiously, can an appropriate policy for European industry help to transform political demands for protection into demands for competitive adjustment?

III. Three types of industrial policy

The contributions collected in this book view this question from various angles. In order to classify them, it is useful to distinguish three (non-mutually exclusive) types of industrial policy, according to their level of aggregation.

The *macro-economic* orientation is the least interventionist and leaves the functioning of industries and firms to the market game. Industrial policy, if any, is then conceived as a policy to improve the general framework within which producer activities and consumer choices take place, and to facilitate an automatic process of industrial adjustment. Such an approach requires an infrastructure of quality, a professionally adapted labour force, accessibility of capital and credit, and a fiscal system which is not opposed to economic rationality. Hence, the proponents of what I called 'market industrial policy' trust that spontaneous competitive forces lead to a price system which emits correct signals and that economic agents react correctly to them. This implies that if the macro-economic environment is 'right', there is no justification for a specific industrial policy.

At a second stage, *sectoral* policies are based on the view that the dynamics of competition are multidimensional; that inter-industry variations are important; that price flexibility will depend upon the characteristics of each market structure;[9] and that without clear micro-economic foundations, macro-economic policies can be incompatible with the effective process of adjustment taking place in real markets. Sectoral policies aimed at certain industries are then justified when market imperfections or 'market failure', such as strong externalities, affect specific industries, e.g. high-technology industries. The precise reasons for the market imperfection or the market failures must then be identified and a policy designed to solve the specific problem directly. Industrial policy is then viewed as being able to provide non-market mechanisms that improve the response given by the market forces existing in the relevant industry.

At a third stage, a *micro-economic* industrial policy can lead government to develop various forms of actions directed towards specific companies or industrial groups. One basis for this approach is the growing importance of the analysis of intra-industry differences in structure and performance, together with development of the notion of a 'strategic group' of firms and intra-industry mobility.[10] A result of this research is that strategic groups, not industries, respond differently to the same market constraint,[11] so industrial policy must take into account this heterogeneity of response. Policies specially directed towards foreign firms, small business, or financial holdings operating in a given industry are a clear illustration of this. The multiple forms of large business/government relations existing in Europe is another. According to an outside observer, 'despite their differences, France, Germany, and Japan believe that government is the senior member of the business/government partnership.'[12] This author then suggests how to develop a better connection between the various corporate strategies and government policies. Not only can industrial policy give domestic firms a better environment by promoting training, investment, and research; it can also develop joint strategies where interactions between large transnational corporations and large national governments are explicitly recognized. Trade negotiations, international transfer of technology, or international joint ventures are, in this view, less explained by the neo-classical model of international trade than by considering elements of game theory, industrial organization, and managerial decision-making. Today several authors even argue that it will help to postulate that countries, like companies, have 'portfolios' of businesses and industries. 'They can influence not only the mix in the portfolio at any time, but also the rate of new business development, the redeployment of human and capital resources to growth sectors, and the withdrawal of those same resources from declining sectors.'[13]

As the reader will notice, the papers presented in this book are loosely ordered according to the former classification. After an examination of the present predicament of the overall European economy and of current industrial policies, the sectoral pattern of adjustment, its process, and its organizational structure in varying circumstances is critically studied. Corporate strategies adopted in a hostile environment are then evaluated and the internal and external constraints met by the European corporations are identified.

IV. Possible Community-level actions

This set of research and discussions leads to several possible actions at the Community level.

Until the crisis, one can say that European industrial policy, if any, has complemented anti-trust policy in favouring the realization of an integrated market. In most cases, the action of the Commission has been 'counter-interventionist', trying to avoid excessive intervention from the member states.

At this level, a constructive European policy could still be developed by offering better information on the Common Market as a whole (operating as a substitute for the information that would be provided by a fully competitive capital market) and by reducing the uncertainties due to the diversity and variability of national policies. European authorities could also encourage efforts at consensus-building among business, governments, and labour. They could limit national protection measures; avoid permanent subsidies (recognizing that quick surgery may sometimes be more effective and less costly than gradual medication); and implement a coordinated policy for the EC as a whole—prohibiting national policies intended to capture 'beggar-my-neighbour' gains and helping national governments to resist lobbying.

The Community could also develop a more voluntary strategy. The basic idea is that the process of an ever-increasing integration has gradually been slowed down by fragmentation of the internal market due to growing public intervention in the national economies. This trend has discouraged the creation of European companies and groupings, and has weakened our industry's ability to meet the challenges posed by the present crisis. European industry is undeniably handicapped on the international markets by the fact that measures to assist firms are taken in a national framework, without any concerted action at Community level. The Community, as such, has virtually no instrument at present for promoting either exports or external investments. Furthermore, the firm organized on a European scale is often treated with suspicion by governments reluctant to afford it the benefits of their various industrial policy instruments: financing R&D aid, public contracts, norms and standards, etc. Thus, such European-scale organization which ought to be a considerable asset in the Common Market, in fact turns out to be a handicap. To alter this it could be proposed that an element of 'Community preference' be added in all cases where industrial development involves the participation of the public authorities.

This would not mean a move towards deliberate protectionism at Community level. Rather, it suggests that officials of the European Community—valuing the political solidarity of the EC—realize that today selective, supranationally supervised, debated, and negotiated agreements could be a second-best policy when compared with a retreat to generalized national protectionism which could cause disintegration both of the European Community and the GATT system. Economic theory suggests that the 'best' industrial policy would involve dismantling the vast majority of measures currently going on in the name of industrial policy and the strict enforcement of anti-trust rules. But under realistic conditions of discontinuous jumps and shocks (considered by the actors involved as exogeneous) with increasing structural unemployment, there is a need for constructive European industrial policies to help the Community reinforce its identity and move with solidarity towards a situation where markets can work better.

Such an orientation could also reduce the instability of international agreements with our North American and Japanese partners and limit disputes over trade and industries among Western nations by presenting a coordinated position on the international scene and by facilitating the implementation of these agreements in the whole Common Market. This issue is crucial, as it is well-known that disagreements in the realm of economic policy have wider impact upon political relations and attitudes, especially with regard to industrial and trade problems.

This more voluntary strategy could also help the EC to face more frankly the inherent danger of a clash between regional and world welfare. When the viewpoint is that of the authorities of one country or an association of countries, only a subset of agents counts in the welfare; foreign consumers' surpluses and foreign-owned firms' profits do not matter.

However, an international coordination requires a much more adequate institutional structure in which to explore these issues. According to many observers, the situation in the United States is not very satisfying. Agencies responsible for procurement, credit, tax, labour, tariff, anti-trust, and trade policies jealously guard their bureaucratic territories,[14] so that the development of a coherent industrial policy presents even more of a political than an analytical challenge. The situation is worse in the EC, where not only is there no recognized focal point to elaborate a coherent action towards a common industrial purpose,[15] but where creating a consensus among the member states is an extraordinarily cumbersome procedure. It is therefore not surprising that without institutional reforms, the potential for pursuing coordinated actions towards industry at the level of the Atlantic Alliance appears very weak.

Finally, it has to be mentioned that in recent publications[16] several European authors have argued that it is necessary to combine industrial and trade policies, in order to elaborate deliberate external protectionism at Community level while maintaining competition within the

Community. Among the arguments, it is stated that labour in Europe and the US is priced at an artificially high level; that all newly industrialized countries (NICs) pursue policies that concentrate development on a limited number of sectors which are subsidized at every level: infrastructure, capital, and the export products themselves, plus protection of the home-market; that the most vigorous and successful example of industrial policy, that of Japan, is certainly heavily protectionist; and that the Community as a whole must conceive itself to be in what amounts to a developmental phase of industrial restructuring. According to this view, anti-dumping duties, selective quotas, and crisis cartels, must be included among the tools of industrial policy; higher concentration and mergers must be promoted at the EC level; and 'picking-the-winners' strategies must be promoted.

The authors of this book have rejected such a view. Instead of a drastic shift towards more protectionism, they believe it is necessary to maintain our decentralized and open economic system, founded on the willingness to take risks, to encourage mobility of resources and creativity. This view does not exclude occasional and temporary protectionism when based on selective and widely debated arguments. It also implies a stronger solidarity between member states, expressed in more powerful common social and regional policies, which are the mechanisms capable of redistributing gains in efficiency.

Notes and Sources

[1] For an analysis of the European situation, see for example J. Pinder (ed.), *National Industrial Strategies and the World Economy*, Allanheld, New Jersey, 1981; V. Curzon-Price, *Industrial Policies in the European Community*, Trade Policy Research Center, Macmillan, London, 1981 and A. Jacquemin, 'Industrial Policies and the Community', in P. Coffey (ed.), *Main Economic Policy Areas of the EEC*, M. Nijhoff, The Hague, 1983. Various aspects of the more recent debate in the US appear in M. and S. Wachter (eds.), *Towards a New U.S. Industrial Policy?*, University of Pennsylvania Press, Philadelphia, 1983, and in L. Tyson and J. Zysman, *American Industry in International Competition: Government Policies and Corporate Strategies*, Cornell University Press, Ithaca, 1983. The Japanese approach and its evolution are examined by, among others, M. Shinohara, *Japanese-Type Industrial Policy*, paper presented at the International Symposium on Industrial Policies for the 80s, OECD, Madrid, 1980; J. Chalmers, *MITI and the Japanese Miracle: the Growth of Industrial Policy, 1925–75*, Stanford University Press, Stanford, 1982; and General Accounting Office, *Industrial Policy: Japan's Flexible Approach*, Report to the Chairman by the Comptroller General, Joint Economic Committee, GAO/10-82-32, Washington DC, 23 June 1982.

[2] See R. Layard and S. Nickell, 'The Case for Subsidizing Extra Jobs', *Economic Journal*, September 1980.

[3] See, for example, J. Pinder, op. cit.

[4] For example, M. Itoh and Y. Ono, 'Tariffs, Quotas and Market Structure', *Quarterly Journal of Economics*, No. 97, May 1982, and B. Spencer and J. Brander, 'International R&D Rivalry and Industrial Strategy', *Review of Economic Studies*,

October 1983. See also M. Kierzkowski (ed.), *Monopolistic Competition and International Trade*, Oxford University Press, 1984.
[5] OECD, *The Industrial Policy of Japan*, Paris, 1972.
[6] For example, J. Chalmers, op. cit., and A. Singh, *Third World Industrialization: Industrial Strategies and Policies in the 1980's*, mimeo, Department of Applied Economics, Cambridge University, 1983.
[7] V. Curzon-Price, op. cit., p. 120. It is interesting to note that A. L. Hillman has proposed a model where protective responses for declining industries are considered when the authorities, rather than seeking social welfare objectives, pursue their own self-interest motives to maximize political support. He concludes that in this case a declining industry will continue to decline and that the authorities may respond either way with respect to the rate of the industry's decline! See Hillman, 'Declining Industries and Political Support Protectionist Motives', *American Economic Review*, No. 5, December 1982.
[8] R. Caves, review of the Chalmers' book, *Journal of Economic Literature*, vol. xxi, March 1983.
[9] A recent OECD study, under the direction of D. Encaoua (1983) and using industrial data for five OECD countries (Canada, Japan, UK, US, and Sweden), concludes that the degree of concentration and of uncertainty of demand negatively affect the degree of price flexibility, while the degree of openness to international trade has a positive effect. See *Flexibilité Cyclique des Prix et Inflation*, Paris, June 1983.
[10] See mainly R. Caves and M. Porter, 'From Entry Barriers to Mobility Barriers', *Quarterly Journal of Economics*, No. 91, 1977. For a recent econometric study of the specificity of the large French industrial groups, see D. Encaoua and A. Jacquemin, 'Organizational Efficiency and Monopoly Power: The Case of French industrial Groups', *European Economic Review*, 19 September 1982.
[11] M. P. Donsimoni and V. Leoz-Arguelles, 'Strategic Groups: An Application to Foreign and Domestic Firms in Spain', in P. Geroski and A. Jacquemin (eds.), 'Symposium on Industrial Organization and International Competition', *Recherches Economiques de Louvain*, No. 3–4, 1981.
[12] B. Scott, 'Can Industry Survive the Welfare State?', *Harvard Business Review*, September–October 1982.
[13] Ibid., p. 75. According to R. Reich ('Why the U.S. Needs an Industrial Policy', *Harvard Business Review*, January–February 1982, p. 75) 'as a theory industrial policy is closer to the strategic planning models used by many companies than to traditional macro- or microeconomics.' A recent article by R. Neilsen ('Should a Country move toward International Strategic Market Planning?', *California Management Review*, vol. xxv, January 1983) presents an interesting review of the main arguments for and against a country moving towards an industrial policy intended to help domestic businesses establish or improve positions in international markets. His very tentative conclusion is that some international strategic planning by government is a logical extension of large multibusiness and multinational corporate strategic market planning.
[14] See Reich, op. cit., p. 80. According to Scott (op. cit., p. 83), the government should make the Commerce Department the centre for industrial policy, broaden its powers, and change its name to the Department of Industry, Trade, and Commerce (ITC)!
[15] The creation of a 'European Industrial Centre', grouping people from industry, administration, and university to provide a forum for discussion and coordination, was proposed several years ago (see A. Jacquemin, *Economie Industrielle Européenne*, 2nd edition, Dunod, Paris, 1979). It is suggested again in a report to the European Parliament by M. Albert and R. Ball (*Towards European*

Economic Recovery in the 1980's, report presented to the European Parliament, working documents 83–4, European Communities, July 1983).

[16] See, for example, W. Hager, 'Industrial Policy in an Enlarged Community', in J. Giraô (ed.), *Southern Europe and the enlargement of the EEC*, Economia, Lisbon, 1982, and, for a French view, J. M. Jeanneney, *Pour un Nouveau Protectionnisme*, Seuil, Paris, 1978.

PART I

THE PRESENT PREDICAMENT OF EUROPEAN INDUSTRY AND CURRENT POLICIES

13 - 38

I

The Changing Context of Industrial Policy: External and Internal Developments

JACQUES LESOURNE*

Ten years ago, most OECD governments would have claimed that the very concept of a national industrial policy was meaningless. The governments had to ensure the maintenance of the three basic equilibria (full employment, constancy of domestic nominal prices, balance-of-payments equilibrium) to manage the welfare state and to correct market imperfections. But the evolution of industrial structures was not a concern for them, and they did not have to interfere, either at the national or international level, with the free competition of firms on the markets. Of course, such a claim did not strictly correspond to reality, but the interventions were on the whole limited.

At the beginning of the 'eighties, both official doctrines and current practices have deeply changed. Industrial policies have become a national preoccupation in many developed countries, even in those traditionally opposed to government intervention. Why? Because of low growth, increasing unemployment, fierce international competition, and the decline of some industrial sectors, almost any European would reply. But such an answer has to be looked at more precisely if we want to understand more deeply the new context in which industrial policies are discussed. Therefore, this chapter will try to describe the main underlying trends which shape this context. In the first part it will analyse how the European economies are now caught between the external pressures coming from the changes in the international economic system and the internal pressures and rigidities resulting from their autonomous evolution. In the second part it will consider the recent transformations in European industry, putting into evidence the similarities and differences between the main EC countries. This diagnosis will lead, in the third and last part, to a presentation of new demands in favour of industrial policies and to a discussion of some of the issues raised by these demands.

* J. Lesourne, Professor of Economics, Conservatoire National des Arts et Métiers, Paris.

I. European economies: between external pressures and internal demands

Since the beginning of the 1970s European economies have been progressively caught between two types of forces: external, as the world economic system has become more and more multipolar and interdependent, and internal, as rigidities have increased with reinforcement of the social oligopoly and new aspirations have generated additional demands. As a consequence, the economic context within which European industry operates has been fundamentally altered.

I.1. Towards a multipolar and interdependent international economic system

After the Second World War the United States was in a position to regulate the world economy. Through their support to free-trade development, technology transfers, and international capital flows, they contributed to European reconstruction and to Japan's take-off. But the very success of these policies within the OECD, and the growing importance of some Third World economies have deeply transformed the structure of the world's economic system. Since the beginning of the 1970s American economic policies, though still having a major influence on the other economies, have no longer been able to generate a co-ordination of economic policies throughout the OECD world, while they have to master much more difficult internal evolution in the US. Several centres of economic power have progressively emerged:—Japan, whose share of the world gross product is regularly increasing,—the EC, whose intra-trade represents approximately half of its member countries' foreign trade,—oil-producing countries, which control a major scarce resource,—newly industrialized countries, which until recently experienced extremely high growth rates of their industrial value added,—Eastern European countries, which have developed their trade with Western Europe. In other words, the world economic system has become more and more multipolar, though it would be misleading to give this term the meaning it has when applied to the geopolitical situation in 1750, 1825, or 1935.

The Statistical Appendix on pages 126-44 illustrates some features of this evolution. Table A.2 confirms that throughout the 1970-80 decade, the GDP growth rates have been higher in Japan, the parts of Asia in rapid development, Latin America, North Africa, and the Middle East than in the EC or the US. Tables A.1 and A.3 propose three complementary pictures of the evolution of the world gross product distribution: the first established with current prices and exchange rates, the second with constant prices and exchange rates, and the third with prices corresponding to purchasing power parities.

In all three cases the share is decreasing for the US economy and increasing for Japan and most of the regions in the developing world. Tables A.4 and A.5 exhibit similar patterns for industrial value added. These progressive transformations in the distribution of economic activities have made the evolution of the world economy far less predictable. Just to give an example, the increase in the real price of crude oil would have been much smoother throughout the 1970s if the supply had continued to be managed by the majors. Only the weakening of American power made it possible for the oil-producing countries to gain control over their own resources and introduce a new suppliers' pricing policy.

But simultaneously the world economic system has become more and more interdependent. The progression was regular during the 1960s; during the five years preceding the first oil-shock the ratio of current exchanges to world gross product increased from 12 to 14 per cent; with the first oil-shock it jumped to 20 per cent; and the second oil shock induced a further increase. Over the decade 1970–80, this growing interdependence transformed the sectoral structure and the geographic patterns of international exchanges.[1]

As far as the sectoral structure is concerned, the major features are the obvious increase in the value of energy trade, the growing importance of invisibles (a consequence of many countries' indebtedness and of the internationalization of production), the relative decline of trade in primary products, the development of exchanges in chemical and metal products (especially electronic and transport equipment), and the lack of dynamism of trade in other industrial sectors (e.g. textiles).

As for the geographic patterns, the main fact is the significant decline of the share of market economies—from 75.9 per cent of current operations in 1967 to 70.8 per cent in 1980. A similar decrease can be observed for socialist economies (8.3 per cent in 1967 to 6.2 per cent in 1980), the beneficiaries being evidently the Third World. Tables A.9 and A.10 of the Statistical Appendix show that the trends are identical for manufactured products. (These tables are interesting because intra-regional trade is excluded, an essential for understanding the EC situation.) From 1970 to 1980 the share of the US, Canada, and EC in world exports of manufactured products decreased from 62.3 per cent to 53.9 per cent. During the same period Japan's share increased from 12.5 per cent to 15.3 per cent and the LDC's (less developed countries) from 8.5 per cent to 11.6 per cent. Tables A.7 and A.8 (which do not exclude intra-regional trade) illustrate the rapid development of South–South trade: though still modest, within ten years it has jumped from 1.33 per cent to 2.39 per cent of international trade in manufactured products.

A more interdependent economic system may, of course, be profitable to many countries, since it enables a more efficient allocation of scarce resources. But in a multi-polar world with political tensions and conflicting economic policies, for European economies it is also a source of vulnerability and of external pressures: pressures on the rate of growth, due to the high elasticity of imports to GDP and to the fierce competition on export markets; pressures on the domestic price stability, due to the increase of international prices; pressures on production structure, due to the differences in inputs, relative prices, and the discrepancies in demand growth rates from one sector to another.

However, it is not sufficient to explain the economic outlook of the 1980s by changes in the world economic system. Internal evolutions within the western industrial societies have also played a major role (for instance in the behaviour of the US economic system, which in its turn has influenced the operation of the world economic system) and have, to a large extent, contributed to the very difficult position of the European economies.

I.2. The social oligopoly and changes in aspirations

We have coined the term 'social oligopoly' to characterize a social structure in which each socio-economic group has organized itself to negotiate with the other groups and with the government. Not only industrial workers and peasants, but also retailers, physicians, car owners, telephone users, etc., are now represented by permanent administrative structures. Though such a phenomenon differs in intensity from one European country to another, its importance cannot be underestimated. It tends to reinforce individual demands for security and collective advantages while repressing demands for autonomy and diversity; it tries to transfer the determination of many economic parameters from the economic market (which confronts demands and supplies, whatever their origin) to the political system (which gives preference to demands strongly articulated by pressure groups); it multiplies rigidities in input reallocations; and it contributes to an evolution of wages, labour costs, and even sometimes output prices independent from market situations. The reinforcement of the social oligopoly was already noticeable at the end of the 1960s and is certainly one of the factors explaining the rise in unemployment, the increase in inflation rates, and the decline in capital productivity which preceded the first oil-shock.

If the reinforcement of the social oligopoly appears to be a natural consequence of the post-war growth period—at least in continental EC countries—the diagnosis is much more delicate for the changes in aspirations. Not only the origin, but even the content and the depth of such changes may be debated. Since a discussion of these issues is obviously out of the scope of this chapter, we shall limit ourselves here to the following conjectural statement: over the last fifteen years, progressive changes in aspirations have occurred in Europe's middle-class youth—though the various groups have experienced them with varying degrees of intensity, and the new aspirations often coexist, in a more or less conflicting way, with former ones. These aspirations are centred on a search for liberty in any of the social roles which an individual plays and on a strong desire to take roots within small groups with rich interpersonal relationships. As a consequence, many of the motivations on which firms base their actions to stimulate productivity increases have been eroded, while managers and politicians have to face many new demands concerning work autonomy, environmental protection, and geographical employment stability.

Therefore, one could say that European societies have now become a mixture of three democracies: the official democracy of parliaments, governments, and local authorities; the corporate democracy of the social oligopoly, which is widely considered as legitimate; and the spontaneous democracy of individuals or small groups trying to express their own demands directly. Between these three democracies the game is unended, and one of its consequences is the existence of internal pressures and rigidities afflicting European economies. Price indexation, lack of flexibility in labour costs, transformation of labour into a fixed factor, increase in the cost of any exchange with the physical environment, and development of the informal economy are just a few examples of such forces. In conjunction with external pressures, they constrain the evolution of European economies.

I.3. The new economic context for European industry

As a consequence of these underlying factors, since the beginning of the 1970s, European industry has been progressively confronted with a totally new economic context. Let us try to describe briefly its five main characteristics:

(i) The GDP growth rate has not only significantly decreased,[2] but it has become much more irregular and very difficult to forecast. The first oil-shock made an inevitable recession more serious, while it reinforced the inflation process already going on. Budget deficits in OECD countries, the demand for equipment from OPEC countries, and the permanence (through increased indebtedness) of the NICs' growth made possible a limited recovery of the Western economies. But the softness of energy policies made these economies vulnerable to a second oil-shock and to its negative impact on growth rates and inflation. The following recession has then been exacerbated by the need to fight inflation, by the increase in real interest rates, and by the decline in imports demand from both the oil-producing countries (because of the evolution of oil prices induced by the drop in oil demand) and the newly industrialized countries (because of their level of indebtedness). At the end of 1982 the growth prospects for the remaining part of the decade appear highly uncertain.

(ii) The rate of unemployment has steadily increased; e.g. the 1973 and 1980 figures are 2.6 per cent and 6.3 per cent for France, 0.9 per cent and 3.1 per cent for Germany, and 3.2 per cent and 7.3 per cent for the United Kingdom. Three types of mechanisms seem to interfere in this growth of unemployment: the Keynesian mechanism (firms do not recruit because of insufficient sales prospects) which has been at work especially in 1974/75 and since 1979; the classical mechanism (firms do not recruit because the relative level of marginal cost of labour is too high); and the adaptation mechanism (jobs are constantly created and destroyed because of the changes in productive structures, but the new jobs require different capabilities). The unemployment situation has increased European industrial firms' difficulty in getting rid of labour in cases of necessity, and therefore has made them more and more reluctant to recruit staff.

(iii) The inflation rate was also definitely higher from 1973 to 1980 than from 1960 to 1973. The figures for the two periods being, for instance, 9.9 per cent and 4.6 per cent for France and 4.3 and 3.8 per cent for Germany. High inflation rates have several major impacts on industrial firms: since accounting is in nominal terms, they make a sound judgement in real terms more difficult; since they differ from one country to another, and since exchange rates often only adapt after a considerable lag, they induce huge fluctuations in external competitiveness; since they are frequently associated with negative real interest rates and rigid real labour costs, they favour labour-saving investment more than capacity investment. This evolution, however, has to a large extent been reversed in the last year with the decline in inflation rates and the occurrence of strongly positive real interest rates.

(iv) A crisis of the Welfare State is noticeable in all western countries, not only because the rise in demand for the corresponding services makes the cost burden less and less bearable by national budgets, but also because the corresponding tax system generates perverse effects in the present economic situation. In some countries for instance, the increase in real labour costs in recent years is more a consequence of rises in social taxes than of augmentations in direct wages.

(v) Finally, European industry has to face pressures for structural adjustment as strong as during the 1960s, but reduced growth, social rigidities, and new demands make the adjustment process much more painful. Technical progress, evolution of demand, changes in domestic relative prices, development of new competitors often having significant comparative advantages, existence of learning curves which privilege the first successful innovator, and government micro-economic policies remain as before some of the most important factors which compel firms to adapt in difficult conditions to remain profitable.

This new context explains to a large extent the present situation of European industry. But to analyse the governments' concern for industrial policy, we have to examine more closely the industrial evolution of the main EC countries.

II. EC countries industrial evolution: similarities and differences

Nothing is more difficult than to describe the industrial evolution of a country or a region, since the economic analyses of the sectors generally considered have two major deficiencies: they do not take into consideration the existence of industrial groups (often transnational corporations), which are the real strategical units pursuing consistent projects; and they give the impression that sectors are at the same time homogenous and comparable, when they are in fact aggregates of activities confronted with widely differing market and production conditions. We shall try to keep in mind these deficiencies in the following analysis, which is to a large extent based on research by Interfutures and CEPII.[3]

To understand the situation of European industry, two broad factors have to be considered first: the trends in technological change and the major industrial evolutions at the world level. It will then be possible to examine similarities and differences in adaptation of industrial structures within the main EC economies. To complement this approach in national terms, however, it is useful to review briefly the changing role of multinational corporations. This will help us to formulate a diagnosis on the EC industrial prospects.

II.1. Trends in technological change

The great technological adventures which are reshaping our industrial future are well known.

First, the electronic complex—which includes informatics, telecommunications, and plant and office automation—is in the process of reorganizing almost all industrial activities as the steam engine did at the dawn of the nineteenth century. It changes production processes, saves labour, modifies existing products and relative costs, and gives birth to a variety of new equipment goods for firms and households. The rapid decline in hardware costs opens huge technical possibilities, the adoption of which will depend on software costs and on information value for users. Though its long-term impact on the level of unemployment is debatable,[4] it alters the professional content of many jobs and changes the relative scarcities of many professional abilities.

Second is the new development in energy production and conversion. The main aspects of the industry are the production of nuclear

electricity, the growing share of electricity in industrial energy consumption, the replacement of fuel-oils by coal, the necessity of energy
saving, the search for off-shore oil, and the take-off (often only at
the research level) of future renewable energy sources, like solar energy,
breeders, biomass, and fusion.

In third place comes biotechnologies. Though their role may not be
essential until the end of the century, major industrial groups have to
take positions now in order to be competitive within ten or twenty
years.

Fourth is the production of new materials (plastics, ceramics, etc.).
According to specialists, these will be conceived to meet a priori
requirements, creating a revolution that will change the whole industrial
procedure with respect to materials.

Finally, we have ocean and space.

To sustain technological competition with Japanese and American
industries is obviously a formidable task for European firms, especially
in the context of the major industrial evolutions now occurring at the
world level.

II.2. Major industrial evolutions at the world level

These evolutions shed some light on the structural non-adaptation of
European industry. Their main features are the following:

(i) In OECD economies the decline in the rate of growth of manufacturing industries started as early as 1967, spreading to the
south after 1975 and to the east after 1978.[5] Simultaneously,
the fluctuations around the trend have become more and more
significant.

(ii) While all sectors have been affected by these two phenomena,
the intensity differs from one sector to another: the range in
growth rate between the sectors with the highest (chemical
industry) and the lowest (textiles) rates diminishes; the food
industry maintains a smooth evolution and is the least affected by
the crisis; contrarily, the metal and steel industry experiences not
only a sharp decrease in its growth rate, but bigger and bigger
fluctuations.

(iii) Within whole agro-chemical sectors, the most severely hit are the
products which had rather high growth rates during the 1960s
(basic chemical products, organic chemistry, plastics and fibres,
paints), while the products which had previously moderate or
low growth rates are less affected (fats, leather and footwear,
clothing, fertilizers, sugar products, beverages, animal foods).

(iv) The most remarkable upheavals occur within the metallic sectors. Shipbuilding, machine-tools, public works equipment,

boiler-making, and electrical appliances are confronted with a huge drop in their growth rates. On the contrary, household electronics, measuring instruments, computers, telecommunication equipment, watch-making, and electronic components maintain high rates of growth or are only mildly affected.

These changes in industrial trends at the world level have had a destabilizing effect on European industry, since many firms have not perceived the implications of these structural transformations early enough and some countries have persisted in massively investing in heavy industries with limited world demand prospects at the very moment these industries are taking-off in some LDCs. Simultaneously, investment in new high-technology industries, like electronics, have not been sufficient to compensate for other sectors' difficulties.

II.3. Industrial adaptation within the main EC economies

To understand the industrial evolution of the main EC economies (Germany, France, and the UK), a comparison with their two main competitors (the US and Japan) is a necessity. The five countries together are responsible for almost 40 per cent of world trade in manufactured products.

The first important features of the 1970s is the growing inter-nationalization of manufacturing activities. Tables A.15 and A.16 of the Statistical Appendix show the jumps from 1970 to 1978 in the ratios of imports to domestic demand and of exports to national production:

	I/DD (%)		E/NP (%)	
	1970	*1978*	*1970*	*1978*
US	5.9	10.4	6.4	9.4
FRG	12.9	16.3	17.7	23.1
France	15.6	20.7	16.7	23.6
UK	20.6	30.3	23.3	31.6
Japan	3.1	3.3	8.1	11.7

The only divergent figure of the above list is the limited increase of manufactured imports on the Japanese market.

A second interesting aspect concerns the respective positions of the five main economies. Over the whole 1967–80 period, Japan has been able to maintain a surplus in its exchanges with the zone constituted by its four other partners and has succeeded in constantly reinforcing her position on their domestic markets. Though also in a surplus situation with its four partners, Germany has experienced, on the contrary, a deterioration of its relative position over the period. Then come, in the following order, the US, France, and the UK, which all experienced deficits with the zone constituted by their four respective partners.

Looking now at international specialization, important differences appear between the countries. Japan is characterized by its great number of sectors with external surpluses. The main exporting industries (measuring instruments, watch-making, transport equipment, electric and electronic appliances, and mechanical machinery) constantly improve their positions. The chemical and steel industries remain in surplus, though their balance deteriorates. On the contrary, textiles and other deficit industries (e.g. agro-food, paper, and basic chemicals) see their deficits increasing.

The same divergence between sectors can also be observed in the United States. The balance becomes more and more positive for exporting industries, such as aeronautics, office machinery, computers, and precision instruments. The position deteriorates for a second group (chemical products, mechanical machinery, and electrical equipment) which succeeds however in maintaining a surplus. For a third group (including textiles, clothing, leather, steel and metal products, transport equipment, optical equipment, cameras, watches, and electronic products—excluding computers) the deficits increase more and more.

In other words, American and Japanese industrial structures tend to be organized around *competitivity* poles, within which the complementarity between activities reinforces external competitivity.

The German, French, and British situations seem to be totally different. One reason is the existence within the EC of two kinds of international firms: subsidiaries of American groups, which have developed strong transnational production processes in Europe, and European firms participating in integrated European programmes (like Airbus or Ariane). Such firms simultaneously generate imports and exports for the same country.

Hence, it is possible to find in Germany three groups of industrial sectors:

— sectors associated with high levels of imports and exports, which include the international sectors mentioned above (office machinery, computers, aeronautics, . . .) and sectors in which LDCs are active (textiles, clothing, and leather);
— domestic sectors corresponding to a low level of external exchange (construction materials, wood, paper, and agro-food);
— sectors with highly positive external surpluses that represent traditionally strong German positions (mechanical and electrical machinery, boiler-making, transport equipment, precision instruments, and chemical products).

But for Germany, according to CEPII, the trade surplus correspond-ing to the five best products only represents 21.5 per cent of total trade against 50 per cent for Japan! France may be characterized by the absence of real competitivity poles. The sectors with high levels of imports and exports can be separated into two: those with exports around 30 per cent and imports around 40 per cent (computers, electronics, precision instruments, and textiles) and those with imports around 40 per cent and imports around 30 per cent (aeronautics, shipbuilding, cars, mechanical and electrical products, steel, and chemical products). A last group includes sectors for which the domestic market is predominant (construction materials, agro-food, wood, and paper).

British industry still seems less structured than the French. The surpluses in a few chemical or mechanical sectors are far from com-pensating for the important deficits in other sectors like automobiles. Tables A.12 to A.17 of the Statistical Appendix illustrate and complete these analyses.

The Commission du Bilan appointed in June 1981 by the French government, concluded:[6]

Over the period 1964–1979, one may observe that on the world markets:

— German industry is in a position of structural withdrawal in almost all fields; the metallic sectors resist but sophisticated industries (electrical engineering, precision instruments) are in sharp decline;
— the United States experiences a decreasing share in high technology industries and withdraws from less sophisticated sectors (metals, cars);
— Japan consolidates its breakthrough; the well-integrated mechanical sectors (steel, shipbuilding, automobile) constitute a homogeneous competitive pole; electrical engineering confirms the steady improve-ment of its share;
— during the same period, French industry has made up a significant proportion of its handicap with respect to German industry on the world market, has generated a stable surplus with respect to the U.K., has resisted relatively well the new European competition (Italy, for instance), but has remained handicapped with respect to the U.S. in the field of equipment goods and has been unable to resist the Japanese breakthrough.

But the tensions generated by industrial adaptation are not limited to their impact on foreign trade and on sectoral growth-rate differentia-tion. They also raise a few other major issues which we have to mention briefly.

From 1960 to 1980 the profitability of industrial activities has steadily declined in the main industrial countries. In 1980 the order of increasing profitability was: United Kingdom, France, Germany, US, Japan. Three factors interfere in this decline: (i) productivity of capital, which generally has had a negative influence; (ii) labour productivity, which had a positive impact throughout the 1960s because of relatively low real labour costs, but which has operated in the other direction during most of the 1970s because of the evolution of real labour costs; and (iii) relative prices (which combine the domestic terms of trade between industry and the rest of the economy and the external terms of trade between the national economy and the rest of the world) which have had a negative influence on the whole. Table A.19 of the Statistical Appendix shows the average annual rates of change of unit labour costs for a sample of industrial countries on a US dollar basis.

Needless to say, the decline in manufacturing's average profitability multiplies the financing problems (especially in countries where own funds have always represented a small share of firms' long-term finance) and augments the number of bankruptcies. This financial situation has an obvious counterpart in the field of investment. While during the last ten years, Japan has quickly increased its capital stock, the capital per worker remained approximately constant in the US and EC since the mid-1970s. For instance in 1979 Japan's share of GDP invested in manufacturing activities was approximately twice the value of the Community and of the United States.

European industry no longer creates jobs. Every year from 1973 to 1980, French, German, and British industry have lost respectively 66,000, 127,000, and 145,000 jobs. Though a part of the loss is compensated by the creation of firms servicing industry, this phenomenon constantly gives rise to social conflicts and to acute political difficulties in regions where declining industrial sectors are predominant. This situation induces some political circles in countries like the UK and France to support a revival of protectionism, either with respect to the NICs or with respect to Japan. But as far as the NICs are concerned, the detailed studies made (for instance by B. Balassa)[7] conclude that the jobs created by their imports outnumber the jobs destroyed by their exports.[8]

In spite of the limited statistical information available, a recent study by the Commission[9] says that the European countries seem to have a relative disadvantage in qualified manpower with respect to the United States and Japan. For instance, scientists and engineers seem to be less represented in European manpower than in the US and Japan. In several member countries, the proportion of students in scientific or engineering disciplines has even decreased in the last ten years. In addition, the professional training given within the Community seems

to be of a lower quality than in the United States, and this phenomenon mainly concerns young generations.

But the description given so far stresses only one aspect of the
evolution of European industry: the competition between nations.
It has the great disadvantage of hiding the other side of the coin: the
competition between firms. The changing context of European industrial policies cannot be understood without taking this dimension into
consideration.

II.4. The changing role of multinational corporations

During the 1960s, the big American corporations devoted a significant
share of their investment to investment abroad. The decline of the
dollar temporarily stopped this tendency, but the movement started
again after 1978. However, since the beginning of the 1970s, American firms have no longer been the only ones to operate at an international level. They have been joined by European and Japanese firms,
compelled by their size to conceive their strategy at the world level and
attracted by the opportunities offered by the various national markets.

Pushed by the chronic difficulties of the British economy and by
the appreciation of the pound, British firms have maintained their
investment abroad, but neglecting Canada, Australia, New Zealand, and
South Africa, they have redirected this investment towards Europe
and the US.

German firms—experiencing difficulties in exporting their manufactured products because of the DM exchange rate—have strongly
increased their investment in the US or in other EC countries. They
have also invested in Brazil and other NICs.

French firms have only followed to a limted extent. From 1974 to
1980, French capital exports only represent two-thirds of the corresponding figure for Germany. But the share of their foreign investment
in other industrial countries, which was of the order of 50 per cent at
the end of the 1960s, now reaches approximately 80 per cent.

On the contrary, Japanese firms have continued to invest predominantly in the Third World, South-east Asia being the most important
zone for this investment along with Latin America and, in particular,
Brazil.

Who would not agree then with the following statement by
CEPII?[10]

The growing internationalization which characterizes not only production, but also distribution and still more banking and financial circuits,
peculiarly alters the efficiency of national policies and partly deprives
of their meaning the analysis and regulation instruments which the
states had at their disposal. To what extent can a production controlled
up to 25 per cent, or 50 per cent, or more by a decision centre located

abroad, or exports made by subsidiaries of a foreign corporation, still be considered as 'national'? What impact may a government policy concerning prices, wages, taxes, and exchange rates have on the competitivity of 'national' products, when a significant proportion of foreign exchanges are through circuits between firms and their subsidiaries and obey different rules from those of classical competition implicitly referred to in government measures?

Without the presently growing industrial interdependence, national incomes of European societies could very well be jeopardized and faced with great threats of sclerosis from the social oligopoly. But in spite of its advantages, industrial interdependence creates internal problems for European governments, all the more difficult because it links partners with very different social dynamics or foreign policy objectives. Thus it raises formidable challenges to the European Economic Community.

II.5. The uncertain prospects of EC industrial evolution

At the beginning of the 1980s the EC industrial scene is obviously characterized by the simultaneous existence of strong solidarities and intense internal tensions. Let us briefly review the solidarities first.

In 1980 intra-EC trade in manufactures represented 21 per cent of world trade in manufactures, and for EC countries as a whole intra-EC exports reached almost 50 per cent of their total manufactured exports. More generally, intra-EC foreign trade corresponds to approximately 12 per cent of European gross product. Such intimate commercial links cannot but create strong solidarities between European economies. For each EC member, the rate of growth of the rest of the Community is obviously a key determinant for its own growth. In addition, EC internal integration is reinforced by the existence of close commercial links between the EC and other Western European countries. The following figures are impressive: while EC manufacturing industry serviced 61.1 per cent of EC markets in 1980, in the same year it covered 61.6 per cent of domestic demand in Northern European countries and 59.6 per cent in Southern European countries. One could say that integration already covers, as far as manufacturing is concerned, the whole of Western Europe.

Another aspect of the solidarity is the fact that EC countries, in spite of national differences, are all confronted with the same industrial problems. All have difficulties with traditional sectors (steel, textiles, shipbuilding, etc.) in the context of low growth and high unemployment; all have problems with the insufficient take-off of high-technology sectors like electronics; and all have to meet Japanese competition in sectors like automobiles, electronics, and mechanical equipment.

But the existence of such solidarities should not hide the progressive development of internal tensions since the mid-1970s. These tensions seem to arise from three different groups of causes. One is the diverging evolution of trade balances in manufactures. In 1980 Germany and Belgium had a strong industrial surplus with the rest of the EC, Italy was in equilibrium, but France and the UK had strong deficits which they had to compensate by their surpluses with the rest of the world. The Netherlands' situation was still more difficult, since the surplus with the rest of the world was lower than the deficit within the Community.

The German trajectory is especially significant. Since 1975 its surplus (in 1975 dollars) with the rest of the world has steadily declined while its surplus with EC countries has become more and more positive. Because of its strength, German industry structures industrial relations within Europe, so French industry—which is more competitive with German industry than complementary—has to look for surpluses outside Europe.[11] In contrast, Italian and German or Italian and French competitivity poles are more complementary. On the whole, the reinforcement of extra-European competition and the decrease in absorption capacities of the Third World have intensified competition within the EC itself.

The second group of causes is the insufficient co-operation between European firms or between governments with respect to industry. Without taking a position on what the respective roles of the market and of government intervention should be, one is compelled to recognize that socio-cultural barriers and national authorities' practices sometimes make it more difficult for a European firm to take advantage of the Common Market than for an American corporation. In addition, for national interests European governments do not hesitate to take measures which will worsen the situation of given industrial sectors in other member countries. The British attempt to attract Nissan to Wales, which may be at the expense of European car manufacturers, is only one example among many others. It is also remarkable that on a national basis EC countries have invested more than $2.1 billion to reinforce their computer industries. These figures are quite high if compared to corresponding figures for Japan and the US, but are still higher when effective results are taken into account.

The third group is the different approaches of European governments. Though the Community has been able until now to protect the existence of the Common Market and to maintain the common trade policy, it is a notorious fact that basic attitudes of European governments with respect to management of the economy are often fundamentally different. In addition, in several EC countries the views on economic issues of the major opposition parties are much more at variance with the government's than in the United States or Japan. This implies that general elections in one or two countries may be sufficient to alter policies which are, in any case, rather heterogeneous compromises.

Thus, the prospects of EC industrial evolution appear highly uncertain. Embedded in economies caught between external pressures and internal pressures and rigidities; confronted with an economic environment characterized by low growth, high unemployment, inflationary risks, a crisis of the welfare state, and structural adjustment; having to face important technical changes; engaged in fierce international competition; experiencing similar problems but having difficulties co-operating, European industrial firms—which are one of the most important European assets—are in a very delicate situation. Hence, it is not surprising if voices ask for industrial policies, with intensities differing from one country to another. But now we have to see, without trying to describe European governments' practices (since they will be covered in other chapters), what issues are raised by the new demands for industrial policies.

III. Issues raised by industrial policies

Industrial policies give rise to two different sets of issues: the first concerns the reasons impelling governments to formulate industrial policies, the second pertains to the instruments employed to reach the goals of industrial policies. We shall briefly discuss these two sets within the European context.

III.1. The rationale for industrial policies

It is more difficult to analyse the rationale for industrial policies than is generally considered because the reasons behind these policies may be discussed:

- within a political or an economic conceptual framework,
- from a descriptive or a normative viewpoint,
- for a closed economy, for an open economy, or for an economy embedded into a community like the EC. (This distinction was introduced at the SIP 1980s symposium.)[12]

We shall adopt this third dimension as the primary division for the discussion.

A closed economy Let us start with *a closed economy* and let us consider first the emergence of industrial policies as a domestic political process. It is well known that governments generally look for a compromise between two objectives: to obtain sufficient support from the population (and in a democracy to preserve their chances of re-election) and to implement into reality their preferred model of a society.

The first objective leads those with political power to make successive concessions to the various minorities which consider themselves under-privileged, frequently at the cost of disadvantages which are more wide-spread but less obvious since they affect the whole population. From that point of view, to give subsidies in order to protect employment in a declining industry may be politically perfectly rational, even if these subsidies will not save the industry, as long as the minority concerned may be convinced that the government has done whatever was possible for them and as long as the rest of the population is not conscious of the cost inflicted on it. In addition, as we have seen, social groups are organized, which means that governments negotiate with them through their representative bodies. So if those in power want to obtain concessions from these groups in some fields, they have to give them advantages in others. Here again this can only be done by neglect-ing the costs or benefits which are spread throughout society. Thus it should not be a surprise to observe that in Europe the claims for indus-trial policies are more vigorous in countries where the social oligopoly is stronger, and that these claims are based above all on the defence of employment. Hence the fact that present European industrial policies often have a strong backward-looking component.

But simultaneously, governments try to change society according to a preconceived pattern of what this society should become. From that point of view, they attach importance to criteria like economic efficiency, equality, freedom, participation, security, etc., and they may consider government intervention in the industrial field necessary in order to improve the performance of society along these lines. This second objective explains why industrial policies also generally contain a forward-looking component related to the development of new innovative sectors. From the French 'Commissariat à l'Energie Atomique' to the European Space Agency and to Airbus, many examples of this second component of industrial policies may be found in the European history of the last two decades. It must be stressed, however, that government policies along this second line cannot be judged on economic grounds alone, since some of the criteria which the governments refer to are out of the economic sphere. For instance, the French socialists claim that the nationalization programme will improve social relations within the industrial groups concerned by the programme.

Let us now consider industrial policies as elements of the economic process, in order to detect which of the reasons proposed in text-books to justify industrial policies are at work in Europe today.

A first bundle of reasons acknowledged by economists derives from distribution issues: the operation of the market may either lead to a permanent income distribution considered as unacceptable, or generate for some individuals transitional adjustment costs judged inequitable.

This last feature is constantly advocated in European countries. But in order to improve the situation of those hurt by economic change, it is obviously better from the viewpoint of economic efficiency to pay unemployment allowances and to organize training, rather than to subsidize employment in present jobs.

Though found in many textbooks, a second group of reasons for government interference with the market has almost disappeared from the present European public debate: existence of a monopoly, presence of external diseconomies, development of restrictive practices, etc. From that point of view, German authorities' justification for their refusal of the attempted Grundig-Thomson agreement—based on the risk of monopoly power—may not be the real one. This diminishing interest in competition policies is even more significant because these policies constituted an important chapter in the Rome Treaty.

Next comes the question of trade-off between present and future. Rightly or wrongly, the political community may consider that the arbitrage made by the market between present and future generations is not adequate for two reasons: (i) the incomplete nature of markets for future transactions, and (ii) the inequality in income distribution which generates a market power that is not considered legitimate for choices affecting the long-term. In nearly all the fields where these choices are fundamental, this problem is present. For instance, energy policies existed in some European countries long before the oil crises. However, a logical consequence of this present/future issue should be government intervention in the capital market and not necessarily measures specific to given industrial sectors. A problem which is only a specific feature of this issue is the question of the survival of firms having acute short-term cash difficulties, but considered as structurally healthy (at least at a reduced production level). Because governments take into account social and economic externalities and discount the future less, they may be more willing than bankers to avoid the bankruptcy of such firms. Nevertheless, we must recognize that many arguments of this type have induced governments to subsidize structurally unprofitable firms.

Another aspect (closely related to the preceding issue) concerns the major risks from the nation's standpoint. Here, too, rightly or wrongly, politicians may consider: (i) that the market for risks is inefficient because of the existence of external economies pushing the economic agents to discount the future more than would be adequate from a collective standpoint, and (ii) that the 'voting rights' given by income are not necessarily acceptable in evaluating the risks to be taken by society as a whole. Such reasons are often proposed by European economists to justify, for example, subsidies for industrial R&D.

I have kept for the end a final phenomenon which has to be taken into consideration even in a closed economy. While until now the arguments could be developed in a one-period or multi-period economic statics framework, this phenomenon relates to economic dynamics: what should be done when the market gives rise to cumulative phenomena, e.g. at regional level when a region begins to decline? Should this cumulative decline and progressive loss of competitive capacity be stopped or not? Is it feasible and how? We must admit that economic theory has not much to say about it yet, since the elements at work in these declines probably concern the social rigidities, the generation of incentives, the diffusion of knowledge, and the creation of human capital. European governments have often justified some of their interventions in industry and banking by their hopes to alter these cumulative processes. (Consider, for instance, the creation of Société Nationale d'Investissement (SNI) in Belgium and of Institut pour le Développement Industriel (INI) in France, and in the past of Istituto per la Ricostruzione Industriale (IRI) in Italy and Instituto Nacional de Industrializacion (INI) in Spain.)

An open economy   Additional issues arise when we pass from a closed to an open economy. First, political considerations now include international issues and, above all, the decision-making autonomy of individual nations. We know only too well that this is a Pandora's box which can be used to justify anything and everything. But in a multipolar world in which each nation is vulnerable to decisions taken elsewhere, one of the jobs of statesmen is to ensure the long-term survival of those nations: hence the preoccupation of these statesmen in maintaining a sufficient degree of autonomy for the national collectivity they have in charge. The more uncertain the future evolution of the world political and economic situation, the more sensitive political leaders become to the disappearance of the last firm producing a given product on the national territory, with the old argument of the armaments industry being extended to many other sectors. A more sophisticated version of the argument is that a country should keep the technical ability to regenerate on its own soil any 'strategic' industrial activity that might be necessary. Hence in an open economy, governments may consider it their duty to sacrifice economic efficiency, to a certain extent, for national autonomy and security.

These political considerations have an impact even when governments restrict their analysis to economic aspects. For instance, the concern for vulnerability tends to make the problems of cumulative divergence much more acute in open than in closed economies. What makes one country competitive *vis-à-vis* others? What makes a country progressively lose this competitive capacity? How do we analyse the social processes which may result, at a given moment, when nations lose contact with others and, if they rely on the market alone, find themselves incapable of facing up to external challenges. There is no doubt that such preoccupations do arise presently in European minds when they compare the situation of the EC with those of Japan and the United States.

The matter is made still more complex by the existence of transnational corporations, since most of these corporations are still managed by a group of individuals having the nationality of the country where the corporation was born and who tend to (or are compelled to) give preference to the interests of that country. For instance, European governments would not have had to support their domestic computer companies if they had not considered IBM as an American corporation. This is all the more significant since IBM is in reality much more multinational than most transnational corporations. From this point of view, industrial policies seem an attempt, perhaps hopeless, to use government intervention in order to stop the decline. But then the crucial question becomes: Are there government policy instruments (and if so, which ones) that allow better evolution of international competitiveness than no government intervention? Without dealing with this question now, we shall only note that the intricate political and economic reasons justifying industrial policies are much more complex for open than for closed economies. This being said, we may pursue the discussion in purely economic terms.

To begin with, we must remember that some economists conveniently ignore the properties of free trade according to economic theory. This theory does not say that everybody gains from free trade. It merely states that if exchange rates are adequate, if perfect competition does exist on international capital markets, and if optimal conditions prevail within each national economy, the situation of the international economy is in a Pareto optimum. Then, the position of one transactor cannot be improved without a loss to another. In other words:

— even if the international economic situation were optimal, there would be no guarantee that all nations would benefit from free trade,
— the impact of free trade is still more ambiguous when it coexists with economic 'imperfections' at national or international levels.

Of course, studies suggest that nations do generally benefit from free trade; but it does not run counter to the theory to ask for econometric evidence in each case.

Under these conditions, one of the goals of industrial policy may be to compensate for the impact on the national economy of 'imperfect' economic conditions abroad through domestic measures. For instance, profits on international markets tend to go to the firms able to obtain dominant positions on these markets. But it may be easier for a country to have such firms in a sector if it also has efficient corporations producing either the necessary inputs or other outputs using the same technology. Hence, the concept of competitivity poles or of industrial networks which are frequently found in the discussions on industrial policies and deserve more precise theoretical elaboration.

Similarly, if the future production cost of a firm depends on its past cumulated output, a government may decide to protect its own domestic market (or the part represented by government orders) to be sure that this firm will ultimately reach a cumulated production level high enough to make it competitive. Just to give an example, this is what the French and the German governments have done (with Bull and Siemens, respectively) to try to have a domestic computer industry. The same issue is sometimes formulated differently: should the governments try to 'pick the winner(s)' in order to have a national champion able to support international competition in a given sector? When there are obviously a certain number of potential 'winners' (as has been the case in Japan for some industries in the last decade), to watch the struggle and wait for the best to win is probably good advice to a government. But what should a government do if there is only one candidate and that is a very vulnerable one? Should it be abandoned to its fate if it operates in a sector having a potentially bright future? The answer obviously depends on the nature of the learning curves. These curves may be such that, in spite of government help, the selected 'winners' will never be able to become competitive.

The existence of dominant positions on international markets is, of course, not the only type of imperfection in world competition for industrial products. Many others exist which refer to financing, technology acquisition, transfer pricing, etc. It is not necessary to analyse them here for the consistency of the discussion.

An economy in a community   The preceding situation—an open economy—does not perfectly describe the situation of EC member countries. In signing the Rome Treaty and in deciding to have a common foreign trade policy, these countries have chosen to deal differently with intra- and extra-EC trade. Hence the key question: Should the arguments developed above for an open economy apply to the Community as a whole or to each country separately? In the first case, the British government should not be concerned by the loss of technical abilities induced by the decline of the British car industry, as long as there remain other car manufacturers within the EC. In the second case the British government should consider Renault or Volkswagen as much competitors as Mitsubishi or Chrysler.

Obviously, the EC's economic, social, political, and military integration has not developed far enough for the governments to completely accept that economic security should only be conceived at the Community level. Therefore two trends coexist. One shows European countries developing industrial policies at the national level while applying the Rome Treaty and, consequently, giving preference to EC firms. The other shows the Commission itself defining a European industrial policy for a few sectors (steel, for instance) and trying to elaborate a more comprehensive industrial policy, but without much support.

Several specific arguments may be given for a Community industrial policy:

— It is easier for the EC as a whole to decrease external vulnerability than for each of the member countries. For instance, firms may have a greater chance to become competitive at the international level if they are offered a significant share of the EC market. The quality of such an argument heavily depends on the sectors concerned. Recent studies in industrial economics seem to prove that its value has often been overestimated.

— National industrial policies within the EC may in the long run endanger the existence of the Common Market, especially if each of the big EC countries insisted on having a (subsidized!) winner in each of the industrial sectors considered strategic. From that point of view also a common industrial policy would be more efficient economically than national policies.

— The transfer of the elaboration of industrial policies from the national to the Community level would contribute to the achievement of the political goal of European integration.

Let us sum up what we have put into evidence until now. If we take into account the first two parts of this chapter, the reasons for the growing interest in industrial policies within the EC should be quite clear:

In a situation of unemployment, structural adjustment generates painful social problems, and because of the social oligopoly governments are under high pressure to alleviate these problems.

In an interdependent economic system, it is impossible to accelerate national growth without improving one's share of the world market and acquiring rents on this market.

In an uncertain multipolar world, to preserve the country's autonomy and to decrease its external vulnerability becomes a legitimate goal.

But the difficulty of European governments is that, although they want to preserve the Common Market, they are not totally ready to transfer the concept of economic security to the Community alone. As a consequence, when an EC country firm formulates its policy with respect to another European firm it has to take into account whether or not that firm belongs to its own country. On these grounds, the European Community is in a situation totally different from that of Japan or the US and cannot avoid being a centre of solidarities and tensions at the same time.

However, the fact that many reasons may be given to justify government attempts to elaborate industrial policies in Western Europe does not imply that instruments exist which make such policies effective, or that governments usually select the adequate instruments. On the contrary, governments often accept goals which are unachievable with the instruments they possess, or select instruments which are not the most efficient.

III.2. The instruments of industrial policies

First it should be stressed that many government policies outside the realm of industrial policies are probably more vital for industry than industrial policies themselves. There are macro-economic and exchange rates policies which have an impact on domestic growth and external competitivity. There are energy policies which progressively loosen the constraint on growth resulting from energy imports. There are employment policies which influence labour costs and hence staff management. There are research policies which may facilitate innovation. There are education and training policies which ease structural adjustment and the development of high-technology sectors. Many, though not all, of the present difficulties of European industries would have been softened if there had been policies moulding the industrial environment. However, a general criticism does not have much meaning since these policies have differed in the main European countries.

As for industrial policies *stricto sensu*, when a government is deciding about its instruments, it must be conscious of its advantages (the importance of its financial possibilities, regulatory power, position of arbitration between social groups, and ability to give preference to the long term). But it should not forget its handicaps (the difficulty in obtaining and in using precise information on markets or on production processes, and hence in putting the problems into their real industrial context; long reaction lags; dispersion of the decision-making process among multiple administrative agents with diverging views; inconsistency of the objectives; and lack of follow-up once a crisis has been settled).

Generally a government has the possibility of choosing among three types of instruments: regulation, introduction of incentives, or direct action.

Regulation policies correspond to the introduction of constraints on the spontaneous evolution of markets. Generally, governments tend to underestimate the interest of such policies, which properly used may increase the efficiency of competition while limiting some market externalities. Unfortunately, they frequently adopt regulations which have a negative impact on industrial competitivity.[13] For instance, in order to fight inflation the French government has for many years maintained a control of industrial prices, which has made the reallocation of production throughout industry more difficult. On the whole, governments should be more conscious that the market has an advantage far more important than its creative power: its destructive capability. It is much better at destruction than governments are because it has the extraordinary feature of destroying anonymously. This is the reason why social groups devote so much time to trying to control the market. But because of this anonymous destructive power the market is also a regenerator of societies, and this is perhaps why it is constantly reborn from its ashes.

Introduction of incentives (which may be positive or negative) is a second possibility. It is by far the best type of instrument for industrial policies, as long as the number of agents concerned is high enough. Generally, government officials tend to believe that these incentives must be given case by case after a careful study. They then impose long and inefficient procedures on industry. Automatic incentives would be much more preferable. For instance, if a government wants to promote the use of computers to accelerate technical change, it is certainly better off reducing the VAT on computers and software than subsidizing specific computer applications selected by a committee.

The third possibility remains direct action. From the concession of public orders to the nationalization of corporations, it often seems to be the preferred course of action of governments, which overestimate by far the possibility of controlling a socio-economic system in this way. It would be especially interesting in this respect to have an analysis of governments' attitudes with regard to state-owned firms in the main European countries since the second oil-price increase.

Hence, the problem of industrial policies is above all a problem of instruments. Governments are often so awkward in adapting these instruments to the industrial issues they try to solve that their policies do not reach the goals which have been defined.

In other words, in the present situation of European industry it does not seem possible on theoretical grounds to reject any kind of industrial policies. Many reasons—political or economic—may justify such policies. However, for these policies really to contribute to the future of Europe two elements seem essential:

(i) Governments should define positive adjustment policies[14] and avoid attempting to rescue lost causes, which only makes adjustment more difficult in the long run, at an increased social cost and often at the expense of sectors with a future.

(ii) Governments should carefully select their instruments and on the whole attach more importance to incentive and regulation than to direct action.

IV. Concluding remarks

What conclusions may be derived from the foregoing analysis? If it is valid, the EC economies should remain caught throughout the decade between external pressures and internal pressures and rigidities; European industry should be submitted to intense international competition and compelled to adapt; similarities and divergences between EC countries' industrial evolutions should simultaneously develop solidarities and intra-European tensions; demands for national or common industrial policies should remain vigorous and be based on social grounds, balance-of-payments problems, and on economic security. But European governments will meet three major difficulties in formulating and implementing these policies:

— They may tend to give preference to conservation of the past rather than facilitate development of the germs of the future.
— They may frequently select inefficient instruments which will consume scarce resources without really strengthening European industry.
— They may be unable to find the proper articulations between the policies at Community and at national levels, thus increasing the tensions within the EC and decreasing the national economic security in the long term because they have conceived it on a short-term horizon and on a narrow geographical basis.

Notes and Sources

[1] See, for instance, Centre d'Etudes Prospectives et d'Informations Internationales (CEPII), 'Economie mondiale: La montée des tensions', *Economica*, Paris, 1983.
[2] See Table A.2 in the Statistical Appendix.
[3] OECD, *Facing the future. Mastering the probable and managing the unpredictable*, Interfutures final report, Paris, 1979, and CEPII, op. cit.
[4] See J. Lesourne, *Les mille sentiers de l'avenir*, Seghers, Paris, 1981, p. 282.
[5] See Statistical Appendix, Table A.5.
[6] Commission du Bilan, 'La France en mai 1981', annex vol 2, *Les activités productives*, La Documentation Française, Paris, 1982, p. 237.
[7] B. Balassa, 'L'évolution de la division internationale du travail dans le domaine des biens manufacturés', *Annales économiques*, No. 17, Editions Cujas, Paris, 1981.
[8] See Table A.18 of the Statistical Appendix.

[9] Commission of the EC, *'La correspondance Economique et Financière'*, étude hebdomadaire, 6 September 1982.

[10] CEPII, op. cit.

[11] This evolution is, of course, partly due to the DM/French franc exchange rate level.

[12] SIP 1980s, *Industry and the Next Decade*, an overview of the work done by the international symposium on industrial policies for the 1980s, organized by the Spanish Ministry of Industry and Energy in co-operation with and under the patronage of the OECD, Madrid, May 1980.

[13] OECD, *Positive Adjustment Policies—Managing Structural Change*, Paris, 1982.

[14] Ibid.

II

Trends in Industrial Policy in the EC: Theory and Practice

CHRISTOPHER WILKINSON*

I. Introduction

Industrial policies are actively discussed today.[1] In the European Community the argument turns around three main themes. First, the essentially political and ideological argument about the role of the State in the economy; second, whether industrial policies are appropriately national or Community in character; and third, the relationship between industrial policies in Europe and industrial developments in other countries, particularly Japan and the United States.

Underlying this policy debate are the large differences in structure and performance of industry in the European economies. These have a real influence over policy, sometimes independently of political considerations. Thus a government's attitude towards policies affecting the automobile or steel industries is primarily affected by whether its country has those industries. Similarly, governments otherwise committed to free trade may become quite protectionist should they happen to have a large, weak textile industry at home.

It is singularly difficult to define industrial policy in this context. For present purposes, *industry* can be taken to include manufacturing and commercial services in both the public and private sectors and *policy* understood to include all the interrelationships between the actions of public authorities and enterprises which affect their economic behaviour. It is very difficult to give a narrower working definition which is useful, although in practice attention focuses on regulations and technical standards, financing of R&D, public purchasing, the size and policies of the public sector in industry, public financing of industrial investment, and all forms of protection which affect the size of markets for industrial products and services.

Consequently, the industrial policy issue is inevitably so broad that

* Head of Strategy Division, European Commission Task Force for Information Technology and Telecommunications. This paper was written while Mr Wilkinson was at the Center for International Affairs at Harvard University.

it cannot be treated properly in a single article, particularly as so many different national policies coexist in Europe. For present purposes we shall have to make do with an over-view of the principal issues, a survey of recent industrial policies in three European countries, and a discussion of the future development of European Community industrial policies. This approach leaves evident gaps, which will in part be filled by other chapters in this book.[2]

Nor will this chapter address the facts and figures of the industrial situation in the Community. To a degree they are only too well known, and a fairly detailed current assessment of the competitiveness of Community industry has recently been published by the Commission.[3]

The theoretical starting point for much of the discussion of industrial policy is the contemporary realization that the Keynesian macroeconomic prescription for stabilization, full employment, and growth is no longer adequate. Increased effective demand does not necessarily lead to an increase in domestic output, even if there are unemployed resources. This can result in inflation (rather than economic expansion), increased imports, and eventually a balance of payments deficit. In short, there is a problem of *supply*, and the Keynesian multiplier no longer has its virtuous effect.

This limitation of the simple Keynesian model has long been recognized in development economics, which has consequently been much more interested in the micro-economic linkages in the domestic economy, both forwards and backwards, and in the source of savings and their application to productive investment. As international economic integration has proceeded during the past forty years (with foreign trade accounting for rising shares of most countries' GDP and consumers preferences changing, quite rapidly in some instances), the industrialized economies have found that the elasticity of supply of goods and factors of production is no longer high, import leakages are high, and the multiplier effect is weak. In some instances even the investment accelerator is unreliable because the requisite capital equipment is not produced domestically—either because the national economy is too small to accommodate specialized capital goods industries, or because these industries have been allowed to become obsolete.

These then are some of the reasons for the contemporary preoccupation with the ability of an economy to supply the products and services required to achieve real growth in output and employment. This approach leads us to consider the input–output relationships in present and future industrial structure, and to address ourselves to the question of whether—qualitatively and quantitatively—the necessary factors of production will be available. Consequently, the availability and price of these factors and products are also major concerns of industrial policy.

In addition to these theoretical considerations, industrial policies in Europe are motivated by the rising level of unemployment, the relative decline in international competitiveness, and strategic considerations.

Unemployment in the Community has reached about 11 per cent of the labour force, or about 12 million people, with far-reaching, undesirable economic, social, and political consequences. Unemployment benefits are a charge on strained budgets and represent demands on resources which may not be matched with additional output; hence they contribute to inflationary pressures. So a major priority for industrial policies is the development of activities where more of the labour force can be usefully employed.

The Commission's report on competitiveness draws attention to the relative decline of international competitiveness, broadly defined, of European manufactured products. This is a matter of concern in several respects. Firstly, the Community is an open market. The emergence of more competitive foreign producers increases the tendency for imports to rise with incomes, which aggravates the balance of payments problems associated with increasing levels of economic activity. Furthermore, with imports—particularly of consumer goods—fewer new jobs are created by economic expansion.

Secondly, the Community has to be able to export manufactured products in order to buy necessary raw materials and energy. However, many European exports are currently threatened: on the one hand by newly industrializing countries, which can sell a wide range of standard manufactured products at low cost, and on the other hand by Japan and the United States, who tend to be more competitive in high-technology products and skill-intensive services.

Finally, there are certain strategic considerations which affect industrial policy priorities.[4] It is important for a large industrialized economy to be able to produce most of the products, services, and technologies it requires, without sacrificing too many of the benefits of specialization. There are several reasons for this. The first is, quite simply, to strengthen the multiplier effect by reinforcing the input–output relationships in the economy. The second is to avoid the prospect of international oligopoly in key technologies. The third is to arrest the decline in manufacturing employment.

The principal difficulty with this 'strategic' approach to industrial policy is where to draw the line between inefficient attempts at autarchy and the risks and costs of excessive dependence on trade.[5] There is no simple rational solution, except that the larger the economic area, the easier it will be to fulfil these strategic objectives of industrial policy. But small economies will find such a strategy much more expensive and difficult to implement, because their small domestic markets lead to inadequate scale economies and lack of resources.

Industrial policies inevitably raise trade-related issues because preoccupation with the relationship between domestic economic structure and growth and employment implies that the outcome of free trade in a purely market economy may not be optimal. This is so. Without going into an elaborate discussion of international trade theory, suffice it to say that there are three important respects in which the modern international industrial economy differs fundamentally from that described by neo-classical trade theory.

First, if firms experience economies of scale (a declining cost curve), international trade theory no longer predicts an outcome where factors of production are optimally employed and trade balances are in equilibrium. Yet we know that many, if not most, manufacturing processes exhibit scale economies up to a certain point. This qualification may not be very important in industries where the world market can accommodate a number of plants operating at optimal capacity, which is also usually the case. However when surplus capacity emerges in a recession, this quite obviously leads to unstable results, of which we have had a good deal of experience in recent years. Indeed, if there is world-wide surplus capacity in an industry where most firms face declining cost curves, then modest shifts in market share can result in quite large shifts in marginal costs, which destabilize the situation even more. Furthermore, there are several industries where international trade is dominated by an oligopoly of firms facing declining cost curves. In the aircraft or semi-conductor industries—to cite two extreme examples—the prospects for neo-classical equilibrium would seem to be slim indeed.

The second respect is the evidence that a firm's costs decline, not necessarily in relation to scale of production, but in relation to cumulative experience of production, particularly in the early stages of producing a new product.[6] The effect of this 'learning curve' is that the first successful firms in a new industry can create a formidable barrier to subsequent entrants by reducing their own costs and prices.[7] This probably can only be overcome by cross-subsidization within a firm or some form of public support or protection. International trade theory does not really address this kind of absolute competitive advantage. In any case, when such cases emerge, as they have done recently, they are clearly not conducive to an optimal equilibrium in international trade.

Third, international trade theory is based on the assumption that national relative endowment of factors of production is given and determines competitive advantage. This no longer describes the world economy. The quality and location of resources are of decreasing importance in determining the location, volume, and competitiveness of industrial production. International trade in raw materials, the reduced resource content of many products, the development of substitutes, and above all the growing international flows of investment and technology all contribute to this trend. Furthermore, crucial elements of comparative advantage can be created, notably by investing in research, technology, and education. Indeed, such improvements in human resources, often at the initiative of governments, are the foundation for most international economic development and they should be encouraged.

From the theoretical point of view, these features of the modern economy undermine the predictive and normative character of much international trade theory, because in such circumstances there is no reason to expect an optimal equilibrium to emerge at any time. If the international trade system is not likely to be moving towards an equilibrium, but rather towards a path of constant evolution, problems of adjustment appear in a different light. Adjustment costs are not necessarily the interim price of moving to a new equilibrium where welfare should be higher for all concerned; they may be a more or less permanent characteristic of a development path which may or may not be advantageous to all participants.[8]

This appears as a particular problem in the world economy today because of the enormous differences in real wages between the developed and developing nations. We do not know whether industrialization in the developing countries will lead to an increase in their wage levels and a consequent decline in their comparative advantages in labour-intensive products, as has been the case in Japan, to some extent, during this century. Nor do we know whether liberal trade policies between developed and developing countries will be to the advantage of the developed countries—in terms of creating sorely needed new markets for their capital goods and high-technology products, or to their disadvantage—in terms of progressive disappearance of major sectors of their economies and the creation of permanent mass unemployment through high levels of imports and the outflow of capital investment.[9]

In conclusion, there are grounds to doubt whether free trade in industrial products will lead to the kind of optimal equilibrium foreseen by neo-classical trade theory. These doubts are reinforced by the problems between the major industrialized and developing countries in the world trade system today.

This is not to advocate or condone protectionist policies as such, but rather to suggest that when trade measures are taken to support industrial policy objectives, they are not necessarily infringing on an ideal free-trade system. Rather they are adding an eventually corrective element to the already highly imperfect and sub-optimal situation which exists at present.

In this context one may note a certain shift in the European Commission's position on external trade. A recent Commission report on the internal market[10] observes that the Community must 'remain open to dialogue and negotiations with its trading partners', and has a clear responsibility to maintain a 'stable and equitable framework for international economic relations'. The Commission proposes, notably, to reinforce common commercial policy by defending against 'unfair trading practices'. So be it. But in today's world, a policy of being open to negotiations is rather different from a policy of being open to free trade.[11]

II. National industrial policies

The development of national industrial policies has generated so much interest in recent years, not only as a by-product of the OECD 'Positive Adjustment' debate, but also because of the success of Japanese industry, the initiatives taken by the new French government, profound concern over the situation in the United Kingdom, and the Commission's proposals for a European industrial strategy.

Such a wide range of different factors are determining national industrial policies that it is virtually impossible to characterize and explain them in a few pages. Consequently, at this stage we shall only address the essential features of industrial policy developments in the Federal Republic of Germany, France, and Greece to illustrate aspects of the current industrial policy debate.

(There are in fact a number of other accessible sources to supplement this inevitably cursory view. The OECD has published the Industry Committee's 'Report to the Council on the Positive Adjustment Policies in the Industry Sector'[12] and an 'Inventory of Adjustment Measures Taken by the Governments of the Member Countries since 1974'.[13] The UK National Economic Development Office has undertaken a comprehensive review of national policies from a British point of view[14] and the European Commission has published a study of industrial policies in the Community.)[15]

II.1. Industrial policy in the Federal Republic of Germany

German industrial policy is of abiding interest, since the FRG is the largest industrial economy in the Community and has the best productivity and growth experience. In recent years the German federal authorities have endeavoured to intervene selectively in industry as little as possible. In particular, the Federal Ministry of Economic Affairs has been persistent and eloquent in its criticism of subsidies to enterprises. Observers have naturally been trying to determine whether German industrial performance has been the result of 'non-intervention', or whether other relationships in the German economy, involving for example the banks or the Länder governments, furnish in practice an effective surrogate for more ostensible forms of industrial policy in other countries.

The German position has recently been restated in the Community, in the OECD, and at home. The federal government's 1982 opinion[16] on the Structural Reports submitted by the five economic research institutes is unambiguous in this respect, fully supporting the institutes' view that the scope of market forces should be increased and that the major subsidy schemes should be reviewed and reduced. One gathers that this recommendation has been supported by the business associations and the Länder governments, but not by the trade unions. However, it should be noted that the bulk of specific federal subsidies in Germany (estimated by the IFW Institute to have been DM 90 billion in 1979) directly benefit the energy, transport, and agricultural sectors. Manufacturing industry benefits principally from tax concessions and regional aids, which are none the less of considerable importance in the aggregate. The Minister of Economic Affairs also set out his philosophy in a memorandum addressed to the federal government in September 1982.[17]

Notwithstanding the official views of the Ministry of Economic Affairs, several observers of the German economy have come to the conclusion that it is no more a competitive market economy than the other principal European economies, but that its characteristics of state influence and of oligopolistic markets differ in important respects from France, Italy, and the UK. The most important difference is the relationship between German industry and the banks. A second important characteristic is the role of the Länder in the ownership and financing of industry. Thirdly, the Ministry of Technology, through the federal financing of industrial R&D, tends to play the role more normally attributed to Ministries of Industry in other countries. (This occasionally introduces an arbitrary bias into the industrial policy discussions in the EC, since the representatives of the Ministry of Economic Affairs do not always speak for the Ministry of Technology.)

Industry and the banks   There is a close, organic link between the major industrial enterprises and the large banks in Germany. This is tangibly expressed in the substantial bank holdings of company stock and in the banks' participation, with substantial voting power, in the supervisory boards of many companies. This system seems to fulfil a need for a long-term, informed relationship between finance and industry. It also gives the banks an overall view of the inter-firm and inter-sectoral relationships.

Elsewhere this view has only been attained through a government-inspired planning mechanism. The corresponding finance/industry relationship is much weaker in other member states. It is difficult to create in the short-term because it presupposes so much about the attitudes and competence of the banks' management and staff, not to speak of their private shareholders. Thus governments in other member states have tried to substitute more direct intervention and control.

A more thorough analysis of the relationship is to be found in John Zysman's book.[18] It establishes the extent to which strong institutional relationships between industry and finance in Germany provide the framework for industrial adjustment, greatly attenuating the need —and the possibility—for direct government intervention in the industrial adjustment process.

It is useful to get an idea of the extent of these links between industry and the banks in Germany. According to a recent study published by the University of Sussex European Research Centre, hardly any of the 100 largest companies in Germany have no representatives of the banks on their supervisory boards, and in many cases the banks even chair the supervisory boards. In terms of their shareholding and voting power (enhanced by the institution of proxy voting), the banks represented (in 1974–5) over 50 per cent of the votes in thirty companies and over 25 per cent in eleven more companies. The three largest German banks (Dresdner Bank, Deutschebank and Commerzbank) account for much of the banking system's influence over the larger industrial enterprises.[19] As a matter of fact, one has to look to Japan to find a similar example of bank–industry co-operation. There, the role of the public Industrial Bank of Japan is pre-eminent, whereas the German case is based ultimately on a small group of major private-sector institutions.

It is arguable that the banks' role in industry is excessive and can lead both to conflict of interests beween a firm's bankers and other shareholders and to maintaining the underdeveloped state of the German capital market (although the powerful anti-trust agency, the Bundeskartelamt, provides a check on some oligopolistic tendencies). It is also arguable that as the profitability and equity base of German industry decline with the current recession, government will necessarily have to take a greater role in financing the restructuring of major firms.

Reforming the institutional relationship has been considered in the past, but no action has been taken. This is understandable in view of the relative success of the present system and the absence of a clear short-run alternative in the current deteriorating situation. In spite of the official anti-interventionist position, several observers expect a growth in State intervention in any event, including financing, because the difficulties in some German firms could become too great for their banks to handle. A 1983 *Economist* survey concluded on this point: 'German banks are not prepared (and probably not able) to hold up heavy industry indefinitely. Recession is driving the wedge of government between them and their corporate customers.'[20] On the other hand, German industry still has advantages in management, technology, and quality. These have engendered almost as much international admiration as the Japanese, and should provide the basis for continued strength,[21] at least in their pre-eminent engineering sector (although concern has been expressed as to whether the German machine tool industry can successfully make the transition from mechanical to electro-mechanical engineering).

The public sector in Germany   In view of the emphasis given to market-economies in Germany, it is sometimes overlooked that there are in fact several publicly-owned industrial enterprises there. These include majority-owned companies in steel, chemicals, aluminium, and minority State participation in automobiles and chemicals. Both federal and *Länder* governments are, of course, also extremely involved in coal mining, electricity generation, transport and other public utilities, as well as nuclear energy.[22] Although public sector industry is a good deal smaller in Germany than in the other large European economies, it has none the less absorbed significant amounts of public resources. These enterprises have a mixed record in their contribution to the efficiency of the German economy. Jürgen Donges questions whether the state sector has achieved its objectives at lowest possible cost, with the possible exception of Volkswagen, whose management has been allowed to run the firm on a more or less private basis. He also points out that public sector enterprises have been slow to adjust to international competitive pressures and draws attention to *de facto* national purchasing policies of the public sector.[23]

Industrial research and development support   In recent years government R&D expenditures in Germany have increased, particularly benefiting economic services, industrial promotion, and energy. Most of this expenditure is channelled through the Federal Ministry of Technology (BMFT). Dr Andrew Black, at the International Institute of Management (IIM) in Berlin, has estimated on the basis of BMFT data that total federal R&D expenditure had reached 0.7 per cent of GDP by 1981, with about half spent on projects of economic, energy, or industrial interest.[24]

The growing interest in innovation is also illustrated by the introduction in 1982 of a system of subsidies to firms covering up to 40 per cent of the costs of micro-electronic systems.

A rather different interpretation of German industrial policy is provided by Victoria Curzon-Price[25] from an avowedly anti-interventionist, free-trade point of view. She argues that the key element in German industrial policy is anti-trust legislation, which she finds compatible with a 'maximum of concertation between employers, employees and the state . . .'. She describes the role of the State as 'discreet', for example in regional aid, in coal (where federal aid has been as much as 30 per cent of value added!), in promoting high-technology, and in occasionally providing adjustment assistance. 'In the case of company failures, the state will not provide assistance although the private banking system may do so.' Regarding the AEG–Telefunken case, Victoria Curzon-Price criticizes what Ralf Dahrendorf viewed as a strength. She says '. . . [the case] shows how far a powerful banking system can go in resisting the verdict of the market and ignoring the best interests of its depositors and shareholders.'[26]

To conclude, it is hardly possible to decide which direction German industrial policies will go in the future. The present government, even more than its predecessor, seems to prefer competitive industries developing through market forces in an internationally open economy. This policy has strongly influenced the federal government's attitude in the Community and in the OECD.

However, there clearly is enough State intervention in the German economy to provide a target for the criticisms of some of the economic research institutes, for example in their Structural Reports. National regulations, standards, and public procurement also appear to be sufficiently effective to provide an obstacle to exports to Germany from other countries, including her EC partners.

There is also the question of the weakening performance of much of German heavy industry. As noted above, some observers expect these problems to get worse because of low growth in the domestic and international markets for German products, declining profitability and investment, and a certain delay in the development of the next generation of technologies, particularly in semiconductors and micro-electronics. Consequently, it is not inconceivable that the role of the state in German industry will continue to be significant, and even increase, political preferences notwithstanding.

II.2. Industrial policy in France

Industrial policy in France has attracted a considerable international literature because it is the only European example of a fairly consistent attempt to organize government–business relationships for industrialization and growth over a considerable period. The principal characteristics of French industrial policies today can be traced back at least to the post-World War II plans, and in certain respects much farther back to the development of the centralized French nation-State during the eighteenth century.[27] Most authors analysing these relationships have identified the same underlying factors:

- centralized public administration,
- a large public sector extending into a wide range of sectors, including banking,
- extensive regulation of the financial markets,
- an unusual degree of symbiosis and interchangeability among the managerial élite in government, finance, and industry.

Thus despite the fact that economic planning as such and the Commissariat General au Plan in particular have become much less important than they were during the 1950s and 1960s, it has still been possible for French governments to exercise considerable control over industrial development in both the public and private sectors. The government's influence over the financial markets is exercised not only through public ownership of banks and credit agencies, but also through the authorization of new issues on the bond market, exchange control, and the various possibilities of interest subsidies for investments corresponding to national priorities.[28] In view of the recent controversy over the present government's nationalizations, it should be noted that France already had a large public sector, which had been growing steadily under previous governments as public sector enterprises diversified into new fields. Patrick Messerlin draws attention to this phenomenon of *nationalisations silencieuses* which accelerated in the late 1970s through the growth of public investment.[29]

By and large it is certain that this interventionist system contributed to the rapid growth of French industry, at least up to the early 1970s. There have, however, been significant and costly errors, some of which might have been avoided. But the question of what might have happened had French policy been less interventionist is hypothetical, except to note that there is little historical evidence in France for the kind of spontaneously entrepreneurial private sector that happened in the United Kingdom in the eighteenth century and in the United States in the nineteenth century. It has been estimated that only three in a thousand engineering graduates of the *grandes écoles* establish their own firms.[30] It may well be that industry in France has needed the reassuring and comforting hand of the State before it would invest and take risks commensurate with the needs of a modern economy.

This having been said, the government of Professor Raymond Barre attempted to introduce a different approach, particularly during 1978–80. It relied more on market forces, deregulating prices, and allowing loss-making firms to go bankrupt if necessary. The episode is described in greater detail by Victoria Curzon-Price.[31] We also know that this approach was politically difficult to sustain, if not controversial.

Christian Soffaës pointed out that the number of industrial bank-ruptcies in France rose from an average of 1,500 per year during 1968-73 to 30,000 per year during 1975-9.[32] In practice, the policy of the previous French government did not go nearly as far towards liberalizing the economy as might have been expected from official statements at the time. Stephen Cohen, James K. Galbraith, and John Zysman have emphasized the extent to which the regulation of indus-trial credit and State guarantees could be and were used during this period to achieve the objective of a '. . . flexible, selective, highly articulated industrial policy . . .'.[33]

In any event, we now know that the relative liberalization of the French economy under the Barre government did not last long. There was a shift back to an active State-conceived industrial policy following the 1981 elections and the constitution of a socialist government under President Mitterand and Prime Minister Mauroy.

It is difficult to describe and assess the present French government's industrial policies objectively. They have undeniably been the subject of a rather controversial debate. Whereas the nationalism which has engendered so much criticism has proved to be more rhetorical than real, the policies themselves have been unstable. There have been four ministers of industry in two years; a new working balance between the interventionist State and the enlarged (but still in principle autono-mous) public sector is yet to be found; and policies have been neces-sarily amended to take account of a deteriorating macro-economic situation and (fortunately) to bring trade measures back into line with European Community rules. Understandable as these developments may be, they give rise to a doubt as to whether what one writes today will still be relevant tomorrow.

French industrial policy[34] aims first to improve industrial structure, which means reinforcing the input-output relationships between its industrial sectors in order to establish or sustain autonomous capabili-ties in all the main industrial fields. Its second aim is to improve the ability of industry to adjust (e.g. support and services for small com-panies) and to improve firms' relationships with their environment (e.g. through finance, training schemes, and standards). The main underlying objectives are to reduce energy dependence, modernize basic industries, maintain competitiveness of secondary manufactur-ing, introduce new technologies (nuclear, aerospace, oceanic, computer, and communications), and the development of agro-industries.

To date the main measures taken to implement these policies have been the extension of the public sector through the nationalization of five large groups and the extension of State control in seven others.[35] The Ministries of Industry and Research have been merged and a new Industrial Development Law is to be presented by the government following consultation and debate with industry and all others concerned.

Business conditions are also being improved by reducing employer social security contributions (which are particularly high in France) and by temporary wage controls. At the same time, price controls, reduced working hours (to thirty-nine hours a week), and the fifth week of paid holiday have increased industrial costs. Measures will also be taken to mobilize private savings for industrial investment. Public expenditure on R&D will be increased rapidly and an attempt is being made to improve the links between the official research centres and industrial users. French industrial policy will continue to address restructuring of basic industries, modernizing manufacturing, and promoting future activities, such as electronics, communications, biotechnology, and energy saving.

In certain respects, the objectives of industrial policy have been overtaken by events in the short-term. A counsel of caution would be to avoid at all costs the experience of the British Labour government during 1965-7, when economic plans (at the time more or less inspired by the French model) were hurriedly abandoned in the face of balance-of-payments crises.

During 1981-2 France's first round of measures provoked considerable criticism in the EC because of their potentially protectionist and discriminatory effects. These measures, which were principally designed to favour machine tools, textiles, furniture, leather goods, and toys and games, seem to have been conceived with a mixture of motives in mind. The first concerns the balance of trade. There is a justifiable concern that in the event of economic expansion, France and the United Kingdom in particular will encounter serious balance of payments difficulties because of the rapid growth of imports of manufactures. This problem will have to be addressed in the EC one way or another.[36] Secondly, the concern about textiles and leather goods is essentially a matter of protecting employment in sectors which are in any case experiencing difficult adjustment problems. (Issues of aid and national protection for textiles are longstanding in the EC, under previous French governments and in most other member states as well.)

More basic industrial policy issues arise in the case of the machine tool industry. Here the problem is the simultaneous recession in demand for traditional machine tools with a boom in demand for numerically controlled machine tools (i.e. those controlled by a programme operating a microprocessor), in which French and indeed most European machine tool manufacturers are still relatively weak. (How can one encourage the modernization of machine tool equipment in industry without decimating the machine tool industry in the process?)

In such a context there is a strong risk that national measures will in practice be discriminatory, particularly if the starting point of the national industry is weak (as is the case with the French numerically controlled machine tool industry) and that national governments may find that they and down stream industry become locked into a costly national policy. The problems which may arise notably concern discrimination between national and other European suppliers in incentive schemes (which would be against the EEC Treaty) or in public purchasing. (For example, procurement of machine tools by vocational training centres or by public sector enterprises would not be subject to Community directives for public purchasing.) In some cases, of course, a national strategy may succeed. But given the size of national markets in Europe, compared with the US and Japan, and the undistinguished starting point of many European firms, one must at least recognize that national strategies are high-risk strategies, the more so if other European governments follow suit.

This argument is implicitly recognized by the French authorities in the case of the electronics industry. In March 1982 a special commission chaired by Abel Farnoux delivered its report to the French government on the *Filière Electronique*, setting out its recommendations for the future development of this field in France.[37] The Farnoux report recognizes that since France represents only 6 per cent of the world market, since French producers will not be able to control all of the national market, and since large volumes will be necessary to cover major investments, the French strategy should be global with world markets in view and European markets in the first place. The report also recommends co-operation between European companies and Community preferences for public purchases and technical standards.

However, these qualifications notwithstanding, the Farnoux report recommends in all other respects an integral, self-contained, national development strategy for the electronics industry which would sustain national independence and deal with all elements of the industry at all levels.[38]

Apart from the inherently high risks which such a strategy[39] involves at a national level, there are two other drawbacks. The first is that similar national strategies in several member states will interact negatively: the inverse of a comprehensive French strategy aimed at the rest of the European market is another member state's strategy aimed at the French market. Parallel national programmes increase the mutual risks of failure. At the same time, the existence of one major national programme is likely to lead to several others. There is some evidence that this is already happening.[40]

The second objection is that although most national strategies pay lip-service to international and European co-operation, in practice there is considerable scope for duplication between them. It may consequently be difficult for the EC governments to reach agreement on the content of European industrial co-operation if they are meanwhile engaged in national policies which aim to some extent at pre-empting leading positions in the European market.[41]

In the medium term, these conflicts between the objectives of national industrial strategies could do far more damage to European industry than the short-term effects of nationalization and balance-of-payments-related protection on intra-EC competition, although it is the latter which have attracted most criticism to date from liberal economic commentators. The nationalizations have been criticized as giving the public sector too easy access to public funds (whereas the French government already had extensive influence over the financing of industrial investment). The protectionist measures have been criticized as being unfair to France's trading partners (which indeed they would be). But there has been more vigorous criticism of these measures' affects on private markets (e.g. furniture and leather goods) rather than public markets, possibly because most governments are discriminating in these fields.

Although the language surrounding French industrial policy still sounds more 'national' than in other member states, there is increasing evidence of a significant shift of policy towards a stronger emphasis on international and particularly European co-operation and trade. As early as November 1982 President Mitterand, addressing a national conference on industrial policy,[42] was advocating alliances between European electronics firms for video products and the EC financing of investments undertaken jointly by several European companies. He also rejected protectionism as a general palliative, supporting competitive business as the way to reduce import penetration and attacking protectionism in France's trading partners, unfair trading practices, and 'surreptitious' alliances with American companies.

By September 1983 the French position had evolved further, as set out in a memorandum to the Council of Ministers.[43] The basic theme now is the penalities that a divided market imposes on European industry. The memorandum argues for greater European co-operation in R&D, creation of harmonized technical standards for new products, opening public procurement to European manufacturers, and a trade policy supporting European industrial objectives.

In view of these developments, the French government's imposition of onerous customs clearance procedures for imports of Japanese VCRs at Poitiers and the resulting furore seems not only out of place, but uncharacteristic. In retrospect that episode was beside the point from the view of industrial policy. It perhaps made some sense in terms of quickly restraining rapidly rising consumer expenditure which was a short-term drain on the balance of payments, but in that case an especially high VAT rate or excise duty would have been a more appropriate instrument. As a salutory gesture to Japan (where similar devices are not unknown) Poitiers was perhaps counter-productive, not because it was unjustified, but because it could not be sustained. On the other hand, it had the desired effect of concentrating the minds of France's EC partners. It also persuaded Japanese companies that they had to license and manufacture their products in France and elsewhere in the EC.

There is, however, a lesson to be learned from this experience. In the case of high-technology products with significant scale economies and learning-curve effects, the time to protect—if one is going to do so—is *before* foreign competitors have obtained most of the domestic market! Some form of protection will be a necessary element of European industrial strategies for new high-technology industries because European industry has so much ground to make up. Given the EC rules on trade and competition, it will have to be European protection, in which case the underlying industrial policies will have to be agreed by the Community as well.

II.3. Industrial policy in Greece

As one of the smaller member states, Greece's industrial policy may be thought to be peripheral to our principal concerns. However, the striking changes in policy introduced by the PASOK (socialist) government do afford an interesting example of radical or socialist policies in a small, peripheral, industrializing country, and may indeed prove to be a thorn in the flesh to the European Community, unused to accomodating such policies within the Common Market framework.

The Greek industrial situation is particular in the European context. To find an analogous situation elsewhere in Europe one must search among the peripheral regions of larger member states, such as the Scottish Highlands or the southern Mezzogiorno, or perhaps look at Ireland at a much earlier date.

In the national economy, manufacturing industry is dominated by tourism, shipping, and a large but hardly competitive agricultural sector. Within manufacturing, apart from a handful of medium-sized firms, there are a host of small-to-very-small enterprises. Textiles, leather goods, food products, and building materials are the largest manufacturing sectors. The construction industry is also a major activity providing business for local manufacturers. Manufacturing activity is inordinately concentrated in the Athens–Piraeus area and to a lesser extent in Salonica.

The principal objectives of Greek industrial policy seem to be:

— to promote food processing on the basis of local agricultural co-operatives,
— to enhance the size, productivity, and innovation of small enterprises,
— to improve the regional distribution of activities,
— to encourage foreign private investment in the selective development of high-technology activities.

The main instruments of policy are still in the process of being set up, so this can at best be an interim description. The initial objective is to re-establish competitiveness through a restrictive incomes policy and through making it much more difficult for public sector employees to go on strike. The principal measure is a new law concerning incentives to support regional and economic development,[44] which supplements those provided in a 1961 law[45] to promote foreign investment. Further efforts are being made by the new government to promote foreign investment with other OECD countries. Thus foreign investment is still welcome in Greece, but with strict development criteria.

The new law provides for subsidies and interest rebates on loans for new economic investments (adjusted according to the nature of the expenditure) and to regional priorities. The government has developed objective criteria for these aids. As a rule the corresponding loans will be made by commercial banks, but the government has reserve powers to ask them to make 'required loans' or, at the limit, to have ETBA,[45] the State-controlled investment bank, make the loans.

The second instrument is the small company promotion agency, EOMMEH,[47] which provides finance for technical assistance for these enterprises.

The new law also envisages state participation in subsidized enterprises (Article 10), although the criteria and objectives of such participation are not clear.

Press reports[48] suggest that this possibility for State participation has been exercised with great moderation to date, but that the prospect has still inhibited foreign investors. If so, this may reflect a reaction on the part of multinationals that benefited in the past from a remarkably generous charter for their activities in the preceding legislation for foreign investment.[49]

No new nationalization of existing manufacturing enterprises has been reported since the PASOK government came to power, in spite of its socialist programme and the public sector's small share in manufacturing compared with other European countries. However, there is a new law (June 1983) providing for workers' participation in control of the administration and public enterprises.

Greek industrial policies relate to their membership of the European Community in several ways. In the first place, the longer-term objectives of present government policies are shared by the Community and should in principle be supported by the EC industrial, regional, and social policies. However, these policies, as they stand at present, may not be very effective for industrial development in Greece. The main burden of regional development, small company promotion, and industrial training will for the time being fall on the Greek authorities.

The second issue (which has been raised by the Greek government) is the longer-term compatibility of established Community policies with the development of the Greek economy. The government's position is set out in a Memorandum addressed to the Council in March 1982.[50] The main requests are for increased Community financial support and exceptions to competition rules to be extended over an adequate period. To some extent the Greek position can be met within the provisions of the Accession Treaty, particularly in the transitional periods, and of the Greek Protocol.[51]

The Commission's position on this subject considered that the Community could to a large extent adapt its policies to the Greek situation and requirements, but could not make exceptions to the Treaties.[52] The Commission recalled that the Community cannot take over the full costs and responsibilities of developing a member state, but can at best support national policies. Furthermore, the Greek government was invited to take account of Community policies in developing its own priorities, particularly in the preparation of the five-year plan.

A second area of potential disagreement concerns Greek aids to exports. These are provided for particularly through the remission of social security and payroll taxes[53] and in Community law can only be remitted for exports outside the Community.[54]

Thirdly and more fundamentally, the Community would not allow protection of newly established enterprises if this involved trade protection against goods from other member states. This position, which corresponds to the Commission's existing philosophy, raises some theoretical and practical issues.

It is difficult on the one hand to argue that the Commission shares the Greek government's analysis of the Greek economic situation and agrees with the need to act resolutely to face up to the situation, and on the other hand to refuse to consider one of the principal instruments of early industrial development: infant-industry protection. At the same time, the Commission admits the desirability of investment aids, particularly to small enterprises, but the Community is not at present in a position to contribute significantly to their costs. Furthermore, the Commission does in practice allow manufacturing enterprises elsewhere in the Community to be protected by a variety of measures, including for example differential electricity tariffs, selective public purchasing, and national technical standards. In those cases where temporary infant-industry protection can be justified in Greece, it would perhaps be wise to admit it subject to review and eventual withdrawal by the Commission, rather than to refuse it in principle and push the Greek government and enterprises towards other forms of protection, which may be more expensive and prove to be more intransigent in the long term. In this context it is not surprising that the Minister of National Economy has emphasized national public purchasing as a major instrument of industrial development in the future,[55] including current purchases, the investment programme of public enterprises and agencies, as well as goods presently purchased by the State, which is the largest single importer.

In the longer term, tensions are likely to arise between Greece and the Community concerning the development of additional capacity in Greece in sectors which are depressed in the Community as a whole.[56]

Such situations are in fact a reflection of more general sectoral problems and should be treated as such. There are, however, a few general principles which are relevant. The first concerns the long-term viability of capital-intensive or energy-intensive activities in Greece, which should be very carefully appraised in the present and foreseeable economic situation; otherwise there is a serious risk of major problems becoming a permanent charge on the Greek economy and budget. Secondly, there is the question of sectors which are protected at the European level, particularly the textile and clothing industries.

To some extent, Community protection will be to the advantage of the low-cost producers within the Community. This has been the case for Italy, and Greek firms could take advantage of the system in the same way. However, there are two limits to this process. First, Community protection is neither absolute nor permanent, so Greek firms will have to take care that their new production will be competitive without protection. Second, the textile industry is protected essentially to allow time for existing producers to adjust; there is bound to be a political reaction within the Community if domestic free trade undermines the gains from protection.[57] This phenomenon is of crucial concern to the Commission because of the effect on its negotiating position *vis-à-vis* textile producers in the rest of the world. They would certainly criticize an 'adjustment' which took the form of transferring Community textile production progressively towards new member states without significant improvements in international market access.

In conclusion, Greek industrial policy is likely to become a recurrent issue in the Community, not so much because of the objectives and orientation of the government, but rather because this is the first time that the government of a small pre-industrial member state has tried to develop its economy in a world recession.

In the event, however, the first clash between Greek policies and the Community has not been a matter of industrial policy, but rather of import restraint to support the balance of payments following the rapid deterioration of the current account balance and the terms of trade which occurred after EC membership. A substantial devaluation of the Drachma had to be accompanied by import restraint to cushion the effects and give Greek industry some time to adjust. Meanwhile, the underlying industrial policy issues remain unresolved.[58]

III. European Community industrial policies

Many of the benefits of integration in the European economy are compromised by problems of structural adjustment and by national measures which are designed to improve the situation (either by controlling the rate of decline of some activities or by promoting new activities), but actually tend to aggravate it by 'renationalizing' parts of the Common Market by accident or design. With very low growth, most markets are the zero-sum game (i.e. what one gains another partner must lose). Furthermore, sooner or later most of these problems come to Brussels because the Commission has to arbitrate whether member states are respecting the EC rules for domestic trade or subsidies, and because the Commission has to negotiate the international trade aspects of domestic industrial problems.

The case for European rather than national industrial policies rests on:

— eliminating the inefficiences of more or less rival national policies.
— reducing the unfairness arising from the fact that few member states have both the resources and the national market to sustain the semblance of a successful national industrial policy. (In practice Germany is probably alone in this respect. These differences contribute to the growing divergency in the performance of the national economies within the EC.)
— reducing the number of zero-sum situations by keeping the domestic market as open and competitive as possible and promoting new activities. (At best, national protectionism improves national access to one national market—which may be growing—at the expense of the other member states' access to that market. Thus dispassionate and agnostic as one may be about the theory of free trade, the national protectionist in Europe has to answer the fairly basic criticism that net benefits are assured only in so far as no other member state decides to behave likewise.)

— Community industrial strategy being both a political and an economic idea. Precisely because there are interferences between one member state's policies and what happens in another economy, the appropriate political level of conception, implementation, and control of industrial policy is the Community itself.[59]

It is useful to review in this context the essential features and some of the principal problems of EC policies for the integration of the domestic market, the promotion of industrial investment, and the development of high-technology activities. These three areas are selected because they are currently the subject of an intensive effort on the part of the Commission and because the other major area of Community industrial policy—steel—is already the subject of an extensive literature.

It is a truism to recall that the Community is an historically immature organization when it comes to taking difficult decisions. The EC institutions' powers *vis-à-vis* the member states are heavily restricted. Perhaps more important, the overall resources (budgetary and otherwise) available to the Community are still so limited that the scope for compensating the losers in any particular decision are excessively limited, and the trade-offs and side-payments, which one would expect to arise in the context of a better integrated organization, are not possible. Consequently, it can be costly and painful to be on the losing side in an individual Community decision.

Furthermore, slow economic integration and successive enlargements mean that there are great and growing divergencies in the structure of the national economies, so in the short term it is rarely evident to the member states that any particular EC measure would be to the advantage of all of them. The fear that Community decisions seeking overall benefits may at the same time impose unacceptable and uncompensated costs on certain interests is a major obstacle to the development of industrial policy in the Community. It also supports the short-term justification for national measures.

III.1. Integration of the domestic EC market[60]

Domestic trade between the member states has been growing until recently as a direct consequence of economic growth and the development of the Common Market. The level of domestic trade is of crucial importance to all member states, accounting for more than half their total trade. Domestic trade has also proved to be more robust than foreign trade, although not immune to the current recession. However, there are major difficulties in sustaining the process of integration.

The problem of non-tariff barriers The panoply of national measures restricting domestic trade between the member states has been thoroughly documented and reported on by the Commission. (The most recent report on this subject provides an inventory,[61] but we do not have space here to give a detailed commentary.) These obstacles are evidently resilient to the Commission's endeavours to remove them.[62] Consideration of the state of the domestic market gives rise to the following observations.

There are substantial areas of manufacturing activities subject to national regulation or purchasing policies which are much less exposed to domestic EC competition than sectors such as automobiles and machine tools. Furthermore, the domestic non-tariff barriers (NTBs) which exist not only have a protective effect and impose costs, but also have far-reaching effects on public opinion and the attutides of business managers.

The second general observation is that if there is a case for preference and a degree of trade management at the level of the Community, why is the analogous argument not equally valid at the level of the member states? In this case would not domestic NTBs consequently be justified? This is clearly a question to be asked, since national protectionism is indeed advocated and practised in the Community. The answer lies first in the sizes of the national economies. Compared with the domestic competition and economies of scale available to industries operating in Japan or the United States—particularly in new, rapidly growing product areas, the Community market cannot afford to remain fragmented.[63] Furthermore, the bulk of national NTBs seems to arise from historical happenstance. They are hardly justified on the grounds of balance of payments, employment, or national industrial policy considerations.

Thirdly, the present condition of the domestic market combined with national protectionism in some of the larger member states will oblige the smaller member states to adopt artificially internationalist policies,[64] relying on foreign investment and free trade rather than integrating their manufacturing economies with the rest of the EC economy. To some extent this reflects the prediction that small economies are most likely to benefit from free trade and are less likely to be penalized for the exceptions that they may make. But this strategy has its drawbacks. The smaller member states are even more dependent on domestic EC trade than the larger member states, and would be the most exposed to increased national protectionism. The strategy also exposes the smaller economies to the future decisions of the multinational companies which have invested in them and which retain their independent ability to disinvest and relocate internationally. The articulated opposition of the multinationals to the proposed Community directive on informing and consulting their employees speaks volumes of the value these companies place on their independence in this respect.[65]

Community preference It is useful to recall the international basis for Community preference, because the EC should extend preferences to domestic firms, at least transitionally, in so far as the national governments are prepared to relax their national discriminatory policies. The GATT recognizes that a customs union is a legitimate exception to general application of the non-discriminatory 'most favoured nation' rule. That is, a customs union which eliminates duties on trade between its members is not constrained to extend those preferences to other GATT contracting parties. Article XXIV of the GATT recognizes that the purpose of a customs union should be to facilitate trade between its members and not to raise barriers to trade with non-member countries. The duties and regulations applied by the customs union to external trade should not be 'higher and more restrictive' than those previously applying in the constituent member states.[66] From the EC point of view this exemption of customs unions from the most-favoured-nation rule implies that 'the community [may] reserve for its members the advantages resulting from an intensification of their mutual ties as long as this does not involve a deterioration in the treatment of non-Community countires by comparison with the earlier situation'.[67]

The issue, then, is whether the Community may institute domestic EC preferences with non-tariff barriers (such as public purchasing or technical standards) by analogy with the application of Article XXIV of the GATT to customs duties. This question is of some importance because the Commission does envisage Community preference within a European industrial area[68] and this proposal is currently criticized as constituting an increase in protectionism, which it does not.[69] Furthermore, there are indications that the GATT and the EC's trading partners do not see things the same way. In particular, the GATT agreements on technical barriers to trade and government procurement[70] make no reference to Article XXIV of the GATT. In fact, Article 9.3 of the Technical Barriers Agreement suggests the opposite, in that members of regional certification systems are expected to ensure access by non-member countries on equally favourable conditions.

Public purchasing A large part of GDP in all EC member states is spent by governments and other public agencies. Significant proportions of their budgets are used to purchase material and equipment. There is a strong and universal tendency for such public purchasing to be restricted to national companies, although to varying degrees competition is organized through invitations to tender.

There are broadly three reasons for wanting to 'open' public purchasing to firms operating in other countries.

— to obtain the benefits of increased competition, principally through lower prices,

— in the event of international financing, to allow companies in the financing countries to tender for the projects,[71]
— to benefit from innnovation or scale economies, at the same time as encouraging standardization in the industry.

In the Community only the first motive has to date had any effect on policy, and that has been limited. The procurement directives provide for publication in the EC's Official Journal of notices of certain projects or orders, which is supposed to allow companies in other member countries to tender for contracts. However the obligation stops at publication. There is no obligation to accept the best value nor to justify the award of contracts. Given the small number of sectors covered by the directives (certain public works and supplies), the small proportion of contracts placed with companies from a different member state, and the widespread feeling that even the modest requirements of these directives are not fully respected, it is not surprising that disillusion is leading national industrial interests to turn back to supporting national purchasing policies. For example, the Confederation of British Industry (CBI) reported that there had been a shift in opinion '. . . away from the belief in the opportunities which liberalization might bring and towards a strict insistence on reciprocity of market access'.[72]

The second motive has had surprisingly little effect in the Community. Investments financed by Community funds, and particularly by the Regional Fund, are only required to conform to the directives; i.e. the procedures must be respected, but the evaluation of tenders is neither reported nor reviewed. The European Investment Bank has tried harder to nudge its borrowers in the direction of more open procurement. The bank's strongest argument evidently is the scope for reducing project costs, but in the absence of an effective Community policy the effect has necessarily been limited.

The third motive for competitive public purchasing proves in practice to be the principal obstacle. Governments are only too well aware of the effects of their purchasing policies on employment and industrial structure. While most EC governments admit that the private sector has benefited from the integration of the domestic EC market, they still have to be convinced that analogous benefits may be available from the integration of markets dominated by the public sector. Recent experience is discouraging, as illustrated by the Council of Ministers' inability to act on the Commission's proposal to open public purchasing for part of the market for telecommunications equipment. It will be interesting to see whether the privatization of British Telecom leads to more liberal procurement policies there.

Part of the problem is different views about the role of Community preference. The principal objective of competitive public purchasing in high-technology industries should be the integration and rationalization of the domestic EC market and industry, rather than simply reducing the price of the equipment purchased in the short term. Consequently, the degree of protection embodied in today's national discriminatory purchasing policies should be translated into an equivalent—but not greater—Community preference. Otherwise the rationale and support for a Community purchasing policy evaporates, at least from the point of view of industrial policy.

An alternative policy is embodied in the GATT public purchasing code, agreed in the context of the 1978 Tokyo round. Article II of the code provides that governments shall provide to *all* other suppliers from GATT contracting parties 'no less favourable [treatment] than that accorded to domestic products and suppliers and that accorded to products and suppliers of any other party'. Furthermore, the parties 'shall not apply rules of origin . . . for purposes of government procurement . . . which are different from the rules of origin applied in the normal course of trade . . .'.[73]

The Community's experience in this field may suggest that the signatories of the GATT code were optimistic. The UK House of Commons Select Committee on the Internal Market reported the CBI's view that both the EC and GATT procurement codes have had 'very little effect' to date.[74]

The way forward out of this quagmire would seem to depend on three essential points:
- placing liberalization of public purchasing for high-technology products firmly in the context of a Community industrial policy;
- recognizing that initially Community preference will replace national preferences and include the possibility of extending Community preference to EFTA manufacturers in certain sectors;
- acceptance on the part of the Community's trading partners that Article XXIV of the GATT applies to the public purchasing code. This would legitimize Community preferences internationally in the same way as the common external tariff is accepted as an exception to the most-favoured-nation clause.

If these steps are not taken, the present situation is likely to continue.

Technical standards Another major area of domestic NTBs in the Community are national technical standards, whether public or private. The Commission's policy in this field has been to negotiate the progressive harmonization of technical standards using the provisions of Article 100 of the EEC treaty. Although there have been a few success stories (notably in the area of automobile components), the overall picture as reported by the Commission is discouraging, not least because of the inordinate time required to negotiate Community technical standards and the rapid development of new national standards.

One telling example is quoted by the CBI, discussing the market prospects of fibre-reinforced composite materials:

Unfortunately, performance standards for composite products have been set independently in each European country. Hence, the mandatory requirements which manufacturers have to meet tend to differ significantly. In their larger home market the United States producers do not suffer from this disadvantage.[75]

This example is not alone. A recent consultant study addresses the extent to which EC companies have developed their corporate strategies on the basis of an EC-wide home market. Referring to instrument engineering, and particularly to weighing and slicing equipment, they observe that:

The key feature is the current switch from mechanical to electronic measurement and operation . . . the harmonization of specifications has failed to keep pace with this switch. Furthermore the inspection regulations for new products leading to the type approved all tend to be slightly different in each member state, and take much too long to complete (up to 36 months, in one case). Safety regulations also vary widely. . . . This . . . undermines the need for maximum economies of scale to compete with the Japanese, who switched to an electronic technology earlier.[76]

With respect to technical standards, the Commission's policy is to pursue the unending task of harmonization and to try to reduce the scope for conflicts of interest by a system of advance information and consultation. This is all very well in so far as national industries and governments are in fact interested in removing differences and creating common standards. However, in view of the slow progress and considerable practical difficulties which have been experienced in recent years, it could equally well be argued that a more far-reaching Community approach is required, especially for new high-technology products, in which case the scope and responsibilities of a European Standards Institute should be considered.

In this context Article XXIV of the GATT gives the EC the right in principle to extend Community preference to the area of technical standards, and it is important that Article 2.2 of the GATT Code on Technical Regulations and Standards be interpreted in this light. However, the EC should exercise this discretion selectively because of the importance of international standards for exporting industries. In any event, it is important that standards are brought as quickly as possible into the public domain, both in principle and in practice; otherwise not only will national standards constitute non-tariff barriers, but private standards will form the basis of oligopolistic positions.

Managing domestic trade imbalances   The prospect of rising domestic protectionism in the Community is sufficiently tangible that its causes and the ways of handling it should be considered as dispassionately as possible, on the basis of a thorough analysis of the relationship between domestic demand, exchange rates, inflation, and the intra-EC balance of payments of each member state.

It is not desirable that the Commission try to deal with what may prove to be a chronic problem, as the member states try to move out of the recession during the next few years, simply on the basis of formally opposing government measures which have the effect of restraining domestic trade (Article 30, EEC) in the absence of any consensus as to the underlying economic forces.

In this context it is interesting to note that the recent difficulties between the Community and France in this respect were implicitly predicted in a study published by the Cambridge Department of Applied Economics.[77] They argued that in the event that reflationary economic policies were to be pursued again, difficulties would arise from the imbalance between the position of the different member states in the Common Market. In particular, since the FRG has lower (albeit rising) unemployment than the other member states, and holds a larger share of all intra-Community trade in manufactures (39 per cent in 1981), the German authorities would be unlikely to agree to reflate enough to stimulate full recovery in the other member states. On the contrary, nationally based reflation—particularly in France and the UK—would have to be bolstered by policies to increase their shares of other EC markets and reduce other member states' shares of their markets.

Analogous conclusions are reached in a recent study of increasing tensions in the world economy by CEPII in France.[78] Their analysis of intra-Community trade flows since 1973 concludes:

The growing imbalances within Europe give grounds, in fact, for even more concern in that the EC member states' trade surpluses of manufactures with the rest of the world (in 1975 dollars) have either been stable or have deteriorated since 1975. Germany's experience is significant from this point of view. Since 1975 her surplus on trade in manufactures (in 1975 dollars) has deteriorated with the rest of the world at the same time as it has got stronger and stronger with the Community. Which makes it all the more difficult for the other European countries to earn the surpluses which they need to pay their oil bills. France is particularly concerned by the imbalances in trade in manufactures within Europe. She is in a deficit with all the countries or zones in the Community with the exception of the British

Isles. The latter are the only other countries whose situation is equally bad.[79]

In addition, a 1981 analysis by Wyn Grant concludes that '. . . the political chances of Britain adopting protectionist policies on an increasing scale in the 1980s are high'.[80]

These potential weaknesses in the domestic EC market need to be addressed because free trade in the Community is a means to an end —greater prosperity and employment—not an end in itself. Furthermore, with the recent reduction in inflation in most member states and the decline in the oil price, the macro-economic conditions for new stimuli for growth and investment are improving. It would be a shame if the benefits from a higher level of economic activity were prejudiced by internal imbalances, not least because this would provide the incentive and justification for national protectionist measures.

In this context, it would be desirable in the first place for the Commission to make its own assessment of the different relationships between imports, growth, and unemployment in the member states.

Secondly, the above argument in no way justifies the perpetuation of national NTBs, which in many cases bear no relation to the underlying imbalances in trade flows, but introduce arbitrary inefficiencies into the EC economy.[81]

On the contrary, should the Cambridge and CEPII predictions be confirmed in practice, domestic EC trade management would be a lesser evil than national protectionism, not least because any restrictions would remain under Community control. Such measures would have to be administratively simple, applying to a few large-volume and fairly standardized products. They would have to be transparent, and there is little doubt that the Community would see to it that they would be temporary.

The alternative development is all too easy to foresee. National NTBs would be maintained and reinforced[82] and—in the absence for the foreseeable future of an internationally co-ordinated reflation —national governments would attempt to protect domestic recovery, if not through higher tariffs then by selective import restrictions.[83]

In extremis, a degree of temporary domestic trade management by the Community would be better than the Common Market ceasing to be a Community policy.

I expect that it will be argued that my approach here involves a substantial departure from the principles of the EEC Treaty. From a formal point of view this is so. But since the present situation also covers extensive and pervasive departures from the same principles (which moreover prove to be politically intractable), I am prepared to consider alternatives which, in my opinion, have a stronger economic rationale than the vested interests of the many firms which benefit from the local protection of various national NTBs today.[84]

III.2. Promoting productive investment

We have already noted the declining level of industrial investment in the EC, with its resulting adverse effects on innovation and competitiveness. In broad non-economic terms it is fair to say that the rate of investment reflects society's interest in the future and concern that resources and opportunities remain commensurate with the needs and ambitions of future generations. Thus, we should endeavour to pass on to the future an enhanced, not depleted, heritage, not only in terms of our culture and environment, but also the economic system.

Several factors together result in weak investment performance, and there is no rigorous explanation of their relative importance. From the point of view of the *incentive* to invest, the recession, high levels of surplus capacity, and low profitability have been important influences. From the point of view of the *cost* of investment, risk aversion on the part of financial institutions and the high cost of capital are additional discouragements. From the technological point of view, opposing forces are at work. New technologies, if successfully introduced, can be very profitable, as illustrated by the Japanese domestic electronics and the American personal computer industries. However, as we have seen, even in profitable new technologies the risks for late entrants are great unless they can reach significant market share quickly, and this reality can discourage investment. On the down-side, the energy crises have made much industrial capacity obsolete, and energy-efficient alternatives are being introduced too slowly. Some energy-intensive processes are migrating to the few areas which still have cheap gas or electricity.

These basic changes in the structure of demand and industrial costs have imposed the need for 'restructuring' investments in the endeavour to recover competitiveness at the same time as capacity and employment are usually reduced. Current changes in technology have also made some kinds of investment particularly capital-saving, such as electronic applications in computing telecommunications or machine tools. The same capacity, or improved service, can be obtained for less investment, in which case it is less significant that the overall rate of investment is lower than before. However, this phenomenon is not an adequate explanation for low industrial investment in the EC, although such changes are certainly on the way.

In the United States (where the rate of industrial investment is also low), it is argued that this is a natural consequence of the shift to a services-based, post-industrial economy combined with the growing domestication of services (the 'self-service society'). This may indeed be a part of the explanation in their case, but the same diagnosis must be treated cautiously when applied to the EC situation. The European economies are much more dependent on exports of manufactured products than the US and, with few exceptions, European service industries are not likely to become internationally competitive in the short term, particularly those services depending on information technology.[85]

These considerations led the Commission in 1981-2 to increase the priority of industrial investment in several policy areas and to make several recommendations and proposals which were adopted by the European Council of 3-4 December 1982.[86]

The Commission's approach can be divided into three areas. First, improving the macro-economic context for private investment decisions, including integration of the domestic EC Market, reduced inflation, control of budget deficits, and reduction of real interest rates. There are great differences among the EC members regarding tax treatment of investments and losses incurred, as well as distribution of the costs of social security, and it is likely that these differences have some undetermined effect on the behaviour of firms. This aspect of the question has given rise to comparative studies (as yet incomplete) regarding the incidence of taxation (corporate taxes and social security taxes) on firms and its possible effect on the incentives for firms to invest and their access to funds.[87]

The second area concerns deliberate promotion of investment in strategically important areas of future development, such as R&D, innovation, energy, biotechnology, information technologies, and industrial conversion.[88] This can be done by reinforcing Community policies, such as steel reconversion or information technologies, or alternatively by relaxing Community State aids or anti-trust rules as they apply to national policies or corporate behaviour.

The third, and perhaps most important, aspect is the Commission's 1983 proposal to expand direct Community lending for industrial investment. This policy was quickly adopted by the Council and the new 3 billion* ECU tranche of Community loans is already being used.[89] This measure is the latest step in a now well-established policy of increasing the Community's role as a financial intermediary between international capital markets and the EC economy. In 1982 total operations (European Investment Bank, European Coal and Steel Community, Euratom, and the new Community loan facility) reached 5.25 billion ECU, 29 per cent for energy loans, 37 per cent for other productive sectors, and the balance for infra-structure.[90] Apart from modest EIB lending for manufacturing and the ECSC loans for steel,

* 1 billion = 1,000,000,000 throughout this volume.

coal, and steel reconversion areas, very little of this growing lending activity has had a direct effect on industry to date. This is now changing. The new tranche of the NCI will be used partially for investments by small companies,[91] and Community loans should be available in the future to finance larger industrial investments when the need arises. Thus in one crucial respect—the provision of long-term loan capital for industrial investment—the Community is using its economic and financial scope to create an industrial policy instrument of considerable importance for the future.

III.3. Technology and employment

The main objective of industrial policy must be to ensure that the economy has available the technologies which are necessary to remain internationally competitive[92] and to take advantage of new possibilities and opportunities for the welfare and enjoyment of the people.

In their discussion of public policy and the development of the firm, Hay and Morris[93] review on the one hand the economic characteristics of R&D expenditures, and on the other hand the divergence between private and social returns to investment in innovation.

There are three major problems with R&D expenditures in a competitive market economy: risk aversion by firms; the difficulty of appropriating R&D results; and the fact that once new information is available, it is socially optimal that it should be freely transferred (whence the well-known debate surrounding the optimum degree of patent protection).[94] Furthermore, there is empirical evidence to confirm the rather common-sense conclusion that in light of the above discrepancies between the economics of R&D expenditure and the competitive market model, there is a significant divergence between private and social returns to innovation.[95]

Consequently, the theoretical case for public intervention in R&D is based on two propositions: that without patents markets confer insufficient returns to the innovator, and that uncertainty induces firms to do less risky R&D than would be socially optimal.

To some extent, private R&D expenditures can be encouraged by tax incentives which reduce the risks or by allowing oligopolies to recoup larger returns from innovation than would arise in a competitive market.[96] In practice, these arguments—as well as more political considerations—have led European governments to support industrial R&D extensively.[97]

In light of the general argument for public support of pre-competitive R&D and the scope for duplication and dissipation of the effort in national programmes in the EC, the Commission has proposed a major long-term European R&D strategy for information technologies.[98] This programme, known as ESPRIT, was approved by the Council in

February 1984 and provides for joint financing by industry and the Community of a 1.5 billion ECU R&D programme during 1984-8. The Commission envisages that this programme '. . . must at least match comparable efforts in the USA and Japan'.[99] The scope and future development of EC policies for information technologies is discussed in Chapter IX.

As new information technologies are developed and introduced into manufacturing and service activities, the Community will have to continue to address employment and other social implications. There will be particular problems if robots are introduced extensively into manufacturing. Then many existing jobs will disappear or be totally transformed, and the new jobs which emerge will very largely be in different firms and different places, and in any case require totally different skills and training. These problems have to be recognized and resolved. If they are ignored, the social and political resistance to new technologies will rise to the point where a low-productivity, protected economy—based essentially on traditional technologies—will necessarily become a serious option.

In their recent study of robotics in the United States, Ayres and Miller[100] are fundamentally optimistic about the effects on the economy and society. Nevertheless the authors are concerned about the displacement of industrial workers and argue for radical policies to accommodate their problems. For example, they envisage a Human Resources Policy which would include a Workers' Bill of Rights. This would comprise an experience-related fund, made up of employer and employee contributions, which would finance retraining and supplementary income in the event of job loss or otherwise be converted to pension rights. The programme would emphasize mid-career retraining and educational up-grading, with a view to more major career changes during a working life.[101]

However, Ayres and Miller also suggest that their proposal should *replace* unemployment insurance. This is unrealistic because many people would experience automation-related redundancies in the near future, long before a new fund could constitute the requisite resources. They also envisage that the fund be self-financing following an initial federal endowment. This is not likely to work either: retraining mid-career people for employment in high-technology skills will not be easy or cheap. Success will be less than 100 per cent. As long as technological change is rapid and unemployment is high, there is no assurance that such a system could be self-financing, nor that the contributions of those successfully re-employed would completely reimburse the training costs of those who had insufficient accumulated contributions.

Ayres and Miller also argue that unskilled, uneducated, and

disadvantaged minorities have 'never' been productively employed and that their problems should be dealt with by different means. This is not so, and raises an issue of general relevance which cannot be ignored. The uneducated and unskilled have indeed in the past been productively and profitably employed at the level of technology and wages which prevailed, for example in Europe in the 1950s and 1960s. Their position in the European and American economies has been recently, and perhaps irrevocably, prejudiced by the growth of unit wage costs and by the increasing international mobility of technology.[102]

The main issue, however, is that not much more than half of the active population has above-average ability and that that bench-mark is very similar from one period to another and from one society to another. In addition, not much more than half the active population has above-average educational attainment. Although the second bench-mark can indeed be influenced, it may take a decade or a generation to do so. Meanwhile the social and retraining problems of high technologies will be with us. But they are not insurmountable, and they must be at the centre of high-technology policy in Europe.

The alternative, which has been outlined and sometimes condemned by several authors, envisages the emergence of a dual society consisting of 'low-wage, unskilled service jobs on the one hand, and high wage "élite" professional jobs on the other hand'.[103] For example, Daniel Bell[104] definitely envisages the emergence of a powerful professional technocracy which will become the largest single group in society. But he is remarkably silent as to the size and activities of his subordinate 'statuses' in society (technicians, clerical, and semi-skilled), admitting however that 'The politics of the future [will be] the concerns of communal society, particularly the *inclusion* of disadvantaged groups.'[105] In another more down-to-earth discussion of the same issue, Jonathan Gershuny[106] develops a convincing critique of post-industrialization, arguing essentially that tertiary activities are indissolubly related to the production of material goods. However, recognizing the effect of the drive for efficiency on employment in the formal sector of the economy, Gershuny would '. . . encourage the development in the rich countries of the northern hemisphere a sort of dual economy'[107] where the informal sector would internalize the production of a wide range of goods and services.

Other authors (particularly those writing about the United Kingdom, where the de-industrialization of the working class has evidently advanced most rapidly in recent years) are arguing that one version of the post-industrial economy is, on present trends, well on the way. Discussing the reasons for successive underestimates of total unemployment in the OECD area (which is now about 35 million people), Giles Merritt comments that 'some OECD analysts wish they had an econometric model . . . which would help forecast the two underlying factors which have already proved the downfall of almost all projections so far—the collapse of manufacturing industry and the rise of micro-technical equipment . . .'.[108] For an even more pessimistic, indeed apocalyptic, interpretation one may turn to Bill Jordan of the University of Exeter, who argues that the de-industrialization of Britain could proceed to the point where it would become a 'colonial' market for world manufacturers. He claims that the main limit to automation is the decline in working-class incomes, with a consequent depressive effect on the market for the products of automated manufacture. Jordan also argues that since the beneficial effects of protection on investment and growth are exaggerated, the only viable strategy would be at least to ensure social justice (and avoid gross political instability) by the allocation of labour and resources on a more or less World War II basis.[109]

In the American context, there is growing concern that even the large continental US economy is subject to analogous pressures. A major new study[110] draws attention to the extent of job-loss in basic industries in the United States, to the small proportion of redundant industrial workers who manage to get new jobs in high-technology industries (perhaps most significant), and to the large wage cuts which many have to take to get any sort of job at all.

In short, it is hardly necessary to labour the point that the unresolved problems arising from the decline of traditional industries aggravate the political and social context for introducing new technologies. Their employment effects will be increasingly in the forefront of public concern. If public policy for R&D in information technologies progressively becomes a major EC activity, as it could and should, then its success will be greatly strengthened by emphasizing technologies which could give rise to new products and services rather than simply rationalizing existing processes; by promoting technologies which lead to domestic EC manufacture and employment rather than simply the application of imported high-technology equipment; and by giving very high priority to retraining and re-employment of people affected by new technologies.

IV. Implementing EC industrial policy

In conclusion, it is important to refer to the way in which industrial policies in the Community might be implemented in the future, bearing in mind that the Commission has an important role but only the authority which it is given through treaties or subsequent legislation or which it acquires by virtue of its own analysis and actions. Furthermore, the EC is a mixed economy and will remain so despite the ebb and flow of the public sector in certain member states. As we have seen, it is precisely in the penumbra between public and private sector decision-making where most EC industrial policy issues arise.

During the formulative stages of EC industrial policies there will be three basic components:

- analysis and information,
- consensus building,
- capacity for implementation.

IV.1. Analysis and information

It is essential for industrial policy to be based on excellent information and analysis about the real situation in Europe and the rest of the world. It is particularly important that this be done at the Community level to generate the mutual understanding of the situation within the Community which will be needed if any action is to be taken. A common understanding of developments in the United States and Japan should also be a prerequisite for trade aspects of industrial policy.

The situation has greatly improved in this respect in recent years. Major reports have been issued on automobiles, textiles, and machine tools.[111] The Maldague reports[112] have greatly improved our knowledge of adjustment in industrial structure and trade in the Community. The more recent report on the Competitiveness of European Community Industry sets out more detailed information for the first time, comparing the EC systematically with the US and Japan.

But most of these efforts have been one-off jobs, resulting from ad hoc temporary work by Commission departments or external advisory groups. The Commission has not yet produced anything to compare with the US Congress's Office of Technology assessment for depth of analysis nor the Department of Commerce's US Industrial Outlook for regular detailed information across the whole range of industrial activities. The Japanese MITI also provides government and industry with sources of information about Japanese industry and its international competition.

This analytical role has been advocated by the Commission in its industrial strategy report, but has not yet been implemented on a permanent basis. Implementation would require a small staff of well-trained people and a modest research budget. Then the Commission could develop the basic specialization and continuity to become a centre of excellence in economic and industrial analysis.

The EC competitiveness report described immediate priorities, which have been endorsed by the Commission and the European Parliament:[113]

- improved industrial statistics,
- improved and permanent analysis of trade data,

— better information about international industrial development (US, Japan, NICs),
— analysis of the service industries,
— more detailed and disaggregated information about the main manufacturing sectors.

A regular flow of high quality, comparative analysis of industrial developments would significantly alter the technical and political context for industrial policy decisions in the Community. The provision of such information should be recognized as a responsibility of the public authorities. Without it the private sector is unable to make good decisions either, so most of the results of this analysis should be published. Most of the Community's industrial and trade data should ultimately be available on-line to the EC institutions, the governments, research agencies, universities, and the private sector, particularly industry itself.

Information of this kind is also a precondition for an EC consensus on industrial policy issues. Firstly, agreement on policy in the Community depends on all the participants knowing and understanding the situation in all the *other* member states. This does not normally transpire from the typical national sources. Secondly, reliable conclusions can only be drawn from *comparable* data. Thirdly, sooner or later many industrial policy decisions involve international discussions, either bilaterally with Japan, the US, or EFTA partners or in the OECD and GATT. It is important that the Community's position in such discussions be based on a common EC data base.

IV.2. Creating the consensus

Even modest industrial policy issues in Europe involve many actors. However convinced or convincing the Commission may be, action will be taken on the basis of a consensus between industry and public authorities in the Community and the member states. There are many ways the Community could develop this consensus about future priorities for development.

It can be argued that the most influential element of Japanese industrial policy today is the consultative and analytical process which gives rise to their 'visions' of the future. Thus coherent action towards a common purpose can be brought about to a large extent without regulatory directive powers. The Commission might consider expanding the existing 'round table' formula, informally and experimentally, to see if an analogous approach proves to be valid in other fields.

Compared with Japan or the US, the problem of creating a consensus in the Community among the member governments is a supplementary and extraordinarily cumbersome procedure. The Commission has deliberately maintained an informal environment for discussions among the member states through the non-statutory 'Directors-General for Industry' group. Similarly, the Council Presidency has preferred to keep most recent Industry Councils 'informal'. Nevertheless, the results during 1981-3 were unimpressive. The extremely slow pace of the consensus-building process between the Commission and the sometimes intransigent national ministries has been the bane of industrial policy in recent years and is a luxury which the Community cannot much longer afford.

One problem has been a tendency on the part of certain delegations to address issues primarily from a philosophical point of view. It is now time for senior officials to take the free market-interventionist polemic as read and to address more practical issues directly.

Another problem is the tendency of most delegations to address issues strictly from the point of view of the effect on their own 'national' industry as they may perceive it. Nearly all member states have been members of the Community for many years, and it is now reasonable to expect that their representatives come to Brussels to discuss EC policies in relation to the Community as a whole. Obviously national interests will be present, but they should not exclude understanding of the overall situation. The Commission's information and analysis is germane in this respect.

Prolonged, repetitive, and inconclusive meetings sap the credibility of the Community at a time of industrial crisis. The same decisions returning repeatedly to the same committees, only to rediscover the same disagreements, are creating a cynicism among the most optimistic and committed participants, not to speak of outside observers.

Compared with the national governments, industry itself could find a consensus in the Community more readily. Admittedly, industry's experience is limited, precisely because so few decisions have escaped from the web of institutional procedures. Obviously there will be difficulties, as there have been from time to time in EUROFER. But the striking thing is that so much can be agreed within industry, as evinced by the Commission's positive experience with the electronics industry round-table. In any event, the nature of the consensus with industry is more flexible because the participation of individual firms is neither obligatory nor susceptible to a veto.

IV.3. Implementation

Finally, how would EC industrial policies be implemented? It is not necessary to answer this question very specifically or comprehensively because the process of analysis and consensus-building will in practice largely determine what needs to be done and how to do it. In some circumstances there will be no call for the Community to 'intervene' on a permanent basis. In other cases it will be sufficient for the Community to give clear signals to the principal participants in a particular industry.

In so far as industrial policies will involve the Commission, the implicit credibility gap may be reduced by referring to areas where the Commission is already implementing aspects of an industrial policy, like steel.

The steel policy is implemented primarily through the Steel Department in the Directorate General for Industrial Affairs, with some support from other directorates general. The Steel Department contains about eighty-five people of all grades. All Community lending for steel reconversion is handled by two small divisions in Brussels and Luxembourg. In 1982 approximately twelve people of all grades handled about 300 million ECU of new loans through a decentralized system of agencies in the member states.

There are several other examples of policies being implemented through the Commission departments, where the Community's administrative effectiveness stands comparison with most other public authorities.

However, there are limits to what can be done with available resources. If some of the ideas presently being advocated in the European Parliament (for example, the industrial reconversion fund) become future policy, there will clearly have to be a reassessment of the allocation of staff resources in the Commission. Taken overall, the problems of implementation can be overcome in practice, provided reasonable staff resources are available to the Commission departments involved.

Implementation is not in fact the main issue. The first priority is to improve the analytical base and the consensus-building process. Experience suggests that the real bottleneck is the difficulty in reaching a political consensus with the member states. Most of the rest would follow.

Acknowledgements

This chapter is the principal outcome of research carried out during the 1982–3 academic year. I am indebted to the European Commission for a year's sabbatical and to the Center for International Affairs, Harvard, for providing the necessary intellectual stimulus and environment. Many colleagues and friends have given me encouragement, comments, editorial assistance, or typographical and secretarial help at various stages of this work.

I would particularly wish to acknowledge the advice, criticism, and assistance of Ben Brown, Raymond Vernon, Robert Putnam, Robert Reich, Jeffrey Hart, Alain Boublil, Wyn Grant, Wolfgang Hager, Lena Tsipouri, Vivian Woodward, Andrew Black, Geoffrey Shepherd, Susan Eldredge Mead, and Eva Morvay. Roger Proserpio and Marianne van Spronsen provided indispensable documentation from Brussels.

Notes and Sources

[1] For example, the *Journal of Public Policy* devoted an entire issue to the theme (vol. 3.1, 1983) and several books on the subject were published in 1982–3.

[2] See Chapters VIII, IX, and XIV.

[3] Commission of the EC, 'Competitiveness of the Community Industry', 1982.

[4] This approach is in many respects analogous to what has come to be known in French as 'strategie de filières'. My main point of disagreement with the current French version is that I very much doubt whether the French economy is large enough for it to succeed. I would also argue that if an autonomous strategy is attempted by one or more of the EC member states, it will become much more difficult for the Community as a whole to achieve a similar objective, particularly in new high-technology activities.

[5] These strategic arguments for an industrial policy are independent of specific military considerations. The military arguments for industrial independence are sometimes too far removed from economic factors. If one assumes that international trade will be interrupted in the event of a war, then there is a tendency to try to ensure that *all* conceivable aspects of any war economy are assured at home. But if one expects a modern war to reach apocalyptic proportions quickly there is little point in incurring long-term costs for the sake of strategic capacities that one might never be able to use.

[6] For a discussion of the evidence regarding learning curves see I. Magaziner and T. Hout, *Japanese Industrial Policy*, Policy Studies Institute, London, 1981.

[7] Verner, Liipfert, Bernhard, and McPherson Chtd., *The Effect of Government Targeting on World Semiconductor Competition*, for the Semiconductor Industry Association, Cupertino (Calif.), February 1983. The most striking contemporary example of the learning curve is the regular and dramatically rapid decline in the historic RAM price per bit as a function of cumulative industry-wide volume in bits. Dataquest (quoted by SIA) estimate that during 1975–80 the price per bit consistently fell by 30 per cent for each doubling of cumulative industry output!

[8] Note that this argument for temporary protection is distinct from the 'infant industry argument'. The latter, recognized by neo-classical trade theory, relates to the fact that the firm operating in an un-industrialized area will not benefit from the same external economies as its competitors in a fully industrialized area. The relevant case is the infant industry *in that area*, and the argument is in fact independent of economies of scale or learning phenomena. The latter are more likely to be relevant in trade between industrialized countries, given that they are usually experienced in relatively new high-technology industries.

[9] See in this connection Wolfgang Hager, 'Protectionism and Autonomy— How to Preserve Free Trade in Europe', *International Affairs*, Summer 1982. Hager draws a dichotomy between 'two socio-economic worlds'. 'One . . . characterized by unfree labour markets and still relatively free markets for allocating real capital. The other of free labour markets (kept free by jailing trade unionists, if necessary) and systems of capital allocation by central plans or strategic consensus.' He argues that there is no natural equilibrium solution to free trade between much different worlds, notably because 'as educational advances proceed, the supply of industrial labour in the third world will approach for practical purposes the infinite . . . (and) the marginal price of labour will remain close to subsistence level . . .'.

[10] Commission of the EC, 'Assessment of the Function of the Internal Market', COM (83) 80 final, 24 February 1983.

[11] The extent and character of existing departures from market principles in the EC's international trade are fully documented in *EEC Protectionism: Present Practice and Future Trends*, European Research Associates, Brussels, 1981.

[12] OECD, IND (79) 3, 25 April 1979.

[13] OECD, 7 June 1979.

[14] *Industrial Policies in Europe. A study of policies pursued in European countries and the EEC and their implications for the UK*, NEDO, October 1981. See also Linda Hesselman, 'Trends in European Industrial Intervention', Economic Working Paper No. 7, NEDO, July 1982.

[15] Commission of the EC, *Industrial Policies in the Community: State Intervention and Structural Adjustment*, Brussels, January 1981.

[16] English Translation circulated to the OECD Industry Committee under DSTI/IND/82.36, 21 June 1982.

[17] Dr Otto Graf Lambsdorff, 'Konzept für eine politik zus überwindung des wachstumsschwäche und zur bekämpfung der arbeitslosigkeit', 9 September 1982. (This document is reported to have contributed to the break-up of the SDF/FDP coalition in Germany that autumn.)

[18] John Zysman, *Governments, Markets and Growth*, Cornell University Press, Ithaca (NY), 1983.

[19] Ernst-Jürgen Horn, *Management of Industrial Change in Germany*, Sussex European Papers, No. 13, Sussex European Research Centre, 1982.

[20] *The Economist Survey: International Banking*, 26 March 1983, p. 56.

[21] For example, see Joseph A. Limprecht and Robert H. Hayes, 'Germany's World Class Manufacturers', *Harvard Business Review*, November–December 1982.

[22] Ernst-Jürgen Horn, op. cit., pp. 29–31, provides a more detailed inventory of state-owned industry in Germany.

[23] Jürgen B. Donges, 'Industrial Policies in West Germany's Not So Market-Oriented Economy', *The World Economy*, September 1980.

[24] Andrew P. Black, 'Industrial Policy in West Germany, Policy in Search of a Goal?', paper presented to ISVEIMER Conference, Naples, 1983.

[25] Victoria Curzon-Price, *Industrial Policies in the European Community*, Macmillan, London, 1981.

[26] Ralf Dahrendorf takes precisely the opposite view on this particular point. Commenting critically on the short-term horizon of bank-industry relationships in the United Kingdom, he observes: 'Still less are directors and bankers inclined to support an enterprise through a trough, help restructure it, appoint new management, discuss possible products, and explore new markets together. The story of AEG–Telefunken in Germany, where all this happened with the help of the Dresdner Bank, is not yet complete. The venture may yet fail. But even to try it without calling for the assistance of the government shows a different attitude by all concerned.' (From *On Britain*, BBC Publications, London, 1982, p. 95.)

The contrast between these two assessments tells us more about the authors' preconceptions than about the merits of the case. In the event, AEG has had to declare itself bankrupt and write off part of its debts. The more successful consumer electronics branch of Telefunken's business has merged with Thomson Brandt. The federal government has offered a state guarantee on a fraction of the bank loans to AEG–Telefunken, but appears nevertheless to have stayed outside the restructuring negotiations.

[27] For a more thorough description of the contribution of economic performance in France see Saul Estrin and Peter Holmst, 'French Planning and Industrial Policy', *Journal of Public Policy*, vol. 3, No. 1, 1982.

[28] For a current description of French banking/business/government relations

see 'Banking on Recovery', in *The Economist Survey: International Banking*, op. cit.

[29] Patrick A. Messerlin, *La Politique Industrielle Française*, Sussex European Research Centre, forthcoming.

[30] Yvan Gattaz, Head of the Federation of Employers' Organizations, quoted by Theodore Zeldin in *The French*, Sussex European Papers, Sussex European Research Centre, forthcoming.

[31] Victoria Curzon-Price, op. cit., p. 44.

[32] Christian Stoffaës, *Industrial Policies for the 80s*, Spanish Ministry of Industry and Energy, 1980, p. 45.

[33] Stephen Cohen, James K. Galbraith, and John Zysman, 'Credit Policy and Industrial Policy in France', in *Monetary Policy, Selective Credit Policy and Industrial Policy in France, Britain, West Germany and Sweden*, a study prepared for the Joint Economic Committee, US Congress, 26 June 1981.

[34] The following summary is drawn from 'Politique Industrielle et Situation de l'Industrie', presented to the OECD Industry Committee, Paris, 22–4 March 1983.

[35] Compagnie Générale de l'Electricité, St. Gobain-Pont à Mousson, Thomson, Pechine Ugine Kuhlman, and Rhone Poulenc were nationalized; the two principal steel companies, USINOR and SACILOR, and C.G.C.T. MATRA, CII-Honeywell Bull, and Dassault were brought under state control. There is also a majority state holding in the pharmaceutical company Roussel-UCLAF.

[36] In so far as the recent nearly $4 billion EC balance-of-payments loan to France is an alternative to French national protectionism, the issue has been temporarily resolved in favour of liberal domestic EC trade. That the question is not solved may be inferred from the concurrent demands by the French Minister of Commerce, Edith Cresson, to the effect that Germany must liberalize its own restrictions on imports (for example, on manufactured food products). This is a line of argument in which the Europeans are now well versed, since it constitutes the essence of their collective case against Japan!

[37] Abel Farnoux, *et al.*, 'Rapport de Synthèse de la Mission Filière Electronique', Ministère de la Recherche et de la Technologie, Paris, March 1982. See especially Annexe VII, 'Les Axes d'une Stratégie Globale'.

[38] Ibid., p. 8, 'This global strategy, which would leave aside no sensitive sector of the industrial structure ("filière"), has to be undertaken at all levels: research, industry, international cooperation, supporting policies, taking advantage of available synergies, and making sure that each action is consistent with the overall policy for the *filière*. Such a strategy is not only necessary . . . it is also the most economic in so far as synergies are realized within and between sectors.' (There are reasons to doubt whether such a policy would be the most economic if applied to *all* aspects of the industry. It is also clear that international co-operation will, if seriously undertaken, lead to specialization which would weaken the strength of the general proposition.)

[39] The following discussion does not imply that the Farnoux report represents French policy in detail, but discusses the strengths and weaknesses of a national electronics strategy, using the Farnoux report as one example of such an approach.

[40] The UK's recent Alvey Committee report specifically refers to the French programme as a justification for a programme 'geared to the UK's needs' which would at the same time reinforce the UK's input to any EC programme. See 'A programme for Advanced Information Technology', HMSO, London, 1982.

[41] This critique of national industrial policies in France, or for that matter in any other member state, is distinct from the liberal critique which envisages an entirely private enterprise-based approach. For example, see *L'Expansion*, 'La Guerre Mondiale des Industries 1981', 6/19 November 1981, or Bela Balassa,

'Une Année de Politique Economique Socialiste en France', *Commentaire*, No. 19, July 1982, p. 419.

[42] Speech by President François Mitterand at the Conference on French Industrial Policy, Maison de la Chimie, 16 November 1982.

[43] 'Une nouvelle étape par l'Europe: un Espace Commun de l'Industrie et de la Recherche', memorandum presented by the French government to the Council of the EC, September 1983.

[44] Law 1262/1982 Concerning Incentives to Support the Country's Regional and Economic Development and Amendment of Provisions Incidental Thereto.

[45] Law 4171/1961 General Measures to Assist the Development of the Country's Economy (as amended).

[46] Hellenic Industrial Development Bank S.A. (ETBA).

[47] EOMMEH (Ellinikos Organismas Mikro Messeon Epichiriseon) is the autonomous public corporation charged with the promotion of small companies and artisanal activities in Greece.

[48] 'Greek Industrial Policy: Anything but Nationalisation', *The Economist*, 10 April 1982.

[49] Legislative Decree 2687/1953: Investment and protection of foreign capital (as amended). This decree has not been repealed by the new government, but implementation is now based on more severe criteria. Legislative Decree 4171/1961 (see note 45).

[50] 'Position of the Greek Government on Greece's relations with the European Communities', Athens, 19 March 1982.

[51] Protocol No. 7, which was modelled to a certain extent on the precedent Protocol contained in the Accession Treaty applying to Ireland.

[52] 'Communication from the Commission to the Council concerning the Greek Memorandum of 19 March 1982', COM (82) 348 final, Brussels, 14 June 1982.

[53] Law 2861/1954, Article 5, Legislative Decree 4231/1962, Article 8.

[54] Greece presently applies a turnover tax. When this is replaced by a value added tax, it will be remitted on exports to the Community and elsewhere in the usual way.

[55] Speech by G. Arsenis, Minister for the National Economy, to financial correspondents, 25 August 1982.

[56] This problem is recognized in the transitional provisions which have been negotiated with Portugal on this issue.

[57] Note that this process would still be accompanied by major job losses in existing EC textile-producing areas.

[58] These issues have been the subject of further discussions between the Commission and the Greek government.

[59] The basic argument for an EC industrial policy has been set out in Alexis Jacquemin's article, 'Industrial Policies and the Community' in P. Coffey (ed.), *Main Economic Areas of the EEC*, Nijhoff, The Hague, 1982, and the Commission's own communication, 'A Community Strategy to Develop Europe's Industry', COM (81) 639, 1981.

[60] The awkwardness of the official translation of this term is noted by the 17th report of the House of Commons European Communities Committee, 13 July 1982: 'One of the EC's prime objectives was to create a single domestic market, often now referred to as the "Internal market".' (It is a psychological error on the part of the Community that the *domus* remains the preserve of the nation state.)

[61] 'Assessment of the Function of the Internal Market', COM (83) 80 final, 24 February 1983. For example, regulation of insurance and banking effectively discourages EC-wide competition; extensive customs, tax, and border controls also impose additional costs on trade between the member states. Furthermore,

differences in health and environmental regulations divide the national markets, and public procurement policies effectively remove important parts of the economy from intra-EC competition.

[62] 'One cannot but feel that civil service inertia has once again carried the day', Commission of the EC, COM (83) 144, 15 March 1983.

[63] For example, the US market is able to accommodate a large number of firms making personal computers.

[64] Telesis, *A Review of Industrial Policy*, National Economic and Social Council, Dublin, February 1982.

[65] It is ironical that the previous Irish government became persuaded of the multinational companies' point of view in this respect.

[66] General Agreement for Tariffs and Trade. See especially Article XXIV, Secs. 4 and 5.

[67] Commission of the EC, 'Assessment of the Functions of the Internal Market', report to the Council, COM (83) 80 final, 24 February 1983, para. 8.

[68] See 'A Community Strategy to develop Europe's Industry', COM (81) 639, p. 87, in *Competitiveness of Community Industry*, 1982.

[69] See, for example, *The Economist*, 14 May 1983, p. 72, and the address by the President of the Federation of Danish Industries at Frederiksdal, 18 May 1983.

[70] The Tokyo round of agreements are published in *Official Journal of the EC*, L71, 17 March 1983.

[71] This system is best illustrated by the World Bank's international competitive bidding procedures.

[72] CBI, *The Internal Market of the European Community*, 16 April 1982, para. 25.

[73] GATT Agreement on Government Procurement, *Official Journal of the EC*, L71, 17 March 1980, p. 45.

[74] House of Commons European Communities Committee, 17th Report, 13 July 1982.

[75] CBI, *Technology, putting it to work: opportunities, prospects, problems*, London, July 1982, p. 35.

[76] Arthur D. Little, *The EEC as an Expanded Home Market for Industry*, September 1982, p. 33.

[77] 'The European Community: problems and prospects', *Cambridge Economic Policy Review*, December 1982.

[78] Centre d'Etudes Prospectives et d'Informations Internationales (CEPII), *Economie Mondiale: la Montée des Tensions*, Ed. Economica, Paris, 1983.

[79] Ibid. (translation), p. 287. For the purposes of this comparison CEPII have aggregated UK and Irish data.

[80] Wyn Grant, *The Political Economy of Industrial Policy*, Butterworth, London, 1982, p. 134.

[81] German NTBs, particularly technical standards, would tend to aggravate the situation in so far as they reduce German import propensities.

[82] See *Cambridge Economic Policy Review*, December 1981, p. 45.

[83] As proposed in the UK by the Labour Party and the TUC. Selective national protection is even being considered by the UK's Social Democratic Party (SDP). See 'Partnership for Prosperity—a Strategy for Industrial Success', SDP Consultative Green Paper, No. 2, 1982, p. 21.

[84] The depth of the problem is illustrated by the *cri de coeur* in the French government's September 1983 Memorandum to the Council of Ministers, op. cit. This document essentially argues for a European industrial policy, but nevertheless concludes on NTBs that 'It is impossible to give up all the existing national

standards. Choosing between them would oblige some to give up in the face of other's success, which could in the short term give rise to extreme difficulties. On the contrary, it is essential that European standards are systematically established for new products which require a large market . . . (and that) a European Standards Office should be set up . . .' The dilemma could hardly be stated more poignantly.

[85] There are several explanations for this intuition. European interests in the liberalization of services is usually argued in terms of the banking, insurance, and international shipping industries, where some European companies may indeed be sufficiently competitive to benefit from international liberalization. However, the growing information-based services, such as software development, data bases, and other forms of information management, are to date dominated by US companies. It will be some time before European companies will be in a position to compete on a balanced basis in the event of international liberalization. Whence my reservations about the potential scope of the current GATT exercise in this field.

[86] Conclusions of the Presidency on the work of the European Council held at Copenhagen, 3–4 December 1982.

[87] Commission of the EC, 'Mesures Fiscales en Faveur de l'Investissement et de l'Epargne Productive', Working Document XV/81/83, 21 March 1983.

[88] Commission of the EC, report on investment to the European Council, 24 November 1982.

[89] Council decision 83/200/EEC empowering the Commission to borrow under the New Community Instrument for the purposes of promoting investment within the Community. See *Official Journal of the EC*, L112, 28 April 1983.

[90] Commission of the EC, 'Coordination of Community Financial Instruments', Staff Paper, Sec. (83) 563, 30 March 1983. See also 'Report of the Borrowing and Lending Activities of the Community in 1982', COM (83) 527 final, and 'Towards Community Financing of Innovation in Small and Medium-sized Enterprises', COM (83) 241 final.

[91] The proposal for Community financing of innovative investments in small and medium-sized companies (COM (83) 241 final) is still being considered by the Council.

[92] Or, more precisely, that R&D based innovations change relative prices and confer an advantage on the initial innovator.

[93] Donald A. Hay and Derek J. Morris, *Industrial Economics, Theory and Evidence*, Oxford University Press, 1979, ch. 17.

[94] See Kenneth Arrow, *Economic Welfare and the Allocation of Resources for Invention in the Rate and Direction of Inventive Activity*, Princeton University Press, 1962.

[95] See E. Mansfield, J. Rapoport, A. Romeo, S. Wagner, and G. Beardsley, 'Social and Private Rates of Return from Industrial Innovation', *Quarterly Journal of Economics*, No. 19, 1971.

[96] Hay and Morris, op. cit., p. 611.

[97] CEPII, *Economie Mondiale: La Montée de Tensions*, op. cit., p. 280.

[98] See Commission of the EC, 'Towards a European Strategic Programme for Research and Development in Information Technologies', COM (82) 287, 25 May 1982, and 'The Foundations for a European Strategic Programme of Research and Development in Information Technology: the Pilot Phase', COM (82) 486/2, 13 August 1982, especially Annex II.

[99] COM (82) 287, para. 43.

[100] Robert U. Ayers and Steven M. Miller, *Robotics: Applications and Social Implications*, Ballinger, Cambridge (Mass.), 1983.

[101] Ibid., p. 310 f.

[102] For a discussion of the effects of international technological transfers on traditional industries in the OECD, see *North-South Technology Transfer, the Adjustment Ahead*, OECD, 1981, cited in Wolfgang Hager, 'Protectionism and Autonomy: How to Preserve Free Trade in Europe', *International Affairs*, Summer 1982.

[103] Ayers and Miller, op. cit., p. 312.

[104] Daniel Bell, *The Coming of Post Industrial Society—A Venture in Social Forecasting*, Heinemann, London. It is remarkable that this treatise, published in 1973 and republished in 1976, contains only three references to unemployment, all of them either minimizing or disparaging.

[105] Ibid., p. 367 (emphasis added).

[106] Jonathan Gershuny, *After Industrial Society? The Emerging Self-Service Economy*, Macmillan, London, 1978.

[107] Ibid., p. 150.

[108] Giles Merritt, *World Out of Work*, Collins, London, 1982, p. 43.

[109] Bill Jordan, *Mass Unemployment and the Future of Britain*, Basil Blackwell, Oxford, 1983.

[110] Barry Bluestone and Bennett Harrison, *The Deindustrialization of America*, Basic Books, New York, 1982.

[111] Commission of the EC, 'The European Automobile Industry', COM (81) 317; 'Situation and Prospects of the Textile and Clothing Industries in the Community', COM (81) 388; 'The European Machine Tool Industry Situation and Prospects', Sec. (83) 151.

[112] See Commission of the EC, *Sectoral Change in the European Economies from 1960 to the Recession*, 1978, and *Change in the Industrial Structure of the European Economies since the Oil Crisis 1973-8*, 1980.

[113] European Parliament, 'Report drawn up on behalf of the Committee on Economic and Monetary Affairs and Competitiveness of Community Industry', 14 March 1983.

III

Employment and Industrial Assistance

DAVID METCALF*

I. Introduction

Industrial policy tends to 'focus on medium to long term (5-10 year) supply side objectives', on things that increase output like 'competitiveness, investment in fixed capital and labour, technology and innovation, basic industries and infrastructure'.[1] The British National Economic Development Council (NEDC) indicates that European industrial policy shifted from concern with basic industries and infrastructure immediately after the Second World War, to size and technology in the 1960s and to industrial structure in the 1970s. In the 1970s there was a shift away from the large sectoral support schemes and rescues, evident between 1973 and 1976, to more concern with rationalization and the basis of future competitiveness.[2]

Analysis of industrial policy is elusive: 'Not only is it impossible to measure effect on objective, e.g. how much extra investment or how many extra jobs resulted from a particular policy, but it is also almost impossible to determine the amount of resources directed through the instrument to the objective.'[3] However, it is possible to collate certain broad items of spending on industrial support. It is clear from Table 1 that large amounts of spending go on subsidizing investment and on supporting particular sectors to rundown, maintain, or increase output. Manpower policies in the form of training and placement, which augment human capital and wage subsidies, also interact with more strictly defined industrial policy.

The implications of industrial policy for employment, and particularly public spending on industrial support, have received very little analysis. Industrial policy has traditionally been concerned with the supply side (output), not the demand side (employment). High levels of unemployment, the rising population of labour-force age in Europe, and the reluctance of governments to pursue reflationary macro-economic policies might, in time, concentrate attention on the implications for employment of certain micro-economic measures like industrial policy. In this paper I raise certain employment-based questions and set

* Professor of Economics, University of Kent.

TABLE 3.1
Spending on selected items of industrial support (£ million)[1]

Measure	Belgium 1978	France 1978	Netherlands 1980	Norway 1980	United Kingdom 1980
Investment incentives[2]	1,000		600	100	6,000
Support for particular sectors[3]	900	3,300	800	400	3,100
Research and development		500			2,400
Manpower[4]		400	800	100	1,200
Total	1,900	4,200	2,000	600	12,700
Total as % of GDP	4	2	3	3	6

[1] For reasons indicated in the text, the figures are illustrative, not comprehensive.
[2] Includes both spending (e.g. grants) and tax expenditures (e.g. capital allowances).
[3] Sometimes incorporates regional policy-based spending as well as industrial policy spending. For France it includes major spending on restructuring steel, for Britain substantial support for public-sector industries like coal, railways, steel, cars (British Leyland), aerospace, and shipbuilding.
[4] Includes special employment measures like wage subsidies, as well as training and placement.
Source: National Economic Development Office, *Industrial policies in Europe*, October 1981, annexes B, C, E, F, and *Industrial policy in the U.K.*, June 1982, annex 2.

out certain principles concerning both the distribution of industrial assistance across sectors (II.1) and the case for preventing closures (II.2). I go on to analyse two instruments of British industrial policy, capital subsidies (III.1) and labour subsidies (III.2), in terms of their employment implications. Summary and conclusions are presented in Section IV.

I am focusing specifically on industrial assistance rather than general industrial policy, which includes, for example, competition and trade policy. Before turning to the interaction between employment and industrial assistance, it is worth setting out the possible justification for any state intervention to support industry. The rationale for industrial support depends on achieving better resource allocation, an improved pattern of effective demand by sector, a lower government budget deficit than that associated with other uses of the money, better income distribution and achievement of macro-economic goals, such as higher employment, lower inflation, and a better balance of payments. Employment will be discussed shortly, but first I wish briefly to analyse some of the other reasons why support might be justified.

The market may fail to allocate resources efficiently because of a divergence between private and social costs and benefits. Such a divergence can be corrected by taxes, controls, and—the focus of our interest—subsidies. First, the credit market might work imperfectly because it provides an inadequate supply of risk capital or because it simply functions badly in a recession. Second, private capital may take a shorter view or have less information than the public authorities. In considering plant rescues, both these two causes of market failure suggest support for acute but not chronic cases. Third, a subsidy may help correct other distortions, such as an overvalued exchange rate or too high real wages, for a particular group or in a particular geographic area. Finally, a subsidy may stop the undesirable externalities associated with the rundown of social and private capital in one place and the need to rebuild such capital elsewhere.

Industrial assistance can be justified to achieve a superior pattern of effective demand among regions, industries, and individuals. The key question here turns on the real resource cost of unemployed labour, which will be considered below. In addition, to the extent that industrial support is concentrated in areas of high unemployment, such spending may have less unfavourable consequences for inflation than alternative uses of the money.

It will be readily appreciated from the preceeding two paragraphs that micro-economic intervention in the form of industrial assistance and special employment measures is difficult to analyse because such intervention is simultaneously attempting to correct for market failure and deficient demand, both concentrated in particular areas or among specific groups.

Gross and net exchequer costs of industrial assistance (as well as real resource costs) must also be examined. A useful device is to calculate the gross and net (i.e. Public Sector Borrowing Requirement (PSBR)) exchequer cost per job supported. This can be compared for example, with the financial cost of keeping a person unemployed, or with using the same sum of money for tax cuts or wage subsidies.

The impact of industrial support on income distribution has been almost entirely neglected. This really is amazing. In 1982 the NEDC[4] put total British assistance to industry at some £20 billion a year. It is likely that this support is regressive: it goes mainly to industries and firms with prime-age, male, unionized labour forces. Feminists would do better to concentrate more on the allocation of industrial subsidies and less on the contents of children's comics if their aim is to improve the position of women in the labour market. There is a further distribution question which we might call 'spatial equity'. At any given national level of employment and unemployment, why does it matter that certain areas bear a disproportionate burden of unemployment? Presumably we worry because an area may be run down cumulatively as its best people leave and its social capital is underused. Consideration of distribution across areas, rather than among individuals, brings out the overlap between policies of regional support and industrial support.

II. Allocation of industrial assistance

II.1. Distribution across sectors

The bulk of industrial assistance goes to manufacturing. What is special about manufacturing? Arguments have been advanced that manufacturing is the engine room of growth, that it is vital to the balance of payments, and that service employment depends on a thriving manufacturing sector. These arguments are discussed below, where I consider the allocation of industrial support within manufacturing.

There is a positive correlation across industries between productivity changes and employment changes. If this correlation is causal (rather than a coincidence), there is a strong case for shifting industrial assistance towards sectors where productivity growth is above average, because then we get more output and more employment. Putting it another way, industrial performance might then be a positive function of assistance, rather than—as at present—industrial assistance being a negative function of performance.

More narrowly, authorities face the difficult task of deciding when to intervene to save a particular plant from closure. Two criteria which might be used to decide whether or not to intervene are analysed in Section II.2. These are the social opportunity cost of the labour and the social value of the output of the plant.

Does manufacturing matter? The lion's share of industrial assistance goes to manufacturing, yet that sector is smaller than often realized:

		Share of manufacturing in (%)	
		GDP	Civilian employment
UK	1981	24	29
US	1977	29	23
FRG	1976	44	36

This raises two questions. First, why is the manufacturing sector deemed so worthy of support? Second, to the extent that employment considerations figure in the allocation of support, which manufacturing sectors should receive support and which should not?

As mentioned, manufacturing is often held to be the engine room of the growth process. Thus Davies[5] points out that in Britain manufacturing output (at constant prices) grew at 3.4 per cent per year between 1948 and 1973 (faster than any other sector) and GDP rose at 2.8 per cent per year; and that between 1973 and 1981 manufacturing output fell 2.5 per cent per year (a bigger fall than any other sector) and GDP only rose by 0.1 per cent per year. The process by which a fast-growing manufacturing sector generates a fast-growing economy is seldom spelt out. It is sometimes held that manufacturing is technologically progressive and is a source of scale economies. But Neuberger[6] questions this: numerous examples of technical progressiveness occur outside manufacturing—in telecommunications and health care, for example—and scale economies are likely to be as important in distribution as in manufacturing.

It is unlikely that a decline in manufacturing can be completely offset by a rise in services, because employment in manufacturing generates demand for service products and manufacturing output is distributed by the service sector. Further, if in the long run productivity in services rises less rapidly than productivity in manufactures, then a switch away from manufacturing will tend to lower the long-run rate of economic growth. Manufacturing is also held to be important because of trade flows,[7] with a higher proportion of value added through exports than in services.

The debate on the importance of manufacturing is unresolved. This is a pity. The NEDC[8] recently calculated that industrial support in Britain totals around £20 billion a year. Some two-thirds of this goes to manufacturing, even though manufacturing accounts for under a third of output and employment. It is vital to know whether output and employment would be better served by a different, less manufacturing-oriented allocation.

Within manufacturing   There is a positive correlation across industries between the change of employment and the rate of growth of labour productivity in an industry. Salter[9] first reported this result for the period 1924–50; it has recently been confirmed for the period 1954–73 by Wragg and Robertson.[10] Amazingly, no work has been done to test whether this correlation is causal or whether it is a mere coincidence. It is causal if the fast rate of productivity growth in an industry lowers costs and thereby raises the demand for output and employment. It is coincidence if it just happens that technologically progressive sectors where productivity growth is high are also the sectors with high income elasticities. If the relationship is causal, it has a clear message for industrial assistance: support should be directed to the growing sectors because then we get a faster rate of productivity growth and we *also* get more employment. Previously much industrial assistance went to sectors where productivity growth was below average—cars, motor cycles, planes, ships, and steel. Would we be better served, in terms of both output and employment, if that support went instead to sectors like chemicals, instrument engineering, and electrical engineering— where labour productivity growth is so much higher?

II.2. Plant closures and rescues

Social opportunity cost of labour In the 1970s the British Department of Industry used shadow values for labour in deciding whether to provide assistance to stop a firm from closing. These shadow values were initially developed to try to determine the optimal rate of rundown of the coal-mining industry.[11] Mines should close when the social opportunity cost of their output rises permanently above the price consumers are prepared to pay for it. Many coal miners experience very long unemployment durations when a mine closes (partly because younger miners tend to get transferred to other pits). Thus, retaining them in mining by delaying the pit closure does not deprive the rest of the economy of any inputs it otherwise might have had. Therefore the social opportunity cost of labour is lower than its financial cost, and a shadow value—to represent the true resource cost to society from the closure—is appropriate.

By analogy, if a firm faces closure, many of the jobs in the national or local labour market will not get replaced, and in deciding whether or not to rescue the firm it is appropriate to value labour below its financial cost. The firm can be public (e.g. British Shipbuilders) or private. The Department of Industry assumed that when a plant closed in an Assisted Area (i.e. an area of high unemployment) 30 per cent of jobs were initially replaced, rising to 100 per cent after ten years. Therefore the correct shadow value of labour to apply to its accounting cost was 0.3 in year 1, rising to 1.0 in year 10. In the rest of the country the corresponding shadow values were 0.5 in year 1, rising to 1.0 after five years. If this approach is adopted, the case for rescuing firms at a time or place of high unemployment is clearly stronger than if mere accounting rules are used.

Shadow values, however, are not without problems. They reduce the downward pressure on real wages, which would otherwise occur to raise employment; they may permit inefficient firms to continue and, for example, delay required labour migration; they probably have perverse income distribution consequences because many firms which get the assistance, once the shadows have been applied, are unionized, male-intensive, high-wage firms. Further, modern macro-economic analysis has pushed real resource costs into the background and put financial costs at the centre, arguing that the subsidy has to be financed somehow and the borrowing or taxation required results in less employment elsewhere in the economy.

If shadow wages are used, the crucial question is the value of the ratios to deflate accounting costs. This turns on the job replacement profile. By how much does employment initially fall, and how long would it take for employment to be restored? Initially it was believed that this could be analysed by following a group of redundant workers through their subsequent labour market experiences to see how long their unemployment lasted. But such an approach is useless because it entirely neglects displacement: when a redundant worker gets re-employed, he may simply displace someone else and lengthen the other person's unemployment. Therefore changes in the stock of employment, not the experience of redundant workers, is the key.

This has been analysed as follows.[12] Employment in nine towns where major redundancies occurred was predicted (either by regression technique or by shift-share technique) to see what it would have been had the closure or redundancies not occurred; this was compared with the actual level of employment. The size of the wedge between predicted and actual employment at various times after the redundancies was then correlated against certain other variables. Among the more important results, the speed of recovery of employment after redundancies was found to be slower:

— the greater the proportion of women made redundant in the closure,
— the higher the unemployment level in the local labour market prior to the closure,
— the larger the size of the redundant group and the firm in the local labour market.

On this evidence, the case for rescuing firms is strongest (i.e. the shadow values are low) where the firm is female-intensive, located in an area of high unemployment, and large relative to the size of the local labour market.

Consumer surplus   The social benefits of rescues are emphasized by Foreman-Peck and Waterson.[13] They indicate that large-scale rescues may be justified because large firms have a significantly lower chance of being taken-over than small ones, so inefficient management in large firms may not get replaced even when a firm gets into difficulties. The government may choose to correct this deficiency by mounting a rescue. Further, in some instances the productivity of the whole firm may be greater than the productivity of the parts, so it may not be sensible to allow individual components of the firm to be sold off. This might occur because of economies of scale in a particular process, economies from the operation of many plants—perhaps permitting overhead costs (such as research or advertising) to be shared, economies of joint production, or because of vertical integration.

The social return, not the financial return, is the key to intervention. From the benefits side the key feature is consumer surplus. A firm generates both profit and consumer surplus: firms buying intermediate products or final consumers gain because the amount they would have been prepared to pay generally exceeds the amount they do pay for the item. Therefore, on this score, intervention should focus on maximizing the ratio of consumer surplus to profit. The key factor determining this ratio is the elasticity of demand for the products of the firm. The more inelastic the demand, the larger the ratio of consumer surplus to profit and the greater the social benefits from intervening.

Two factors have an important influence on the elasticity of demand. First, demand will tend to be more inelastic for intermediate goods than for final goods, because intermediate goods only account for a modest proportion of the cost of the final goods. Second, new products tend to be in inelastic demand relative to old-established products because of their novelty value or their very specialized use. So micro-chips—new, intermediate products—should represent good value for such intervention.

Various industrial characteristics related to the case for intervention to maximize net social benefit are presented in Table 2. The case for intervention is stronger the higher the fraction of intermediate production in total output, the higher the spending on research and development (because such spending generates new products), the larger the scale economies and joint production economies, and the larger the growth in output (because then the rescued firms will have a long-run future).

It would seem that the case for supporting metal manufacture and vehicles, two sectors which have received substantial assistance from European governments, is 'not proven'. By contrast, on these criteria there is a strong case in Britain for providing assistance to firms in chemicals and in electrical engineering, but no case for intervening to rescue firms in textiles or clothing and footwear.

III. Capital subsidies and labour subsidies

Although industrial assistance comes in many forms—e.g. tax allowances, cash grants for investment, and selective support for particular sectors like steel and vehicles—the bulk of such assistance boils down to subsidies on capital or labour. Hesselman[14] indicates that 'the most common direct instrument of industrial policy in Europe is financial assistance in the form of tax relief, special depreciation allowances, grants and soft loans.' In Section III.1, I discuss the scale and substitution

TABLE 3.2

Selected characteristics of British industry relevant to intervening to maximize social benefit

1968 SIC order[1]	Inter-mediate-ness[2]	Research[3]	Joint-ness[4]	Scale econo-mies[5]	Produc-tion growth	Case for inter-vention
5 Chemical and allied	M	H	H	M	H	Yes
9 Electrical engineering	H/M	H	M	M/L	H	Yes
6 Metal manu-facture	H	L	H	L	O	?
11 Vehicles	M	H	H	H/M	O	?
13 Textiles	L	L	L	L	O	No
15 Clothing and footwear	L	L	L	L	O	No

H = high, M = medium, L = low, O = zero

[1] Standard Industrial Classification.
[2] Calculated from census of production.
[3] Indicates relative spending on R&D.
[4] Joint production, measured by ratio of firms in SIC order that have plants in other orders to firms that do not.
[5] Measured by minimum efficient size of plant.
Source: J. Foreman-Peck and M. Waterson, 'Industrial policy for a market economy in recession', *The Business Economist*, Spring 1981.

effects of capital subsidies. In Britain there is evidence that the substitution effect dominates the scale effect and that the industrial distribution of the subsidy has perverse consequences for employment. In the last decade much industrial support has taken the form of wage subsidies of one type or another. These labour subsidies are analysed in Section III.2, which presents evidence on the industrial distribution of the major British labour instrument, the Temporary Employment Subsidy.

III.1. *Capital subsidies*

By far the largest single measure of industrial assistance in Britain over the last decade has been the Regional Development Grant (RDG). This is a capital subsidy in the form of a cash grant towards the purchase of buildings, works, plant, and machinery. Gross spending on RDGs in 1972–82 was some £6 billion (in 1981 prices). Unlike much other industrial assistance, RDGs are available for projects offering no net increase in the number of jobs.

RDGs are clearly designed to contribute to many goals: increased efficiency, higher output, improvements in the balance of payments and the inflation rate, and equity among regions. But are they a sensible instrument to generate employment? The impact of a capital subsidy on employment has two dimensions—a scale effect and a substitution effect. The scale effect comes through the way in which the subsidy lowers costs and prices, and thereby causes an expansion in the demand for output and thus employment. If the aim is to maximize employment, the subsidy should go to those sectors with a high price elasticity of demand. The substitution effect refers to the extent to which firms substitute capital for labour, as the price of capital falls relative to the price of labour consequent on the subsidy. Again, the subsidy should go to sectors where the elasticity of substitution between capital and labour is low, if the aim is to minimize adverse employment consequences of such industrial assistance.[15]

Evidence on the industrial distribution of these capital subsidies and the elasticity of substitution across industries is given in Table 3.3. It seems clear that the industrial distribution of the subsidy has harmed employment. The correlation (across industries) between the RDG and the elasticity of substitution is +0.44: the industries which have received the most capital subsidy per head are the ones which make the biggest substitutions away from jobs. The favourable scale effect of the RDGs will need to be large to offset the adverse employment effect associated with the substitution effect.

Richards[16] has analysed additional dimensions of capital subsidies by comparing money spent on RDGs with using the same money for cuts in income tax. First, the gross exchequer cost per net job created by RDGs is put as high as £100,000 by Gudgin et al.[17] If the job lasts for three years, the gross cost would be similar to that of generating extra employment by income tax cuts. It will be noted that both capital subsidies and income tax cuts are massively more expensive in gross and net exchequer cost per job than more selective special employment measures, such as marginal wage subsidies. Second, the RDG will have a smaller unfavourable effect on inflation than tax cuts, because the capital subsidy is concentrated in regions of high unemployment which do not lead the process of wage inflation. Further, the capital subsidy may have a favourable effect on productivity by encouraging firms to install the most up-to-date capital equipment. Third, the capital subsidy scores better than tax cuts on balance-of-payments grounds because it reduces costs and has a favourable impact on net exports. It is noteworthy that the chemical and allied industry, which received almost a quarter of RDG spending in 1972–8, exports 28 per cent of its sales—around twice the fraction exported by the rest of manufacturing. Finally, the spending on RDG has a complex impact on distribution: it is equitable across regions, but probably compounds pay inequality between men and women and the skilled and unskilled.

TABLE 3.3

Employment change, elasticities of substitution and spending on the Regional Development Grant, by industry

SIC order	Absolute change in employment 1972–8 (ΔE)	Elasticity of substitution (σ)	Spending on Regional Development Grant 1972–8 (£ per head at 1981 prices)
Food, drink, tobacco	−17,400	0.776	807
Coal and petroleum	−3,300	1.841	7,328
Chemical and allied	+14,000	1.225	2,504
Metal manufacture	−41,700	1.696	2,110
Mechanical engineering	−7,700	0.953	2,542
Instrument engineering	−1,300	0.512	433
Electrical engineering	−5,900	1.084	403
Shipbuilding and marine	−7,900	0.936	667
Vehicles	−5,900	1.408	335
Metal goods NES	+5,600	1.424	428
Textiles	−89,500	1.760	315
Leather goods and fur	−2,000	1.347	286
Clothing and footwear	−34,800	1.104	147
Bricks, pottery, glass, cement	−15,400	1.060	498
Timber and furniture	−5,300	0.764	477
Paper, printing, and publishing	−9,400	0.823	541
Other manufacturing	+5,800	0.584	436

$r\sigma$, RDG = 0.469; $r\sigma$, ΔE = −0.452; rRDG, ΔE = 0.127.

Note: Employment change across manufacturing by region excludes the South-East, West Midlands, and East Anglia regions, which are not eligible for RDGs.

Sources: Employment figures calculated from *Department of Employment Gazette*, August 1976, pp. 839–49, and March 1981, Table 1, pp. 142–4. M. J. Tooze, 'Regional Elasticities of Substitution in the United Kingdom in 1968', *Urban Studies*, No. 13, 1978, pp. 35–54. Regional Development Grant: spending calculated from various *Annual Reports* on the Industry Act 1972. Denominator for £ per head figures is employment (defined above), June 1976.

III.2. Labour subsidies

In the face of rising levels of unemployment many countries have turned to wage subsidies as a form of assistance to industry.[18] Such subsidies can be paid on behalf of the whole of a firm's stock of employment ('average stock'), or to preserve or increase employment at the margin ('marginal stock'), or on behalf of new recruits. Subsidies to preserve employment and stop redundancies have been widespread. They can take the form of subsidies to output (like the British Temporary Employment Subsidy and the Swedish Employment Maintenance and Training Subsidy), or of subsidies to leisure (like the short-time working subsidies in Germany, France, and, more recently Britain). Naturally, the international repercussions—exporting unemployment—are greater in the case of measures which subsidise firms to produce output, than short-time working subsidies, which instead pay firms not to produce output. Much industrial support for particular sectors—coal, steel, vehicles, and shipbuilding, for example —amounts to marginal employment subsidies which go towards subsidizing the output of 'nearly viable' firms.

To boost employment in a recession (in any one country) a marginal employment subsidy is likely to be superior to using the same money spread thinly across the whole stock of employment. This is because, for any given subsidy, the average cut in wage costs is the same whether it is spread across the board or concentrated on incremental employment. But marginal costs are clearly cut more by a marginal subsidy. So a marginal subsidy is unlikely to have any less impact on employment than an across-the-board subsidy and, as many firms are price takers in world markets, it is likely to raise employment by far more. This is why the net cost per job is less for the marginal subsidy than an across-the-board change, such as a cut in the payroll tax.

The major British measure of this kind was the Temporary Employment Subsidy (TES), which paid firms £20 a week for up to a year for each redundancy averted. In their evaluation of TES, Deakin and Pratten[19] find that for every 100 jobs initially supported:

39 jobs were preserved by TES,
29 jobs would have continued without the subsidy, i.e. deadweight,
12 jobs were put in jeopardy because of competition from firms which
    also received the TES subsidy, i.e. 'domino',
11 jobs were lost,
 9 jobs were lost at firms not supported by TES, i.e. displacement.

The net effect—some 2 jobs in 5, representing a net gain for TES— is very impressive from the British viewpoint. But from a European perspective it is plausible that the net increase in employment associated with TES (compared to what it otherwise would have been) merely means that employment elsewhere in the EC is correspondingly lower. This is why the EC forced Britain to switch to a short-time working subsidy to replace TES in 1979. The demand by the EC for such a switch is quite understandable. But it is puzzling that the EC is content to permit member countries to support directly particular sectors—steel, vehicles, etc.—to such an extent, when such support amounts to a marginal wage subsidy. Perhaps the support is allowed because of the threat to employment in these sectors from outside Europe.

The industrial distribution of TES payments has been analysed by Richards.[20] The incidence of the subsidy was relatively *high* in industries:

- hit by the recession: no surprise because this was the criterion on which the subsidy was allocated;
- where average pay is low, reflecting the flat rate (cash) nature of the subsidy, which comprises a larger part of labour costs where pay is low than where it is high;
- where the unskilled form a small part of the labour force, reflecting the need to retain specifically trained skilled workers;
- where unionization is extensive, probably reflecting unions' concern to maintain employment;
- where the industrial structure is atomistic rather than concentrated, reflecting the lack of any excess profits to tide them over the recession.

However, there does not seem to be any association between the incidence of the subsidy and the factors which influence the elasticity of demand for labour: the elasticity of demand for the product, the elasticity of substitution, and labour costs in total costs.

IV Summary and conclusions

The rationale for public spending on industrial support (rather than other things) turns on achieving better resource allocation, faster output growth, an improved pattern of effective demand across sectors, a lower budget deficit, a more favourable balance of payments, a higher level of employment, and a more favourable income distribution. The employment implications of industrial assistance are virtually unknown.

Most industrial assistance goes to manufacturing, but it is not clear why. Within manufacturing it tends to go to industries with below-average growth of labour productivity. It is possible that the employment effects of such support would be stronger if it were switched towards sectors with a higher growth in labour productivity.

When deciding whether to rescue a firm (i.e. to stop it closing down), the authorities should consider resource costs and benefits as well as financial costs and benefits. The case for intervening to stop a closure is stronger where the shadow value of labour is low—in an area of high unemployment, for example—and where the demand for the product of the firm is inelastic.

Capital subsidies form the core of industrial assistance. To the extent that employment matters, such subsidies should be directed away from those sectors where it is easy to substitute capital for labour and towards those sectors where the substitution possibilities are limited.

Much selective assistance to particular sectors amounts to a marginal wage subsidy to preserve employment. Such subsidies tend to be effective inside one country, but have thorny international repercussions.

Acknowledgements

Section II.1 draws on research by Hilary Metcalf (no relation) on redundancy and re-employment. Table 3.3 is taken directly from work by John Richards, Ph.D. student, University of Kent. We acknowledge with thanks financial support from the Leverhulme Trust for research on special employment measures and selective industrial assistance.

Notes and Sources

[1] L. Hesselman, 'Trends in European Industrial Intervention', Economic Working Paper 7, National Economic Development Council, July 1982.

[2] Ibid., paras 8 and 14, and National Economic Development Council, *Industrial Policies in Europe*, October 1981.

[3] L. Hesselman, op. cit., para. 26.

[4] National Economic Development Council, *Industrial Policy in the U.K.*, June 1982.

[5] G. Davies, 'Revolution—the fourth phase: the collapse of manufacturing in a long-term context', *The Economics Analyst*, Simon and Coates, Vol. 2, No. 9, September 1982.

[6] H. Neuberger, 'Does manufacturing deserve special status?', *Socialist Economic Review*, 1981.

[7] A. Thirlwall, 'De-industrialization in the United Kingdom', *Lloyds Bank Review*, No. 144, April 1982.

[8] National Economic Development Council, *Industrial Policy in the U.K.*, June 1982.

[9] W. Salter, *Productivity and technical change*, Cambridge University Press, 1966.

[10] R. Wragg and J. Robertson, *Post-war Trends in Employment, Productivity, Output, Labour Costs, and Prices by Industry in the U.K.*, Research Paper 3, Department of Employment, June 1978.

[11] H. Christie, 'The shadow value of labour', HM Treasury, 1981.

[12] Hilary Metcalf, 'Do redundancies matter?', Working Paper 10, Special Employment Measures Project, Kent University, March 1983; R. Rowthorn and T. Ward, 'How to run a company and run down an economy: the effects of closing down steel-making in Corby', *Cambridge Journal of Economics*, No. 3, 1979, pp. 327–40.

[13] J. Foreman-Peck and M. Waterson, 'Industrial Policy for a market economy in recession', *The Business Economist*, vol. 12, No. 2, Spring 1981.

[14] L. Hesselman, op. cit., para. 24.

[15] M. Tooze, 'Regional elasticities of substitution in the U.K. in 1968', *Urban Studies*, No. 13, 1976, pp. 35–44; R. Harris, 'Estimates of inter-regional differences in production in the U.K. 1968–78', *Oxford Bulletin of Economics and Statistics*, August 1982, pp. 241–59.

[16] J. Richards, 'The employment implications of selective industrial assistance', Labour Workshop, University of Kent, 23 February 1983.

[17] G. Gudgin, B. Moore, and J. Rhodes, *Cambridge Economic Policy Review*, vol. 8, No. 2, December 1982.

[18] Organization for Economic Cooperation and Development, *Marginal Employment Subsidies*, Paris, 1982; D. Metcalf, 'Special employment measures: an analysis of wage subsidies, youth schemes and worksharing', *Midland Bank Review*, Autumn/Winter, 1982.

[19] B. Deakin and C. Pratten, *Effects of the Temporary Employment Subsidy*, Occasional Paper 53, Department of Applied Economics, Cambridge University Press, 1982.

[20] J. Richards, 'The distribution of the temporary employment subsidy', Working Paper 11, Special Employment Measures Project, University of Kent, April 1983.

99-144
2212
6160
4200 4220
6370
EEC

IV

The Logic of EC Commercial and Industrial Policy Making

JEAN WAELBROECK*

I. Free trade doctrine

I.1. Free trade as a desirable policy: the principle and the assumptions on which it is based

We start from the corner-stone of trade theory: the *optimality of free trade*, which goes like this. If a country has perfect competition in its domestic market, and if it does not influence export and import prices, it is in its interest to abolish trade barriers. This is true if certain assumptions about technology are made, if there are no external economies or increasing returns to scale and finally, if full employment is assumed.

The argument which lies behind this classical result is very straightforward. For example, let us assume that relative to the cost of producing machinery, Japan can produce cars much more cheaply than the Community. Then the latter should import cars from Japan and export machinery to the world (not necessarily to Japan). External trade makes what may be called an 'external contribution to productivity'. Exchanging cars for machinery is as effective as carrying out the perhaps impossible task of raising the efficiency of Europe's car factories to the Japanese level.

The assumptions made are hardly realistic. But relaxing them *on the whole* reinforces the theorem. The assumption about the lack of impact on world prices is a notable exception (see section below on economic power). The phrase 'on the whole' warns the reader that when the assumptions are relaxed, the conclusions are less clear-cut than the findings of the optimal free trade theorem.

The additional gains which trade permits under more realistic assumptions are generally referred to, somewhat improperly, as '*dynamic gains*' and we shall follow this custom. Both theory and empirical analysis suggest that they are probably much larger than those implied by the classical analysis: greater realism reinforces the classical view

* Professor of Economics, Free University of Brussels and Senior Fellow, Centre for European Policy Studies.

that free trade is in general a good rule of conduct. But it also weakens it by suggesting that clever policies may be even better.

Domestic markets are in practice not *perfectly competitive*. There is every reason to expect that opening the economy to trade makes them more competitive and reduces the losses due to market imperfections. This is not a mathematical result capable of proof; it is a reasonable inference, confirmed by experience. The impact of trade on competition is a first source of dynamic gain.

What about *external economies* and *increasing returns to scale*? There are undoubtedly synergies between industries, via such mechanisms as the accumulation of know-how and skills, the ease of co-operation with nearby suppliers and clients. Large-scale plants are often more efficient than smaller ones. The well-known 'infant industry argument' emphasizes that protection may help a country to exploit such sources of productivity increases.

We shall return to this important problem in the section on industrial policies. There are, however, some qualifications to be made. First, all governments know about scale economies and externalities and heavily subsidize the industries where they are thought to be large. This competitive subsidization reduces the profitability of high-technology sectors. Apart from this, it is not even certain that any such help is necessary for such a powerful economy as the Community, which offers large markets to its firms and has large producers strong enough to set up plants of the required size. Furthermore, all that the argument establishes is that in special cases it may be true that it is useful to foster an infant industry artificially. But the best general rule of conduct remains open trade, as this obviously increases opportunities for scale economies, and enables producers to exploit synergies with producers abroad as well as with those at home. A more realistic view of the world therefore reveals a second source of dynamic gains from trade.

Lastly, what about the assumption regarding *unemployment*? Here, too, the optimal free trade principle is strengthened. Take the reasonable assumption that countries have to keep their trade in balance in the medium run, and that as a result of implicit or explicit price indexing of wages in particular, real wages are hard to reduce. Under such assumptions, protection tends to destroy jobs, instead of creating them.[1] This is a third way of generating dynamic gains from trade. The reasoning goes like this.

Of course protection helps employment in the industry concerned. Steel import quotas from third countries are being cut down. Perhaps this will save the steel mill at Ravenscraig in Scotland from closure. But the Community's clients will have less to spend. They will (perhaps not at once) cut down their purchases of EC goods, causing an export loss which offsets the relief brought about by the import cut.

This mechanism has been quantified many times in calculations of the 'employment impact of a balanced increase or decrease on change of trade'.[2] The studies indicate that the job loss due to the export drop is slightly less than the gain caused by the import cut. This reflects the difference in productivity between import substitution and export industries: it is because the economy has become less efficient, so the calculations indicate that a balanced drop in trade creates more jobs than it destroys.

These calculations, however, neglect the inflationary implications of this drop in productivity. As workers strive to maintain real wages in spite of the loss in efficiency, protection increases wages and prices; it can be shown that except in extreme cases, the net effect of an increase of protection is to reduce employment.[3]

I.2. Some practical implications of the analysis

Many of the conclusions are quite obvious. On the hotly debated issue of *selectivity of safeguards*, it is clear that if for social reasons the decline of an industry hit by new competitive producers needs to be slowed down, the exports that should be cut back are those of other, more expensive, suppliers, not of the low-priced suppliers. Why spend more than is necessary? Of course the selective safeguards which the Community has been demanding for years are not of this type: we go into other explanations of the EC position below.

There is also a *symmetry between tariffs and subsidies* which treaties and agreements do not reflect,[4] perhaps because they are written by lawyers. But the symmetry is increasingly recognized by policy makers, and to a certain extent by international codes of conduct and by EC regulations which have given the Commission an increasing power to regulate subsidies. Production subsidies remain widespread, however, and are a source of domestic market distortion which in the case of some products may exceed the tariffs which the Common Market did away with.

Likewise, subsidies *are equivalent to negative indirect taxes*. Economic logic would imply that a Belgian exporter of machinery to Germany should not only enjoy a refund of the Value Added Tax on the steel which he has used, but should also pay back the subsidy which the steel producer received. This would, of course, please German steel producers, and in fact the Tokyo Round subsidies code appears to imply international acceptance of this view. (Should and could an EC member attack another under a Tokyo Round code ?) This code was invoked by US producers in the recent EC–US steel trade dispute.

According to the *marginal principle*, it is the marginal tariffs and subsidies which measure market distortion: from this point of view

US producers were kind in last summer's unfair trade practices suit: the compensatory duty asked for Cockerill Sambre steel should have been equal to the per tonne subsidy needed by the obsolete Seraing mill, not the per tonne subsidy of the company as a whole. The marginal principle appears to be understood by the Commission in its difficult negotiations on cutbacks of steel capacity. It remains to be seen whether the decisions eventually taken are rational: only too often the Council has transformed sensible proposals by the Commission into economic monstrosities.

The marginal principle also implies that, although most of Europe's trade in 'highly sensitive' clothing articles, such as T-shirts, is not subject to tariffs or other impediments to trade, the true rate of protection for these goods is the roughly 100 per cent tariff required to raise T-shirt prices of low-cost suppliers to the Community level.

Even within the Community, barriers are high, as countries and producers manipulate norms and technical standards to prevent outside competition. There are a wealth of funny stories about technical ways of keeping goods out, amusing ancient German laws about the purity of beer, Belgian insistence that margarine be packed in cubes, and the London City Council's insistence on Englishmen being able to sit upright in taxicabs with top hats on their heads. The implications of such obstacles are less amusing for the consumers. For instance, automobile prices in the UK are 50 per cent above the Benelux level,[5] and this is only one of many price differences which persist in spite of the Commission's efforts to guarantee that consumers can buy from the cheapest source of supply.

The fact that large market distortions exist points to the importance of what may be called *the square law of protection*. This asserts that the waste due to protection is proportional to the product of the sensitivity of imports to a tariff change and the square of the tariff rate. This law has useful policy implications. Other things being equal, it is twice as useful to eliminate a 100 per cent tariff covering 1 per cent of imports, as a 50 per cent tariff covering 2 per cent: the high tariffs should be the first to be removed. Likewise (contrary to what we might imagine), it is better to eliminate an obstacle to trade if the result is an 'import surge' than if imports are sensitive to the tariff cut.

The last idea—perhaps the most important one in the present context of the Community's lack of industrial dynamism—is that protection of one industry makes the others less competitive. This is the result of *equilibrium price adjustment*. In the medium run, especially in a period of flexible exchange rates, countries tend to return to a balance of payments equilibrium. If imports are cut, exports will drop, a mechanism mediated by changes in exchange rates and in domestic costs. Helping weak sectors weakens the strong ones. It is as though a racing stable owner transferred handicap weight from his slow to his fast horses before the big race. Some of the strength of Japan's successful industries stems from that country's willingness to phase out less successful ones: and some of Europe's inability to break into the markets of the future is the result of excessive efforts to prop up ailing firms and industries.

The same mechanism means that a country hit by trade discrimination will tend to develop other exports—Japan is a good example. Its shipping industry, which today 'sets the world price' for ships, would quote higher prices in US dollars—and EC ship-building would thus be in a sounder state if the yen had not been weakened by automobile exports curbs.

Here also dynamic effects should not be overlooked. Because saving the weak weakens the strong, the preoccupation with supporting ailing industries has prevented more efficient firms from acquiring the winning edge which, in growth industries where accumulated know-how and economies of scale are vital to success, makes the difference between rapid progress and stagnation.[6] It has therefore been a direct cause of the lack of dynamism in the growth industries.

II. The case for protection

II.1. Protection, income distribution, and risk reduction

Efficiency is not the only goal of economic policy, whatever its importance in restoring the vitality of the Community's economy. The modern welfare state has other major goals. Improving income distribution and reducing the risks to which its members are exposed are also important.

Protection of course causes large *income transfers*. It makes members of the protected industry richer and impoverishes the rest of society. Proponents of a protection measure often argue that better prices are needed to help poor members of the industry: small farmers, underpaid clothing workers for example. Should such measures be part of the armoury on which the modern welfare state draws to assure a just distribution of income?

On reflection, it becomes clear that this is not the case. Protection is an extremely inefficient way of helping the poor, because its benefits cannot be shot at an accurate target. The Common Agricultural Policy (CAP) is a good example. According to Commission estimates, three-quarters of the Community's farmers produce one-quarter of output: out of every franc or pfennig which the policy takes from consumers, only 25 centimes go to persons who may be needy. In fact the proportion is even worse, because the poor farmers are mostly in the Mediterranean area, and, for both practical and political reasons, northern products are better protected than the Mediterranean ones. The CAP's price impact on consumers is hard for the poor, since they spend more money on food, comparatively speaking, than the well-off.

The proper way to improve income distribution is through taxes and transfers. That this is not what the industrial lobby is demanding is hardly surprising: it likes the waste of funds implied by protection, knowing that most of the gains it provides slop over into the pockets of the richer members of the industry. Using the pretext of helping the poor, import cuts enrich all the lobby's supporters.

A more subtle argument is that protection is a *risk reduction device*. In general there are no grounds for this: countries were no more secure economically in the protectionist 'thirties than in the free-trading world of today; free trading Hong Kong and Singapore have withstood the recession better than more protectionist Korea, not to speak of Brazil. The prevalent belief that open economies are more exposed to shocks has no foundation in fact.

It would make more sense, at first sight, to argue that protection may be desirable to give an industry time to adjust to a sudden deterioration in its competitive position. It would, it is claimed, provide firms with time to introduce new technology and/or give workers time to move to other occupations.

As before, however, it can be argued that specific, careful transfer targets are preferable. The US Trade Adjustment Act is an example of an experiment inspired by this idea. On the other hand, the economic cost of temporary protection, phased out over a period of, say, five years, ought not to be excessive.[7] Unfortunately experience suggests that—once introduced—protection is not phased out.[8] The promise that, thanks to import control, an industry will become competitive, is a Trojan horse, helpful in deceiving public opinion. But once protection is granted the hoped-for return to competitiveness does not take place, and the protection stays.

In an interdependent world, finally, each country's efforts to reduce risks for itself increase the risks for others; if all act in the same way, the world is no safer. The 1977 voluntary export restraints for textiles and clothing which the EC imposed on developing countries shifted pressure to the United States, which responded by taking similar measures. Risk was pushed back to the Newly Industrialized Countries (NICs), as the quotas froze their most lucrative exports.

As a result they were hit harder by the second oil price shock than by the first, and today there is concern that they will be forced into a debt repudiation which would seriously weaken the monetary system of the developed world. There is no maternal womb where the Community can hide 'safe from the big bad world'.

II.2. Using economic power

Contrary to what is assumed by the optimal free trade theorem, world prices are not fixed for a large trading unit like the EC. If the Community reduces imports, import prices will fall as foreign suppliers struggle to maintain a foothold in a shrinking market. As its exports drop, prices will rise as EC goods become scarce. The result is a *terms of trade gain*.[9]

Recognizing this has sweeping implications. If world markets are imperfect in the sense just defined, free trade is no longer optimal. There is an 'optimal tariff level' which maximizes the country's welfare (it can also be proved that even then, some trade is preferable to none: the 'gains from trade theorem').

This is however a negative sum game. The gain of the country which resorts to protection is more than offset by the loss inflicted on others. Adoption of such policies by every country would impoverish them all. *Free trade is still optimal for the world.*

Society prevents its members from playing such games by laying down rules: thieves go to jail if they are caught.[10] Countries cannot be jailed, but they can be made to pay penalties which discourage them from resorting to protectionism. In Papua New Guinea, a man who kills a member of another tribe has to compensate the tribe by giving it pigs, the number of which is settled in long and difficult negotiations. If he does not, tribal war breaks out. The Australian administration has done its best to encourage pig-giving as an alternative to war. The GATT has been less successful in persuading members to provide compensation when they resort to import cuts to safeguard their producers.

Society does not permit robbery even by specially designated people. Curiously, the GATT exempts developing countries from obeying its rules as a curious way of redistributing income in the world. How to change this has been the object of much debate, and has been at the centre of the work of the Framework Group, created during the Tokyo Round negotiations. The conditional most-favoured nations clause built into some Tokyo Round codes is meant to persuade developing countries to give up that privilege. The Community was right to insist that provisions for graduation of the advanced Newly Industrialized Countries should be built into the GATT rules.

Power may also permit rule-breaking, or be used to enforce changes in the rules. US power introduced the grandfather clause into the GATT, which legalized practices not consistent with that Treaty when they were embodied in existing legislation. The Community is using power when it gives its developing country partners to understand that if they do not sign voluntary export restraint agreements for textiles and clothing, they will be subject to selective import curbs, a violation of the GATT rules.[11]

Finally, power is one of the two basic justifications for the Common Commercial Policy (CCP). One reason this has been so successful is that member countries know that by negotiating as a unit they can obtain better results than if each country defended its interests alone.

The optimal tariff theorem is of course only as good as its assumptions. In particular, it assumes away increasing returns to scale and imperfections of domestic markets, two major sources of dynamic gains from trade. Even if a country is able to improve its terms of trade by protection, free trade may be optimal if when imports are restricted, it becomes more difficult to exploit economies of scale and domestic markets become less competitive. Also when unemployment and real wage rigidity are present, the optimal tariff may be zero.[12]

It is also necessary to think of long-term consequences. Experience shows that protectionist measures tend to be extremely hard to eradicate even when they were originally intended to be temporary.[13] While a country does have some power to change its terms of trade in the short run, any attempt to do so will, in the long run, bring forth new competitors and other changes in supply and demand that will largely eliminate the initial gains (for example, OPEC today).

The misuse of power has political implications because it triggers off coalitions of victims. We can see this in connection with the Multifibre Arrangement, where developing countries have begun to coordinate their negotiating positions and to use, as in the case of Indonesia, their intrinsically strong bargaining position.[14] Such shifts do not happen in a day—but once they have come about they are difficult to reverse. The Community's founders saw how 'negative sum' antagonistic trade policies had contributed to worsening political relations and helped to trigger the last World War. They believed strongly that open trade would make a vital contribution to peace within Europe. The Community's generosity in opening trade with the developing countries has stimulated much goodwill. Closing its frontier would lead to hostility and conflicts.

III. Customs unions, negotiaions, and interest groups

III.1. Theories of customs unions and of negotiations

Viner was the first to point out that a customs union may decrease the welfare of its members as well as increase it.[15] It may cause *trade diversion*—replacement of efficient producers outside the union by less efficient ones within it. Or it may lead to *trade creation*, for example, if protected inefficient producers in one member country lose market shares to more efficient producers in others. A priori there is no particular reason to expect that one of these effects will predominate.

A second effect is at least as important from the political point of view: it is the *transfer of purchasing power* resulting from the price changes caused by the union. In the Central-Latin American Common Market, for example, the less-developed members were quick to realize that free trade with more advanced partners led them to buy expensive goods from the more advanced countries, instead of the cheaper—but tariff burdened—products sold by the rest of the world. Through this mechanism the UK can buy Danish butter at Common Agricultural Policy prices, even if Danish farmers are efficient enough to survive at world prices.

The second effect is particularly damaging politically, because it pits countries against each other over trade issues. The resulting tensions can be contained if the protection level is low, if such gains and losses are more or less balanced, or as long as the issue is not understood by consumers. Experience of developing countries suggests that the first condition is crucial, and that 'you can fool all the consumers some of the time, some of the consumers all of the time, but not all the consumers all of the time', to steal a line from a former US president. A customs union will crumble if it is closed to the outside world.

This rather pessimistic conclusion about the likely welfare impact of a customs union may be corrected using *the theory of negotiations*. This envisages a group of agents who seek to improve their welfare by a process of negotiation, without in any way giving up their autonomy. Obviously, such agents must be in agreement. They can lump issues together freely in packages so that what an agent loses on one issue is compensated for by a gain in another. (The UK can veto farm price increases if its budget contribution is too high.) Usually, the reasoning leaves out of the equation negotiation and information costs.

When this type of decision-making takes place, a customs union cannot reduce welfare, if (and this is also a critical assumption) the negotiators really have their respective country's welfare at heart.

The implication, interestingly, is that there is nothing wrong in requiring unanimity decisions. This de Gaulle understood—presumably without close study of the economic theory of negotiations. There is no special merit in majority voting apart from its usefulness in speeding things up.

This does not mean that all problems disappear, even in a world of perfect information where the negotiation process costs nothing. The difficulty that remains is that there are usually a number of solutions which would be beneficial to all. Each agent opts for those which are best for him. It is impossible to forecast which solution will be adopted: the choice will be influenced by a complicated game of bluffing and menaces, using alliances to pool the closely matched interests of particular agents. Threats to resort to tactics which would make everyone poorer, to frighten other agents into agreement, may even be used.

Disagreements about sharing gains are, however, less painful than suffering actual losses. And, since the players in the negotiation game which the EC Council plays are evenly matched, each will win some and lose some. It is safe to say that though each country is convinced that others are making off with the biggest gains, the true situation will be more or less balanced. If it is not, the losing country should lay the blame on its own incompetence rather than on the system.

In spite of the lack of realism in the assumptions made, this argument says something interesting about the reason for the solidity of the European Community. It has been said that it was the political goals which brought it into being. I would venture that, a quarter of a century after Messina, it is the considerable net economic gains which each member has accumulated in complicated, sometimes excruciatingly slow, negotiations which are keeping it together.

This bold claim needs to be qualified by saying that the agents who helped the Community to become what it is and who value its achievements may not reflect their countries' interests faithfully. We now turn to this point.

III.2. The political economy of protection

The grand perspective of the last two paragraphs may well seem far-fetched to people who experience European policy-making on a daily basis. Indeed, the theory, with dashing insouciance, sweeps under the carpet the complications of contacts between the Commission, the Council, Parliament, the Court of Justice, the member states' governments and even their oppositions, the multiplicity of languages, the Economic and Social Committee and the different lobbies, contacts with large firms whether nationalized or not, etc. It skips over the sharp bargaining tactics and deceit, breaches of commitments and exploitation of loopholes in regulations and, last but not least, the ever-present and multifarious brinkmanship of delegates, always eager to wait longer than their partners to dot the last 'i' on a deal.

Sometimes friends make an agreement that the last to arrive should pay for the drinks: should there not be a Council rule saying that the country which has most held up decision-making should foot the bill for the next year's 'Problème Anglais'?

In practice, the negotiations process is immensely complicated. To take part in it successfully requires vast knowledge of rules and precedents. A twilight world of lawyers, consulting firms, and lobbies floats around the 'European Quarter' of Brussels and draws a rich living from this complexity.

There is money to be made by influencing Community decision-making, sometimes directly, more often by lobbying a member government. To take an extreme example, a profit-maximizing steel industrialist, especially from a weak firm, serves his shareholders better if he lobbies his government and DG3 rather than worrying about raw material costs and the like. The Hanoun Report that was suppressed in France showed that 51 per cent of specific government aid went to five large industrial groups, which obviously found it advantageous to keep the manna falling from heaven. Krueger[16] first gave a name to this behaviour in an article on the *'rent-seeking society'*.[17]

Whatever their concern for the common good, politicians have to get elected. For this votes are needed. Moreover, a minister needs the trust of those whom he administers if he hopes to make a good impression: a Minister of Agriculture would not keep his job for long if he attacked the farm lobby head-on.

Bureaucrats also have to reconcile selfish desires for promotion and so on with their concern for the common good. Bureaus are ever-anxious to expand their sphere of influence—from the local authority office wishing to check on housing facilities for immigrants, to the General Directorate of the Commission looking for an additional mandate. Should we follow Messerlin[18] in attributing to them a perverse interest in complicated administrative solutions which (as no one else understands how things should be done) ensures their immunity from outside meddling in running their activities? Anyone who has delved even cursorily into the regulations organizing the Common Agricultural Policy, or the Multifibre Arrangements' import controls, will find it hard to reject Messerlin's suggestion outright.

Those who have little to say are the people who should matter most —consumers. To take the recent example of import curbs on consumer electronics products, what weight does the consumer's desire to buy cheaply and well have when set against the self-interest of participants in the Council's negotiation game, or the French government's wish to announce spectacular achievements in 'reconquering the domestic market', or German concern over Grundig, or Holland's feeling that what is good for Philips is good for the country, or the UK government's wish to encourage more Japanese firms to invest in a country which is sometimes called 'Japan's aircraft carrier for invading the EC', or the Commission's desire to have something more exciting to manage than some dying industries?

IV. Pointers for EC policy-making

It is the privilege of denizens of the ivory tower to be bold in their view of what the world should become. The advice they hand out, therefore, is often annoying and useless, but occasionally, it helps practical people to see more clearly. Signs abound that the Community is in need of new directions, and armies of counsellers have jumped up to offer advice. Building on the trade theory set out above, I shall add my own twopence worth.

IV.1. The grand long-term world view

Our discussion here can be brief. We shall dismiss the view that the Community must accept as inevitable a future trading system in which the EC, or Europe, or a North Atlantic Grouping, or such a grouping extended to Australia and New Zealand, practises free trade internally but is 'driven by realism' to protectionism with respect to third countries.

Protectionism has no natural frontiers, as indicated by the multiplicity of groupings conjured up in conversations. The United States has been as quick in moving against European steel as the EC against US artificial fibres, Swedish steel, or Korean cotton cloth. Europe may discriminate against US computers tomorrow just as it is doing against Japanese videotape recorders today. And certainly Australia/New Zealand and the Community have not been shy about restricting each other's imports. Today as well as yesterday, lobbying for protection is part of firms' profit-maximizing strategy. An import curb is money— and money does not smell and knows no frontiers.

Yet a protectionist scenario is possible. With clockwork regularity the same well-rehearsed scenario is repeated, smooth and polished like a Harvard Business School case, in the US, in the EC, in Australia or in Sweden. It goes something like this.

An industry is faced with a grave threat, heightened by unspeakable yet secretive practices of perfidious foreigners. The problem is only temporary, but unless something is done very quickly irreparable damage will result. There is no time to get good data. 'We' (whoever we may be) are not protectionist but cannot afford to let others cheat any longer. In Community versions of the scenario one or two member countries will take illegal measures, the Commission and Council will panic at the threat to the integrity of the domestic market, crumble when castigated for their weakness in facing up to a grave outside threat. Voters assent, not very sure that all this will create jobs. What else can they do, since they are not consulted?

But if the slide into protectionism cannot be arrested, the Community will die. Already the Common Agricultural Policy is causing bitter controversy; the Multifibre Arrangement has split the Common Market into seven trading zones, made countries introduce regulations on markings of origin and sparked off other disputes; external protection for steel is matched by heavy domestic protection via subsidies. The EC prospered while it was playing positive sum games. It will crumble away if it shifts to the welfare-decreasing game of trade diversion.

The Community, whose power of coercion is negligible, lives through respect for rules: its regulations, the decisions of the Court of Justice, and above all the Treaties. It cannot violate the GATT order without undermining its own authority. It threatened last year to leave the Multifibre Arrangement and replace it by import controls which are not compatible with that Treaty; it continues to hope for a selective safeguard clause which has no chance of being accepted by the developing countries' majority in the GATT, and which would gut whatever weak guarantees that Treaty offers to less powerful countries; it refused in the 1982 Ministerial Meeting to seriously discuss most issues on the agenda. But the domestic market is not spared from the protectionist trend. France is introducing *de facto* import controls on other Community members. Several members are stubbornly refusing to eliminate the subsidies which distort steel trade. Every year brings its two or three small agricultural trade wars. Like protection, disrespect for rules knows no frontiers. Can we hope, if the GATT system disintegrates, that the 'Europe des Patries', as de Gaulle realistically described the Community, will hold together?

IV.2. The fast-growers' club and the Community

Through various mechanisms, not all of which are well understood, growth begets growth. This was very clear in European economic history as industrialization spread from the United Kingdom first to France and Belgium, then further out. After the war, rapid and then slow growth in the Community have coincided with a striking reversal of the fortunes of the 'Southern tier' of EC new entrants. Until recently, the relatively good performance of France and the Federal Republic of Germany cushioned recession in the rest of the Community. Similarly, Japan's strength has helped the successful growth of the East Asian Newly Industrialized Countries.

Japan and the NICs have been the fast-growers' club in the recession. They have had to import more and the increase in their imports of raw materials in particular has been crucial in protecting less advanced developing countries from a catastrophic deterioration of their terms of trade. Directly—or indirectly through triangular trade—they have provided support for EC exports at a time when the growth of other markets was very poor.

Inevitably they have broken vigorously into export markets— the dramatic upswing in Newly Industrialized Countries' textiles and clothing exports after 1973, Japanese automobile exports a couple of years ago, Korea's surge into Middle East contracting. But every dollar, and more, that these countries have earned has been spent.

The Community has been cutting itself loose from the fast-growers' club through the Multifibre Arrangement, the Common Agricultural Policy restrictions on exports of tapioca and soon perhaps of fats and oils, informal and formal restraints on automobiles and consumer electronics. This is not going to slow these countries down very much in the long run, though for the moment they are going through a difficult period. All that will happen is that through the equilibrium exchange rate mechanism, the Community will find itself pushed out of one offshore market after another—after steel, automobiles, and construction projects. It will lose markets for arms and for many kinds of machinery, as its efforts to save sunset industries jeopardize the chances of others which are competitive enough to export. This can only make recovery more difficult. The Community's abuse of its economic powers (referred to earlier) has long-term political implications that would inevitably polarize the world into hostile groups.

Perhaps the Community's trade restrictions are a legitimate retaliation against the fast-growers' protectionism? My research has not indicated serious grounds for the accusation that Japan is indulging in a carefully hidden system of protection, of a kind worse than the covert protection practised by all countries. There are stories about norms, public procurement practices, and about MITI-industry collusion. They could be told about any country. What is true is that Japan has 'natural protection' as a result of distance, domestic market size, pervasive cross holdings of shares by firms, an inefficient trading network—not to mention a difficult language. Is Bolivia protectionist because it is up in the Andes?

For the Newly Industrialized Countries the accusation is more firmly grounded; in fact some trade restrictions in Korea and Brazil, for example, are plainly foolish. But while the Community has rightly insisted that developing countries should take on the obligations as well as the privileges of membership in the GATT trading system, this insistence has been purely verbal. Moreover, developing countries like Hong Kong or Singapore which have practised free trade have been treated no better than the others.

A sound long-term policy should start from the recognition that it is in the Community's interest to be closely linked with the most dynamic component of the world economy. This will require adjustment, as dynamic partners break into markets which had seemed secure ('growth is change'), but will provide a steady basis for expansion for Europe's competitive industries. Differences in factor costs provide a natural and mutually profitable basis for trade with Newly Industrialized Countries, while with respect to Japan, Britain has led the way in realizing that close economic contacts offer invaluable opportunities to draw benefits from the technology and management methods which lie behind Japan's success in mass-produced goods.

Not too much should be hoped for from reasoned arguments. It is necessary to fight fire with fire, to counter the domestic lobbies' ability to manipulate political processes by reinforcing the 'foreign lobby'. This is represented by the 119 embassies of countries which have recognized the Community, and by the committees that accompany the EC's Lomé and other external agreements. To use the GATT jargon, these constitute a 'disputes settlement system' which has proved effective in ironing out countless small disputes. From a higher perspective, they are instruments of the Community's embryonic foreign policy. Enhancing their role is one way to halt the slide into protectionism. What is even more important perhaps, it would arrest the political estrangement from the developing world and Japan which is resulting from more restrictive trade policies.

IV.3. Defensive industrial policies

Industrial policies are a firmly rooted component of European economic systems. Like a two-headed Janus, they stare firmly in opposite directions. Most of the money goes to support sunset industries. Some goes to prestige 'high-tech' sectors. There is little left over for the rest of the economy.[19]

So far it is declining industries which have absorbed the Community's energies. Using the military metaphor currently popular with trade experts, we could say that in the trench warfare over competence between the Rond Point Schuman bureaucracy and bureaux in member countries, the latter have conceded some low ground, holding steadfastly to the high ground of the 'industries of the future'.

Have the Eurocrats—and with them Europe's economic and political future—fallen into a trap? There are reasons to think so.

The Common Agricultural Policy probably redistributes income from the poor to the rich. It is ridden with price distortions.[20] It eats up to 70 per cent of the Community's budget. Because Agricultural Councils set prices too high year after year, production creeps up relative to consumption, making further increases in spending inevitable. Through the budget solidarity principle, each member is encouraged to promote overproduction and can do so because structural aids are still controlled at the national level. The decision process remains extraordinarily centralized; even tiny decisions require long and bitter negotiations by the Council. The complexity of the regulations under which the Policy operates is a rich source of fraud and evasion—often with the complicity of the countries themselves in whose interest it is to tolerate violations by their farmers, knowing that, thanks to the solidarity principle, others will be footing the bill.

The Multifibre Arrangement has also generated an incredibly complicated system of regulations that inevitably encourage evasion. Instead of providing roughly equal protection to all producers, as would be desirable under the 'square law' defined above, the system rigidly safeguards the interests of the very uncompetitive producers of highly sensitive goods. By depriving developing countries of export earnings, it holds back exports of capital goods, which are subject to increasing return to scale and externalities and therefore have a low marginal cost to the Community. From the diplomatic point of view the rigid and restrictive negotiating mandate imposed on the Commission by the Council has caused serious damage to the EC's image in developing countries, yet even in terms of jobs in the textile and clothing sectors, this mandate has produced results that are hardly any better than what would have happened had the politically far more acceptable proposals the Commission initially put before the Council been adopted.

Europe needs an efficient steel industry if it hopes to continue to be a competitive exporter of capital goods. Capacity is excessive, and it is quite clear which plants should be shut down. An easy task apparently, but governments of member countries have been confronted by a muscular lobby, happy to break windows in capitals and at the Rond Point Schuman and to set fire to buildings. The obvious decisions have been delayed, perhaps indefinitely, and heavy subsidizing continues. Since the Simonet Plan, the Community has found itself pushed into establishing ever more rigid steel controls. This has blocked adjustment rather than promoting it. Only in periods when the cartel seemed to be falling to pieces have governments consented to take vigorous measures of rationalization.

The automobile industry has reached the stage of maturity where demand has ceased to grow rapidly, though technical progress continues apace. It is the latest sunset industry. Here trade restrictions are still at the national level: watertight like the tiny automobile import quota maintained by Italy against Japan or not yet firmly rooted, like the voluntary export restraints forced on it by the Benelux and by the Federal Republic of Germany. Existence of these national restrictions violates the spirit of the Common Commercial Policy. They have also led countries to stymie the EC's efforts at unifying the internal market. In other words, governments have done what they could to help firms keep prices high on markets from which Japanese cars are excluded.

Where shipbuilding is concerned, rapid rationalization of the industry has taken place, although the regulation on subsidies permits substantial support. There is no prospect of the industry becoming competitive again, though special branches like warships, passenger ships and oil-drilling rigs may survive thanks to acquired know-how, geographical chance and moderate protection.

The message of trade theory is unambiguous: protection of sunset industries should be rolled back to help the Community to climb out of the recession. Of course it cannot be eliminated at one fell swoop, for familiar social reasons and there is no danger that this will happen. Any progress will need more than declarations about the evils of protectionism and reminders about the events of the 1930s. It will be necessary to reconsider dogmas which—though they are not in the EC treaties—have come to be regarded as unalterable pillars of the Community.

In agriculture there are two lines of improvement of the *Common Agricultural Policy*. The low-track approach is to make it economically efficient, using the marginal principle. Koester[21] has made interesting and constructive proposals to that effect, as have others. Any economist can have a field-day gambolling in the unkempt garden of the CAP, wondering why subsidized sheep push out less subsidized forests in Scotland, why butter is heavily subsidized and sunflower oil needed for margarine taxed little, why obvious defects of the Monetary Compensatory Amounts system incite re-routing of exports and imports via hard currency or soft currency ports. Unfortunately, the Agricultural Council will in all probability not be interested.

A high-track approach is in any event needed to confront the problem of steadily rising surpluses. It is not enough to hope that the 1 per cent ceiling of Value Added Tax income which limits the EC's budget receipts will force the Agricultural Council to be reasonable.[22] No real progress is possible without changing hallowed principles.

The first principle that has to be changed is that it is a normal duty of the Community to redistribute income from town to country.[23] (Though the Rome Treaty prescribes an agricultural policy, it is later interpretation which has so firmly enshrined this peculiar idea.) Why should the EC be concerned with one narrow aspect of income distribution, using a range of instruments (restricted in the main to prices) that is far more limited than those available to member governments? The EC might have a comparative advantage if the goal was to shift money from rich to poor countries, but it is the opposite which is happening, and the 'Problème portugais' for agriculture will be even worse than the 'Problème anglais'.

Governments do engage in such income redistribution even today— French grants to young farmers and the like. Shifting the responsibility for helping their poor farmers back to countries would clear the way for a substantial reduction of farm prices, free EC budget resources for more valuable tasks, and do away with the *Problème anglais*. Only rich farmers would lose, and they would doubtless use their control of the agricultural lobbies to fight the change tooth and nail.

The second basic idea follows from three facts: one, the Community is the largest importer of agricultural products; two, world markets for some products are quite narrow; and three, all countries protect their agriculture in some way, even Australia.

This means that William Brock's* idea of GATT negotiations over agriculture is sound: co-ordination of agricultural policy-making is a positive sum game. A small example of what is feasible is the Tokyo Round codes for beef and dairy products, which have made world markets for these products more orderly. The Community has co-operated tacitly in efforts to stabilize sugar prices.

International co-ordination would mean acceptance of rules, and this would deprive Agricultural Minister Mueller and Congressman Smith of their yearly bouts of valiant combat about hand-outs to agriculture. Would they regret this? Might they not be grateful to be able to say that 'of course we understand what must be done, but international agreements stand in the way of what you or I would like'?

The third deeply rooted idea that should go is that the CAP should be organized around the defence of every single price. The result is *not* justice between farmers: there are surprising differences in year-to-year changes in agricultural incomes in different countries and on different types of farms, and of course between farmers. It would be better to have a more flexible system in which funds are shifted between commodities according to the situation;[24] inevitably this would shift authority from the Agricultural Council to the Commission, subject to appropriate regulations.

If for *textiles*, as for agriculture, free trade is judged politically impossible, the shift should be towards transparency by replacing the extraordinarily complicated import control system by a (decreasing?) tariff against low-price exporters. The tariff should not be any higher for sensitive than for other goods. The domestic market should be unified, suppressing the present seven zones. Half-way solutions are possible to ease transition, for example a low tariff coupled with elimination of import quotas from smaller exporters.

Of course outward processing can be fitted into such a system under standard provisions about treatment of exports for reimport. If the Community is serious about its legitimate feeling that protection in the developing world deprives it of significant export markets, free-trading developing countries could be given preferential treatment, as well as the poorest. These proposals, of course, break with the philosophy of the first three Multifibre Arrangements, but such a break is necessary to arrest the trend to trading arrangements that would insulate textiles and clothing as completely as agriculture is insulated today. Four years are left until the third Multifibre Arrangement has run its course: they should be used for constructive thinking along such lines.

* United States Trade Representative.

Under the 'square law' of protection such a system would increase productivity and welfare. Above all, it would be transparent: consumers would know the cost of textiles and clothing protection; it would be easier to reduce trade barriers through negotiation, in trade rounds in which the Commission could press for less protection in the developing world. For these reasons it would be as unpopular with Comitextile as the CAP reform sketched out above would be with COPA.

For *steel*, present practice contradicts economic logic. Subsidies are negative indirect taxes, and the FRG government exhibits sound logic in hinting that it will impose countervailing duties on subsidized steel imports. More basically, the problem—as with the New Guinea tribe—is to enforce laws of conduct through appropriate penalties: thus it is necessary to put teeth into Council decisions about the elimination of subsidies and the reduction of capacity. As for agriculture, there is reason to believe that many politicians would be relieved at being able to resist lobbies by pointing to the need to conform to Community rules. As to what the teeth should be, a West German border tax is clearly undesirable, though it is useful as a threat. A better idea—German again—is to reduce quotas as a penalty for refusal to phase out uneconomic plants.[25] This policy would meet fierce resistance. But what is at present the most likely outcome—consolidation of an inefficient steel industry—is far worse. It would handicap forever the large and vital steel-using industry.

For *automobiles*, the EC does not control protection. It can be predicted that a coming skirmish in the trench warfare for competence between the Rond Point Schuman and the national bureaux will consist of efforts by the former to complete the Common Commercial Policy by merging national restrictions into a Community System. Through the Lowest Common Denominator Law the latter will be more restrictive than the aggregate of national restraints. It would be better not to renew the voluntary export restraint agreements for Japanese exports into markets such as the West German one, where the government professes to be opposed to protection. There is evidence that these restraints are to a certain extent redundant today. There could be precautions to prevent diversion of exports to the liberalized markets: the EC anti-dumping procedures are quite flexible enough to instil wisdom into Japanese exporters about the desirability of avoiding this.

For *shipbuilding*, policy has followed the right lines, though progress is becoming more difficult because the remaining shipyards, in West Germany for instance, are those which are politically most sensitive. As in other areas, it is unclear what should be done to cushion the effects of the French socialist government's sensitivity to pressure groups. But the approach taken, based on gradually more stringent curbs on subsidies and efforts to prevent capacity increases, should be pursued.

IV.4. Industrial policies in growth industries

Are industrial policies in growth industries an area where the competence of the EC should be extended? This is a crucial issue today, about which I have doubts. What light does the trade theory on which this paper is based shed on this question?

In the main, industrial policies seek to exploit returns to scale and externalities. It is impeccable trade theory to assert that if these exist, free trade is only better than haphazard protection; very clever industrial policy can do better still.

The main qualification of this statement is that since the very clever policy would be profitable, it could be agreed on by producers and there would be no need for the government to get involved. Somewhere in the reasoning there is the belief that civil servants are better informed, more far-sighted, more understanding than businessmen. Whether this is true I will let each reader decide, according to how he stands on the unidimensional left-to-right scale along which West Europeans instinctively rank political beliefs.

Do these policies work? Again, it is doubtful. The Federal Republic of Germany and its *Sozial Marktwirtschaft*, and France with its *plans indicatifs* have done equally well. A Frenchman will feel sure that Germans plan without acknowledging it, a German that French planners give themselves a feather in their caps for what industrialists would have done anyway. There is truth in both views.

One thing appears clear, and that is that industrial policies for growth (and for sunset) industries are a divisive force, because of the tendency of governments to help national rather than foreign firms, and because so much money hangs on good relations with governments. This has hampered co-operation across borders. Shifting some of the financing to the Community level would counter this tendency.

The other fact is that surprisingly often these funds are wasted. *Concorde* and the *Plan Calcul* are the best-known white elephants, but the field is strewn with similar cadavers. On the other hand, industry is risky and private industrialists also make mistakes. Obviously a good deal of nerve, expertise, and ruthlessness is required on the part of the civil servants who run industrial policies. Do all businessmen possess those qualities? Any extension of the Community's role in this area would have to be matched by more flexible rules of recruitment and more ruthless elimination of less efficient staff members. Should the Council give up the *juste retour* doctrine and other causes of inefficiency and shift to a more brutal style of personnel management?

Following these agnostic remarks, I will try to evaluate the case for such industrial policies. The popular *strategie de filière* (process chain strategy) provides an appropriate framework. This regards the economy as a chessboard, in which pieces support each other via input/output links. The vertical links are emphasized: e.g., there are process chains for food, textiles and clothing, etc. The planner uses economies of scale and externalities to strengthen particular links and reinforce the whole chain. These become poles of dynamism.[26] The textbook example of such a strategy is Korea's climb up the textiles and clothing chain. Basically the strategy emphasizes marketing and research externalities. For example, protection of television sets and video recorders will, it is said, enable European producers to achieve economies of scale; it will also provide them with the stable income needed to fund research on the consumer electronics products of tomorrow. Barring such protection, European industry would have to retreat forever from a promising industry. (But the price increase which the EC force the Japanese to implement will provide them with a much larger extra profit, which will also surely be ploughed back into research.) There is something naïve about the idea of the planner pushing buttons— a couple of billion dollars here, a trade war there—as he advances his pawns on the board. But this in fact is what businessmen do, in particular in growth industries where technology and the relative strength of participants change rapidly. Of course businessmen can—and do— lose everything they have, and there is no penalty for wasting $2 billion in subsidies or for a trade war causing irreparable damage.

The real danger of the approach is that it draws attention away from the role of competition in weeding out inefficient producers and clearing the way for fast growth of the efficient ones. It creates a 'soft market', with manipulated prices and quantities, where the prizes go to the Krueger rent-seekers who are most skilful in prying funds and price support from eager civil servants. If there is a mistake, it is easy to hide it by manipulating the market, by means of public procurement, import curbs, subsidies, and the like.

The other weakness is that the best industrial planners cannot know where the next opportunities will be—the Sony Walkman, microcomputers, electronic games, to mention recent examples in consumer electronics. Xerox did not exist at the end of the war and IBM specialized in Hollerith machines to sort punched cards. The roots of European industrial policies go far back into the past, and it is instructive to remember the seventeenth- and eighteenth-century efforts of France, even then preoccupied with prestige durable consumer goods, to dominate the *filière porcelaine* and wrest from Germany the lead secured by Böttger's breakthrough. Thanks to public procurement and efforts to gain access to technology and to the raw material kaolin, Sèvres did prevail over Dresden around 1750, though this was more the result of Frederic II's invasion of the Electorate of Saxony than a victory for the day's indicative planning. But the industrial revolution did not start in porcelain.

Should the Community run an industrial policy for consumer electronics? It should not. Every such involvement by the Community has sunk into the quicksand of protection and excessively detailed regulation. This judgement does not imply mistrust of EC staff; it reflects the proven inability of the cumbersome Commission/Council system to steer such policies efficiently.

Has the Community no role then? Industrial policies to promote growth industries are a European reality. They are practised in Japan and less explicitly in the United States. At present the EC does little in this area, compared with member states' governments. If a 'Europe of industry'[27] is to come into being, it must rest on much more co-operation by twos and threes between firms of different countries. Such co-operation will not flower as long as governments are the only major sources of funds.

The Community has a large lending programme, which appears to be well administered. This could be expanded and the lending need not be limited to ventures by EC firms only. The EC research programme is very small and its effectiveness should be improved. For one thing, Council supervision is far too detailed. Figures such as a doubled lending programme and, if management can be improved and CAP spending reduced, research and development support amounting to 15 per cent of the Community's budget would not be absurd medium-term targets.

IV.5. Opening up the domestic market

There is, however, a far cheaper way to exploit synergies and economies of scale, and this is to open up the domestic market.

As protectionism has increased against third countries, EC members have also turned inwards. There has been little progress in opening up the domestic market in the last few years. Recourse to article 115 and other legal ways of blocking trade has increased sharply, and violations have become more frequent.

The problems are well known, and may be recalled briefly:

(i) Border procedures are almost as complex for intra-trade as for trade with third countries. There are obvious ways of simplifying procedures, through co-operation in levying the Value Added Tax and simplification of forms and procedures.

(ii) Progress in agreeing on common technical norms is extremely slow. Such progress is of vital importance, particularly for the growth industries that everyone agrees need fostering, since these are dependent on externalities and scale economies.

(iii) There has been negligible progress in opening up public procurement to competition, even in the vital communications sector, but not for lack of trying by the Commission. There is reason to believe that covert protection in this area often reaches 50 per cent or more.

(iv) In the parallel military area (which is outside the scope of Community actions), an extraordinarily wasteful system of allocating funds through complicated lobbying prevails, almost regardless of efficiency. As well as being wasteful, by weakening defence industries, it reduces the research spillovers into civilian industries, which are so important in the United States, for example.

(v) There is no common policy for transport, a flagrant gap in fulfilling the Rome Treaty. Even truck norms are not unified, in spite of obvious benefits in terms of economies of scale in the truck industry. Prices of air transport are absurdly high. Traffic would increase sharply if fares dropped to the US level, giving the aircraft industry a more secure basis than the subsidies which have been poured into Concorde, Airbus, and other projects. One initiative—EC support for the UN liner code—is regrettable, as it will foster cartelization in this sector still further.

(vi) There has been negligible progress in liberalizing services. Not only would this be beneficial in itself, but a modern services sector would be a natural market for the industries of the future.

This lack of progress is not simply a reflection of resurgence of protection. It is also the result of the stubbornness of Messerlin's bureaux. Their relish for the established procedures on which their authority rests, and their sensitivity to low-level lobbying by producers (and even, if I am to believe business friends, quite a bit of corruption). Progress is also held up by a doctrinal dispute in the Council between France and the FRG about the desirability of giving preference to 'real' EC producers over subsidiaries of foreign multinationals. The Commission has just launched another effort to open up the domestic market, but there is little hope for progress with the present procedures, unless the recession ends.

Is there room for a *Europe à la carte* approach? The Benelux countries have progressed further in certain areas than the rest of the Community. A group of countries could implement a regulation on norms, or agree on simplifications of border procedures. This is not a popular idea, but as attempts to remove obstacles to trade between members fail one after the other, it is beginning to appear that a *Europe à la carte* offers the only hope for progress.

V. Summary and concluding remarks

This chapter has reviewed the theoretical arguments which are relevant to the Community's economic policy-making, and used the conclusions drawn to answer the question put to me by the editors of this book, 'what should the EC do'? The proposals put forward are deliberately bold. The European Community is in difficulty, and sharp reforms are needed if Europe is to move forward again.

Trade theory in general justifies a liberal policy stance, close to that which inspired the Treaties. Two important qualifications to this have been shown up, however. Firstly, a country (e.g., the EC) can do better by using its economic power than it could under free trade but this puts it at the risk of retaliation. Secondly, as a result of externalities and economies of scale, clever planning can lead to better results than market forces. The second topic discussed, customs union theory, points to the key role of negotiations mechanisms in assuring that a customs union is beneficial to members. Last but not least, the chapter stresses the role of interest groups in triggering protection and other welfare-reducing measures.

Community economic policies should reflect a vision of Europe's role in the world trade system. It is an illusion to believe that the EC could be protectionist against third countries yet be engaged in free trade internally. The choice is one of an open trade stance or of withdrawal of each member country inside its borders. It is a choice between respect for international rules of conduct and arbitrary import restrictions. On another issue, cutting loose from Japan and the NICs would be damaging from an economic point of view. It would also tend to create a polarization of the world that would be politically dangerous in the long run.

As for industrial policies, the Community must extricate itself from its role as caretaker of sunset industries. Again, both economic and political arguments make this desirable. As for industrial policies in growth sectors, the Community should not devise industrial policies for specific growth industries, for example, consumer electronics. But it should play a much greater role in supporting investment and research, although, for research especially, this may require changes in decision procedures and management methods.

The main contribution which the Community can make, however, to Europe's economic dynamism is to eliminate obstacles to trade between members. Prospects for rapid progress in this direction are poor. Would an á la carte approach similar to that of the International Labour Office conventions make it possible for the more free-trading Community members to move forward in areas such as norms, border procedures, and transport regulations? This would be desirable only provided that no discrimination against other member countries results.

Notes and Sources

[1] J. Waelbroeck, *Protection, employment, and welfare in a 'stagflating' economy*, Working Paper 8201, Centre for Econometrics and Mathematical Economics, Brussels Free University, 1981.

[2] D. Schumacher e.g., *Handel mit Entwicklungsländern und Beschaftigung in der Europäischen Gemeinschaft*, Duncker Humbolt, Berlin, 1981.

[3] The assumptions that the balance of payments is constant and that real wages are rigid are useful mainly in simplifying the argument; they do not affect the conclusion. Protection may improve the balance of payments and create employment through the Keynesian multiplier mechanism, but a similar change obtained through a devaluation will create more jobs. Protection which causes a real wage cut may create jobs, but the same wage cut without protection will provide more employment. This assumes that the net contribution made by additional workers to output is less than that of workers already at work. This is reasonable given that the factories and workers which have to be drawn back into production to increase output tend to be less efficient and less suited to the needs of employers than those which withstood the pressure of the recession. Reversing this assumption, as is done by the Cambridge Economic Policy Group (T. E. Cripps and W. Godley, 'Formal analysis of the Cambridge Economic Policy Group Model', *Economica*, 1976, pp. 335–48), would change the conclusion stated. For a critique of their work, see M. F. G. Scott, W. M. Corden, and I. M. D. Little, 'The case against general import restrictions', Thames Essay 24, Trade Policy Research Centre, 1980.

[4] A. P. Lerner, 'The symmetry between import and export taxes', *Economica*, 1936, pp. 306–13.

[5] BEUC, *Report on Car Prices and the Private Import of Cars in the EEC Countries*, Bureau Européen des Unions de Consommateurs, Brussels, 1981.

[6] A 'winning edge' could be assured by a well-targeted subsidy. This raises the issue of whether such targeting is practicable. See the remarks below on rent-seeking.

[7] This is the kind of protection hoped for by those who have been advocating that countries should adopt a Safeguard Code, allowing them to impose degressive import restraints.

[8] There are very few exceptions to the rule. A notable one is the elimination by President Reagan of the (not very effective) restrictions on imports of shoes and colour TVs.

[9] Market power may be used for other purposes, of course. Examples are the US embargo on equipment for the USSR/Western Europe gas pipelines and Arab countries' use of the oil weapon to weaken support for Israel.

[10] 'Pas vu pas pris': under this title *Le Monde* recounted how, at the cost of a negligible fine, the French government and the shoe trade were able to hide evidence of a 'voluntary import restraint' on shoes from the EC. Similarly, the Community claims that Japan is practising under-cover protectionism on such a scale that it negates the tariff and other concessions that country made in the Tokyo and other trade rounds.

[11] Within the EC the larger countries seem to get away with more open rule-breaking than the smaller ones. There is reason to believe that in the shoe example just referred to, the fine would have been higher had the guilty party been Danish.

[12] Richard A. Brecher, 'Optimal commercial policy for a minimum wage economy', *Journal of International Economics*, No. 4, 1984, pp. 139–49.

[13] The 'Short Term Agreement on Cotton Textiles' of 1961, ancestor of today's Multifibre Arrangement, is a famous example. In trade, as in other areas, 'c'est le provisoire qui dure'.

[14] Developing countries are very large net importers of manufactured goods and export raw materials which are essential to the industry of developed countries. Blocking their exports would force them to stop borrowing, which would make debt repudiation an attractive policy option.

[15] Jacob Viner, *The Customs Union Issue*, Carnegie Endowment for International Peace, New York, 1950.

[16] A. Krueger, 'The political economy of rent-seeking', *American Economic Revue*, June 1974.

[17] As pointed out to me by L. Ohlssen, it is amusing that one of the inventors of rent-seeking entrepreneurship was A. Krueger's namesake, the Krueger of Swedish Match, who offered loans to governments in distress against monopoly rights for his match factories.

[18] P. Messerlin, *Bureaucracy and the political economy of protection: reflections of a continental European*. World Bank Staff Research Paper, Washington DC, 1982.

[19] This contrast is less marked in countries (e.g. Sweden) which have emphasized regional objectives. But even here the politicians' fascination with the two types of industries is apparent (see L. Ohlssen, *Swedish specialization and recent industrialization policy*, World Bank Staff Working Paper, 1984).

[20] See for example, U. Koester, *The EC grain economy and trade in grain*, International Food Policy Research Institute, Washington DC, 1982.

[21] Ibid.

[22] The ceiling can be revised, for instance, on the pretext of clearing the way for enlargement of the EC. Or income can be generated within agriculture by raising prices paid by consumers more than those received by farmers, through such devices as co-responsibility levies for dairy products.

[23] This is the basic message of H. Dicke and H. Rodemer's provocative papers, 'Gesamtwirtschaftsliche und Finanzwirtschaftliche Kosten des Agrar Schutzes in der EG', Kieler Arbeitspapiere, No. 146, 1982, and *Financial problems of the EC and the reform of the Common Agricultural Policy*, Institute for World Economy, Kiel, 1982.

[24] To some extent, this is how the generous subsidies handed out to farmers in agricultural exporting countries, like the USA, are distributed.

[25] The summer 1983 decision renewing the EC's article 58 powers envisages rewarding firms that cut capacity by granting extra quotas. There is much that is bizarre in that decision, arrived at after a meeting that failed to achieve its objectives. It remains to be seen whether this provision will be implemented.

[26] Presumably the strategy would emphasize to an equal extent 'poles of stagnation', such as the steel industry today, and would stress the need to remove the protection that sustains these sectors' inefficiency.

[27] CEPII, *L'économie mondiale 1970-1990: la troisième revolution industrielle en jeu*, 1982.

Other sources

B. Balassa, *The Newly Industrializing Countries in the World Economy*, Pergamon, 1981.

R. E. Baldwin, 'The Political Economy of Protection', in J. N. Bhagwati, ed., *Import Competition and Response*, NBER, Chicago University Press, 1982.

M. Borrus, J. Millstein, and J. Zysman, *US-Japanese Competition in the Semiconductor Industry*, Institute of International Studies, University of California at Berkeley, No. 17, 1982.

A. E. Buckwell, D. R. Harvey, K. J. Thomson, and K. A. Parton, *The Costs of the Common Agricultural Policy*, Croom Helm, London and Canberra, 1982.

R. B. Cohen, *Internationalization of the Auto Industry and Its Employment Impacts*, SAE Technical Paper Series, February 1982.

R. B. Cohen, 'The prospects for trade and protection in the auto industry', presented at the conference on Trade Policy in the Eighties, Institute for International Economics, Washington, June 1982.

Commission of the EC, *Les activités d'emprunts et de prêts de la Communauté en 1981, Economie Européenne*, September 1982.

Commission of the EC, eleventh report on competition policy, 1982.

A. J. Cornford and R. B. Glasgow, 'The process of structural change in the world economy: some effects of the rise of the shipbuilding industry in developing countries', *Trade and Development, an Unctad Review, 1981*, pp. 103–32.

V. Curzon-Price, *Industrial Policies in the European Community*, for the Trade Policy Research Center, Macmillan, 1981.

D. Diegel, 'The Future of the European Electronics Industry', Data Resources European Conference, November 1982.

J. B. Donges, C. Krieger, R. J. Langhammer, K. W. Schatz, and C. S. Thuroe, *The Second Enlargement of the European Community*, J. C. B. Mohr, Tübingen, 1982.

I. Frank, 'The graduation issue in trade policy towards LDCs', World Bank Staff Working Paper No. 334, June 1979.

W. Hager and R. Taylor, *EEC Protectionism: Present Practices and Future Trends*, vol. 2: *The Geography of Protection: the Community's Instruments and Options*, European Research Associates, January 1982.

H. Hughes and J. Waelbroeck, 'Can developing-country exports keep growing in the 1980s?', *The World Economy*, June 1981, pp. 127–47.

J. M. Jeanneney, 'Concurrence internationale et structures économiques', in J. L. Reiffers, ed., *Economie et Finance Internationale*, 'dédié au Doyen Marcy', Dunod, Paris, 1982.

T. E. Josling and S. R. Pearson, *Developments in the Common Agricultural Policy of the European Community*, United States Department of Agriculture, Economic Research Service, report 172.

D. B. Keesing and M. Wolf, *Textile Quotas Against Developing Countries*, Trade Policy Research Center, 1980.

B. Kohler, 'Decision-making in an enlarged Community', in J. A. Girao, ed., *Southern Europe and the Enlargement of the EEC, Economia,* January 1982, pp. 159–72.

P. Mishalani, A. Robert, C. Stevens, and A. Weston, 'The pyramid of privilege', in C. Stevens, ed., *EEC and The Third World: A Survey*, Hodder & Stoughton, 1981.

M. Noelke and P. Taylor, *EEC protection: present practice and future trends*, vol. 1, European Research Associates, June 1981.

P. Oliver, *Free Movement of Goods in the EEC*, European Law Centre, Eastern Press, London and Reading, 1982.

R. S. Taylor, 'Protectionism: recent developments in national and community policies', presented to the European Research Associates seminar on Protectionism and Trade Policy, Brussels, April 1982.

P. M. Wijkman, 'Effects of cargo reservation: a review of the Unctad code of conduct for liner conferences', *Marine Policy*, October 1980, pp. 271–89.

M. H. Wolf, 'The EEC and trade policy', British Association for the Advancement of Science conference, September 1982.

A. J. Yeats, 'Agricultural protectionism: an analysis of its international economic effects and policy options', *Trade and Development*, an Unctad Review No. 3, Winter 1981.

Statistical Appendix

Part I. Evolution of world gross products and its regional distribution

A.1 Regional distribution of world gross products at current prices and exchange rates, 1970–80 — 128

A.2 Annual growth rates of regional gross products at constant prices, 1970–80 — 129

A.3 Regional distribution of world gross product at prices corresponding to purchasing power parities, 1970–80 — 129

Part II. Evolution of world manufactured value added and of its regional distribution

A.4 Growth rates of regional manufactured value added at constant prices, 1970–8 — 130

A.5 Growth rates of manufacturing industries, 1960–81 — 130

A.6 Regional distribution of world manufactured value added at current prices and exchange rates and at constant prices and exchange rates, 1970–8 — 131

Part III. World trade in manufactured products

A.7 Regional distribution of world trade in manufactured products in 1970 at current $US (intra-regional trade included) — 132

A.8 Regional distribution of world trade in manufactured products in 1980 at current $US (intra-regional trade included) — 133

A.9 Regional distribution of world trade in manufactured products in 1970 at current $US (intra-regional trade excluded) — 134

A.10 Regional distribution of world trade in manufactured products in 1980 at current $US (intra-regional trade excluded) — 135

A.11 Evolution of trade in manufactured products by region, 1970–80 (intra-regional trade excluded) — 136

Part IV. Industrial structures of the main EC countries

A.12 Industrial value added as a percentage of GDP in the main EC countries, 1970–9 — 137

A.13 Structure of industrial value added in the main EC countries, 1970–9 — 138

A.14 Structure of industrial value added in constant prices for the five main industrial economies, 1970–9 — 139

Part V. Foreign trade in manufactured products for the main industrial countries

A.15 Ratios of Imports/Demand and Exports/Production for nine sectors in the five main industrial countries, 1970 — 140

A.16 Ratios of Imports/Demand and Exports/Production for nine sectors
      in the main EC countries, 1978   141
A.17 Surpluses and deficits by sector for the five main economies,
      1970–80   142
A.18 Impact on employment of trade in manufactured products
      between developed and developing countries, 1976   143

                  Part VI. Evolution of labour costs in the EC
A.19 Average annual rates of change of unit labour costs for a sample of
      industrial countries, 1960–81   144

             Part VII. Transfers and subsidies to industry in EC countries
A.20 Transfers and subsidies to industry and commerce in EC countries,
      1973–5   144
A.21 Share of subsidies in gross investment for a few industrial countries,
      1960–77   144

Code Names for Regions

USA:	United States
CAN:	Canada
EC:	European Community
JAP:	Japan
OWEC:	Other Western European Countries
ANZ:	Australia and New Zealand
SA:	South Africa
UEE:	USSR and Eastern European Countries
LA:	Latin America
ARD:	Asia in rapid development
NAME:	North Africa and Middle East
OAC:	Other Asian Countries not centrally planned
SSA:	Sub-Saharan Africa
CHI:	China, including North Korea and Mongolia

This appendix was prepared by Philippe Guinchard and Said Ighilariz. Unless otherwise noted, tables are based on data kindly made available by Centre d'Etudes Prospectives et d'Informations Internationales (CEPII), Paris.

TABLE A.1

Regional distribution of world gross product at current prices and exchange rates and
at constant prices and exchange rates, 1970–80[1]

(1975 values)

Region	Current prices and exchange rates				Constant prices and exchange rates (1975)			
	1970	1980	Growth rates of regional shares		1970	1980	Growth rates of regional shares	
			1970–3	1973–80			1970–3	1973–78
USA	31	22	−4.5	−2.9	27	24	−0.6	−1.0
CAN	3	2	−0.5	−2.4	3	3	1.3	−0.5
EC	20	23	3.7	1.0	22	20	−0.9	−1.0
JAP	6	9	9.8	0.6	8	9	1.9	0.4
OWEC	6	7	4.9	0.1	8	7	−0.2	−0.6
ANZ	1	1	7.2	−2.2	2	2	−0.8	−1.0
SA	1	1	−0.1	1.4	1	1	−1.2	−0.2
UEE	17	16	−3.2	−0.7	15	16	0.5	1.2
LA	5	6	−0.1	3.3	5	6	2.1	2.0
ARD	1	2	5.3	7.0	1	1	5.7	4.5
NAME	2	4	6.5	9.9	3	3	1.0	2.8
OAC	3	3	−3.3	1.6	4	4	−1.3	1.3
SSA	1	2	2.2	4.3	1	1	−0.6	0.1
CHI	3	2	−2.2	−0.1	2	3	1.5	1.8
World total	100	100	—	—	100	100	—	—

[1] Figures concerning shares have been rounded up to 1 per cent.

TABLE A.3

Regional distribution of world gross product at prices corresponding to purchasing power parities, 1970–80[1]

Region	1970	1980
USA	23.0	21.0
CAN	2.0	2.0
EC	19.0	17.0
JAP	7.0	8.0
OWEC	7.0	7.0
ANZ	1.0	1.0
SA	1.0	1.0
UEE	13.0	14.0
LA	7.0	8.0
ARD	1.0	2.0
NAME	4.0	5.0
OAC	8.0	8.0
SSA	2.0	2.0
CHI	5.0	5.0
World total	100.0	100.0

[1] Figures have been rounded up to 1 per cent.

TABLE A.2

Annual growth rates of regional gross products at constant prices, 1970–80 (%)[1]
(1975 exchange rates and domestic prices)

Region	Growth rates	
Code	1970–3	1973–80
USA	4.8	2.3
CAN	6.8	2.8
EC	4.4	2.3
JAP	7.4	3.8
OWEC	5.2	2.7
ANZ	4.5	2.3
SA	4.1	3.2
UEE	6.0	4.6
LA	7.6	5.4
ARD	11.4	8.0
NAME	6.5	6.2
OAC	4.0	5.2
SSA	4.8	3.4
CHI	7.0	5.2
World total	5.4	3.3

[1] Figures for Vietnam, Cambodia, and Laos are not included.

TABLE A.4
*Growth rates of regional manufactured value added
at constant prices, 1970–8
(1975 prices and exchange rates)*

Region	Growth rate (%) 1970–8
USA	3.4
CAN	4.4
EC	2.7
JAP	6.4
OWEC	4.4
ANZ	3.5
SA	2.5
UEE	5.5
LA	6.4
ARD	14.0
NAME	11.0
OAC	6.6
SSA	5.4
CHI	5.7
World total	4.5

TABLE A.5
*Growth rates of manufacturing industries, 1960–81
(yearly rates in %)*

Region	1960	1967	1971	1975	1978	1981
West[1]	6.6	5.0			2.0	
South[2]	6.3		7.3		5.7	
East[3]		8.9		6.6		4.7

[1] Developed market economies.
[2] Developing market economies.
[3] European centrally-planned economies.
Source: CEPII, *L'économie mondiale 1970–1990. Enjeux d'une troisième
révolution industrielle*, Paris, 1983.

TABLE A.6

Regional distribution of world manufactured value added at current prices and exchange rates and at constant prices and exchange rates, 1970–8

Region	Current prices and exchange rates					Constant prices and exchange rates (1975)		
				Growth rates of regional shares				Growth rates of regional shares
	1970	1973	1978	1970–3	1973–8	1970	1978	1970–8
USA	25.90	22.00	19.34	−5.3	−2.5	22.24	20.30	−1.1
CAN	1.76	1.73	1.44	−0.5	−3.6	1.73	1.72	−0.1
EC	20.37	22.35	22.22	3.1	−0.1	24.60	21.31	−1.7
JAP	7.52	9.66	10.65	8.6	2.0	7.71	8.88	1.8
OWEC	4.19	4.91	5.35	5.4	1.7	5.41	5.39	0.0
ANZ	1.08	1.17	0.89	2.7	−5.2	1.20	1.11	1.0
SA	0.40	0.41	0.34	0.8	−3.6	0.41	0.35	−1.9
UEE	29.00	27.60	28.20	−1.6	0.4	27.00	29.18	1.0
LA	3.65	3.94	4.25	2.6	1.5	3.83	4.41	1.8
ARD	0.54	0.69	1.09	8.5	9.5	0.52	1.07	9.4
NAME	0.61	0.69	0.96	4.2	6.8	0.53	0.90	6.3
OAC	1.35	1.31	1.57	−0.9	3.7	1.33	1.56	2.0
SSA	0.33	0.34	0.48	1	7.1	0.40	0.44	0.9
CHI	3.30	3.20	3.20	1.0	0.0	3.07	3.38	1.2
World total	100.0	100.0	100.0	—	—	100.0	100.0	—

TABLE A.7

Regional distribution of world trade in manufactured products in 1970 at current $US
(intra-regional trade included)

Exporting countries	Importing countries														Total[1]
	USA	CAN	EC	JAP	OWEC	ANZ	SA	UEE	LA	ARD	NAME	OAC	SSA	CHI	
USA	–	3.86	3.28	1.00	1.02	0.49	0.24	0.08	2.44	0.48	0.32	0.55	0.22	0.00	14.60
CAN	3.65	–	0.63	0.08	0.08	0.08	0.04	0.01	0.21	0.02	0.07	0.01	0.01	0.01	4.90
EC	3.59	0.69	19.16	0.60	8.18	0.87	0.79	1.51	1.84	0.47	1.52	0.81	1.29	0.20	42.03
JAP	2.74	0.30	0.66	–	0.51	0.34	0.15	0.20	0.52	1.19	0.27	0.92	0.45	0.27	8.54
OWEC	0.80	0.17	4.03	0.16	2.91	0.12	0.11	0.84	0.48	0.12	0.27	0.11	0.29	0.04	10.50
ANZ	0.05	0.01	0.10	0.05	0.01	0.12	0.03	0.00	0.01	0.04	0.00	0.13	0.01	0.00	0.62
SA	0.08	0.01	0.14	0.04	0.02	0.01	0.00	0.01	0.01	0.01	0.02	0.01	0.07	0.00	0.42
UEE	0.06	0.03	0.55	0.08	0.54	0.01	0.00	9.06	0.09	0.00	0.14	0.12	0.01	0.14	10.84
LA	0.54	0.01	0.46	0.07	0.09	0.00	0.00	0.15	0.35	0.00	0.01	0.00	0.00	0.01	1.70
ARD	0.63	0.04	0.27	0.08	0.07	0.04	0.06	0.07	0.04	0.15	0.09	0.23	0.05	0.03	1.83
NAME	0.01	0.00	0.12	0.00	0.02	0.00	0.00	0.08	0.01	0.01	0.08	0.01	0.01	0.00	0.36
OAC	0.49	0.04	0.23	0.14	0.05	0.04	0.02	0.20	0.01	0.04	0.08	0.04	0.04	0.05	1.51
SSA	0.02	0.00	0.60	0.15	0.10	0.00	0.03	0.02	0.01	0.00	0.01	0.03	0.03	0.02	1.02
CHI	0.00	0.01	0.05	0.03	0.01	0.02	0.00	0.19	0.00	0.10	0.04	0.04	0.02	0.00	0.52
Total[1]	12.66	5.17	30.74	2.49	13.71	2.15	1.46	12.40	6.01	2.62	2.87	3.13	2.50	0.77	100.00

[1] Totals sometimes differ from sums of column or row figures due to discrepancies between import and export figures.

TABLE A.8

Regional distribution of world trade in manufactured products in 1980 at current $US

(intra-regional trade included)

Exporting countries	Importing countries														
	USA	CAN	EC	JAP	OWEC	ANZ	SA	UEE	LA	ARD	NAME	OAC	SSA	CHI	Total[1]
USA	0.00	2.76	2.69	0.82	0.70	0.35	0.19	0.07	2.49	0.80	0.80	0.55	0.16	0.12	12.77
CAN	2.26	0.00	0.30	0.08	0.05	0.04	0.01	0.03	0.17	0.05	0.05	0.05	0.02	0.02	3.14
EC	2.88	0.41	20.94	0.54	6.99	0.45	0.55	1.55	1.40	0.61	3.60	1.35	1.35	0.19	42.42
JAP	2.63	0.23	1.27	0.00	0.47	0.34	0.15	0.29	0.70	1.53	1.19	0.98	0.33	0.45	10.57
OWEC	0.62	0.10	4.70	0.16	2.07	0.09	0.07	0.94	0.47	0.14	0.84	0.16	0.26	0.06	10.71
ANZ	0.09	0.01	0.09	0.09	0.01	0.10	0.00	0.00	0.01	0.06	0.01	0.10	0.00	0.02	0.75
SA	0.25	0.01	0.17	0.05	0.02	0.01	0.00	0.01	0.03	0.01	0.02	0.04	0.04	0.00	0.60
UEE	0.09	0.02	0.76	0.06	0.44	0.01	0.00	0.49	0.06	0.00	0.20	0.07	0.02	0.26	8.46
LA	0.72	0.03	0.38	0.12	0.12	0.01	0.00	0.13	0.50	0.01	0.04	0.01	0.04	0.02	2.14
ARD	1.51	0.11	0.85	0.34	0.18	0.12	0.02	0.02	0.04	0.43	0.40	0.18	0.06	0.11	4.36
NAME	0.02	0.00	0.24	0.01	0.04	0.00	0.00	0.05	0.02	0.02	0.14	0.02	0.01	0.01	0.58
OAC	0.38	0.01	0.40	0.12	0.07	0.03	0.00	0.11	0.00	0.12	0.14	0.07	0.03	0.01	1.52
SSA	0.06	0.00	0.31	0.06	0.02	0.00	0.00	0.02	0.01	0.00	0.02	0.03	0.05	0.02	0.62
CHI	0.07	0.01	0.11	0.08	0.03	0.02	0.00	0.07	0.01	0.12	0.11	0.02	0.02	0.00	0.67
Total[1]	11.59	3.69	33.85	2.54	11.22	1.56	1.00	9.78	5.91	3.90	7.57	3.06	2.39	1.29	100.00

[1] Totals sometimes differ from sums of column or row figures due to discrepancies between import and export figures.

TABLE A.9

Regional distribution of world trade in manufactured products in 1970 at current $US
(intra-regional trade excluded)

Exporting countries	Importing countries														
	USA	CAN	EC	JAP	OWEC	ANZ	SA	UEE	LA	ARD	NAME	OAC	SSA	CHI	Total[1]
USA	0.0	5.7	4.8	1.5	1.5	0.7	0.4	0.1	3.6	0.7	0.5	0.8	0.3	0.0	21.5
CAN	5.4	0.0	0.9	0.1	0.1	0.1	0.1	0.0	0.3	0.0	0.0	0.1	0.0	0.0	7.2
EC	5.3	1.0	0.0	0.9	12.0	1.3	1.2	2.2	2.7	0.7	2.2	1.2	1.9	0.3	33.6
JAP	4.0	0.0	1.0	0.0	0.8	0.5	0.2	0.3	0.8	1.7	0.4	1.4	0.7	0.4	12.5
OWEC	1.2	0.2	5.9	0.2	0.0	0.2	0.2	1.2	0.7	0.2	0.4	0.2	0.4	0.1	11.2
ANZ	0.1	0.0	0.1	0.1	0.0	0.0	0.0	0.0	0.0	0.1	0.0	0.2	0.0	0.0	0.7
SA	0.1	0.0	0.2	0.1	0.0	0.0	0.0	0.0	0.0	0.0	0.0	0.0	0.1	0.0	0.6
UEE	0.1	0.0	0.8	0.1	0.8	0.0	0.0	0.0	0.1	0.0	0.2	0.2	0.0	0.2	2.6
LA	0.8	0.0	0.7	0.1	0.1	0.0	0.0	0.2	0.0	0.0	0.0	0.0	0.0	0.0	2.0
ARD	0.9	0.1	0.4	0.1	0.1	0.1	0.1	0.1	0.1	0.0	0.1	0.3	0.1	0.0	2.5
NAME	0.0	0.0	0.2	0.0	0.0	0.0	0.0	0.1	0.0	0.0	0.0	0.0	0.0	0.0	0.4
OAC	0.7	0.1	0.3	0.2	0.1	0.1	0.0	0.3	0.0	0.1	0.1	0.0	0.1	0.1	2.1
SSA	0.0	0.0	0.9	0.2	0.2	0.0	0.0	0.0	0.0	0.0	0.0	0.1	0.0	0.0	1.5
CHI	0.0	0.0	0.1	0.0	0.0	0.0	0.0	0.3	0.0	0.1	0.1	0.1	0.0	0.0	0.8
Total[1]	18.6	7.6	17.0	3.7	15.9	3.0	2.2	4.9	8.3	3.6	4.1	4.5	3.6	1.1	100.0

[1] Totals sometimes differ from sums of column or row figures due to discrepancies between import and export figures.

TABLE A.10

Regional distribution of world trade in manufactured products in 1980 at current $US

(intra-regional trade excluded)

Exporting countries	Importing countries														
	USA	CAN	EC	JAP	OWEC	ANZ	SA	UEE	LA	ARD	NAME	OAC	SSA	CHI	Total¹
USA	0.0	4.0	3.9	1.2	1.0	0.5	0.3	0.1	3.6	1.2	1.2	0.2	0.2	0.2	18.4
CAN	3.3	0.0	0.4	0.1	0.1	0.1	0.0	0.0	0.2	0.1	0.1	0.0	0.0	0.0	4.5
EC	4.2	0.6	0.0	0.8	10.1	0.7	0.8	2.2	2.0	0.9	5.2	1.2	1.9	0.3	31.0
JAP	3.8	0.3	1.8	0.0	0.7	0.5	0.2	0.4	1.0	2.2	1.7	1.4	0.5	0.7	15.3
OWEC	0.9	0.1	6.8	0.2	0.0	0.1	0.1	1.4	0.7	0.2	1.2	0.2	0.4	0.1	12.5
ANZ	0.1	0.0	0.1	0.1	0.0	0.0	0.0	0.0	0.0	0.1	0.0	0.1	0.0	0.0	0.9
SA	0.4	0.0	0.2	0.1	0.0	0.0	0.0	0.0	0.0	0.0	0.0	0.0	0.1	0.0	0.9
UEE	0.1	0.0	1.1	0.1	0.6	0.0	0.0	0.0	0.1	0.0	0.3	0.1	0.0	0.4	2.9
LA	1.0	0.0	0.6	0.2	0.2	0.0	0.0	0.0	0.0	0.0	0.1	0.0	0.1	0.0	2.4
ARD	2.2	0.2	1.2	0.5	0.3	0.2	0.0	0.0	0.1	0.0	0.6	0.3	0.1	0.2	5.7
NAME	0.0	0.0	0.3	0.0	0.1	0.0	0.0	0.1	0.0	0.0	0.0	0.0	0.0	0.0	0.6
OAC	0.6	0.0	0.6	0.2	0.1	0.0	0.0	0.2	0.0	0.2	0.2	0.0	0.1	0.0	2.1
SSA	0.1	0.0	0.5	0.1	0.0	0.0	0.0	0.0	0.0	0.0	0.0	0.0	0.0	0.0	0.8
CHI	0.1	0.0	0.2	0.1	0.0	0.0	0.0	0.1	0.0	0.2	0.2	0.0	0.0	0.0	1.0
Total¹	16.7	5.3	18.7	3.7	13.2	2.1	1.4	4.8	7.8	5.0	10.7	4.3	3.4	1.9	100.0

¹ Totals sometimes differ from sums of columns or row figures due to discrepancies between import and export figures.

TABLE A.11

Evolution of trade in manufactured products by region, 1970–80
(intra-regional trade excluded)

Region	Share of world imports			Share of world exports			Share of world exports minus share of world imports		
	1970	1980	Difference	1970	1980	Difference	1970	1980	Difference
USA	18.5	16.7	−1.9	21.5	18.4	−3.1	+2.9	+1.7	−1.2
CAN	7.6	5.3	−2.3	7.2	4.5	−3.2	−0.4	−0.8	−0.4
EC	17.0	18.7	+1.7	33.6	31.0	−2.6	+16.6	+12.3	−4.3
JAP	3.7	3.7	0.0	12.5	15.3	+2.8	+8.8	+11.6	+2.8
OWEC	15.9	13.2	−2.7	11.2	12.5	+1.3	−4.7	−0.7	+4.0
ANZ	3.0	2.1	−0.9	0.7	0.9	+0.2	−2.3	−1.2	+1.1
SA	2.2	1.4	−0.8	0.6	0.9	+0.3	−1.6	−0.5	+1.1
UEE	4.9	4.8	−0.1	2.6	2.9	+0.3	−2.3	−1.9	+0.4
LA	8.3	7.8	−0.4	2.0	2.4	+0.4	−6.3	−5.4	+0.9
ARD	3.6	5.0	+1.4	2.5	5.7	+3.2	−1.1	+0.7	+1.8
NAME	4.1	10.7	+5.6	0.4	0.6	+0.2	−3.7	−9.1	−5.4
OAC	4.5	4.3	−0.2	2.1	2.1	0.0	−4.4	−4.2	+0.2
SSA	3.6	3.4	−0.2	1.5	0.8	−0.7	−2.1	−2.6	−0.5
CHI	1.1	1.9	+0.8	0.8	1.0	+0.2	−0.3	−0.9	−0.6

TABLE A.12
*Industrial value added as a percentage
of GDP in the main EC countries, 1970-9
(at current market prices)*

Country	1970	1979
Belgium	30.9	25.8
FRG	38.1	33.8
France	26.8	27.2
Italy	29.5	31.0
Netherlands	26.6	19.1
UK	30.0	27.0

Source: Commission of the EC,
Eurostat, Brussels, 1980.

TABLE A.13

Structure of industrial value added in the main EC countries, 1970–9 (%)
(at current market prices)

Sectors	Belgium		FRG		France		Italy		Netherlands		UK	
	1970	1979	1970	1979	1970	1979	1970	1979	1970	1979	1970	1979
Minerals, ferrous and non-ferrous metals	12.8	8.4	5.7	5.3	7.4	5.4	7.1	6.0	5.2	4.2	5.7	6.2
Non-metallic products	7.6	6.2	5.9	5.7	5.2	5.5	7.6	7.0	5.5	5.5	4.0	5.2
Metallic products	8.1	8.5	11.0	10.4	11.9	11.2	7.4	7.4	8.7	8.5	7.9	6.0
Chemical products	8.5	10.9	8.2	9.8	8.7	9.2	8.9	9.1	13.8	14.9	7.8	8.7
Equipment	7.1	8.6	11.2	12.0	7.6	7.3	6.6	7.3	6.8	7.8	11.6	11.1
Office precision instruments	0.2	0.3	3.2	3.9	3.5	2.5	1.6	1.6	0.7	1.3	2.5	3.7
Electrical	7.3	8.7	10.1	10.9	7.3	7.3	7.0	6.7	12.2	11.7	8.6	8.7
Transport equipment	6.2	8.8	7.0	8.3	10.1	14.3	6.2	6.7	6.4	5.7	11.2	11.8
Food and agro industries	16.6	16.0	14.2	12.4	15.1	15.9	15.8	12.8	18.2	17.3	15.0	15.6
Textiles, clothing, leather	12.3	8.7	8.3	5.7	10.1	8.2	16.1	18.4	7.4	4.4	10.4	8.8
Paper	5.5	5.4	6.2	6.2	5.4	5.3	5.6	5.9	8.4	10.6	8.4	7.1
Rubber, plastics	2.0	2.9	4.0	4.3	3.5	3.3	3.5	3.9	2.0	2.5	2.9	3.1
Others	5.7	6.7	5.0	4.9	4.2	4.5	6.6	8.2	4.8	5.6	3.9	4.0
Total	100.0	100.0	100.0	100.0	100.0	100.0	100.0	100.0	100.0	100.0	100.0	100.0

Source: Commission of the EC, *Eurostat*, Brussels, 1980.

TABLE A.14
*Structure of industrial value added in constant prices for
the five main industrial economies, 1970-9 (%)*

Sectors	US	France	FRG	UK	Japan
Construction materials					
1970–3	3.6	5.0	5.5	3.9	5.6
1976–9	3.3	4.7	5.2	3.8	3.7
Metals and metallic products[1]					
1970–3	15.8	16.5	15.7	13.2	19.9
1976–9	13.8	14.4	15.2	11.7	17.5
Textiles					
1970–3	8.0	10.0	8.2	9.4	6.9
1976–9	7.8	7.7	6.6	8.8	6.2
Mechanical equipment					
1970–3	16.3	10.2	16.2	14.9	13.1
1976–9	15.7	9.8	16.3	14.9	13.2
Electrical equipment					
1970–3	14.3	10.4	11.6	9.7	8.5
1976–9	15.6	13.6	13.5	10.5	13.4
Transport equipment					
1970–3	9.4	10.6	10.3	12.4	11.7
1976–9	10.2	12.0	11.5	11.0	13.4
Chemical products					
1970–3	12.5	12.4	13.8	11.2	11.9
1976–9	13.7	12.8	15.0	13.3	12.9
Agro-food industry					
1970–3	10.9	14.9	10.0	12.1	7.3
1976–9	11.7	14.7	9.1	12.7	7.0
Paper, wood, and others					
1970–3	9.3	9.8	8.7	13.5	15.6
1076–9	8.6	9.9	8.2	13.4	13.0
Total	100.0	100.0	100.0	100.0	100.0

[1] For France, only the total (mechanical equipment and electrical equipment)
is comparable to the other countries' figures, since electrical equipment data
include products considered as mechanical equipment in other countries.

TABLE A.15

Ratios of Imports/Demand and Exports/Production for nine sectors in the five main industrial countries, 1970

Sectors	US	France	FRG	UK	Japan
Construction materials					
I/D	3.4	12.7	9.0	17.5	0.4
E/P	2.5	11.7	9.7	22.0	4.1
Metals and metallic products					
I/D	5.8	20.1	15.7	23.6	2.7
E/P	4.4	17.1	17.8	19.8	8.1
Textiles					
I/D	7.3	10.3	18.1	16.3	2.1
E/P	1.9	16.6	11.7	20.3	12.4
Mechanical equipment					
I/D	5.2	28.0	14.8	21.9	4.0
E/P	12.8	26.6	32.7	40.2	8.6
Electrical equipment					
I/D	8.0	21.1	9.9	14.4	3.4
E/P	10.5	19.2	18.6	22.1	14.0
Transport equipment					
I/D	8.2	15.5	13.5	12.9	2.3
E/P	9.5	27.1	28.2	30.0	15.2
Chemical products					
I/D	4.7	19.8	14.4	22.8	4.4
E/P	10.0	22.6	24.6	35.0	8.8
Agro-food industry					
I/D	4.3	7.5	8.4	22.4	4.4
E/P	2.3	7.9	3.2	10.4	2.1
Paper, wood, and others					
I/D	5.7	12.7	10.8	25.5	2.6
E/P	3.7	8.7	7.1	10.8	4.2
Total					
I/D	5.9	15.6	12.9	20.6	3.1
E/P	6.4	16.7	17.7	23.3	8.7

E = Exports; P = Production; I = Imports; D = Domestic Demand.

TABLE A.16
Ratios of Imports/Demand and Exports/Production for
nine sectors in the main EC countries, 1978

Sectors	US	France	FRG	UK	Japan
Construction materials					
I/D	5.6	15.3	10.9	88.4	0.6
E/P	3.5	15.0	11.8	90.5	4.4
Metals and metallic products					
I/D	9.1	24.3	16.4	22.5	1.9
E/P	3.9	24.6	24.1	17.6	10.1
Textiles					
I/D	14.5	21.0	32.5	31.0	6.0
E/P	4.2	20.9	21.2	28.9	8.2
Mechanical equipment					
I/D	11.1	31.9	17.8	40.5	3.3
E/P	19.3	37.7	36.7	53.6	19.0
Electrical equipment					
I/D	16.7	28.9	15.4	27.0	3.2
E/P	16.7	29.2	25.2	31.5	22.3
Transport equipment					
I/D	14.6	21.0	16.9	36.0	1.9
E/P	13.6	36.8	32.8	38.2	25.6
Chemical products					
I/D	9.0	26.1	18.4	34.2	4.2
E/P	13.6	29.9	27.8	47.9	7.9
Agro-food industry					
I/D	5.7	11.0	9.7	18.6	5.5
E/P	4.6	11.4	6.7	12.9	1.0
Paper, wood, and others					
I/D	8.5	16.5	13.1	30.1	3.3
E/P	5.0	11.7	10.6	14.4	3.5
Total					
I/D	10.4	20.7	16.3	30.3	3.3
E/P	9.4	23.6	23.1	31.6	11.7

E = Exports; P = Production; I = Imports; D = Domestic Demand.

TABLE A.17

Surpluses and deficits by sector for the five main economies, 1970–80

(Surplus (+) or deficit (−) of a sector divided by trade value in manufactured products)

	Construction materials	Metals and metallic products	Textiles	Mechanical equipment	Electrical equipment	Transport equipment	Chemical products	Agro-food industry	Paper, wood, and others	Total
US										
1970	−0.4	−3.8	−7.8	+15.6	+3.5	+3.2	+7.9	−5.9	−4.7	+7.7
1980	−0.4	−4.8	−5.6	+14.0	+1.3	−1.1	+9.1	−1.4	−3.1	+8.2
France										
1970	+0.4	−1.8	+4.8	−1.3	−0.1	+9.0	+2.5	+1.8	−2.1	+13.4
1980	+0.1	+1.3	−1.3	+0.8	0	+7.6	+2.3	+3.1	−2.4	+10.6
FRG										
1970	+0.9	+3.9	−3.8	+21.1	+6.2	+13.9	+10.7	−6.0	+0.2	+47.2
1980	+0.4	+6.3	−6.1	+15.7	+4.0	+13.3	+8.9	−2.1	−1.1	+39.3
UK										
1970	+1.1	+1.6	+2.2	+11.4	+2.0	+11.6	+5.1	−8.4	−3.7	+22.8
1980	+0.6	−1.9	−2.3	+7.0	+0.4	+0.5	+5.4	−1.4	+4.1	+4.1
Japan										
1970	+2.4	+22.2	+14.9	+9.5	+19.5	+23.8	+8.1	−4.2	+3.4	+99.6
1980	+1.8	+20.4	+2.0	+20.5	+25.2	+38.1	+4.2	−8.3	−0.1	+103.9

TABLE A.18

Impact on employment of trade in manufactured products between developed and developing countries, 1976
(thousands of jobs)

	OECD			US			EC			Japan		
	Exp	Imp	Bal	Exp	Imp	Bal	Exp	Imp	Bal	Exp	Imp	Bal
Textile yarns	138.9	192.2	−53.3	15.4	62.5	47.1	48.7	74.3	−25.6	61.7	18.8	42.9
Clothing	40.8	218.2	−177.4	13.0	81.5	−68.5	19.8	90.1	−70.3	3.4	13.7	−10.3
Wood and wood articles	10.4	26.3	−15.9	2.0	11.5	−9.5	5.2	8.9	−3.7	0.3	2.2	−1.9
Furniture and appliances	19.7	10.6	9.1	3.4	4.1	−0.7	12.8	3.4	9.4	1.7	1.6	0.1
Paper and allied products	33.3	2.8	30.5	8.6	1.0	7.6	6.5	1.2	5.3	3.6	0.1	3.5
Printing and publishing	25.0	2.7	22.3	4.5	0.8	3.7	15.3	0.8	14.5	1.4	0.2	1.2
Chemicals and allied products	163.4	23.4	140.0	37.5	10.4	27.1	73.8	6.6	67.2	28.8	2.8	26.0
Petroleum products	1.1	0.0	1.1	0.0	0.0	0.0	0.7	0.0	0.7	0.0	0.0	0.0
Manufactured rubber and plastics	32.2	63.1	−30.9	4.4	41.8	−37.4	16.0	11.5	4.5	8.1	3.2	4.9
Leather and leather apparel	10.1	36.2	−26.2	2.5	15.1	−12.6	3.7	13.7	−10.0	3.1	2.0	1.1
Stone, clay, and glass products	51.6	10.9	40.7	6.6	4.5	2.1	25.7	3.2	22.5	11.0	1.3	9.7
Basic metals and allied products	94.2	27.7	166.5	25.7	11.9	13.8	77.4	9.8	67.6	73.1	2.8	70.3
Metal products	91.9	7.3	84.5	15.9	2.8	13.1	22.3	4.5	17.8	17.2	1.5	15.7
Non-electrical machinery	527.4	18.7	508.7	142.7	6.4	136.3	261.7	6.6	255.1	71.5	1.6	69.9
Electrical equipment	417.3	122.7	294.6	106.3	77.9	28.4	187.1	29.9	157.2	88.6	10.8	77.8
Transport equipment	486.2	13.7	472.5	108.0	2.6	105.4	145.1	5.0	140.1	177.4	3.0	174.4
Instruments and allied products	72.7	17.8	54.9	16.3	9.5	6.8	22.3	4.5	17.8	17.2	1.5	15.7
Other manufactured goods	47.7	58.0	−10.3	9.1	27.2	−18.1	25.3	18.3	7.0	9.4	6.3	3.1
Total	2,363.8	852.5	1,511.3	521.9	371.5	150.4	996.7	289.9	706.8	573.8	72.3	501.6
Sum of positive balances			1,825.4			344.3			816.3			513.8
Sum of negative balances			314.1			193.9			109.5			12.2

Source: B. Balassa, 'L'évolution de la division internationale du travail dans le domaine des biens manufactures', *Annales Economiques No. 17*, Editions Cujas, Paris, 1981.

TABLE A.19
Average annual rates of change of unit labour costs for a sample of industrial countries, 1960–81 (%)
($US basis)

	1960–73	1973–81	1978–9	1979–80	1980–1
US	1.9	7.7	8.6	11.0	8.7
Canada	1.9	6.4	5.4	12.6	7.7
Japan	4.9	7.2	−6.5	−3.5	7.0
Belgium	4.6	10.8	9.1	5.6	na
France	2.8	9.5	14.2	16.9	−11.2
FRG	6.1	9.2	12.5	8.8	−15.4
Italy	5.4	8.1	12.0	8.9	−10.6
Netherlands	6.1	10.6	10.4	4.7	na
UK	2.6	15.0	27.7	34.8	−5.4

Source: US Department of Labor, Bureau of Labor Statistics, Washington DC.

TABLE A.20
Transfers and subsidies to industry and commerce in EC countries, 1973–5

Country	% of GDP
Belgium	0.95
FRG	0.34
France	1.10
Italy	0.88
Netherlands	0.94
UK	1.31

Source: OECD Evolution of public expenditures, June 1978.

TABLE A.21
Share of subsidies[1] in gross investment for a few industrial countries, 1960–77 (%)

Country	1960	1970	1975	1977
FRG	3.0	5.0	7.0	7.0
France	7.0	8.0	11.0	11.0
Italy	6.0	7.0	14.0	13.0
Netherlands	7.6	6.3	9.1	12.2
Belgium	10.0	11.8	16.7	20.1
UK	10.0	11.0	20.0	12.0
US	1.0	3.0	2.0	2.0

[1] Direct subsidies, tax reliefs excluded.

PART II

SECTORAL PATTERNS OF
ADJUSTMENT AND INTERVENTION

V

Sectoral Development and Sectoral Policies in the EC

4233
~~6300~~ 6160
2260
OECD
U.S.

HENK W. DE JONG*

I. Introduction

The first twenty years of the Community were marked by continuous growth, with fluctuations in the rates of economic development rather than around absolute levels. This has changed since the mid-1970s and at the beginning of the 1980s overall stagnation is clearly visible throughout the Common Market. It would be wrong, however, to focus too much attention on the macro-economic entities. The European economy is (notwithstanding extensive government influences on the functioning of the economic system) primarily a market economy. One of the most prominent aspects of a market economy is the growth and decline of markets. This is visible on the one hand in the rise of some firms and branches of industry, and on the other hand in the recession, accompanied by the shrinkage, reorganization, and failure of firms and branches. Such sectors also generate a good deal of the rising unemployment. Such changes mean that the sectoral composition of a market economy is shifting continuously, both in a quantitative and in a qualitative sense.

Many problems follow from this: economic crises are demarcations of the compository set-up of the market economy. The European cyclical crises of the post-war period were recognizable from this point of view; a real problem is why they extended throughout an increasing range of sectors in the course of time. The very moderate recession of 1957-8 was limited to coal mining and the traditional textile industry. The recession of 1966-7 saw problems arising in shipbuilding, steel, shoes, and clothing, whereas in 1974-5 building and construction, basic chemicals, and motor cars (even if temporarily) also went into the doldrums or worse. The most recent set-back, in 1981-3, has extended the list again: the stagnation in automobiles is now fairly general and investment goods (such as machine building, oil refining, and even telephone equipment and aircraft construction) have stopped growing. The crises have become longer in duration, too. In 1957-8 it was

* Professor of Economics, University of Amsterdam.

a matter of months; in the mid-1960s the recession lasted for about a year; in 1974-5 about two years; and now the growth of industrial sectors is more the exception than the rule.

Two main questions pose themselves in looking at these extending crises. First, what is the cause—or if one prefers, what is the mechanism—behind all this? Second, were governmental policies directed at industrial sectors a solution to the problem? I will take up these questions in succession.

II. The economy as a composition of sectors

The European economy—i.e. the economy of the EC—has gone through a series of dynamic changes since its foundation in 1958. These can be roughly divided into two major periods with remarkably different characteristics. The period between 1958 and 1973 was marked by fast expansion, full employment, heavy investment, low energy and raw materials prices, and, until 1971, a relatively modest increase in prices of most end-products and stable exchange rates. In contrast, the period 1973-82 saw a reversal of nearly all these aspects: much slower growth, increasing unemployment, modest (and later declining) investments, rising raw materials and end-product prices, and fluctuating exchange rates.

II.1. First period

During the first period, the development pattern of the main sectors in the various member countries showed a remarkable *convergence*, even though the quantitative dimensions of growth per sector were different. The majority of the growth industries of this period were represented in all or nearly all countries. They consisted of chemicals, oil products and other energy sources, electrical and electronic goods, machinery, iron and steel, means of transport, and similar industries. Likewise, the relatively declining industries were shared by the member countries and consisted of agriculture, coal mining, textiles, and clothing (with the important exception of Italy, where the textile industry grew satisfactorily).

These convergencies in sectoral developments were a reflection of supply and demand factors, operating rather uniformly throughout the Community of the six. For example, expenditure for investment purposes grew markedly, while consumption expenditure declined relatively in total demand. Within the consumer share shifts occurred from food and other basic consumer goods towards durable consumer goods. The share of government expenditure in total consumer demand also rose. Coal was substituted for oil and gas; the more capital intensive character of the production processes spurred the investment goods industries, while the decline of sectors with low value-added in total output mirrored the sluggish demand for such goods.

Another aspect of the sectoral development during this period was the tendency towards national integration of the sectoral composition of the economies of member countries. Instead of the expected specialization of broad sections between countries, European integration prompted countries to round off their industrial structures. No country freely gave up its industrial sectors to the benefit of other member states, where such sectors might be more efficient. On the contrary, countries have founded new broad sectors or expanded small existing ones, even in cases where those sectors were already far developed in other member states. When they lost out, it was through the force of competition. Iron and steel in the Netherlands and Italy, food and transport (other than motor cars) in West Germany, and investment goods in France and Belgium are cases in point.

A third and shared experience was the rise in the commercial-services sector, in terms of added value, employment, and fixed capital investments. Whereas manufacturing industry's share of added value and employment hovered around 30 per cent in the EC as a whole, the market-services sector grew, especially in terms of employment and fixed capital investments. The flow of productive resources—labour, knowledge, capital—towards the sector of market services was ample. The expansion of this sector also added several new qualitative elements to European industry: research and development, sales promotion, market research, management development, and a much extended use of office machinery and control systems.

Finally, the general economic expansion was driven forward by the broad capital investment process. This lasted in all member countries —though in varying degrees—until 1973, and necessitated increasing amounts of semi-manufactures and machinery. The rising capital intensity of the production process occurred in all EC countries and in all sectors, but sectors shed labour (e.g. in agriculture, textiles, and coal mining) or increased their total employment (e.g. in the chemicals and automobile industries and in market services) depending on the growth rate of final demand.

II.2. Second period

During the second period—1973 to 1981-2—these tendencies were reversed. Three particular phenomena stood out very clearly: the decline in capital investments, the accelerated rise of the services sectors (commercial and non-commercial), and the rising prices of energy and raw materials. These tendencies are clearly visible in the shifts of the sectoral structure of the six leading EC countries. Table 5.2 gives these shifts in added value, employment, and gross fixed investments during

TABLE 5.1

Total employment and major sector shares in US and EC, 1960–81

	1960	1970	1973	1979	1980	1981
Total employment (000's)						
US	65,778	78,678	85,064	98,824	99,303	100,397
EC	99,218	101,854	102,509	103,650	103,901	103,567
Share in total employment (%)						
Agriculture						
US	8.5	4.5	4.2	3.6	3.6	3.5
EC	17.2	10.4	8.9	7.5	7.3	7.2
Total industry (including building and construction)						
US	35.3	34.4	33.2	31.3	30.5	30.1
EC	42.7	42.4	40.7	38.1	37.8	36.8
Manufacturing industry						
US	26.8	24.6	23.7	21.3	21.4	21.2
EC	29.7	30.1	30.3	27.9	27.3	26.6
Services						
US	56.2	61.1	62.6	65.2	65.9	66.4
EC	40.1	47.3	50.5	54.4	55.0	56.0
Share of women in total professionals employed (%)						
US	33.4	38.1	38.9	42.2	42.6	42.9
EC	—	34.3	35.2	37.5	37.8	37.2
Rate of unemployment (%)						
US		4.8			7.1	7.6
EC		2.0			6.0	7.8

Source: Commission of the EC, *Economic Annual Report*, No. 14, November 1982, Table 7.3 (adapted).

TABLE 5.2
Sectoral structures of added value, employment, and fixed investment in the EC-6[1]
(1975 prices and exchange rates)

	Added value			Employment			Fixed investment		
	1970	1973	1979	1970	1973	1979	1970	1973	1979
Agriculture	4.8	4.2	3.9	9.9	8.6	7.2	4.0	4.2	4.6
Energy	5.0	5.2	5.6	1.9	1.7	1.7	7.0	6.7	8.2
Industrial products	32.1	30.5	29.4	30.9	30.2	27.9	22.5	18.7	16.5
Semi-products	6.7	6.5	6.4	5.0	4.9	4.5	8.0	6.2	5.0
Investment goods	12.4	12.0	11.7	12.5	12.6	11.9	7.4	6.2	6.3
Food and drinks	4.8	4.3	4.2	3.0	2.9	2.8	2.6	2.4	2.1
Other consumer goods	8.1	7.8	7.1	10.3	10.0	8.7	4.5	4.0	3.1
Building and construction	7.6	7.6	6.6	8.7	8.5	7.8	2.3	2.0	1.8
Commercial services	39.0	39.7	41.6	33.0	34.1	36.8	48.8	54.1	55.7
Non-commercial services	11.6	12.8	12.9	15.7	16.9	18.7	15.5	14.2	13.2
Total	100.0	100.0	100.0	100.0	100.0	100.0	100.0	100.0	100.0

[1] Belgium, Germany, France, Italy, the Netherlands, and the United Kingdom.
Source: Commission of the EC, Economic Annual Report, No. 10, November 1981, Table 8.1 (adapted).

the 1970s, while Table 5.1 makes the comparison in terms of the employment variable between the EC and the US for the longer period 1960-81.

Table 5.1 indicates that the US economy has been a bigger creator of employment since 1960: no less than 35 million new jobs arose, against some 4 million in the EC countries. Also, by 1981 the US rate of unemployment was less than the EC, even though the US level was initially higher. Finally, in the US the share of women in the total of professionals employed had risen to 5.7 per cent more than in the EC.

It is clear that new US sectors (particularly in the service industries) have provided big new opportunities for jobs. This is also clear from both the increase in the rate of participation (total professional population as a percentage of population in the productive age class, 15-64 years) and the increase in the rate of employment (total employment as a percentage of population in the productive age class, 15-64 years). The former rate rose in the US from 67 per cent in the 1960s to 71-2 per cent in the late 1970s; the latter rate increased from 64 to 67 per cent. In contrast, the EC countries saw both rates decline from about 67 per cent in the early 1960s to some 65 per cent and 61-2 per cent in the late 1970s.[1] The EC therefore seems to be currently less efficient in utilizing its labour in the productive age class.

Nevertheless, Table 5.1 shows that the sectoral shares in total employment have moved in the same direction for both economies. In both the US and the EC, labour in goods production has declined substantially in the long-term, while employment in the service sectors has risen appreciably. The shift in the EC countries was nothing less than spectacular: from 40 per cent to 56 per cent employed in service, which means that on average some 800,000 new jobs arose every year.

Manufacturing industry's share fell continuously in the US economy, but in the EC it only started falling after 1973, giving rise to the idea of 'de-industrialization' within this economy. The shifts towards services employment in the US and in seven European countries are also expressed in Figure 5.1, which shows the long-term relationship between real per capita income and the employment share of the services sector.[2] There seems to be a distinct relationship in each country between service employment and real per capita income. Nevertheless, the services sector has been growing in all the countries charted and in some (the US, UK, Benelux, and Italy) at an accelerating rate. The acceleration may be debatable from a policy point of view, but there can be no question as to the long-term, spontaneous movement of the European and American economies.

As Figure 5.2 demonstrates, the growth in services employment cannot be sufficiently explained by per capita productivity growth. The reverse was thought to be the case earlier, the argument being

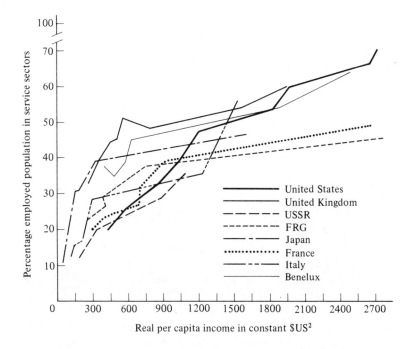

Fig. 5.1: Relationship between percentage service employment and real per capita income.[1]

[1] The lines for the US, the UK, France, and Italy were drawn through points indicating the years 1860, 1880, 1900, 1913, 1929, 1952-4, 1960, 1970, and 1979-80. For the FRG no figures are available for 1860. For Japan none are available for 1860 and 1979-80. The USSR has a line through the years 1928, 1940, 1960, and 1970. Benelux years are 1900, 1913, 1929, 1952-4, 1960, 1970, and 1979-80.
[2] Base year is 1970.
Sources: Per capita incomes for 1860-1960 from L. J. Zimmerman, *Arme en rijke landen*, Albani, The Hague 1964, pp. 136-7; for 1970 from J. B. Kravis, 'A survey of international comparisons of productivity', *The Economic Journal*, No. 86, March 1976, p. 19; for 1979-80 from *EC European Economy*, Nos. 10 and 14, 1981 and 1982. Employment in services from J. Kuznets, 'Industrial distribution of national product and labour force', in *Economic development and cultural change*, No. V, University of Chicago Press, July 1957; F. Decker, *Einführung in die Dienstleistungsökonomie*, F. Schöningh, Paderborn, 1975; R. Livshits, 'Industry in the economic structure of the USSR', in *Problems of Economics*, No. XVIII, January 1976; Commission of the EC, *Economic Annual Report*, Nos. 10 and 14, 1981 and 1982.

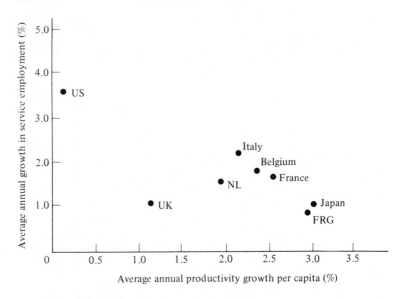

Fig. 5.2: Relationship between growth of service employment and per capita productivity growth, 1960–79.

that fast productivity growth would displace manpower, which would be taken up by new industries (very often with low productivity growth, as in services).[3] It is therefore difficult to go further than stating that there is a relative saturation with goods in the western economies, and that the crisis which we have been experiencing since the middle of the 1970s may be seen as an expression of this shift from goods to services.

Focusing our attention on the sectoral shifts in the EC-6 in Table 5.2, we see that investment in agriculture kept rising during the 1970s, but the sector's share in employment and added value fell. The sharp reduction in employment indicates that labour-productivity in European agriculture has continued to rise. But the contrasting movements in added value and investment point towards a declining productivity of fixed capital investment. In other words, the increasing capital intensity of agricultural output generates lower and lower rewards in Europe, which casts doubts on the economic sense of continuing protectionism for this sector.

In the energy sector, investment and added value have shifted in the same direction by about the same magnitude (0.6 vs 1.2), though employment declined. These tendencies mirror increasing energy prices and the penetration of natural gas.

In industry, the various sub-sectors behaved differently. The basic industries, like metal production and chemicals, saw their shares in added value and employment fall to a lesser extent than their share in fixed investment, indicating the need for less investment as over-capacities arose on a larger scale, particularly since 1973-4. The investment goods sector consequently went through an output and employment decline, though this did not apply to some particular branches such as means of transport, office machines, and electrical materials, which were still in expansion during the 1970s. Food and other consumer goods sectors lost ground, as did building and con-struction.

Within the Community, no industrial-goods producing sector has been able to keep its early 1970s share in added value. At the centre of this de-industrialization process, these sectors are approaching zero net investment in the early 1980s, followed by a practical standstill in the investment-goods and semi-products sectors—once the driving force behind West European expansion. Thus the troubles in the steel, chemical, oil refining, and artificial fibres industries became notorious.

Table 5.3 gives the main characteristics of the investment goods industry in the six leading EC countries from 1970 to 1979. Since that year the situation has deteriorated further, though no detailed figures are available yet. However, the overall behaviour of fixed investment within the total EC economy is a clear indicator: whereas those invest-ments (expressed in 1975 prices) still rose by +2.3 per cent in 1980, they declined by −5.6 per cent and −3.0 per cent in 1981 and 1982. (See Figure 5.3.)

It is apparent that the recession has taken a heavy toll from the investment-goods producing sector during the past decade. This will also have its implications throughout the rest of the 1980s. First, the existing overcapacities in goods production are not easily overcome and will hamper a quick upturn.

Second, the zero growth rate of the past decade means a relative obsolescence of the European production process. In a number of cases, these production processes may have already become technically obso-lete, but as long as average variable costs of the old plants are still covered, this may not be so economically. The picture is complicated by government subsidies, which are not used sufficiently for moderniza-tion; they are meant to keep employment or just to conserve ailing firms. (See Section VI.)

Third, a sluggish investment process does generate negative multiplier effects on specialized supplier firms and on other industries. Through vertical linkages it may even distort the networks of specialized know-ledge and capacities, which may get lost permanently.

The long-term decline in the growth of investment, which is vividly

TABLE 5.3

Investment goods in the EC-6, 1970-9

	Added value[1] % change p.a.			Total employment % change p.a.			Fixed investments[2] % change p.a.		
	1970-3	1973-5	1975-9	1970-3	1973-5	1975-9	1970-3	1973-5	1975-9
Metal products	2.5	-1.3	1.4	-0.1	-2.1	-1.4	0.1	-14.3	1.5
Machinery for agriculture and industry	2.8	-0.4	1.2	-1.2	-1.1	-0.9	-1.8	-5.8	3.2
Office machinery, EDP	7.9	5.6	7.8	0.4	-1.3	0	3.9	-2.5	3.9
Electrical materials	6.1	2.1	4.2	1.1	-0.7	-1.2	2.5	-2.8	2.3
Means of transport	4.9	-2.9	4.8	1.0	-2.4	0.8	-5.2	-0.8	6.7
Total investments	4.2	-0.25	3.2	0.2	-1.6	-0.7	-1.1	-5.4	3.8

EC-6: Belgium, Germany, France, Italy, Netherlands, United Kingdom.

[1] Gross added value at market prices (E.U.A. 1975).
[2] Gross investment in fixed assets (at prices E.U.A. 1975).
Source: Commission of the EC, Economic Annual Report, No. 10, November 1981, Table 8.2 (adapted).

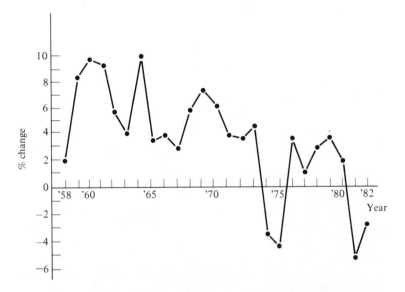

Fig. 5.3: Volume of gross investment in fixed assets in EC, 1958–82 (% change on previous year).

illustrated in Figure 5.3, raises a question as to its causes. On average, investments in fixed assets have come to a standstill during the past decade: since 1973 the negative rates have been as important as the positive rates, with the number of years on both sides of the balance about equal. The reason for the stagnating total investment rate—which in its turn has been the main reason for the overall stagnation of the European economy for a number of years—is not hard to find: the structural shift from industrial to service sectors (analysed in the previous paragraphs) has also brought about a shift in investments. As Figure 5.2 and Table 5.2 indicate, gross fixed investment fell in manufacturing industry and its four main sectors, but rose appreciably in commercial services. During the four year period 1975-9, 2.3 million jobs were created in the commercial services sector and 1 million jobs in the government sector within the Community as a whole, and these people had to be provided with offices and tools. On the other hand, the stagnating demand for basic industrial goods, such as cement, chemicals, steel, oil, and means of transport led to overcapacities in these sectors because the investment process was too strong in the years preceding the first oil crisis.[4] The present crisis is therefore mainly an industrial crisis, reflecting a relative saturation with goods, but not services.

Before we return to the overcapacity problem in these industries, another dimension has to be discussed. This relates to the interaction between the sectoral processes and the market co-ordination mechanism.

III. The dynamics of a market economy: structure and process

There is a conventional, definitive difference between the notions of sector and market, which is neglected in the rest of this article: the sector refers only to *suppliers* of some economic activity (goods or service). Basically, markets or sectors are the result of specialization, which promotes efficient allocation, learning by doing, and invention and innovation. Specialization and markets are like a pair of twins: they are two different individuals, yet hardly distinguishable and derived from the same source.

Nevertheless, a market completes and unifies specialized activity in a double sense. It completes the productive action with a sale, putting a societal value on what was initially an individual value, and it unifies specialized activities in sectors through co-ordination. The co-ordination, obviously, is necessary to secure order in markets and, in a wider sense, society.

In contrast to the neo-classical or the general equilibrium theory (with its emphasis on the pivotal role of price in reaching equilibrium in markets and securing in this way a stable and static order) it is held that the co-ordination of specialized economic activities is attained in essentially three ways: competition, co-operation, and control. These concepts correspond to some fundamental human needs relating to economic activity: the need to discover and undertake new things, to imitate such 'innovations', to effectuate co-operation in tasks which are of super-individual nature, and the desire to decide on the organization of resources (control) in the interests of stabilization and security. In modern economic language we speak of competition, combination, and concentration as being the co-ordinating methods used by economic agents (individuals and companies) to improve their positions both in an absolute and relative sense. Price is one of the action parameters (and perhaps the most important) used by those economic actors to achieve their goals, but it is still only one amongst many others: product, product variety and quality, promotion, service, location, etc.

It is essentially these co-ordinating methods which constitute and delineate sectors and markets. Sectors cannot be distinguished on the basis of physical characteristics such as materials or processing activity, as is being done by statistical bureaus and government agencies. For many economic purposes this makes no sense. Neither can they be delineated with the aid of only prices and related concepts, such as cross-price elasticities or substitution gaps.[5] The sector or market is *the area of competition* or of its counterbalancing methods combination and concentration, as has been held in anti-trust literature and policy decisions for a long time. If dairy farmers constitute a co-operation to exploit a milk-processing plant, they are in the same sector, even though they do not compete in price; if one half of them deliver self-made cheese to the market, they are not. It is the same with cigarette manufacturers, who engage in struggles which have practically nothing to do with price, but depend on life cycles of brands, and the 'strategic competition' of licensing, take-overs, and mergers, i.e. control.[6]

In addition, the economic process and its structure are closely interrelated: the dynamics of a market economy follow from the interactions between structure and process, which mutually influence each other. Market or sector processes are dynamic because sectors rise, stagnate, and decline. Market structures are dynamic because the competitive, combinatory, and control relationships between firms change all the time. Generalizing, one may say that process and structure are linked through competition and expansionary or declining markets, whereas combination or control are connected with market maturity and stagnation. This basic picture can be distorted by governmental action: for example, when a sector saddled with overcapacity would normally try to escape the fierce competition through reorganization, but is prevented from doing so by government subsidies.

It would be wrong, however, to lay much stress on one or the other, emphasizing the exclusivity, because sometimes the rivalry is continued once combinations are formed or the control is established. For example, shipping conferences may counter price competition through either minimum price agreements or reduction cartels. Apart from outside competition and the rivalry associated with establishing common tariffs, there are several control aspects involved in such agreements: price discrimination to discipline infiltrating tramp lines, control of shipping tonnages through restrictions on departures, tonnages, or ports, or the joint pooling of profits or loads. Notwithstanding such far-reaching agreements, the 100-year history of shipping conferences is one of ups and downs, in the sense of competition breaking through when new chances could be exploited.

Another example is the book-publishing industry. There is a long-standing cartel in the Netherlands, including the booksellers, which regulates collective resale price maintenance at the retail level, stipulates that publishers must adhere to the price fixed at the introduction of a new book title for a period of two years, and splits up the Dutch-speaking market into the Netherlands and Flanders, with prohibitions on re-importing books shipped to Flanders. Nevertheless, the leading publishers have actively participated in the rise of book clubs and book chain stores which have undercut the cartel agreement with appreciable reductions, the latter especially when the growth of book sales slowed down.

It is rare when sectors of activity do not show similar cross-currents of behaviour by economic agents. Thus, a necessary prerequisite for discussing sector policies, apart from defining the sector, is to study its process and its organizational structure in varying circumstances.

A simple, first approach is given in Table 5.4, which distinguishes the phases of development of sectors and the types of structures to be found in them. The various growth phases of individual industries

TABLE 5.4
Development phases of a sector: structure and process

Process →	Introduction	Expansion	Maturity	Decline
Structure ↓				
Competition	innovatory pioneering	imitative improving	differentiative segmenting	destructive rationalizing
Combination	joint-venture		cartels, concerted practices, joint-ventures, restrictions	structural cartels, protection
Concentration	innovatory monopolies, patents, copyrights, trade marks	franchises, licensing, subsidiaries	mergers, take-overs, holding companies	deconcentration, splitting-up of firms

are not so difficult to distinguish: a comparison of the growth rate with some relevant aggregate standard, such as GDP, manufacturing industry, or the service sector is usually sufficient to establish expansion (rate of growth above average), maturity (rate of growth below average), or decline (negative growth). Looking at the growth rates of the EC economy as a whole since 1958, we see that the first ten years were a period of expansion, when innovatory and imitative competition was the main mechanism of co-ordination, joined by innovatory monopolies. Since the end of the 1960s, there has been a clear tendency (at least in GDP and investment in fixed assets) for the rate of growth to fall back —on average—to modest rates. In accordance with the scheme of Table 5.4, the slow rate of growth of the maturing sectors in the European economy in 1968–78 was accompanied by intensive merger and take-over activity. Combining activities (mainly in the form of joint ventures with restrictive aims) and concerted practices also spread. Finally, during the recession of 1974-5 and especially since the end of the 1970s, the pronounced decline in the rates of growth of GDP, industrial output, and investment have accompanied the emergence of fierce and even destructive competition; companies have gone through failures and had to be dismantled and split up. Combination between firms increasingly takes the form of structural cartels or joint protection, as in steel, automobiles, chemicals, and textiles, often supported by import regulations and government aid.

Of course, the above is too crude a sketch of the interactions because:

— individual sectors have had their own phases of development which did not necessarily coincide with the course of the aggregates. For example, steel reached maturity and decline earlier than automobiles, which did rather well during the second half of the 1970s (after the 1974-5 recession) because of higher real incomes. Also, some sectors are still growing, like computers, video discs, and surf boards;
— individual sectors have often been influenced by specific government measures, varying according to countries. For example, in tobacco processing the high tax rates have made price competition well-nigh impossible, and government licences have made building behave differently from what would have been expected in a free market. Still, it is worth mentioning that a monopolistic industry like telephones went through the various phases of sectoral development. This sector has stagnated for about a year, after declining rates of growth during most of the 1970s.
— of the competitive parameters used in the process as shown in Table 5.4. The maturing consumer goods sector in the 1970s widened assortments, differentiated products, and segmented markets. But for about the past three years, the growth of private consumption within the Community has stopped and strong price competition has returned in retail trading and many other sectors.

It is also worth mentioning here the difference between the types of sector pricing and the relationship of this difference with organizational forms. John Hicks (and long before him, Gardner Means) distinguished between 'fix-price' and 'flex-price' markets. It would seem that flexible pricing is often associated with competitive industries and fix-pricing with combining and concentrated industry structures. In view of the foregoing it should be clear that the demarcation lines, both in sectors and in time, are not rigid.

IV. The growth of overcapacities

The most general reason I can think of as to why problems have arisen in sectors is the growth of overcapacities. This seems fairly simple, but it is not. There are two problems of identification: first, what is excess capacity? and second, why and when has surplus or excess capacity arisen?

As to the first problem, three capacity concepts have to be distinguished: namely, installed capacity, which is generally the highest capacity estimate, taking into account all the potentially productive installations; technical or operational capacity, which refers to the maximum production rate that can be sustained for longer periods and which is normally below installed capacity and allowable capacity; or economic capacity, which takes into account existing structures or regulations within a market, e.g. governmental or cartel rules, or agreements between oligopolies. Excess capacity measures current demand against these standards and thus may vary by definition. Games between firms locked up in rationalization problems in an industry nearly always have to do with such definitions and form another reason why government-inspired or government-imposed solutions are often sterile. The European steel industry offers one example of the difficulties which are to be overcome in this respect.

Another example is the Dutch bread baking industry. It got into problems through take-overs of the large industrial bakeries, and then proposed a solution in which the government and the consumer financed the withdrawal of its excess capacity. This was defined as installed capacity that was based on a three-shift system, whereas actual working hours normally equalled a two-shift system.[7] The Reorganization Committee paid Dfl 700 to reduce operating capacity by one bale (50 kgs), but a reduction of idle capacity was only rewarded by Dfl 100. The costs of the 'restructuring' of capacity (Dfl 30 million) were paid by the government and by a tax on wheat flour, causing the bread price to rise by 1 to 2 cents for a period of 4 to 5 years. Small wonder the industry continues to be plagued by the same disease.

The second problem is still more complicated. Simply stated, over-capacity is the surplus of producible output over demand at a price which covers long-run total average costs. The reasons why it arises can be on the demand side (e.g. an absolute reduction or a reduction in the growth rate) or on the supply side (e.g. over-investment of the firms in the industry, or replacement of capacities by the capacities of new suppliers, or innovations in processes). However, this is complicated by the time dimension (is the reduction in demand of a cyclical or a structural nature?), by the visibility of overcapacity, and by the policy question: can the acknowledged overcapacity still be used elsewhere or for other purposes, or does it just hang over the market?

The diagnosis of the reasons and circumstances for overcapacities arising in particular sectors requires another rather complex analysis; yet it must be undertaken because policy solutions depend on it. Again, a general reason is the relatively high proportion of constant costs in the total cost structure. Those heavy fixed investments also have a long durability, so the problem is not a passing one. Another reason is the combination of high overhead costs with a diversified type of firm. The allocation problem is not easily solved or not solved at all, and losses in activity A are paid for by profits made in activities B, C, or D. Artificial fibres are a case in point: surplus capacity has existed for more than a decade now, but the losses were financed in diversified firms by profits made in pharmaceuticals, food products, and the like. At the end of 1982 European producers had to agree on on further capacity reductions.

These two sources of overcapacity correspond fairly closely to the two ways in which firms or sectors have come into troubles: either they have built or acquired production facilities that were too large, based on past growth rates which could not be sustained, or they have acquired too heavy a superstructure of general costs as a result of intensive merger and take-over activities. In the latter case, these concentrations arose from the strategic manœuvering of firms for market shares, but in many cases the required rationalization was not effected. The necessary 'streamlining' of operations was omitted, this clearly being an unrewarding task. Management errors were, in the final instance, the source of the casualties; but governments aiding those companies have either not seen this or closed their eyes to it. The majority of the big firms which came into troubled waters in the various European countries were of this kind. Still other, though less general, causes of the overcapacities have been the rise in capacities of non-European countries (oil-refining, petrochemicals, or clothing) or innovations replacing older products (e.g. typewriters). However, it would be too far-fetched to discuss these here.

V. Meso-economic policies

Alongside macro-economic policies directed towards influencing aggregate entities in the national economy, so-called structural or sectoral or *meso-economic* policies have been developed (mostly in a haphazard manner, though some countries, such as France, have done it more systematically). Types and names vary between countries and making a catalogue is out of the question. Some classification of structural policies can nevertheless be undertaken and this will show how much meso-economic policies differ within the EC.

The object of meso-economic policies is the market, its structure and process, and the firms operating therein. At the same time, interventions in the market can be distinguished according to their degree of 'public-ness', ranging from private policies undertaken by firms or groups of firms, to semi-public policies (e.g. institutions like the Industrial Reorganization Commission in England, the Bundeskartellamt in West Germany, the Institut National d'Economie and Institut de Développement Industriel in Belgium or France, or the Nederlandse Herstructurerngsmaatschappij (Nehem) in the Netherlands), to full public intervention. This double approach gives one the opportunity to classify structural or meso-economic policies on the basis of both criteria. The questions are then:

(i) whether the policy conforms with the operation of the market, or whether it aims to replace or eliminate the market;

(ii) who conceives and executes the policy, i.e. the distinction between private and public structural policies. These may be reinforcing, but can also be exclusive; e.g. public policies can prove ineffective because companies have already regulated their behaviour among themselves.

A matrix of possible policies can thus be made on the basis of these criteria, giving various types of policies which can be recognized in actual, historical occurrences and episodes. A name in the matrix designates the place and basic characteristics of a type of policy. Horizontal lines indicate the range of the policy; vertical lines indicate interconnections between policies. (If there are many interconnections, a policy becomes more consistent.) Finally, by putting some names of policies in frames one may get a shorthand view of a country's com-position of meso-economic policies. This has been done for the Nether-lands in the matrix in Table 5.5. It can be seen at once that in the Netherlands private sector policies are threefold.

(i) Firms organize themselves in corporations covering sectors: e.g. Royal Dutch Shell in oil, Unilever in foods, Philips in the electro-technical business, Akzo in fibres, Royal Blast Furnaces and Steelworks in steel making, etc.

(ii) Cartels and syndicates arise if sectors do not lend themselves to corporate organization. A 1956 law only forbids their abuse of power positions, and they are hardly ever prosecuted. Thus traditionally there are hundreds of cartels in the country—591 in 1979.

(iii) Strong co-operatives exist in the agricultural processing sector—one

TABLE 5.5
The meso-economic policy matrix

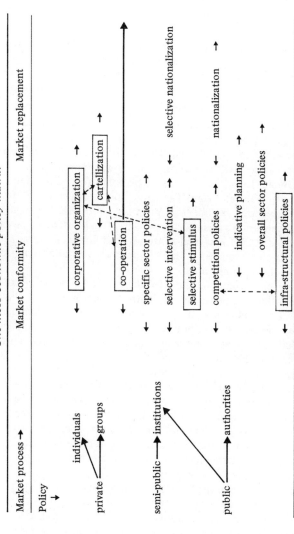

Source: H. W. de Jong, 'Dutch structural policy: the visible finger on the invisible hand', in *Sectoral Policies: Opportunities and Limitations.* Studies accompanying the report, the present position and the prospects for Dutch industry, Staatsuitgevery, 's Gravenhage, 1980.

of the most prominent sectors in the Dutch economy—and extended joint ventures have arisen in the manufacturing sector.

Because of this thorough organization of the private sector, the government's meso-economic policies have never stood much of a chance. The Dutch government has therefore confined itself to basically two tasks in this field:

(i) creation of the conditions for sectors to be able to operate, the so-called infra-structural policy (see last row of Figure 5.5);
(ii) selective stimulation of sectors in cases where the risks were too large for private groups or where there was a threat from a lag in comparison with foreign sectors.

Mainly, such policies were started in support of private initiative, were subsidiary in nature and sector-orientated, and took off in post-war periods (after 1815, 1918, and 1945). In contrast, other types of policies—such as nationalization, which was important in France and the United Kingdom, indicative planning (France), competition and anti-trust policies (West Germany and the United States), or selective intervention of the type practised by the IRC in England—have never even stood a chance of being adopted, let alone being carried out. This holds true for several centuries; Dutch policies have been of the same type for a long time, though there were variations in intensity according to the circumstances.

Similarly, one would be able to characterize the meso-economic policies of other European states. Without venturing into this field too deeply (it is more my aim to describe the system rather than the contents of meso-economic policies), I think that French policies, for example, have also been of the same type throughout history. There has been a preponderance of indicative planning, or what is called in the Netherlands a sector-structural policy, with the State ordering and co-ordinating sectors of activity, setting goals to be achieved, and providing means (mainly of a financial nature) if necessary. To a large extent, this is the reverse of the Dutch situation, because large private corporations, strong co-operatives, and broadly organized cartels have been relatively absent in the French economy and the State has stepped into the void (or as some historians have it, has prevented the private sector from developing commensurately).

In West Germany and the United Kingdom, on the other hand, meso-economic policies have changed several times through history. West Germany's friendly policies towards cartels and trusts of pre-war times were replaced by pro-competitive policies in the post-war period, and successive governments abstained from sectoral policies, at least until the mid-1970s (with the exception of a few sectors, like energy). Now the German course seems to be changing again in the direction of national and branch-embracing solutions (e.g. aircraft, steel, ship-building).

In the United Kingdom the frequencies of change in meso-economic policies have been much greater, with probable negative effects on the functioning of industries. As George and Joll state in a recent book: 'More noticeable has been the lack of consensus on industries policy. It is doubtful whether any other industrial country can match the UK for shifts in policy and for creating an uncertain environment for industry to work in. The creation and subsequent abolition of the National Board for Prices and Incomes (born 1965, died 1970) and the Industrial Reorganization Commission (born 1966, died 1970), the frequent shifts in regional policy, and the running battle between the two major political parties over State ownership of industry are just a few examples.'[8]

VI. Meso-economic policies: concentration and financial support

On the basis of the preceding discussion it is easy to see that in a matur-ing economy (such as the EC's during the late 1960s and 1970s) structural adaptations have to follow, which lead to increased combina-tion and concentration. This was extensively documented by the EC Commission in some of its annual competition reports. I will not repeat what was written in those reports but emphasize the two main findings: an appreciable increase in both market concentration and in overall concentration.[9] In the period up to the mid-1970s many dominant positions were established; in many national markets within the EC, leading firms acquired market shares of over 50 per cent. Even if some of these dominant positions were not tenable, they led to '. . . a tendency away from single-firm dominance accompanied by spreading duopolistic or triopolistic dominance',[10] i.e. to many opportunities for combination.

These structural changes stifled competition in many sectors during the 1970s. Concentration and stagnation mutually reinforce each other, not only because fewer decision centres come forward with fewer initiatives, but also because these centres have an interest in preserving the status quo. Their positions having become important and established, change could only mean deterioration for them. There is nothing new in this coincidence of stagnation in the economic process and the tendency towards concentration: the US trust movement as well as the German cartellization movement of the 'eighties and 'nineties in the nineteenth century coincided with the prolonged recession of these decades. Again, the stagnation of the 1920s and 1930s was accompanied by the formation of large combines such as I.G. Farben, Vereinigte Stahlwerke, Unilever, ICI, AKU, etc. Concentration and merger activity have had a tendency to lead the cyclical movement, as several authors have underlined.[11] The main reason is that in maturing industries, the external growth of firms displaces inernal growth, both horizontally and vertically, because the latter takes too much time and business strategy is preponderant. In turn, higher concentration has the effect of promoting rigidity in market structures. What was new in recent European history was the fact that national government policies promoted concentration well into the 1970s. The errors of this policy have since become clearly visible, especially for those firms which have taken part intensively in concentrations (mergers and take-overs) and have failed or come into difficulties. The list is too long to mention here, but AEG, British Steel, British Leyland, Nederhorst (building), Akzo (synthetic fibres), and RSV (shipyards) are just a few examples.

When the consequences of this erroneous policy manifested themselves in the second half of the 1970s, European governments again did the wrong thing: they supported the shaky organizations with *ad hoc* finance for so-called social and employment reasons, and protected the dominant positions by means of market restrictions, aid, favoured positions, etc. Governments pursued what Professor H. R. Peters has called a neo-mercantilistic sectoral policy. What he reproached the FRG government for can also be laid at the door of other European governments: 'The political decision makers in the Federal Republic have fundamentally proclaimed a market conforming sectoral adaptation policy and practised a preponderantly neo-mercantilistic sector protection and sectoral conservation policy.'[12]

The four main reasons why these policies were wrong can be summarized as follows:

Firstly, the problems of the concentrated large firms were long term in nature; most of the errors were made long ago. To remedy such problems with *ad hoc* financial aid is simply senseless: no cures can be or were provided. On the other hand, the aid seriously worsened the States' budgetary troubles.

Secondly, protection and financial aid did not clear away the overcapacities, but prolonged and even extended the sectoral crises, because these policies falsify the competition. Profitable firms saw their positions undermined. The aid became repetitious and hidden, and distorted the market.

Thirdly, not only did the so-called specific regulations concerning aid falsify competition, but the so-called generic aid had a similar effect. Firms are increasingly multi-product, multi-sectoral, and multi-national in nature, so while aid given within a particular sector may not distort competition in this sector, it may nevertheless have effects on other sectors. Firms will take this aid into account in devising their strategies for the whole group, with the result that cross-subsidization occurs, and effects on rationalization, investment, and employment can no longer be traced. The aid, as a high Dutch civil servant once said, 'will just disappear'.

Finally, politically speaking, aid has had a divisive effect instead of promoting a consensus on industrial policies, which is often said to be its main virtue. Interest groups—firms, communities, trade unions, etc.—have fought for the largest possible slice of the cake, and the so-called tri-partite, integral, and sectoral conceived models tried in the Benelux countries have floundered.[13] Governments have not sufficiently realized that a sector is composed of competing firms, bent on promoting their own interests, instead of so-called sectoral interests, which are products, production processes, exhibitions, trade associations, and the like.

VII. Summary and concluding remarks

The sector is an economic reality because it is composed of firms competing with each other or making combinations to try to gain control. These methods of co-ordination determine the structure of a sector.

The various configurations of structural relationships between firms change with the phases of the economic process. Rivalry for markets is prominent during expansion, when it does not hurt, and during decline, when it hurts seriously because the firms are saddled with over-capacities. In maturing and stagnatory phases of the economic process, combination and control get the upper hand, because price competition works like a boomerang—it no longer stimulates demand. Competition —least of all, price competition—does not pay in a stagnant market; moreover, it is not the urgent necessity that it is during the declining phase. These natural tendencies of market development have been intensified, instead of countered, by the two types of meso-economic policies pursued by European governments during the past fifteen years: the promotion of concentration between 1966 and 1975 (and in some cases, also in later years) and the conservation of overcapacities since then through financial aid and the protection of firms and sectors. Both types of policies have intensified the economic crisis by creating dominant positions and/or weak organizational structures and by prolonging the adaptation process and spreading the negative effects to other firms and sectors. On top of this these policies have contributed to the disarray of government finances by increasing debts, the rise of interest and tax rates, and the consequent burden on the remaining viable part of the market sector.

These developments were most prominent in the industrial sectors. In service sectors, growth has continued, whether measured by added value, employment, or fixed investment rates. As far as the figures go, they show an increasing impact of the service sectors. But the rate of growth may be expected to slow down under the influence of the economic recession during the 1980s. Two main factors will probably account for this: first, the non-commercial services are likely to feel the backlash of governments' restrictive budget measures, and second, the commercial services are to some extent interrelated with industrial sectors and may especially feel the stagnation of real per capita incomes. On the other hand, current innovations in electronic equipment, data processing, telecommunications, and the like are moving the cost functions of the provision of many services sharply downward, and through price abatements many new applications of services may be anticipated. Thus the lead in a renewed economic upturn is likely to be taken by such commercial service sectors, pushing the economy still further along the road towards a service-economy, which, for all its changes, will remain a predominantly market-oriented economy.

Notes and Sources

[1] See Commission of the EC, *Economic Annual Report*, No. 10, November 1982, graph 7.2.

[2] Adapted from H. W. de Jong, *Structuur, Orde en Welvaart,* Stenfert Kroese, Leiden, 1976, p. 20.

[3] J. Gershuny, *After industrial society. The emerging self-service economy*, Macmillan, London, 1978, p. 133.

[4] See Table I.13 in A. P. Jacquemin and H. W. de Jong, *European Industrial Organization*, Macmillan, London, 1977.

[5] See H. W. de Jong, '*The relevant market*', in J. A. van Damme (ed.), *Regulating the behaviour of monopolies and dominant undertakings in Community Law*, Bruges Week, De Tempel, Bruges, 1977, pp. 524–38.

[6] Proceedings in the case of EC Commission *vs.* Ph. Morris/Rothmans. See replies by Ph. Morris, Dr Gutowski (economic counsel for Ph. Morris), and my opinion on behalf of R. J. Reynolds. In the Netherlands, 80 per cent of all cigarettes are sold at exactly the same price per cigarette; this percentage does not differ in magnitude in other European countries.

[7] See Commission of the EC, *Report on the Dutch food industry*, No. 43, Brussels, 1982, part 4.

[8] K. D. George and C. Joll, *Industrial organization. Competition, growth and structural change*, third edition, Allen & Unwin, London, 1981.

[9] See Commission of the EC, *Competition Policy Reports*, Three, 1974; Six, 1977, No. 293; Seven, 1978, Nos. 284–5; Overall concentration—the share of the hundred largest firms in the EC's total domestic product for all sectors—rose from 23 per cent in 1969 to nearly 30 per cent in 1979. G. Locksley, *The structure of the top 100 EEC enterprises*, Research paper 13—PCL, School of Social Science and Business Studies, London, 1981.

[10] Commission of the EC, *Ninth Report on Competition Policy*, No. 223.

[11] See the discussion in H. W. de Jong, *Dynamische concentratietheorie*, Stenfert Kroese, Leiden, chapter 7, 1972.

[12] H. R. Peters, 'Konzeption und Wirklichkeit der sektoralen Strukturpolitik in der Bundesrepublik Deutschland', in G. Bombach, B. Gahlen, and A. E. Ott (eds), *Probleme des Strukturwandels und der Strukturpolitik*, J. C. B. Mohr, Tübingen, 1977.

[13] H. Daems wrote about the 'disastrous policy of solidarity between strong and weak firms and between strong and weak sectors'. The Belgian government has damaged the dynamics of the market economy, necessitating government intervention, so that the aid policy justifies itself. H. Daems, *De Belgische industrie, een profielbeeld*, Uitgeverij De Nederlandsche Boekhandel, Antwerp/ Amsterdam 1981, pp. 66–73.

VI

Intra-Industry Trade Adjustment and European Industrial Policies

GEOFF WHITE*

I. The adjustment imperative

The debate about the role of industrial adjustment in contributing to competitiveness and economic growth has been injected with a sense of urgency in recent times. All countries are having to cope with the problems of slower growth in the world economy, inflationary pressures, and increasing unemployment. This conjunction of circumstances is seen to have imposed external constraints on the ability of individual nations to achieve faster growth. The consequence is that nations have looked internally to the deployment of their own industrial resources and the efficiency with which they are used.

The notion of industrial adjustment that emerged seemed to derive largely from the theoretical principles about comparative advantage drawn from conventional trade theory. This was reinforced by the very real phenomenon of the rapid penetration of newly industrializing countries (NICs) into world competition in a particular range of products. The emergence of the NICs seemed to illustrate the principle of comparative advantage that, as certain countries exploited their endowments of low wage, relatively low skill labour supplemented by foreign or subsidized capital equipment, so industrialized countries would have to move to higher ground and concentrate their resources on 'higher value-added', 'high-technology' products. The terms which were used to characterize sectors under pressure from the NICs—'mature', 'declining', 'sunset', 'smoke-stack'—and those into which industrialized countries would have to move—'sunrise', 'knowledge-intensive', 'high-technology'—have provided enduring images of the kind of industrial adjustment required.

Another phenomenon which reinforced this image of industrial adjustment was the swarming of microelectronic-based innovations in information technology, production technologies, and telecommunications. These developments appeared to offer prospects of the higher

* Senior Economic Advisor in the Department of Trade and Industry.

ground to which industrialized countries could advance. For the country lagging behind the leading edge of these industrial developments, the prospects seemed grim indeed: caught between the upper millstone of the successful industrialized countries and the nether millstone of aggressive NICs in a slower growing world economy.

This image of industrial adjustment is essentially inter-sectoral in nature. It implies that industrialized countries will have to concede comparative advantage to the NICs in a whole range of productive sectors, and adjust into and exploit new areas of activity. There are reasons for accepting some of the underlying features of this model. In particular that

- over the period 1973-8 the NICs' share of world exports increased by 5 per cent yearly and was concentrated in certain sectors— e.g., textiles, clothing and footwear, consumer electronics;
- analyses of trade between industrialized and industrializing countries found quite distinct patterns of specialization between the two blocks, with the industrialized nations' comparative advantage being found in sectors characterized by high intensity in human capital and skills and technology.

The studies (by Wolter,[1] and Smith et al.[2] suggest that competition from the NICs would be characterized by certain features which made intense competition more likely and survival less likely for certain sectors in the advanced countries. However, the studies do not provide much justification for the view that NICs will 'wipe out' whole sectors, nor that they will advance inexorably to erode whole areas of the industrial base of advanced countries, nor that preoccupation with NIC competition should dominate our image of industrial adjustment.

In the first place, studies of comparative advantage are general. They use proxy indicators and measurable inter-industry data to inform our understanding of some broad tendencies in trade flows. They do not provide the basis for precise predictions.

Secondly, the NICs have been an increasingly important feature of world trade over the last decade, but their impact generally still remains small except in certain areas. Trade between industrialized countries remains the dominant source of competition. And in this competition a significant role is played by intra-industry trade— i.e. trade flows between countries within product categories which can be measured. It is the phenomenon of intra-industry trade which this chapter will explore, to see if it offers paradigms and images of industrial adjustment which differ from those inherited largely from conventional trade theory and our perception of NIC competition.

II. Intra-industry trade and adjustment

Intra-industry trade is a significant form of international specialization and has been growing. Similar countries (i.e. with similar endowments of physical and human capital) not only trade with each other a great deal and to an increasing extent, but also trade with each other in similar products. First, some characteristics of intra-industry trade:

- *It is significant.* Grubel and Lloyd[3] found that in the late 1960s the intra-industry trade of ten major OECD countries comprised over 60 per cent of total trade. More recently, Finger and De Rosa[4] estimated that in the trade of fourteen major industrialized countries during 1974-6, 117 out of 144 product groups had intra-industry trade in excess of 50 per cent of their total trade.
- *It is more than a statistical phenomenon.* Most studies of intra-industry trade have been conducted at the three digit SITC (Standard International Trade Classification) level, and there may be some suspicion that the phenomenon simply derives from the use of general (and not economic) classifications of products. Grubel and Lloyd,[5] Balassa,[6] and Aquino[7] have explored different levels of disaggregation. While the phenomenon is reduced by statistical disaggregation, it does not disappear, and indeed remains at quite high levels.
- *It is growing.* Most analyses of intra-industry trade have concentrated on industrialized countries and have found it to be growing faster than total trade. Moreover, those few analyses of developing country trade have discovered that the phenomenon is growing here as well, even in trade with industrialized countries. This suggests that it would be premature to infer from NIC competition that there is a kind of linear model of transformation of comparative advantage, by which developing countries seize comparative advantage in an increasing number of sectors, which then have to be conceded by the industrialized countries. Rather the findings imply that developing countries are increasingly trading like developed countries trade with each other: on the basis of intra-industry specialization.[8]

Confirmation of the predominance and persistence of intra-industry trade can be found in estimates of the convergence of industrial output and trade patterns between countries. Some unpublished statistical work by the author with H. Ergas and R. Gonenç has confirmed this convergence. Using recently compiled World Bank series for production and trade at four digit ISIC (International Standard Industrial Classification) level for the main OECD countries, this work found that for some 180 product groups, the correlation of import penetration and export-output ratios remained high over the period 1970-80, and in a number of cases had increased. A high and rising correlation was found even in those product groups threatened by NIC competition—such as clothing, textiles, and household equipment.

It was also demonstrated, using the same data, that there was a striking similarity between the product structure of manufacturing output for the US, Germany, Japan, the UK, and Italy. The intercountry correlation of the shares of 180 products in total manufacturing output significantly exceeded 0.9 in each case, and by and large the correlation coefficients tended to increase over the last decade. This confirms the findings of other studies that differences in levels and changes of productivity could not be attributed to any great extent to industrial structural differences.[9]

The explanation for persistent and increasing convergence of such patterns and intra-industry trade has rested very heavily on product differentiation in a world characterized by differing and complex consumer utility functions and economies of scale. In particular, five factors have been adduced to explain intra-industry trade:[10]

— *Functionally homogeneous products.* The influences of transport, storage, selling, and information costs may not be insignificant in certain products, and can give rise to border trade, particularly in common trading markets.
— *Product differentiation and scale economies.* Where non-trivial product differentiation is relevant to consumer satisfaction, where the differentiation does not require radical changes in the production process (but could be disruptive if embodied in one production flow), and where scale economies exist, then the effect is most likely to be intra-industry rather than inter-industry specialization. As Krugman[11] points out, if there is a wide range of potential products, each produced under conditions of increasing returns, then each country will produce only a limited sub-set of the products in each industry.
— *Technology.* Grubel and Lloyd[12] observe that technology-gap trade can become intra-industry trade in cases where research and development produce a rapid turnover of products which are protected by patents and copyright and serve specialized requirements in different segments of the market and parts of the world (e.g. pharmaceuticals).
— *Joint costs, marketing, and distribution systems.* A variety of factors exercise an influence here, ranging from the joint costs associated with integrated production facilities (as in the case of certain chemical products), to joint marketing costs (e.g. those that car manufacturers tend to incur to span the model range), to joint system costs (like those incurred by computer equipment manufacturers to have compatible hardware and software systems).

— *The extent to which multinationals' joint requirements in production, marketing, and distribution are met by international trade
flows between affiliated companies.* As Caves[13] points out, such
flows include goods for resale—to fill out the affiliate's product line
—as well as intermediate goods.

It has to be said that few of the empirical tests of the determinants
of intra-industry trade have proved completely satisfactory. There
remains a strong commitment in the literature to the explanatory
power of scale economies and product differentiation. But only relatively weak support is available from the empirical tests so far (see
Caves, Loertscher and Wolter, and Toh[14]). The empirical problem is
undoubtedly one of model specification combined with data limitations.

What are the normative implications which arise from the increasing
significance of intra-industry trade? These are not at all easy to tease
out, and the literature has by and large been reluctant to step into still
muddied water. The theoretical underpinnings of intra-industry trade
and their empirical verification remain sufficiently open for normative
judgements to be premature at this stage. Nevertheless, some tentative
observations can and have been made.

Firstly, the recognition of the intra-industry phenomenon must alter
the use and interpretation of measures of competitiveness. In a world of
intra-industry trade, the level and growth of import penetration can be
very high and yet signify very little. What matters for competitiveness
is the net trade position.

Secondly, the process of specialization and product differentiation
within industrial sectors will mean that industrialized countries may
seem a little obsessional in their preoccupation with attaining the higher
ground represented by 'high-technology' sectors. It is not an essential
characteristic of industrial adjustment that it should involve discarding
'mature' sectors and adopting and developing 'sun-rise' sectors. The
adjustment process in an intra-industry world can be envisaged as
a possibly much less painful switch of resources *within* sectors than
between them. This may come as some relief to those who have observed
that the higher ground of 'high-technology' sectors actually comprises
a rather small proportion of total output and employment.

Thirdly, the intra-industry process of adjustment can mean that
successful corporations can be found in virtually any sector of manufacturing and services, even in those hardest hit by NIC competition.
In other words, even within the general framework of comparative
advantage which has developed countries at a disadvantage, there will
be the prospect for successful corporate adjustment strategies in
the industrialized world. Where scale economies/product differentiation prospects are particularly pronounced and the framework of

comparative advantage much weaker (e.g. between industrialized countries with similar factor endowments), there will be enhanced potential for all countries, companies, and factors to gain from trade.[15]

Finally, the gains from trade are not necessarily jeopardized simply because the specialization which follows may tend to be more of an intra-industry than an inter-industry kind. It is not necessarily the case that 'positive' adjustment is being neglected simply because it does not appear to take the form of inter-sectoral shifts from 'declining' to 'growing' industries.

III. Adjustment in the EC

The existence of the European Community has been associated with a considerable expansion of trade within the EC, which far exceeded the growth of trade outside the EC. It has also been observed that this growth of trade within the EC was not characterized to any great extent by inter-sectoral specialization among member countries. Rather it seemed as if the structural patterns of output and trade among member states were converging; i.e. the growth and specialization of trade appeared to be of an intra-industry kind. In part this must be attributable to member states' reluctance to incur the adjustment costs which might be associated with full-blown inter-sectoral specialization. For example, non-tariff trade barriers through public purchasing policies will have hindered this process of specialization. However, it must also be recognized that the apparent lack of inter-sectoral specialization may also be attributable to the phenomenon, which has been observed elsewhere,[16] for integration efforts to contribute to increased intra-industry trade specialization.

It was noted earlier that intra-industry trade need not jeopardize the gains from trade. Indeed, various commentators have pointed to the gains secured for consumer welfare from the availability of a wide variety of products within each industry and the opportunities for the achievements of scale economies through long production runs of particular varieties of products. However, Franko[17] has noted that if the observed intra-industry trade is only the result of inefficient market-sharing by oligopolist firms at sub-optimal output and scale, the phenomenon may in fact generate welfare losses.

In recent years the world recession and external competition from the US, Japan, and the NICs have revealed weaknesses in the response of the EC and its member states to an increasingly hostile environment. Trade performance has deteriorated and serious over-capacity has emerged in a range of industries.

Where the growth of demand is low (particularly relative to expectations) and external competition proves capable of penetrating the

EC market, it may be that much more difficult for EC firms to pursue product differentiation at volumes which permit scale economies to be achieved. In such circumstances it becomes less easy for member states and firms to accept the inter-penetration of their markets which had been a feature of intra-industry trade. In other words, to use the jargon of perhaps a more special case, oligopolist equilibrium may become destabilized.

In Chapter XII Ergas[18] outlines various corporate adjustment responses to this situation of destabilization. In one respect his review of corporate strategies might suggest an increase in intra-industry trade in these circumstances. Increased focus and specialization of manufacturing and technology strategies in the horizontal sense will tend to increase intra-industry trade. Firms will explore advances in production technology (particularly, flexible manufacturing systems) which permit product differentiation at lower minimum efficient size of plant and production runs. However, this may not always prove possible, for example in products where, almost by definition, product differentiation is not an available option: i.e. commodity products, such as bulk chemicals and steel, requiring high capital intensity and large dedicated plants. In these circumstances it seems likely that companies and governments of individual member states will seek to defend their chosen areas of product specialization and associated capacity, either by means of vicious price competition or, where this becomes too painful, by protection, subsidies, and orderly marketing arrangements which attempt to sustain the status quo.

Another aspect of corporate adjustment outlined by Ergas[19] is the process of 'de-verticalization' of industrial structure, by which the co-ordination mechanisms *within* firms are replaced by contractual relations *between* firms. Such contractual relations may take a variety of forms, often of an international kind: joint ventures in research, development, production, and even marketing; long-term contracts; out-sourcing and dual sourcing of components; 'swap-deals'; and 'quasi-integration'. Examples of these arrangements are to be found in vehicles, white goods, chemicals, aerospace, telecommunications, and computers.

The conventional wisdom with regard to relationships of this type is that they reflect periods of corporate disequilibrium. As such, they are thought likely to be highly unstable—an instability aggravated by the problems of intra-firm co-ordination. Member governments and companies may be less inclined to see the virtues which may be associated with limiting vertical integration, particularly when restricted to an EC context. Companies which have been competing on an intra-industry basis within Europe may prefer to arm themselves with the strengths of non-European partners in order to continue the fight on the European battleground.

In any event, the substitution of vertical integration by contractual relations between firms may be viewed as less than desirable if it means that reliance has to be placed on supplies from a single source in another country. This is an important factor in cases where the components are regarded as technologically critical, e.g. semiconductors. Moreover, such substitution may also require the untangling of existing vertically integrated processes, with all the associated adjustment costs (e.g. in petro-chemicals).

The thrust of the above a priori reasoning is that the very phenomenon of intra-industry trade, which was associated with trade growth and welfare gains in times of strong demand growth, may weaken EC corporate response in tougher times. In other words, intra-industry trade emerged naturally in good times. But it may only be sustainable in bad times, when fierce price competition becomes too costly, by inefficient explicit or implicit market-sharing arrangements bolstered by government protection and subsidization, and/or when contractual relations between companies not necessarily all of EC origin become unstable.

IV. Managed adjustment

So far this chapter has argued that intra-industry adjustment has been, and probably will continue to be, an important feature of the process of international specialization. It has suggested that the phenomenon and theory of intra-industry trade specialization provide a fuller potential explanation of some of the puzzles of industrial adjustment than a model based on inter-industry specialization. However, it has to be conceded that intra-industry trade is a more complex phenomenon which does not lend itself as readily as the inter-industry trade model to predictions of shifts in competitiveness and comparative advantage. As such, it does not offer clear guidelines to industrial policy making. This is likely to be the case in national industrial policies, but it is even more likely to be true of industrial policies sought across national boundaries. It was suggested in the previous section that European-level policies might be as much confounded by the natural phenomenon of intra-industry trade between EC member states as by the political obduracy of member governments. Indeed the latter might be seen as a reflection and a defence of the former. It is to the policy-making implications in an EC context that this chapter now tentatively turns.

A first implication of the argument is that in a world characterized by intra-industry specialization, public-policy options are much more complicated than in an inter-industry context. Thus it makes little sense to select some statistical aggregates called 'industries' and term some 'winners' and others 'losers'. The adjustment process can no longer be characterized as convincing industry and government to abandon 'declining' sectors and enter 'growing' ones.

What replaces this sectoral shift perspective will in large part depend on political choices and, in particular, on the stance adopted towards industrial policy. Two extreme approaches are often envisaged in this regard.

The first is the 'hands-off' stance. Given that it makes little sense to target certain sectors as winners and others as losers, proponents of this approach would argue that policy should be sectorally neutral. A European industrial policy would, in this perspective, focus primarily on 'environmental' objectives and instruments aimed at creating a framework within which mutually beneficial intra- and inter-industry specialization could occur. The main areas for action would be:

- harmonization of company law and fiscal regimes;
- accelerated development of European standards;
- tighter monitoring of national industrial policies (primarily with regard to subsidies and public purchasing) to avoid distortions to trade;
- reviewing the impact of competition policy on specialization agreements between firms;
- improving the public infrastructure for firms via programmes of education, training, research, transport, energy, and technology transfer.

By such endeavours the EC could provide a framework for the development of specializations without controlling their particular manifestations.

At the opposite extreme is the 'hands-on' stance. In this approach *all* sectors would become the object of public policy, which would aim at ensuring that firms in each industry adopt viable competitive strategies. Faced with a process of international horizontal specialization, the European Commission would seek to manage this specialization process and to allocate tasks between firms and countries. The primary instrument would presumably be company specific agreements, perhaps along the lines of the development contracts in France. Through those agreements companies would enter into detailed European-wide planning commitments, in exchange for which they would receive discretionary assistance.

In fact neither of these approaches seems viable or appropriate at a European level. The 'hands-off' approach claims to be neutral and non-selective in sectoral terms. However, this neutrality must inevitably be violated. Given the limited resources which can be devoted to policy formulation and implementation, priorities would have to be established. Moreover, inherent in these 'neutral' ambitions for improving the environment in which firms operate, there would have to be selective choices between priorities. In which areas will education/training and research have to be fostered? In which particular areas should specialization agreements be allowed to develop by competition policy? Further, since environmental measures will not have an equal impact on all sectors, devoting greater resources to some measure rather than others will have a sectorally biased effect. Even with a 'hands-off' stance, the European Commission would have to exercise choice; and if the implied choices were not explicitly recognized and embodied in decision-making, the most likely result would be a 'muddling through' in response to political lobbying.

The 'hands-on' approach, while appealing to those who consider that specialization can be managed, implies a very considerable capability and expertise in the Commission to make judgements and difficult choices on corporate matters. As this paper suggested earlier, trade theory based on the inter-sectoral model provides not much more than general guidelines to the Commission—and nothing which can facilitate precise predictions about future desirable shifts of specialization. A 'hands-on' stance would place great strain on the legitimacy of the Commission's decision-making, on its resilience in the face of powerful lobby groups, and on the Commission's transparency and accountability. Furthermore, it would almost certainly acquire a sectoral bias, as the Commission's activities would be diverted to negotiating agreements with the large EC companies to the relative neglect of new and small/medium-sized firms.

Thus the depiction of policy as 'hands-off' or 'hands-on' does not seem particularly helpful. Priority-setting seems inevitable—most obviously with the 'hands-on' approach, but also with the so-called neutral 'hands-off' approach. So what framework should be established for priority-setting, and what elements should it contain?

The argument of this paper is bound to suggest that a sectoral framework would prove inadequate, particularly in isolation from other considerations. National experiments in juggling with diverse sectoral criteria to establish industrial policy priorities have not proved successful. Witness the UK and French sectoral priority ordering of the mid-1970s.

However, any priority framework would clearly need an industrial dimension. How to give this dimension a context is the problem. In a chapter as short as this there is always the risk of suggesting a framework for priority-setting which may sound fine in abstract, but prove virtually impossible to operate in practice. This risk has to be incurred. The following elements for a priority-setting framework are suggested:

— *Needs assessment.* There are major social trends unfolding which will create changes in the social and private demands on technology and industry: e.g. demographic and medical trends altering the balance of the population in terms of sex, age, health, and disability; locational trends which have led to a 'counter-urbanization' shift in a number of countries since the mid-1970s, income and consumption trends which suggest growing service and leisure activities; employment and occupational trends; public infrastructure requirements in transport, housing, sewerage, inner-urban facilities, and communications; and so on. It is salutary and refreshing to turn the pages of the *Long-Range Vision*[20]—produced by Japan's Ministry of International Trade and Industry more than eight years ago—and find a classification of the social and private demands on technology and industry that anticipates in some detail current European preoccupations.

— *Technological and industrial potential.* Recent thinking in the academic literature[21] has developed the notion that taxonomies can be proposed which capture the essential characteristics of the different industrial and technological 'trajectories' on which certain groups of firms, industries, and technologies find themselves. While much work needs to be done to refine the taxonomies—in particular, to understand the process of change and dispel the impression of technological determinism, they still offer the prospect of a fresh insight into the ways in which groups of industries and technologies will be more or less able to respond to changing demands on them. This will be especially important if the existence of such 'trajectories' can be established to have created a certain blindness to social and technological developments which, while occurring outside the field of vision, may nevertheless have a major impact. This is likely to be particularly the case in the area of 'enabling' technologies, such as information technology, materials technologies, and production technologies, and in areas where different technologies are coalescing and being systematized in cross-sectoral applications (e.g. transport control systems). In such cases a public-policy intervention may be appropriate.

— *Policy levers which are realistically at the control of the Commission.* Considerable caution must be exercised here. The range of instruments presently available—and likely to become available in future —to the Commission is strictly limited. This is not only because member states are likely to resist a transfer of the control levers (e.g. in public purchasing) to the Commission, but also because of the phenomenon of intra-European intra-industry trade which has developed.

The integration of these three elements is a major analytical and policy task. The report of the FAST (Forecasting and Assessment in Science and Technology) programme[22] indicates the extent of the analytical and co-ordination problems encountered in the extensive work it has undertaken on needs assessment and technological potential. Further and much more significant, the FAST report notes that 'if the EC also wants to benefit from the [FAST] capability, the necessary "relay" structures for implementing the recommendations must be established'. In what follows the FAST report does not express great confidence in the Commission's capability to do this, essentially because of problems of internal coherence. This is a worrying admission, particularly in the light of the diversity of conflicting interests within the EC, and suggests that the third pillar in the suggested priority-setting framework may be the most difficult to establish.

This chapter will conclude by discussing how the Commission's effective control of policy levers may be limited by the phenomenon of intra-industry trade. In a world characterized by complex interlocking trade relationships, the problem for the public-policy maker is the difficulty of predicting—even broadly—the likely response to any particular policy initiative. Protection is a good example. Though the static welfare losses associated with protection may be lower in markets with a high level of intra-industry trade (because by definition an indigenous capability will exist to substitute for imports in the protected market), two factors make protection in such circumstances an unpredictable and unreliable instrument for encouraging specialization.

The first factor is retaliation. In fact there does not need to be an overt retaliatory response for the consequences of protection to backfire. The complex exchanges in components, final products, joint ventures, and other transfers which make up intra-industry trade flows are such that protection at one point in the flow can have serious effects elsewhere. (The reported confusions arising from the recent agreement between the EC and Japan on video-recorders may be a case in point.) In an intra-industry world, the possibilities for retaliatory action are quite extensive.

The second factor is that protection, particularly quantitative restrictions, may often have a perverse impact on intra-industry trade specialization. Under quite general conditions, quantitative restrictions provide strong incentives for producers in the country protected against to move 'up-market', into the items having the highest value-added content within the protected product-line. This effect has been reported in textiles and clothing (under the MFA) and colour TVs (under the arrangements between the US and Japan).

However, it should be noted that Krugman[23] has suggested that a combination of intra-industry trade conditions and technology gaps might lead to a justification for some kind of infant-industry protection.

It is to the area of infant technologies and industries that this paper will finally turn. It will attempt to demonstrate the constraints imposed by intra-industry trade and the limits to Commission control in one positive area of industrial policy which has emerged from the FAST programme: international collaboration in what has been termed pre-competitive research and development.

V. Collaboration on R&D

There has perhaps been a tendency for Commission initiatives on international collaboration to seek rather too hard for full-scale integration. Franzmeyer[24] suggests that in the past the Commission has based its concept for an industrial policy in advanced technological areas on the assumption that an integrated structure is required where common European needs can be identified and where wasteful duplication of high development costs can be eliminated. Not only have such integration initiatives come up against national preferences and interests, they have also encountered opposition on competition grounds and run straight into the competitive pressures which this paper has suggested characterizes intra-industry trade within Europe.

The forces which lead to intra-industry specialization suggest that individual national companies, while participating in international collaborative ventures, could still find justification in refusing to concede to the pressures for more 'complete' specialization. In other words, it may not simply be nationalistic obduracy which causes national companies in joint ventures to wish to maintain a 'total capability'. Clearly, the requirements of national independence will have been a factor in restricting complete specialization in some of the more common areas of European international collaboration, notably in weapons and aircraft development and procurement.

This has been demonstrated by Dosser, Gowland, and Hartley[25] in the European collaborative arrangements in aircraft development and production. They register the point that there may be national constraints on the choice of least-cost suppliers, with each partner requiring a share in each sector of the technology being developed. This does not arise, however, simply because of the strategic defence requirements of each participating nation.

The additional costs incurred on joint international collaborative R&D projects are not insignificant relative to the 'go-it-alone' or purchasing options. Given that participating organizations will have invested a considerable amount of time, resources, and funding in the establishment of collaborative projects, they will want to hedge against the risks of the project—or their particular part of it—coming unstuck by retaining an option on the exploitation of most aspects of the results. If there is synergy in the joint research work, then it is likely that each participant will have had to develop an understanding and some degree of expertise in a range of the technologies being explored. When it comes to production there will clearly be some incentive to specialize. But each participant may also consider that its own market outlets and capabilities for product differentiation may justify developing a production capability which can exploit a wide range of the developed technologies. This will be particularly true if the prospects for the output of the collaborative project are uncertain. Companies may then wish to retain the option of uncoupling their activity from that of the joint venture.

Dosser, Gowland, and Hartley's survey of the US and UK aircraft industries suggests that, compared with the European approach, American aircraft firms prefer *ad hoc* international consortia rather than the formation of new, permanent, international companies involving governments. US firms were unanimous in emphasizing that it was the competitive nature of their aircraft industry which was one of the major factors in its success. The three authors raise the question whether the European arrangements have suffered not so much from diseconomies of scale, as from cumbersome and over-arching bureaucratic procurement procedures, which should perhaps have allowed a greater degree of competition. Franzmeyer[26] confirms that 'industry prefers more flexible forms of co-operation and the possibility of resource to varying solutions in the way of company structure'.

How can the Commission encourage the process of integration and specialization and at the same time step back from too much involvement in determining the particular form which specialization might take? One possible mechanism is that of 'pre-competitive' collaborative research programmes. The ESPRIT programme of the Commission is a major new initiative of this kind in information technology. Such programmes are not easy to initiate, manage, and sustain. Indeed, some would argue that in a highly innovative area like advanced information technology the collaborative rather than competitive mode is quite inappropriate. Certainly the European industry has diverse and conflicting interests, and this must increase collaborative and management problems. Some general thoughts are offered as to how the fundamental technological capability of European industry can be enhanced, at the same time as accepting and indeed exploiting its diverse industrial strengths.

The main purpose of fundamental research initiatives is to explore and resolve major areas of uncertainty. When confronting major technical uncertainties, 'the problem is not one of choosing among specific end-product alternatives, but rather a problem of choosing a course of action initially consistent with a wide range of such alternatives; and of narrowing the choice as development proceeds'.[27] Williamson[28] has translated this principle to mean that a sequential approach should be adopted to procurement programmes in high-technology areas, with discrete stages for incremental review of the options, characterized by competition at each stage. It is this kind of process which underlies the 'fly before you buy' policy which has been used on occasion in US aircraft procurement.

This sequential approach has the following virtues:

— technical risks and capabilities can be explored in more tightly defined areas, and responsibilities can be more clearly allocated;
— industrial and commercial spin-offs can be explored and encouraged at each stage;
— more participants can be encouraged to participate in increasingly well-defined areas, thus permitting small-to-medium sized operations to participate and widening the technological and industrial capability which can be involved;
— better judgements can be made about the appropriate methods of financing.

Competitive tendering would thus occur for all parts of the programme—even in its initial conceptualization and definition, with options closed, kept open, or actively pursued at each stage. It might even be desirable to encourage duplication in certain areas, since duplication is often the cost of resolving technical uncertainties. By their very nature, programmes which seek to advance fundamental knowledge and understanding tend to generate inventions and innovations in indirect, serendipitous, time-consuming, duplicative, and often unexpected ways. Even the consensus Japanese approach allowed for two very large-scale integration programmes—sponsored by MITI (Ministry of International Trade and Industry) and NTT (Nippon Telephone and Telegraph)—in which some closely similar technologies were explored.

Such an approach would undoubtedly incur problems for management and co-ordination of the programme. Certain infrastructural facilities (e.g. data networks and testing facilities) would have to be provided and their installation and maintenance costs would need to be met. Property rights would also be a source of conflict and negotiation. The problem of late entrants (and potential free-riders) would have to be dealt with. Nevertheless, this kind of competitive and sequential approach may help to overcome the problems which Brooks[29] has identified with government-managed innovation programmes: namely, 'a tendency to narrow down prematurely to a single technical option, excluding competitive approaches, . . . to take too small risks in the early stages of an innovation and too large risks in the later stages instead of following a strategy of evolutionary technical risk reductions'. The clustering of vested interests and constituencies around a particular technological effort (regardless of technical or economic merit), which Brooks has observed and deplored, would be encouraged by the 'club' approach to collaborative research programmes and should be resisted.

Even subject to careful selection of programme areas, to segmented structuring of the programme itself, and to due attention being paid to technology transfer activities, it is still important not to expect too much from European collaborative research ventures. Three basic points can be made in this regard.

Firstly, it remains to be demonstrated that collaborative ventures, even when undertaken by firms for purely commercial motives, are an efficient way of carrying out R&D. In effect, the innovation literature is virtually unanimous in stressing the importance of tight integration between the R&D, marketing, and commercial functions within firms as a factor in the success or failure of development efforts.[30] It is generally extremely difficult to secure such integration within a collaborative venture.

Secondly, even when a collaborative venture might be efficient as a framework for R&D, there is no a priori reason for believing that the optimal pattern of collaboration is between EC firms. Often, in fact, it makes much more sense for EC firms to collaborate with non-EC firms, since the latter offer clearer technological, commercial, and strategic complementarities. There is no particular virtue to intra-EC collaboration when collaboration with firms outside the EC would yield a greater return on innovation effort.

Thirdly, even if an intra-EC collaboration venture might prove useful, it is by no means clear that the EC Commission is the right institution for organizing it. In a well-known survey of collaborative R&D ventures, Hochmuth[31] persuasively argues that these are only likely to succeed in a specific institutional framework: in particular, a framework which provides for strong leadership; a clear division of responsibilities between the venture managers and the participating firms; a skilled, technically-competent, and independent secretariat; and a highly effective buffer between the venture and governments. It remains to be seen whether the Commission can provide such a buffer.

VI. Conclusions

What, then, can be expected of a European industrial policy? First of all, it is impractical for such a policy to even envisage managing the process of international specialization. The Commission has neither the resources, nor the mandate, nor the instruments required to face the highly complex process of intra-industry specialization.

Secondly, given this incapacity to manage the process of specialization, the Commission should work with the grain of trends in inter- and intra-industry specialization, seeking to allow their implications to emerge. This would suggest that the 'hands-off' stance described earlier should be the one to accept and 'environmental' policies the ones to pursue, while recognizing that such an approach does not obviate the need for selectivity and choice.

Thirdly, such 'environmental' policies need to be pursued with vigour in the context of a framework of priorities, as outlined in Section IV, and with an internal coherence and focusing of effort within the Commission.

Fourthly, the 'environmental' policies should be generously defined to include education/training, research and development, and technology transfer. This paper has considered the role of the Commission in collaborative research projects. While it cautions against excessive optimism and expectations about the degree of integration which can be hoped for, it suggests that success in this area can be achieved if four factors are given due regard:

— that the areas for collaboration should emerge from an assessment of needs and technological/industrial potential;
— that a cautious, segmented, and competitive approach should be adopted, avoiding crude and meaningless targets and giving much scope to competing and alternative approaches;
— that a greater emphasis should be given to fundamental research in 'enabling' technologies;
— that other efforts of the Commission in education/training, competition policy, technology transfer, etc., should congregate around such initiatives to ensure that they are fully exploited; i.e. that resources not be solely or even primarily devoted to the collaborative venture itself.

Notes and Sources

[1] F. Wolter, 'Factor Proportions, Technology and West German Industry's International Trade Patterns', *Weltwirtschaftliches Archiv*, vol. 113, 1977.

[2] S. R. Smith, *et al.*, 'UK Trade in Manufacturing: The Pattern of Specialization in the 1970s', Government Economic Service Working Paper No. 56, Department of Industry and Trade, London, 1982.

[3] H. G. Grubel and P. J. Lloyd, *Intra-Industry Trade*, Macmillan, London, 1975.

[4] J. M. Finger and D. A. De Rosa, 'Trade Overlap, Comparative Advantage and Protection', in H. Giersch (ed.), *On the Economics of Intra-Industry Trade*, J. C. B. Mohr (Paul Siebeck), Tübingen, 1979.

[5] H. G. Grubel and P. J. Lloyd, *Intra-Industry Trade*, op. cit.

[6] B. Balassa, 'Tariff Reductions and Trade in Manufactures Among Industrial Countries', *American Economic Review*, vol. 56, 1966.

[7] A. Aquino, 'Intra-Industry and Inter-Industry Specialization as Concurrent Sources of International Trade in Manufactures', *Weltwirtschaftliches Archiv*, vol. 114, 1978.

[8] See S. Laird, 'Intra-Industry Trade and the Expansion, Diversification, and Integration of the Trade of the Developing Countries', *Trade and Development— An UNCTAD Review*, No. 3, Winter, 1981, and the work quoted in P. K. M. Tharakan, 'The Economics of Intra-Industry Trade: A Survey', *Recherches Economique de Louvain*, vol. 47, 1981.

[9] A. D. Smith, D. M. Hitchens, and S. W. Davies, 'International Industrial Productivity: A Comparison of Britain, America and Germany', *National Institute of Economics Review*, No. 101, 1982.

[10] See H. G. Grubel and P. J. Lloyd, op. cit., and P. K. M. Tharakan, op. cit.

[11] P. Krugman, 'New Theories of Trade Among Industrial Countries', *The American Economic Association Papers and Proceedings*, May 1983.

[12] H. G. Grubel and P. J. Lloyd, op. cit.

[13] R. Caves, 'Intra-Industry Trade and Market Structure in the Industrial Countries', *Oxford Economic Papers*, vol. 33, 1981.

[14] R. Caves, ibid.; D. Loertscher and F. Wolter, 'Determinants of Intra-Industry Trade: Among Countries and Across Industries', *Weltwirtschaftliches Archiv*, vol. 116, 1980; K. Toh, 'A Cross Section: Analysis of Intra-Industry Trade in U.K. Manufacturing', *Weltwirtschaftliches Archiv*, vol. 118, 1982.

[15] See P. Krugman, op. cit.

[16] See B. Balassa, 'Intra-Industry Trade and the Integration of Developing Countries in the World Economy', in H. Giersch (ed.), *On the Economics of Intra-Industry Trade*, op. cit.

[17] L. G. Franko, Comments in H. Giersch (ed.) ibid.

[18] See Chapter XII.

[19] Ibid.

[20] Industrial Structure Council (advisory committee to the Minister of International Trade and Industry), *Japan's Industrial Structure: A Long Range Vision*, the Japanese External Trade Organization, 1975.

[21] See R. Nelson and S. Winter, *An Evolutionary Theory of Economic Change*, Harvard University Press, 1982, and K. Pavitt, 'Patterns of Technical Change— Evidence, Theory and Policy Implications', *Papers in Science, Technology and Public Policy*, No. 3, Imperial College, London, Science Policy Research Unit, Sussex, 1983.

[22] Commission of the EC, 'The FAST Programme', Brussels, 1982.

[23] P. Krugman, op. cit.

[24] F. Franzmeyer, *Approaches to Industrial Policy within the EC and its Impact on European Integration*, Gowes, Aldershot, 1982.

[25] D. Dosser, D. Gowland, and K. Hartley, *The Collaboration of Nations: A Study of European Economic Policy*, Martin Robertson, Oxford, 1982.

[26] F. Franzmeyer, op. cit.

[27] B. Klein and W. Meckling, 1958, quoted in O. E. Williamson, op. cit.

[28] O. E. Williamson, 'The Economics of Defense Contracting: Incentives and Performance', in R. N. McKean (ed.), *Issues in Defense Economics*, Columbia University Press, New York, 1967.

[29] H. Brooks, 'Towards an Efficient Public Technology Policy: Criteria and Evidence', in H. Giersch (ed.), *Emerging Technologies: Consequences for Economic Growth, Structural Change and Employment*, J. C. B. Mohr (Paul Siebeck), Tübingen, 1982.

[30] See, for example, E. Mansfield, *et al., The Production and Application of New Industrial Technology*, Norton, New York, 1977.

[31] M. S. Hochmuth, *Organising the Transnational: The Experience with Transnational Enterprise in Advanced Technology*, Sijthoff and Noordhoof, Leiden (Netherlands), 1974.

VII

Industrial Change in European Countries: the Experience of Six Sectors

GEOFFREY SHEPHERD*

I. Introduction

Manufacturing industry continues to live in a fast-moving environment in spite of recession. Technical change continues apace, especially as the impact of micro-electronics is felt almost everywhere. The continuing growth in Japan's industrial strength—and to a lesser extent the Newly Industrializing Countries'—promises a continuing challenge to the economic supremacy of the old industrial world.

To some extent these developments have been diffused and sustained by post-war trade liberalization, a process that was particularly strongly felt in Western Europe as a result of the EC's development. As tariffs have continued to fall and as recession has set in, European governments have increasingly turned to industrial policy in response to the demands of the individual to be protected from the workings of the market. But in many cases the increase in intervention has also been intended to do what the market apparently could not: improve the competitive position of individual firms, sectors, and countries in the international league.

The study of the process of industrial change and the role of governments in promoting, directing, or hindering it is not easy, as everyone knows. First, rapid change implies great uncertainties about the future. This makes industrial *strategy* (for instance, the particular goals followed by firms in changing the organization and processes of production or the design and marketing of products) an important subject of study. Firms within industries may be usefully characterized by the particular strategies they adopt (including such factors as their market objectives and what they seek from governments).

Second, we are becoming increasingly aware of the institutional factors—or 'business environment'—that influence industrial performance, for instance the structure and attributes of the banking system,

* Acting Director of the European Research Centre, University of Sussex.

government, or labour market.[1] Given the complexities of industrial change and the business environment, it is small wonder that public intervention itself is very difficult to understand. Is it an exogenously determined force? Is its effectiveness or ineffectiveness the consequence of a particular set of institutional constraints and relationships?

This chapter draws on a body of recent research which has looked at industrial adjustment and government intervention in Western Europe, primarily through a study of a cross-section of industrial sectors in the four major Western European economies: Germany, France, the UK, and Italy.[2] The particular merit of this comparative national and 'micro' approach is that it allows elements of the complex picture of national business environments to be built up. In particular, it makes the constraints on national industrial policy-making clearer.

The six sectors reported on in this chapter include: two (textiles and steel) normally considered mature and associated with Europe's most painful adjustment problems and strongest doses of intervention; three long-established or 'maturing' industries (motor cars, electrical power plant, and telecommunications), where a combination of recession, international competition, and often quite radical technical change has created strong adjustment pressures; and one 'new' industry (semiconductors) which is thought to be at the heart of our future prosperity, but where Europe's competitive position *vis-à-vis* the US and Japan is weak.

The four countries compared represent the heart of the Western European economy, since they account for three-quarters of its industrial output and nine-tenths of EC industrial output. Comparisons between these economies gain from the rough similarity in their sizes and income levels, the similarities in their political ('social-democratic') and economic (mixed-economy) systems, and the similarities in some of the major policy environments their industries face. Nowhere is the latter more obvious or important than in the competitive pressures imposed by international (GATT and EC) trade policy. Some sense of this can be gleaned from Table 7.1, which compares 'trade-intensity' ratios of the major industrial countries for the six sectors covered in this chapter and for manufacturing as a whole. Especially when compared to figures for the US and Japan, the four countries show a certain homogeneity in the level and evolution over time of their openness to foreign competition (as measured by the share of imports in consumption) and their dependence on exports (as measured by the share of exports in output). For the four countries trade grew significantly in relation to production and consumption in both the 1960s and 1970s and generally reached very high levels by 1980. Trade remained somewhat unimportant for the US (though it did grow relatively). For Japan imports remained modest, while export ratios grew strongly for certain sectors.

II. Textiles[3]

Superficially, textiles are near to a textbook example of a mature sector. Relatively simple technologies, unsophisticated products, and the modest average size of production units indicate a potential comparative disadvantage for Western Europe, which low-wage countries have long since been exploiting. Yet improvements in machinery and the innovation possibilities offered by new chemical fibres, changing fashions, and new industrial uses for textiles have made profitable survival feasible in high-wage countries.

Indeed, much of the pressure for further change in this industry now comes from the intensity of trade *among* Western European countries. Slow growth, even stagnation, in textile consumption combined with continuing high rates of productivity increase to create job losses in Western European textiles in the 1970s that were as large as in any other major manufacturing sector. While industry output levels may have stagnated in the last two decades, the intensity of structural change is evident from the vastly increased importance of imports and exports relative to consumption and production since 1960. (See Table 7.1.)

Western European textiles and clothing production are over-whelmingly located in non-oligopolistic markets and in private hands, with the result that the formulation of strategies for survival has largely been out of government hands. At the same time, most industrialized countries have actively assisted in the defence of these industries by providing extensive non-tariff protection against imports from major low-wage exporters. The European Community considerably tightened this protection with the renewal of the Multifibre Arrangement (MFA) in 1978 and again in 1982. National subsidies to ailing firms and sectors have become an increasingly important second line of defence. In spite of similarities in national rates of job loss, levels of trade, and inter-vention policies, the strategic paths followed by representative firms in the individual industries of the EC countries have been significantly different.

Germany's textile industry entered the 1960s relatively well pro-tected, but with clear expectations that trade would be liberalized in the future. Many leading firms favoured a 'mass-market' strategy of vertical and horizontal concentration and capital-intensification aimed at producing cheap standard textiles in spite of high wage levels. A small number of firms opted for a strategy of market niches—or specialization—through more flexible production methods and

TABLE 7.1
Major industrial countries: levels of trade intensity for selected products, 1960-80[1]

	FRG		France		Italy		UK		EC[2]		US		Japan	
	I/C	E/P	I/C	E/P	I/C	E/P	I/C	E/C	I/C	E/P	I/C	E/P	I/C	E/P
Textiles: woven cloth (by weight)														
1962	12	13	6	25	5	15	31	15	3	13	4	1	..	..
1970	24	22	23	25	33	29	36	19	10	13	5	3	2	29
1980	59	59	59	46	62	56	74	51	35	20	7	6	8	36
Steel (by crude-equivalent weight)														
1961	16	32	27	41	26	11	3	19	3	20	4	3	2	10
1970	28	34	41	41	30	13	12	19	9	18	12	7	–	24
1980	40	52	53	59	31	30	24[3]	26[3]	12	27	15	5	2	31
Motor cars (by no. of units)														
1960	9	46	4	42	5	33	7	42	–[4]	23[4]	7[5]	1[5]	2	4
1970	31	55	23	43	34	37	14	42	2	26	16[5]	1[5]	1	23
1980	42	60	36	46	62	35	57	39	16	20	30[5]	2[5]	2	56
Power plant: steam turbine deliveries (by capacity in GW)[6]														
1955–75	(5)	38	–	37	(5)	..	–	38	..	..	..	8	..	12
1975–87	(5)	50	–	17	(5)	24	–	55	4	25	9	7	9	52
Telecommunications equipment (by values)														
1976	4	14	5	12	9	9	9	14	..	..	2	4	1	24
Semiconductors: integrated circuits (by values)														
1982	..	..	..	..	..	..	..	..	66	18	8	19	1	24
All manufactures (by values)														
1960	11[7]	17[7]	..	..	..	..	10	15	6	11	4[8]	5[8]	14	31
1970	17	21	15	17	18	22	17	18	8	12	7[8]	7[8]	5	10
1978	21	28	20	22	22	31	25	25	9	14	10[8]	9[8]	4	12

:: = not available

— = nil or negligible

[1] I/C = Imports/Consumption (production + imports − exports) × 100; E/P = Exports/Production × 100.

[2] Nine members, excluding intra-member trade.

[3] 1979 figures. The 1980 figures, affected by a long strike, are: I/C, 42 per cent, E/P, 30 per cent.

[4] I/C and E/P for all of Western Europe.

[5] Excluding trade with Canada.

[6] 'Delivery' means the moment of the commissioning of completed plant. Note that delivery lead times have now lengthened to as much as ten years.

[7] 1962 figures.

[8] North America (including intra-US–Canada trade)

Sources: Textiles (woven cloth of cotton and man-made fibres): Textile Statistic Bureau, *Quarterly Statistical Review*, Manchester, various issues; UN, *Commodity Trade Statistics: Series D*, New York, various issues. Steel: OECD, *The Steel Market in 1981 and the Outlook for 1982*, special supplement, Paris, 1982. Motor cars: Motor Vehicle Manufacturers Association, *World Motor Vehicle Data, 1982 Edition*, Detroit, 1982; Society of Motor Manufacturers and Trades, *The Motor Industry of Great Britain 1982*, London, 1982. Power Plant: Science Policy Research Unit, Turbine Generator Data Bank. Telecommunications: OECD, *Telecommunications: Pressures and Policies for Change*, Table A3, Paris, 1983. Semiconductors: *Business Week*, 23 May, 1983, p. 83. All manufactures: for Germany, France, Italy, and the UK: M. Sharp and G. Shepherd, *The Management of Industrial Change in Britain*, Table 2.14, mimeo, Sussex European Research Centre, Brighton, 1983; for the EC-9, North America, and Japan: estimated from UNCTAD, *Handbook of International Trade and Development Statistics*, New York, Table 5.10a of *Supplement 1977, 1978*, Table 5.10b of *Supplement 1980, 1981*, and Table 10c of *Supplement 1981, 1982*.

concentration on export markets. By the mid-1970s, with the continuing liberalization of imports and a rising real wage, the mass-market strategy had collapsed. The regional (*Land*) governments and the banks rescued some of the victims of this collapse, but the federal government maintained its distance. There was a steady conversion of firms towards the specialization strategy; this was accomplished by a mild tendency to deconcentration in the 1970s.

Germany's industry appears to require less protection than other EC textile industries and it is the world's largest textile exporter. This relatively successful survival was the outcome of a process of free competition between the strategies of a substantial number of modern, strong firms. The government influenced the general environment by providing protection, but did not seek to influence the structure or strategies of the industry. Yet the competitive process might not have worked the way it did in Germany in the absence of other environmental factors, such as the strong inherited entrepreneurial base, the favourable conditions provided by DM undervaluation and protection in the 1960s, a system of harmonious labour relations, and a dynamic economy able to mop up textile job losses.

The French textile industry emerged from the last war altogether more backward. Government policy, particularly as far as colonial markets were concerned, tended to encourage the industry to rely on protection for the future. With the shock of competition after entrance into the EC, some of the larger textile firms embarked on a process of concentration which gained government support. By the 1970s the industry came to be dominated by a small number of large textile groups. Unlike Germany, however, these firms appeared to pay more attention to diversification outside textiles than to rationalization within textiles. The government strongly supported the strategy of these large firms, and it was only at the end of the 1970s that policy emphasis shifted from concentration to rationalization. Since 1981 the new Socialist government has somewhat turned back towards policies for employment preservation.

The UK was relatively early in liberalizing its textile import regime in the 1950s, but liberalization of low-cost imports from the Commonwealth encouraged the industry to press for protection. More than anything, this passive response reflected the sense of pessimism that had continued to pervade the industry ever since its decline from dominance of world markets in the earliest part of the century. In some desperation at the prospect of losing large parts of its domestic market, one of the UK's dominant man-made fibre producers, Courtaulds, undertook an ambitious form of private intervention. It acquired a very large share in textile processing capacity and began to pursue a mass-market strategy, aiming at direct competition with low-cost imports. It also used its newly acquired market position to gain government concessions on protection. Courtaulds' entry induced other giant textile groups to emerge, either in defence of their market position or in imitation, to the point where the UK textile industry became by far the most concentrated among the large industrialized countries. In effect, the government encouraged this concentration process through both a policy of protection and a permissive competition policy.

The UK's external trade balance in textiles continued to deteriorate rapidly in the 1970s and the UK is now among the most protectionist of the EC countries. The mass-market strategy has manifestly failed; now there is a belated move in the industry towards a specialization strategy, and perhaps even deconcentration. The mass-market strategy failed partly because the British market was too small; it has proven a good deal more successful in the US. But outdated labour practices have also held back productivity growth. While competition of the many failed to produce a positive approach to adjustment in the 1950s, the more positive approach that emerged in the following period, if ultimately only partly successful, was accompanied by a strong move to concentration. In both periods the government acted somewhat as the captive of the industry: it was rarely the main 'institutional' mover.

Up to the mid-1970s at least, the protection that the Italian textile industry enjoyed was higher than in the UK. The Italian government's propensity to sustain 'lame ducks' through nationalization and subsidies has proven second to none in the EC. In the face of this potential 'feather-bedding', a quite spontaneous process of 'decentralized production' has occurred. This has involved the replacement of large integrated firms by a complex system of sub-contracting among many smaller firms, which combines co-operation with competition.

The initial impetus for decentralization resulted from the problems imposed by a high level of union organization in large firms, but it was discovered that the new structures helped in the adoption of flexible, export-oriented specialization strategies. Segmented labour markets— underpinned by family labour, putting-out systems, and the evasion of social security payments—have also contributed to the viability of an industry less concentrated than in any other EC country. The government has proven far from inactive in policies for textiles. But these policies have proven less effective than political factors (such as the weakness of central government and the strength of trade unions), which have encouraged the emergence of self-reliant, small entrepreneurs and helped sustain segmentation in labour markets.

While intervention can be associated with failed strategies in France and the UK, and its relative lightness with relative success in Germany, it is simplistic to see a line of causation running from type of intervention to type of strategy. An equally valid interpretation is to see intervention as a public response to failed strategies. It seems that entrepreneurship and the competitive process have proven stronger in Germany and Italy, no doubt largely for historical reasons. In the UK and France, public policies to influence the structure of industries (and by implication their strategies) did not succeed in turning weakness into strength, though it may be true that the French and UK textile industries now have a greater potential for healthy survival than twenty years ago.

III. Steel[4]

International competitiveness in non-speciality steels is based on scale, the exploitation of up-to-date techniques, and the minimization of labour costs. Scale has traditionally been associated with the size of the market and modernity of plant—through the vintage effect—with the market's rate of growth. This model of comparative advantage is not as strongly determinant in favour of low-wage countries as that, say, of textiles, since exports to world markets can to a large extent compensate for restrictions in the size or growth of domestic markets.

In fact since 1960 European Community steel production, like that of the US, has been declining constantly as a proportion of world production, mostly in favour of Japan, which has come to dominate world exports, and the developing countries, which have mostly substituted for imports. This development can be primarily related to the slow growth of consumption in industrialized countries and its rapid growth in developing countries. The EC countries attempted to counter it with greater reliance on world export markets in the 1970s, yet increasing import penetration began to weaken overall trade balances as early as 1969–73, *before* the recession (see Table 7.2). In contrast, Japan has enjoyed growing net exports. This evolution of trade reflects the evolution of production costs. European costs were lower than both Japanese and American in 1960; by 1978 they had almost reached US levels and were about 1.4 times those of Japan. European adoption of the latest techniques of production—such as the oxygen process and continuous casting—was relatively slow, while Japan's was rapid. The gap with Japan had almost been closed by 1975, but by that time recession was underway and the demand for steel fell substantially. In effect, the Europeans failed to modernize and to reduce their labour force in the fat years, so that the political difficulties of adjustment to excess levels of capacity and employment have been made worse in the lean ones. The evidence points towards this being, at least in part, an effect of the progressive cartelization and protection of the European industry, which has been facilitated by the provisions of the European Coal and Steel Community (ECSC).

The forms and intensity of intervention in the steel industry by the major European countries have been much more similar than differences in declared doctrine (ranging from free trade to nationalization) might suggest. The levels of both nominal and effective subsidy to the industry have been surprisingly similar in Germany, Belgium, and France, though somewhat higher in Britain and Italy, rising in all cases after 1975, particularly in the form of subsidies to investment. Despite these similarities and the trend towards a more formal EC cartel, culminating in the compulsory production quotas of the 1980s, responses have differed significantly from country to country. Leaving aside Italy, the national industries fall into two groups: on the one side Germany and Luxembourg, on the other France, Belgium, and the UK.

Germany has proved more interventionist in steel than in many other sectors, not only in State and Federal subsidies, but also in government acceptance of the cartel practices permitted by the ECSC (regional sales organizations in the German case). German firms have made extensive rationalization agreements with each other—an effective alternative to the public merger policies pursued elsewhere—and have also pursued strong policies of exporting and diversifying. A number of the major firms (Thyssen, Mannesmann, Krupp), along with Arbed, the dominant Luxembourg firm, launched strategies of diversification before the recession began—some as far back as the mid-1960s. German firms, with long traditions of vertical integration (interrupted in 1945), increased their control over downstream activities in user industries, while Arbed diversified geographically.

The French, British, and Belgians did neither. The Belgian firms were subject to the financial strategies of their owners, principally the banks, so that until the mid-1970s specifically steel-related strategies had not been pursued. The firms were effectively nationalized in 1979. In Britain the nationally owned British Steel Corporation (BSC), like the private companies from which it was formed in 1968, has been severely handicapped by low British growth rates and quasi-permanent political uncertainty and delays. As a result its ambitious expansion plans were launched too late, in 1975, when the recession had already begun. In France state intervention in the 1960s was principally aimed at concentrating the industry. But it prevented steel companies from making high profits in the short boom periods (through price controls), inhibited private investment in steel-making as a result of the uncertainties it created, and failed to choose or promote appropriate strategies of rationalization. In the face of impending bankruptcy, the industry was virtually nationalized in 1978 (and formally so in 1981).

Italy's industry experienced a different history. After the war it grew rapidly from a small size, on the basis of rapid growth in domestic demand as the Italian economy caught up with north-western Europe's consumption levels. The growth of the industry was successfully spear-headed by a publicly owned firm (within the IRI—Istituto per la Reconstruzione Industriale—group). Yet when recession finally hit the industry in the late 1970s, this firm began to face political problems in adjusting to overcapacity and surplus employment that have become familiar in the Italian context. Like Italian textiles and mechanical engineering, the steel industry also has a dynamic private, small-scale sector.

In steel, strategies cannot be improvised overnight, since they typically take ten to fifteen years to mature. As a result, those firms in the Community best placed to weather the current cyclical and structural crisis seem to be those that entered it with long-term strategies already underway. In both the Luxembourg and German cases an important factor in this may have been the firms' expectations that their governments would only support them up to a point (in Germany, partly because of the importance of cheap steel to the country's consumer industries).

IV. Motor cars[5]

A large workforce, a few giant firms, and significant linkages with the rest of the economy make the car industry highly visible—a kind of barometer of national industrial performance. Car production is characterized by important economies of scale in production and distribution and very long strategic horizons. As a result, the industry is one of the most concentrated and internationalized in the world.

Until the 1960s there was a certain stability in the structure and growth of the world industry. It has since been in a phase of structural transformation, which imposes enormous pressures on individual firms and threatens the existence of national industries in the weaker producing countries.

The most immediate pressure comes from the reduced prospects of growth in domestic markets, as a result of market saturation, recession, and the oil crisis. In addition, the internationalization strategies of the US car producers and the development of Japanese car exports have also had fundamental effects. US firms, whose foreign investment has played a leading role in developing the European industry since the 1920s, dominated strategic changes in the world industry until about the mid-1970s. In the 1960s they initiated a trend towards the international integration of national product-design and production facilities; i.e. one 'world-car' model would serve many markets and would be assembled from components produced in several countries. Meanwhile, by the early 1970s, Japan had emerged, in an incredibly short space of time, as a significant new competitive force in world markets—the result of the unique levels of productive efficiency it was able to achieve.

European governments have been closely involved in the car industry for a long time. This has been most notable in the French case. The government fostered the emergence of two large, competitive car firms, Renault (nationalized) and Peugeot. Government and industry have come to work closely to pursue, if a little late in the day, a strategy of modernization and foreign investment (within Europe, but also in the US). Since 1977 the government has unilaterally limited Japanese imports to 3 per cent of the domestic market. It has allowed virtually no inward foreign investment from whatever source. It stands ready to provide the subsidies that its 'national champions' might need for their survival, though Peugeot has so far resisted this.

The federal German government, in contrast, has intervened but lightly in the industry. When Volkswagen (itself a product of intervention in the 1930s) nearly foundered in the early 1970s, the government helped cement the necessary consensus on strategy between the major parties (banks, other shareholders, labour, etc.) and then withdrew again. The banks, in fact, have played a greater role in strategic planning, blocking some foreign investment in the industry and (with the regional governments) rescuing several ailing firms. Volkswagen has adopted a successful strategy of producing up-market cars at home (like Germany's smaller, specialist producers) and the mature product abroad (for instance, the Beetle in Brazil). In 1981, when the US government forced a 'voluntary' export restraint (VER) on Japanese car makers, Germany—the largest remaining non-protected market in the old industrial world—reluctantly followed its lead and secured its own VER with Japan.

The major public support to the Italian car industry has been long-standing quotas against Japanese imports, together with protection against all inward foreign investment. With this protection, Fiat flourished in the past at arms length from the government. Now it has lost its former international advantage in engineering and design, and acute labour problems have forced it into a strategy of automation and diversification. This strategy may well not succeed, and the threat to Fiat's future as a viable car producer may increasingly force it into the arms of the government.

The basic problems that have brought British Leyland, the UK national champion, to the verge of collapse reflect a familiar litany of British industrial ills: poor management, technical weaknesses, the inability of large plants to manage labour relations, etc. The creation of BL was engineered in the 1960s with government money and pressure; it was sustained in the 1970s by nationalization, increasing subsidies, and, since 1976, a Japanese VER. However, both government and management were very slow—indeed, for a long time politically powerless—to attack the fundamental structural weaknesses of the firm. That these problems are now being tackled—with some signs of success, if at great cost, indicates that a learning process about intervention has taken place in the UK. The government and industry also appear to have stumbled into a strategy of seeking a Japanese role in the industry's recovery. BL has begun a promising programme of co-operation with Honda, while the government has been negotiating to get Nissan to produce in the UK.

It is certain that national intervention has kept more European car firms alive than would otherwise have survived on a more open market (BL, BMW, Alfa Romeo, to name some major examples). The importance of minimum efficient size strongly suggests that European, rather than national, solutions would have been optimal; yet fundamental differences in national strategies and in the health of national car industries have precluded a European-level public strategy. Non-tariff protection against Japan is, for example, on a completely national basis. The rapid growth of inter-firm co-operation agreements in Europe suggests that the private firms are far more willing Europeans than their governments.

On the other hand, the introduction of electronics into the industry further threatens the strategic directions that US firms, and to a lesser extent some larger European firms, have been taking. Many experts now think that electronic controls and robotization will allow far greater factory-floor flexibility. This has undermined the 'world-car' concept and may afford Europe's producers better chances of survival than hitherto.

V. Electrical power plant[6]

At the core of the power plant industry are a few, very large firms with broadly based electrical and mechanical skills, producing large steam turbine generators and, increasingly since the 1950s, designing and constructing nuclear power stations. US, German, and Swiss firms (often engaged in a broad range of electro-mechanical activities) have led in heavy electrical technology since the end of the last century, followed by UK, French, and Italian firms. Nuclear power has essentially developed as a spin-off from the military programmes of the victors in the last war. It has been dominated by US technology of light-water reactors, though both the UK and France tried to develop an independent technology of gas-cooled reactors. Power plant equipment generally tends to be lumpy, custom-made (i.e. not mass-produced), and subject to long lead times and cycles. Nuclear plant is particularly reliant on R&D and its cost effectiveness is subject to the familiar learning curve. These characteristics have led to a high degree of concentration.

The concentration and strategic nature of the industry and the public ownership or regulation of electricity supply in all countries have led to close relationships between the industry, utilities, and governments. This in turn has led to a high level of protection through utility procurement policies in most countries (see the very low ratios of imports to consumption in Table 7.1) and a large potential role for governments in industrial strategies. Centralized (usually publicly owned) utilities have tended to encourage monopolistic structures in the power plant industry in order to capture economies of scale, while decentralized utilities (particularly US and German) have preferred a structure permitting at least some competition among suppliers. In nuclear power the size of investment costs and safety and proliferation issues have further increased the role of government and of the political process.

Important changes in the structure of the power plant industry occurred from the mid-1960s to mid-1970s as Japanese and continental European producers made in-roads into world markets and US foreign investment attempted to establish a foothold in Europe. The European response was a wave of national rationalizations. In the 1970s the Third World provided the most dynamic export opportunities, though import substitution is now reducing these. But the major adjustment problem stems from a series of misjudgements that have led to substantial over-capacity: the growth of electricity consumption in industrialized countries was hit by the post-1973 recession; the rising price of oil (and hence of oil-based electricity generation) affected the financial strength of many utilities; and the nuclear option became far less attractive as a result of cost, safety regulations, political opposition, and concern over weapons proliferation. Over-capacity was compounded by the increasing unit size of generating plants.

Two common European reactions to this adjustment problem have been increasing subsidies to electricity production and an intensification of the export drive, often with governments playing important roles. This export drive may even have increased the rate of technology transfer to developing countries.

The German industry entered the 1970s in a strong position. It retained its traditional strength in non-nuclear plant and was an early licensee of US nuclear technology. In the first half of the 1970s, the two major producers merged their power plant interests into a single firm, which made itself independent of US nuclear licences in order to compete more strongly in the world nuclear market. In the event, and in spite of Germany's technological lead within Europe, the later 1970s saw a declining market for the German industry, which was further affected by growing political disagreements on nuclear power. On the whole, industrial strategy appears to have been the preserve of the private industry.

In France, on the contrary, government and utility have played a leading role. An independent nuclear power technology was renounced in 1969. The government initiated a thoroughgoing industry rationalization in the early 1970s to produce sole suppliers in turbine generators and in nuclear reactors, and to lessen significantly the presence of foreign investment in the industry. In 1974 the government embarked on an ambitious programme of domestic nuclear expansion, based on the production of standardized reactors under US licence. It gained independence from its US licences in 1981.

France's strategy is now proceeding more cautiously under the Mitterrand government, but none the less represents a bold attempt at world leadership in nuclear power technology (at a time when the US, the present leader, is looking towards non-nuclear technologies). It runs, of course, all the risks associated with the nuclear option. The apparent success of France's strategy so far reflects the political strength of the government and the effects of past market growth on firms' willingness to rationalize.

The UK, facing similar industry-structure problems to those of France, has suffered from low growth. In the mid-1960s there were already some rationalization moves within the industry in the face of losses of world markets. The government further rationalized the nuclear reactor industry by creating a partly nationalized sole supplier in 1973. This, however, continued to face difficulties due to the lack of consistent home demand and continuing uncertainties about British nuclear technology. Moreover, the government was unable to promote the further rationalization in the non-nuclear part of the industry that it sought. In 1979 it decided that licensed US technology would play an important part in future nuclear expansion, though it has not yet given up its independent option. During the 1970s advanced ordering and maintenance were used to help tide the industry over a period of very low orders. Government problems in rationalizing the industry partly reflect the weakness of the procurement tool in a period of slow growth.

Since 1973 the Italian government has rationalized the nuclear power industry to create a sole supplier (within IRI). It has also rationalized power plant exports through the creation of a partly nationalized company. The industry remains essentially a technology follower. The nuclear industry also faces substantial domestic political opposition and has not yet resolved internal disputes on choice of technology.

European governments now face great uncertainty over the direction in which the structure of the power plant industry will and should move. Given the perception that a strong industry may be needed to meet higher demand in the late 1980s and the 1990s (particularly in the light of growing oil scarcity), and given the obstacles to further rationalization of the industry (inevitably involving cross-border changes given the degree of national concentration), there are strong incentives to attempt to maintain their status quo. However, the political and economic costs of support are rising, competition in world markets is intense, and capabilities risk being eroded by the lack of orders. Structural change may, therefore, become unavoidable for the industry. Rivalries and the requirement for equity and national control stand in the way of a wide-ranging negotiated European solution to the problem of over-capacity. Instead, new technical and marketing alliances may be forged between the major firms. These could eventually lead to reorganization at the production level.

VI. Telecommunications[7]

The telecommunications equipment industry has shot into prominence in recent years as an area for 'high' industrial politics because of the enormous developments in information technology. Telecommunications are one of the most obvious areas for application of semiconductor technology. This gives them a potential role as one of the user industries around which the growth of the electronic industries (seen as the possible basis of future industrial strength) can be nurtured and guided. This preoccupation is clear in the French *télématique* strategy and the European Commission's recent targets for the sector, in which telecommunications play a central part along with semiconductors and computers. The convergence with electronics also means a basic reshaping of the technical bases of the century-old industry.

Wireless and digital transmission, especially through space satellites and semiconductor techniques, make it possible to use existing communications cables far more cheaply, or to by-pass them altogether, while multiplying the devices for feeding in or retrieving data. These are associated with such notions as the 'automatic office of the future'. Accordingly, the industry is generally considered to be poised on the edge of a revolution, the first since the telephone was developed a century ago. This has at least three major implications for the industry and the part it plays in the economy.

The first relates to employment. Very high growth rates in demand for products made much cheaper by rapid technological advances are likely to keep the world industry expanding at around 8–10 per cent per annum, so that the actual numbers employed may not fall. But the types of labour will change, with a higher relative demand for programme designers and operators at one end of the scale and unskilled operatives at the other, and a sharp fall in the proportion of skilled mechanics in between.

The second major change is the breach of the natural monopoly, thought to be constituted by the traditional telephone networks operated by national PTT administrations or the regulated monopoly in the US. The economies of scale at the base of this natural monopoly are falling rapidly in switching and transmission equipment, currently 75 per cent of the market. This is making it possible not only to multiply the terminal devices at each end of the communication line, but also to concentrate more of the market in terminals (possibly half instead of today's quarter), where the economies of scale are least. The result is a potential for opening up the systems to competition, virtually for the first time since the early telephone companies established their lead.

The third new factor is that many of these changes are being introduced essentially by the computer industry, which is to some extent distinct from the telecommunications firms, especially in the United States. The computer industry is much more competitive and market-oriented than the regulated telecommunications industry. Yet it, too, has strong elements of oligopoly. Thus, there is a question as to whether the changes underway in telecommunications foreshadow a more competitive system, or a gradual shift away from the present oligopoly of dominant firms to a new oligopoly where the electronic sector plays a larger part.

In the United States, the Bell monopoly began to be weakened in the 1970s. The result was a rapid penetration by firms such as IBM and Xerox (investing in direct satellite communications to service private intra-firm communications, by-passing the telephone network), by Japanese firms (whose market share is expected to grow), as well as by L. M. Ericsson (of Sweden), Northern Telecom (of Canada), and a significant number of small, innovative suppliers in the terminals market. So far competition seems to be encouraging growth and innovation. It is too early to say if Bell's near-monopoly will really be undermined and, if so, what the costs might be (excessive duplication of investment, realignment of tariffs with cost increases for subscribers in sparely populated areas, etc.).

In Europe the PTT administrations of the main producer countries have taken steps towards freeing the terminals market as part of a policy of encouraging microelectronics development. It looks unlikely, however, that the switching and transmission markets will be deregulated. Both Britain and Germany have suffered costly setbacks in developing switching systems (in the UK System X and in Germany the EWS fiasco). France, hurrying to transform its telecommunications industry as part of its strategy to break into the electronic era, has so far pursued a relatively more successful policy of rapid growth in demand from high public procurement, slightly more competition, and restructuring of the sector round a few firms. But despite some spectacular deals, France still has to establish itself, for instance as a leading exporter alongside American, Japanese, and German firms, or even L. M. Ericsson and Philips. The British and Italians might encounter some difficulties in future, though the Italians are doing well in specialized markets, such as microwave radio and satellite equipment.

In some ways, the telecommunications market resembles that for aerospace. There is the same emphasis on public procurement and government subsidies for competition on open markets (notably in the Third World); the same trend in every producer country towards national champions; the same stress on technological linkages. This might argue for joint procurement (in effect with national quotas) by producing countries of the Community.

In practice, the resistance by national PTTs towards increased standardization seems overwhelming. One reason seems to be the rapid decline in economies of scale in terminals and, probably, transmission equipment. Even R&D in new electronic components, though very high, is not comparable to the development costs of a Concorde or Airbus. The argument for a European solution may be stronger in switching, where R&D costs are growing rapidly. Failure to reach such a solution may recreate, if on a smaller scale, the costly errors associated with national go-it-alone policies in aerospace in the 1950s.

Another reason for resistance to European procurement is the tendency for telecommunications equipment to account for only 10–20 per cent of the turnover of Europe's largest electronics firms, like Siemens, Philips, or even CGE and GEC. Costs can be cross-subsidized and in-house markets provided for upstream products. Most of the main producer countries have more than one such enterprise, usually multinational.

The relaxation of the monopoly on the US market may give significant opportunities for increased exports, especially in terminal equipment (though Japan, Canada, and Sweden have already established strong positions in the US). Nevertheless, the fragmentation of European markets will continue to pose a severe structural problem for the European industry, though probably at the level of the electronics sectors as a whole, rather than telecommunications as such.

VII. Semiconductors[8]

The semiconductor industry, barely 35 years old, is at the heart of the electronics-based revolution that is beginning to change production methods, the provision of services, and broader aspects of society—such as patterns of employment. The speed of technical advance in semiconductors continues to be rapid by any standards, especially in the most 'intelligent' semiconductors—the integrated circuits (including memories and microprocessors) at the heart of the information-technology revolution. The 'learning curve' accompanying rapid technological change means that barriers to entry for new producers, or barriers to catching up for old, can be substantial.

Many people perceive an important mutual stimulation of demand (or 'synergy') between semiconductor producers and users. As a result, many governments strongly feel the need for a domestically owned semiconductor industry that is internationally competitive if their countries are to acquire or maintain a commanding position in the future international division of labour. The struggle now taking place is not only between countries, but also between firms. Established large electronics and electro-mechanical firms are having to face competition from new would-be entrants, and the industry will remain in a state of fundamental structural transition for some years.

At the birth of the industry, Europe—or more precisely Philips—was surprisingly close to the US in technology. Just as it did in other high-technology sectors like aerospace, the US forced the pace and profoundly influenced the direction of technical change in the 1950s and 1960s, through massive military and space programmes aided by the existence of massive research institutions (like Bell Laboratories) operating in the regulated telecommunications sector. With this initial stimulus, a process of intense competition in the US (and subsequently in Japan) was able to take over as the driving force in technological change.

Europe's technological lag increased in the 1960s with the introduction of the more powerful integrated circuits and the subsequent wave of US investment in Europe. This investment, together with predatory pricing policies, severely undermined much of Western Europe's semiconductor industry.

Until the mid-1970s, most of Europe's semiconductor industry operated in a free-market environment, except for some modest military programmes in the UK and France. Virtually the only healthy survivors in the market for standard devices (as opposed to the much smaller custom market) were Philips (Netherlands, but producing as a quasi-national company in the US and major European countries), Siemens (Germany), and to a far lesser extent, SGS (Italy)—but they were all still behind the technological frontier. The survival of Philips and Siemens appears to have been due in part to long-term growth strategies that had been pursued for decades, in contrast to the manifest (and equally rational) orientation of UK and French firms to more immediate financial profitability. The large size of these two firms also enabled them to bear the burden of long-term strategies through cross-subsidization, while their vertical integration (mostly into industrial and consumer applications) enabled them to internalize the producer-user synergy by physically concentrating in one firm the technical resources that were scarce in Europe. (Vertical integration and size were not so important in the 'first-comer' US industry, where the market was able to perform this synergetic function as a result of a relative abundance of technical resources.)

The precariousness of Europe's survival (too few firms and too large a technological gap) under market conditions in an industry as strategic as electronics provided a strong argument for public support. This kind of realization prompted a wave of government promotion of the computer industry in Germany, France, and the UK from the mid-1960s to the mid-1970s. This was at best partially successful (most notably in the case of the UK) and it helped to prompt these governments to move more directly to promote the 'heart' of the electronics industry: semiconductors. In the 1970s Germany, France, Italy, and the UK all developed specific (and growing-over-time) semiconductor support programmes, often related to more general promotion of the electronics industry. The common features of intervention have been a concentration on the provision of R&D and investment funds to existing firms and, except in Germany, structural policies to promote stronger firms. Public procurement has been a secondary tool, while trade protection has not been significant.

In general, the dominant philosophy behind European intervention has been to support existing firms' own survival strategies, rather than substitute new, more ambitious, 'catching-up' strategies. In this way public money may have been wasted, inasmuch as it merely helped firms to go where they would have gone in any case.

Germany's intervention stands out as having been the most effective. A large programme attacking supply-side constraints across much of the electronics spectrum was introduced relatively early in support of existing strategies of German-owned firms. As a result of this, and of the inherited strength of these firms, the German semiconductor industry has emerged in relatively strong shape. But it has emerged no stronger than the 'European' firm Philips, which receives some government incentives but has probably not been fundamentally influenced by them.

The French government has used subsidy and structural (national champion) policies to wage a long fight for the survival of a standardized semiconductor industry, virtually against the inclination of the electronics industry itself. In 1982 the leading firms were nationalized. Some fruits are now being reaped from the government's long fight. But it also threw its weight behind a spate of joint ventures in the late 1970s that, in effect, exchanged French cash (mostly from non-electronics firms) for American technology. Finally, a broad offensive is now underway to encourage electronics-user industries across the board. French policy constitutes a fairly clear bid, if from some way behind, to catch up with the world technology leaders.

Faced with the determination of UK producers to quit the standardized market, government structural policies and historically small subsidies were not very effective. (They probably would not have been effective even had the programme been larger.) A government reply to this 'abdication' by the private sector was to create a firm, INMOS, to 'leap-frog' into the high technology of very large-scale integrated circuits. The future of this ambitious act of state capitalism remains to be seen. The government is also hedging its bets (as in the car industry) by encouraging, partly with regional subsidies, US and Japanese firms to set up UK subsidiaries.

Italy's national champion SGS (now part of IRI) is potentially able to profit from a new programme of pan-electronics support reminiscent of German programmes. Yet the signs are that this support is too little and too late and likely, in any case, to suffer badly from the inefficiencies of the state administration.

In contrast with Europe's battle to survive, the Japanese semiconductor industry has rapidly developed to the point where, in many areas, it is level with or ahead of the US and is making important inroads on the European market. While European government intervention has basically sought to encourage the strategies of existing firms within existing constraints, the more comprehensive Japanese policy approach has been to seek to remove these constraints, albeit in the presence of a number of large, strong, vertically integrated firms. These policies have been characterized by: strong controls on foreign investments and (until the mid-1970s) on imports; promotion of common technological targets; making technical information licensed from abroad available to all domestic firms; and support of co-operative basic research by these firms. Consensus, rather than a dominant role played by government, has been a key to the successful implementation of this approach.

The socio-economic features of European countries are not likely to support the kind of consensus essential to a Japanese-style policy. None the less, Europe's best chances of moving towards the technological frontier in semiconductors lie in making national policies as comprehensive as possible and achieving as much European co-operation as possible through cross-border mergers, 'Airbus'-style co-operation, and common basic research. Failing this, and with a continuation of present, often piecemeal, national policies, the best outcome might be the survival of technologically-lagging national champions in each of the major countries; the worst outcome the survival of only Philips and Siemens.

VIII. Conclusions

One of the most important generalizations that can be made from the sector reviews is that change—whether in the form of new processes, new products, or new forms of organization—is very important across a range of industrial activities. Textiles, motor cars, and telecommunications are 'mature' or 'maturing' activities that have experienced—or at least begun—a cycle of rejuvenation. This is less marked in the steel or electrical power plant industries—the latter if only because the nuclear option has gone sour for a number of reasons.

The process of change has helped reinforce the competitive process in spite of recession and the growth of public intervention. First, international competitive pressures increased rapidly for Western European countries in the 1970s. (See Table 7.1 for the growth in trade-intensities.) Second, our sectoral evidence undermines notions of the inevitability of increasing concentration. Micro-electronics now appear to offer possibilities of deconcentration in motor cars and telecommunications, while some deconcentration has already occurred in textiles as a result of new forms of business organization.

The structural peculiarities of each sector limit the value of typologies of or generalizations about sectoral patterns in adjustment. None the less it appears feasible and useful to seek to identify adjustment strategies that characterize (at least at the margin) certain sectors in certain countries. Clearly, one strategy may dominate where there is monopoly or very heavy government intervention; but characteristic or dominant strategies are also often observable where there are larger numbers of decision-makers. The most obvious example from this chapter is textiles, where—in spite of competition of the many— different strategies appeared to dominate in different countries.

Moreover, the evidence suggests that different countries pursue characteristic strategic themes across sectors. One can note, for instance, the promptness of German firms to move into more specialized markets (e.g. in textiles, steel, and cars); the strong public role in French industrial development and a tendency to go for broad, ambitious offensives (full-range car producers on a European scale, a 'mass-market' in nuclear energy, the *télématique* strategy); the recent and growing British propensity to seek co-operation with Japanese firms (in cars, semiconductors, and machine tools); the ubiquity and past success of Italian public enterprise and the current success of small-scale, co-operative production in that country. These 'strategic' patterns cannot be taken too far, but they do indicate systematic differences in behaviour between countries. These differences concern both national capacity for reacting to opportunities for industrial change and the way in which these capacities are organized.

Of the four countries we have looked at, Germany and the UK are the polar examples of relative capacity and incapacity for change across the broad range of industries. To date France appears to have innovated better in the intermediate and new industries than in the mature, while Italy tends to have fared better in small-scale, rather than large-scale industry.

The sector summaries in this chapter have provided *some* elements —though no more—of the differences in national business environments that help to explain why capacity for change differs across countries. It can perhaps be said that the unifying factor for these four countries since the Second World War has been an economic nationalism, determining—even if in a vague and uncodified way— that they should maintain (Germany and the UK) or acquire (France and Italy) a competitive and, if possible, indigenously-owned presence in a full range of industrial activities. This full range includes both high-technology sectors (such as aerospace and electronics) and 'strategic' industries (which, in the most generous definition, appears to cover any industries, such as textiles and steel, where employment is significant).

In Germany, a relatively successful history of adjustment appears to be the consequence of an environment in which both competition and co-operation flourished and where public intervention was light by European standards. The private sector's success in finding its own profitable forms of adjustment *may* be explained by the nature of this intervention and German firms' expectations that the public authorities would not bail them out if they got into difficulties. On the other hand, it can equally be argued from the evidence that intervention was light precisely because the private sector was strong—a strength inherited from many decades of industrial dominance.

France, entering the post-war period as a comparatively backward industrial power, sought to become strong across a broad range of industries. But it did not—and still does not—have the German option of encouraging a process of competition among a number of strong national firms. This helped to steer France towards a highly interventionist approach (albeit under the powerful constraint of increasingly opening the economy to international competition). The partial success of French intervention partly reflects national traditions of étatism and centralized authority, not to mention the industrial and political ineffectiveness of trade unions until the change of government in 1981. French intervention appears to have succeeded best in industries where firms are large and there are no long-established industrial structures and strong pressure groups.

The British industrial system appears to possess little of the 'cement' provided by government links with industry in France, and by the banks, inter-firm co-operation, and harmonious labour relations in Germany. Indeed, the poor relations among firms, unions, and governments have often proved debilitating, for instance in the long-running debates on steel nationalization and nuclear energy options. In addition, the longer-established industries (e.g. textiles, steel, shipbuilding, and motor cars) have clearly suffered from poor labour relations or labour rigidities.

Industrial intervention in the UK has grown considerably, albeit at first unwillingly, against this unpropitious business environment. British intervention was far more concerned to influence industrial structures than the German for instance, yet far less technically efficient and influential in doing this than the French. It tended in some cases to be a captive of pressure groups (for instance, the textile or nuclear lobbies) or to find itself occupying ground that the private sector was intent on abdicating (standard semiconductors, for instance). On the other hand, there are signs of a learning process in intervention: some technological ambitions have been scaled down and Japanese firms have been sought as investment partners.

Part of the particular quality of Italy's business environment is the product of its political system: a succession of weak governments of the centre-right, subject to factional pressures from within their own ranks and to substantial opposition from the political parties and trade unions to their left. This system has made the operation of larger firms very difficult. On the one hand, it helps to explain the emergence of the state-holding company (principally IRI) as a historically effective formula for the development of risky new activities, such as semiconductors. On the other hand, it helps to explain the remarkable growth of 'decentralized production' (often a form of collective entrepreneurship among small firms) in the 1970s.

To an extent, then, different national business environments can be explained by the characteristics of existing institutions and arrangements, such as the capacity and political authority of government or the nature of labour relations. But a large part of the explanation—like the existing institutions themselves—has a deep-rooted history: many of the weaknesses in British textiles, like the strengths in German mechanical engineering, go back to the last century. These inheritances are not immutable, but they are the raw material on which public policies have to operate.

Notes and Sources

[1] Shonfield's work on modern, mixed-economy capitalism provides an important forerunner in this area. See Andrew Shonfield, *Modern Capitalism: the Changing Balance of Public and Private Power*, Oxford University Press, London, 1965.

[2] Most of these sectors, along with some others, are treated at some length in Geoffrey Shepherd, François Duchêne, and Christopher Saunders (eds), *Europe's Industries: Public and Private Strategies for Change*, Frances Pinter, London, 1983. This chapter draws on the sector studies from the book, as well as longer monographs by the same authors. However, the interpretations of the sector studies in this chapter are my own.

[3] This section is based on the chapter by G. Shepherd in G. Shepherd, F. Duchêne, and C. Saunders, op. cit.

[4] This section is based on a chapter by Patrick Messerlin and Christopher Saunders in G. Shepherd, F. Duchêne, and C. Saunders, op. cit., as well as on Patrick Messerlin, *The European Industrial Adjustment Policies: The Steel Industry Case*, mimeo, Sussex European Research Centre, Brighton, 1981.

[5] This section is based on the chapter by Daniel T. Jones on motor cars in G. Shepherd, F. Duchêne, and C. Saunders, op. cit., as well as on Daniel T. Jones, *Maturity and Crisis in the European Car Industry: Structural Change and Public Policy*, Sussex European Papers No. 8, Sussex European Research Centre, Brighton, 1981.

[6] This section is based on the chapter by John Surrey and William Walker in G. Shepherd, F. Duchêne, and C. Saunders, op. cit., as well as on John Surrey and William Walker, *The European Power Plant Industry: Structural Responses to International Market Pressures*, Sussex European Papers No. 12, Sussex European Research Centre, Brighton, 1981.

[7] This section is based on Jürgen Müller, *Public Policy Issues in the Telecommunications Equipment Industry*, mimeo, Sussex European Research Centre, Brighton, 1980.

[8] This section is based on the chapter by Giovanni Dosi in G. Shepherd, F. Duchêne, and C. Saunders, op. cit., as well as on Giovanni Dosi, *Technical Change and Survival: Europe's Semiconductor Industry*, Sussex European Papers No. 9, Sussex European Research Centre, Brighton, 1981.

VIII

6312
4233
EEC

Steel: a Case Study in Industrial Policy

ALBERT KERVYN DE LETTENHOVE*

I. Introduction

In 1960 the steel industry in the present EC member states was the largest in the world, with production exceeding that of the US, and a dominant position in export markets. It was, however, predominantly composed of small firms, operating medium- or small-scale plants. It has since been swept by a wave of mergers, from which a number of large-scale producers emerged. Although these mergers have occasionally cut across national boundaries, the industry has remained basically national, and less concentrated than its US or Japanese counterparts. (In 1981 the four largest firms accounted for 39 per cent of production in the EC, as against 49 per cent in the US and 64 per cent in Japan.)

These modern European firms, however, inherited a motley array of small dispersed plants, often located in industrial suburbs where there was no room for the layout of a complete modern plant. Of course, many small plants were closed down (more than 50 of them between 1975 and 1981 alone) and some integrated mills were built on new sites, generally located on the coast (notably in Italy, France, and more recently in the UK).

In sharp contrast to Japan, where modern integrated mills were built with over 100 million tonnes of capacity, the European picture essentially remains one of modernizing older plants on their traditional sites. This often involves extra cost in the flow of materials from one stage to the next, as well as energy losses.

Still, the modernization effort has been substantial, and the European industry went over to the oxygen converter for steel-making well ahead of the Americans. (By 1981, no steel was made in Europe on the older open hearth or Bessemer processes, which still accounted for over 25 per cent of production in 1973.) The more recent change-over from ingot to continuous casting is still in progress: from 12 per cent of

---

* Professor of Economics, Catholic University of Louvain-la-Neuve.

crude steel output in 1974, continuous casting accounted for 45 per cent in 1981 (with the UK and the Benelux countries trailing behind Germany, France, and Italy).

Efforts have also been made, though on the whole less successfully, to take advantage of economies of scale. Continuous strip mills for flat products have been built in all countries and the size of blast furnaces and converters has been increased, althoguh here the variance remains considerable. Both the data and their incomplete results are illustrated by the following data:

TABLE 8.1
Number of blast furnaces and oxygen converters

Number of blast furnaces		
Hearth diameter (metres)	1965	1978
< 6	255	90
6 to 9	124	137
9 to 12	11	49
> 12	–	5
	390	281
Number of oxygen converters[1]		
Capacity per hearth (tonnes)	1965	1978
< 100	24	88
100 to 200	15	55
200 to 300	2	32
> 300	–	18
	41	193

[1] Beetween 1965 and 1978 nearly 500 open-hearth and Bessemer converters were scrapped.

These data show that while investment has been important, the proportion of equipment meeting a criterion of optimal size remains fairly low. It must be stressed, however, that keeping up with constantly changing standards would involve very large invetments with very low financial yields. Thus replacing two medium-sized blast furnaces by one large one would slightly improve the technical efficiency of the plant, but also increase its total costs (including financial charges).

Thus, the traditional process (starting from iron ore and proceeding to steel through pig-iron) increasingly requires large-scale production; the major technical indivisibility lies downstream, in the continuous strip-mill for the production of coils, from which all finished flat products are derived. At the same time, new types of 'mini-mills' have been gaining a competitive edge. Working from scrap and using electric furnaces (typically smaller than oxygen converters), they dispense with the upstream process. Here small-scale operations are efficient for products where economies of scale are not important in the downstream process (reinforcing and wire rods, special steels). Since prices are far more flexible for scrap than for iron ore, the cost advantage of small electric plants grows in periods of recession. The destabilizing impact of the 'Bresciani' is well known: since capital costs are low, there is easy entry into this segment of the industry, and cartel arrangements are difficult to enforce.

The current crisis in the steel industry has made it an important testing ground for industrial policy, both at the national and Community levels. Addressing this issue, this chapter is divided into four parts:

— Situation and prospects of the steel industry,
— Cost and market structures,
— Adjustment problems: market failure and inefficiency of government intervention,
— Possible guidelines for community policy.

I. Situation and prospects of the steel industry

Steel production capacity in the EC stood at around 200 million (metric) tonnes 1982. Such a figure is of course no better than an order of magnitude; despite apparently rigorous definitions, it is not always clear what is being measured, or indeed that all firms use common standards.

The EC Commission's Eurostat figures report that production of crude steel in the Community (including Greece) was 126 million tonnes in 1981, but only a little more than 111 million tonnes in 1982, a decline of nearly 12 per cent. The 1982 drop in production resulted from a decline in net exports (from 16.4 to 10.6 million tonnes) and domestic consumption (from 77 to 71.6 million tonnes).[1] For the first half of 1983 the rate of output is not expected to rise above its level for the end of 1982, some 10 per cent below the year's average. Thus, early in 1983, the steel industry will be operating at about 50 per cent of its capacity.

From the cyclical peak of 1973 to the next peak in 1979, consumption of steel products in the EC-7 (excluding Denmark, Ireland, and

Greece) declined from 89 to 80.2 million tonnes, or approximately 1.7 per cent per year, while GDP in the area grew at the reduced rate of 2.4 per cent per year. Despite the margin of error in the figures, it is clear that steel use per unit of GDP significantly declined, and this trend clearly continued into 1982.

For the coming years, recently issued projections of the Commission foresee a fresh decline in the GDP trend rate of growth to 1.6 per cent from the 1979 peak to 1986-7. (This growth rate is of course much higher if the recession year 1981 is taken as a basis.)

It is not, however, legitimate to extrapolate future trends on that basis. Part of the decreased use of steel is due to a change in the composition of final demand and output: a decline in the share of investment and an increase in the share of services. From 1973 to 1979, investment grew by only 1 per cent per year, against 2.4 per cent for GDP.

It is investment that absorbs the greater share of domestic use of steel; the automobile industry accounts directly for only 13 per cent. Statistically, fixed investment is the better regressor, with approximately unit elasticity, and an exogenous declining trend of about 1.7 per cent per year. This trend is to be explained by technological factors, such as an increasing share of electronics in the value of equipment, a decline in the weight of machinery in terms of its cost and performance, and in a few cases the substitution of plastics for steel.

The Commission's projections envisage that after a period of running down the capital stock, investment will show some revival. A growth rate of 3.6 per cent per year is forecast from 1983 to 1987, faster than GDP's 2.5 per cent for the same period. (Both figures are, of course, much lower from a 1979 basis.)

Such estimates may be on the optimistic side. If realized, however, they imply no better than a return by 1986 to the 1979 level of apparent steel consumption, or a flat trend from peak to peak.

Net exports increased until 1974, when they reached over 20 million tonnes of steel products. They went through a secondary peak in 1981 with 16.4 million tonnes, but fell off sharply in 1982. It appears unlikely that the 1981 level will be easily regained. With slow growth and difficulties in many developing countries, excess capacity will appear, notably in Latin America. It is also likely that access to the US market will remain limited in the long run. The proportion of world steel production accounted for by the EC is likely to go on declining, as it did from 1970 (23 per cent) to 1980 (18 per cent).

The trend in net exports will of course partly depend on pricing policies within the EC. Internal prices (at current rates of exchange where $1 = DM 2.4) are well below US domestic prices, about on a par with Japanese internal prices, but significantly above world prices, as reflected in quotations for exports to third countries. Any sharp decline in the dollar would of course alter these price relations. (Pricing policies will be discussed later.)

Thus, extrapolating from the present relation between production and apparent consumption is likely to be optimistic. It would imply that the production figure of 1979, around 140 million tonnes of crude steel, stands as the upper limit of likely productions for the foreseeable future. With present capacity in the 200 million tonne range, excess capacity may then be estimated at over 25 per cent of the total.

II. Cost and market structures

Some of the policy problems are bound up with the structure of costs and markets. A brief reminder of these may be useful before proceeding further.

A typical modern steel plant includes a series of processing stages: upstream a sintering plant (and sometimes coke ovens), blast furnaces, and then steel converters with ingot or continuous casting; slabbing or blooming mills; and downstream rolling mills for flat or long products or wire rods. In some cases transformation is carried further, in wire drawing, tube mills, or sheet coating (tinplate, etc.).

Dealing with an integrated system, all stages will operate at the same rate. In a modern plant, variable costs are essentially constant, in the range of 50 to 90 per cent of capacity utilization. With older plants (or multi-plant firms), this will not be strictly true. Some older blast furnaces may coexist with new ones, or an old rolling mill will be held in reserve until its more modern counterpart is fully used. In such cases, beyond a certain rate of capacity use, marginal costs will be higher.

The same may occur when a firm has more modern installations for flat, say, than for long products. If it can arrange for an exchange of quotas with another firm with the opposite cost structure, marginal cost will again be lower when only the more efficient plant is used. (Such cases are unfortunately not frequent.)

Apart from the case of mini-mills, average costs are generally much above marginal costs, and therefore declining with the scale of output. The difference, of course, increases when output is lower.

Marginal costs depend essentially on the technical characteristics of the plant. In practice, this can be identified with its age and layout. Fixed costs, on the other hand, are much more dependent on the quality of management, but also depend on past investment and its financing. Firms which have built large plants with borrowed money in the last ten years carry particularly heavy financial charges.

On the market side, the price elasticity of demand is very low in the short-run: steel consumption is a function of the demand for products in which steel represents a maximum of 25 per cent of the cost. In the medium-term, the elasticity is of course somewhat higher, mostly as a result of the export trade in metal products, but also through substitution possibilities. The latter appear limited, however, and may be linked to technical change as much as to relative prices.

At the level of the firm, the elasticity of demand is of course much higher. However, competition is far from perfect. Although products appear fairly standardized, there can be significant quality differentials which can be used to justify premiums in some cases, or more usually nowadays, rebates well beyond what is allowed by the basing point system. The market is thus far from transparent, and firms are tempted to act as discriminating monopolists. As long as such special rebates apply to a small volume of sales, they do not appear to entail a general lowering of prices.

In fact, these imperfections in the market have tended to encourage non-collusive behaviour. Some firms appear to pursue individual short-term profit maximization rather than joint oligopoly optimum, thus breaking away from (implicit or explicit) cartel rules. The number of firms pursuing such aggressive tactics is sufficient, under present conditions of excess capacity, to drive the price down to the level of the marginal cost of the aggressive firms (or of the least efficient firm whose output is needed). It must be stressed, however, that such behaviour is far from uniform, and differs across both countries and product types.

III. Adjustment problems:
market failure and inefficiency of government intervention

The previous discussion suggests that in the absence of market organization (i.e. some form of cartel), internal EC prices could well fall below current international prices and lead to a situation where even the most efficient firms would incur heavy losses.

Restoration of some kind of market equilibrium would then depend on the closing down of a sufficient number of plants—or the bankruptcy of a sufficient number of firms—to eliminate excess capacity and allow the survivors to raise prices to the level of average costs.

Such a competitive market solution need not be the most efficient. Survivors may be selected on the basis of financial reserves, enabling them to last out their competitors, rather than on the basis of efficiency of operations. In addition, a protracted recession might leave the industry with an insufficient capacity to meet a revival of demand.

Such a market solution is in any case precluded by government intervention. Employment in the steel industry is very lumpy, and the closing down of a large plant constitutes in every case a major social problem. In addition, the location of the steel industry often makes it the major employer in its area, and this regional aspect then aggravates the social problem. Furthermore, in the UK, France, Italy, and Belgium the industry is in large part nationalized, so the final decision regarding survival depends on the government. The invisible hand thus becomes highly visible, political pressures have an obvious target, and the temptation to protect the domestic market could in some cases spell the ruin of European integration.

Even where this is not the case (Germany, Luxembourg, and the Netherlands) governments have intervened with subsidies, although in the case of Germany on a far smaller scale than elsewhere. Some governments are clearly more sensitive to the employment problem and are prepared to subsidize a far higher level of losses than others. This creates a major factor of inequality.

The importance of the employment problem is shown in the following table, which gives both current figures and the trend since 1974—the peak year in most countries. (In Germany and the UK, employment had already declined by 20 per cent or more between 1965 and 1974.)

TABLE 8.2
Employment in the steel industry, December 1982

	Numbers ('000)	Index Dec. 1974 = 100
FRG	177.3	76.4
France	95.5	60.5
Italy	92.3	96.5
UK	75.7	40.0
Belgium	42.2	66.2
Netherlands	20.1	80.1
Luxembourg	12.3	52.3
EC-7	515.4	65.1

The trend difference between the UK and Italy is striking. However, it must be remembered that between 1965 and 1978 the Italian industry carried out very large investments, both of extension and modernization. As a result, its equipment is on average the most modern in the EC, but it also carries the heaviest debt burden. Italy is also the only country where production rose from 1974 to 1981, mostly thanks to the development of the Bresciani.

In the first recession, that of 1975, firms attempted to maintain output, and prices fell by 35 to 45 per cent. The EC Commission then intervened to negotiate a programme of 'voluntary restrictions' of production. But in the second recession (1982) it went further and applied articles 58 and 61 of the Rome Treaty to declare a situation of 'manifest crisis'. This enables it to impose production quotas and/or minimum prices.

So far, quotas have been imposed (and their application controlled) and a price level has been 'recommended'. In fact, production quotas appear to be the only available instrument to hold the price line. Thus, the unexpected drop in demand in the middle of 1982 immediately brought about a decline in effective prices, which fell in some cases to 15 to 20 per cent below posted prices. Thus the reduction in quotas for late 1982 and early 1983 aims at getting effective prices back to the level of April 1982 posted prices.

The EC Commission thus assumes at present the essential responsibility for steel policy. One may deplore the fact that the powers which were vested in it in order to maintain competition had to be used in order to build a cartel. However in the short-run it is inevitable.

The immediate objective is to prevent cut-throat competition that would be ruinous to all firms. In the medium-term, the aim is to organize a reduction of capacity and to reach a level of efficiency that can ensure the viability of the surviving plants. A necessary condition is to limit the power of the national governments, since rationality at the Community level can run into conflict with national interests, as perceived by governments.

At the Copenhagen meeting of the Council of Ministers in 1982, the Commission obtained an agreement in principle that overall capacity should be reduced by 20 per cent. However, most governments faced with the social problems this entails wish the cuts to be made elsewhere and are defending the line that their domestic capacity should be reduced less than their neighbours'. Apportioning the cuts will thus involve complex and protracted negotiations.

In theory the Commission retains a dominant position. The rules of competition allow it to forbid public subsidies. It has used this legal power to rule that no national subsidies will be allowed after 1985. This will be a major test of power and every effort must be made to hold on to this deadline. Weakness in this respect would compromise the whole effort to establish a viable industry.

All investment programmes must also be approved by the Commission. It has ruled that no such programmes will be accepted unless accompanied by a restructuring plan of the firm, which would normally involve a reduction in total capacity. Should a proposed investment increase capacity in one plant, this should be offset by a reduction elsewhere in the firm.

Legal instruments therefore exist. Their essential importance may reside in enabling the governments to shift on to the Commission the responsibility for unpopular decisions. Still, the use of such instruments will have to be negotiated.

The first problem for the Commission will lie in defining the policy criteria it will attempt to enforce, and it is to this issue that we now turn.

IV. Possible guidelines for Community policy

In the short-term, the policy problem focuses essentially on the appropriate price level. In the medium-term (1985–6), prices are still a main issue, but bound up with the decision regarding the level of capacity to be retained and the amount of modernization investment required. Finally there is the micro-economic problem of defining criteria for choosing which plants to retain.

The following discussion will pay most attention to the medium-term problem, since short-term pricing policy depends on medium-term objectives.

It was mentioned above that the EC is still a substantial net exporter. Thus the first question that arises is whether capacity targets should be based on maintaining this situation. This appears to be primarily a question of relative prices.

But the problem of external cost competitiveness appears intractable. Rates of exchange at the end of 1982 ($1 = DM 2.4) put domestic US prices for many products well above European prices. One may, however, consider the US dollar as overvalued. Should it decline substantially in real terms (that is, taking into account relative inflation rates), the price relation might be upset. Domestic Japanese prices are also above world market prices. One must also ask how relevant relative costs are for the imports of semi-finished steel from Eastern Europe. At the present stage, it is clear that international quotations are more or less dumping prices and a poor guide to the allocation of resources.

In terms of markets, the situation is clearer. The geographic distribution for the last two years on which data are available is shown in Table 8.3. The stability of the trade with the first five areas contrasts with the volatility of the last three, where large gains were posted in 1981 and the largest declines (presumably) occurred in 1982. Markets in Asia and Latin America may be lost to Japanese competition or the build-up of local capacity. There would still remain a substantial amount of net exports to markets protected in some form or another (be it by transport costs or long-term contracts). While net exports are likely to shrink in the future, they will remain substantial in the medium-term.

Domestic demand is also liable to violent shocks, since stocks can

TABLE 8.3

EC net exports of steel products (10^6 tonnes)

Markets	1980	1981
Other W. European	2.5	2.1
Soviet Union	2.3	2.0
Other E. European	−1.4	−1.5
African	2.7	2.7
Middle Eastern	2.3	2.0
United States	2.5	4.8
Other American	1.4	2.0
Other Asian, etc.	1.0	2.3
Total	13.2	16.4

represent three to four months' output. Capacity to be maintained could then correspond to consumption at the cyclical peak, plus some marginal allowance for stock accumulation. This could imply rates of capacity utilization of 70 to 90 per cent, according to cyclical phases.

The previous discussion was based on the continued prospect of slow growth, which suggested that 140 million tonnes might be the maximum capacity required. Uncertainty about the macro-economic projections does, however, call for prudence. Should the miracle of rapid growth take place, another 10 million tonnes of capacity might be needed by 1987.

In any case, starting from a level of 200 million tonnes, the agreed 20 per cent reduction of capacity is very likely to be insufficient, and further cuts may well be required later. This also is, to some extent, a question of relative prices.

The EC is primarily an exporter of finished products based on steel. Metal products, machinery, and transport equipment (excluding planes) account for about one-third of exports to third countries, and thus play an essential role in the balance of payments.

Steel inputs do not, however, weigh very heavily in the cost of these products. (At the lower limit they account for 7 per cent of the value of machinery, according to the German input–output table for 1975.[2]) Still, the EC is essentially an indirect steel exporter, and its basic interest lies in maintaining its competitive position in the more sophisticated products which embody a large proportion of value added. In this perspective, the domestic price of steel should be as low as is compatible with the maintenance of a viable steel-producing industry.

The present system of quotas, allocating production among all firms, stands immediately condemned on this criterion. Indeed, it is inefficient in two respects: the price that goes with it should cover the costs of *all* firms, and costs are reckoned for operation at, say, 60 per cent of capacity. Compare this with a situation where the 25 per cent least efficient plants have closed down, and the same volume of production is concentrated on the remaining equipment, operating at 80 per cent of capacity.

Since marginal cost at the level of the firm can be assumed constant in the 60 to 80 per cent range, the elimination of high-cost producers would reduce the industry's marginal cost for the same total output. At the same time, overheads would now be spread over a larger production, and unit total costs would be reduced for each surviving firm. On both counts, the industry's equilibrium price (reckoned on the basis of full costs) would be lower.

Such notional cost curves for various levels of output and capacity could be computed, using the technical data of the firms. They could be used to define a set of medium-term target prices, which (at present costs of inputs and labour) would of course be substantially lower than the prices which have to be set on the basis of the quota system.

These reference prices should be used by firms in planning their medium-term reorganization. Firms should be asked to show whether they are capable of covering their costs at these prices and at what capacity. In order to avoid overly optimistic estimates of progress, they should indicate how they plan to come down from their present cost levels to the reference price.

There are, of course, substantial complications behind the previous simple-minded statement. The first relates to complementary investment. Many firms can lower their costs by removing bottlenecks in the production flow, or by replacing obsolete equipment at some stage of the process. Indeed, if given enough money at no cost, most firms could become technically efficient and increase their capacity as well. This is liable to be a temptation to some governments. It must, however, be stressed that the social yield of investments which would justify the maintenance of redundant capacity in terms of costs is nil—or negative.

Thus such proposed investment should be subject to a strict rule of financial accounting. Even if governments are prepared to supply funds on an equity basis, a fairly high real rate of return should be required.

The most effective safeguard lies in the Commission rule mentioned earlier: investment programmes will be accepted only if attended by a sufficient reduction in capacity.

The medium-term objective may then be redefined in terms of obtaining the minimum cost with the minimum investment outlay. Of course firms would be expected to reinvest their internally generated funds, and thus to increase over time the efficiency of their plant. This factor should indeed be taken into account when setting price targets.

Other problems arise on the price side: all firms do not sell on the same markets or under the same terms. Some are integrated down-stream and sell a substantial part of their output to subsidiaries, which offer a fairly stable outlet. In some cases, long-term contracts also offer protected markets. Some firms, on the other hand, sell mostly semi-finished products and face a greater part of the risks and lower quotations of exports to third markets.

Location factors can also play a role, not only on the cost but also on the price side. Some firms must absorb higher transport costs than others in order to reach their markets. A common reference price (meaning, in effect, a posted price) does not imply a common average sales price per tonne.

Such factors must be taken into account when assessing the viability of firms: cost effectiveness is not the only criterion.

It is clear that the type of criteria suggested here would not meet all cases. However, it could be hoped that firms would realize that for part (or the whole) of their capacity, they would in any case not be capable of meeting the target prices, and that this could substantially facilitate the painful and difficult process of allocating the reductions in capacity. In this respect the announcement effects of the December 1982 Copenhagen decisions (stating that existing capacity was 20 per cent above foreseeable demand) are likely to be even more important.

Even in the short-run, pricing policy has a role to play: not only could lower target prices be announced for the medium-term, but a progressive reduction of posted prices could be announced. The main object would be to maintain pressure on firms and shake them out of the complacency arising from the reconstituted cartel.

In this respect it would be useful to encourage the use of the market mechanism. Firms are already free to exchange quotas for different types of products. Should the sale of quotas also be permitted in order to help weaker firms bow out gracefully? It must be recognized that the exchange (or sale) of quotas, if it is to become a regular medium-term flow, may require partial change in ownership. Thus if a rolling mill is to be fed with steel from two different firms, it may have to be made into a joint subsidiary.

Notes and Sources

[1] These figures are from Eurofer data and refer to steel products. They exclude Denmark, Ireland, and Greece and differ slightly from the Eurostat figures.

[2] As published by Eurostat, Brussels, March 1982.

IX

The European
Information Technology Industry

MAURICE ENGLISH*

European opinion[1]

'The battle is already over and Europe has lost; the best we can hope for are partnerships with Japanese and American companies using access to our market as a negotiating tool.'

(Board Member of major EC IT company.)

'The main problem with the European IT industry is the Japanese; without them, there would be no European IT problem.'

(Former national government minister.)

'The European lag in IT is not a problem. I will buy components and equipment from anywhere in the world.'

(EC automobile company board member.)

'Unless one or more of my suppliers masters the technology, my business is destined to fail because I'll always be "late to market" with my products.'

(Director of a numeric control machine tool company.)

'I think we should restrict the use of robots and automatic controls until we can reduce the number of working hours.'

(Member of a government-sponsored study team for automation.)

'In the past, we have made mistakes, but our new programmes in IT should reverse the past downward trend in several sectors.'

(Senior civil servant with responsibility for national IT programme design.)

I. Introduction

The importance and the promise of the information-technology industry is best summed up by Kenneth Baker, Minister for Information Technology in the United Kingdom.

* Head of Intelligence Unit, Information-Technologies Task Force, Commission of the EC.

Information Technology is the fastest developing area of industrial and business activity in the Western World. Its markets are huge, its applications multitudinous, and its potential for increasing efficiency immense. Without doubt it will be the engine of economic growth for at least the rest of the century. Britain's economic prosperity depends on the success with which we manufacture its products and provide and exploit its services.[2]

Although it is difficult to be precise about an industry in which technology and manufacturing methods are changing rapidly, if current market and productivity trends continue, the world IT industry will top $1,000,000,000,000 a year in the early 1990s.[3] Given the size, and more importantly, the strategic importance and high growth rate of the IT sector, Europe must become or remain competitive in technology and price with the US and Japan. Europe's deteriorating performance in this high-technology area and Japan's increasing success will be clearly demonstrated in this chapter. The ability of even the largest EC member states to match US and Japanase competitors must be doubted.

Undoubtedly there is much waste and duplication of effort by rival member states and their 'national champions'—Siemens, Thomson, ICL, etc. In addition, as the structure of the European industry and its market is examined—from mainframe computers and components through consumer electronics, telecommunications, and broadcasting —it will become obvious that small, protected, national markets and their accompanying attitudes, policies, laws, and regulations have in generally severely handicapped IT developments in Europe.

In a sector as wide and pervasive as IT, isolated examples can be found to support almost any view. Nevertheless, in the absence of comprehensive statistics, it is only by examining a series of illustrations and examples that we can form an impression of the nature of the policies required to resolve their difficulties, favour their growth, and establish their competitivity on world markets.

The evidence forces recognition that possibly only the creation of Community scale markets could support the leading edge that producers and applications require. These markets do not at present exist. Further, it will be shown that in many cases only a truly European market, even if based on some kind of market pooling and sharing, could provide the competitive stimulus and scale of production required if Europe is to match its competitors' technologies and production costs.

The information technologies market has demonstrated a remarkable degree of independence of economic cycles, showing little more than a hesitation in growth during periods of recession. Growth in hardware shipment value is much slower than in volume of units shipped, owing to the tremendous improvements in price/performance ratios. But growth has continued even during periods of recession.[4] Average annual growth in sales during 1980–5 is estimated at 14 per cent a year.[5]

TABLE 9.1
Market potential in Western Europe for Electronics
($ billion)

Sector	1979	1981	1984*	1991*
Electronic data processing	15.58	23.00	41.76	50.00
Components	15.58	19.00	23.04	45.00
Consumer	13.94	15.00	14.04	24.00
Telecommunications	12.30	15.00	18.72	42.00
Communications and military	8.20	11.00	15.84	22.00
Medical and industrial	3.28	3.50	5.76	12.00
Control and instruments	9.02	11.00	15.84	32.00
Office	4.10	5.50	8.64	17.00
Total	82.00	103.00	144.00	244.00

* Forecasts.

Sources: *Mackintosh Electronics Yearbook*, 1981, and I. M. Mackintosh, in Gareth Locksley, *The European Telecommunications Industry: Competition, Concentration and Competitiveness*, Commission of the EC IV/669/82, p. 44, 1982.

I.1. The IT market structure

In Europe, information technology markets are dominated by US multinationals. ICL, CII-HB and Siemens in the UK, France,[6] and Germany, respectively, have substantial market shares only at home (as Figure 9.1 shows). Systematic international shares are held by US multinationals making or buying peripheral equipment from US groups, rather than from more nationalistic Japanese firms

IBM dominates world data-processing markets with 60 per cent of total value, and Burroughs, Honeywell, National Cash Register, Control Data Corporation, and Digital Equipment Corporation have substantial shares. These firms set price levels, standards, and performance. For many years IBM supplied complete systems with applications software at an overall 'bundled price' in which system costs have little relationship to hardware manufacturing costs. Rental charges were, and are, often based on use. Even now when unbundling is possible, only sophisticated customers can create their own system. Most customers rely on back-up and support by major system suppliers, who are usually the manufacturers and who usually help users set up their systems.

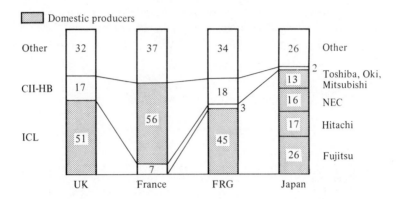

Fig. 9.1: Share of market of major computer products in Europe and Japan
(excluding IBM).

Source: ICL, 'Government Policies and the Computer Industry', Yano
Research Institute.

The major system suppliers clearly specify their system in terms of
their own products and can thus pressure users who wish to add non-
proprietary elements to their systems. Further, non-proprietary peripherals must necessarily conform to supplier software and interface
specifications.[7]

The peripherals and system components A powerful *de facto*
standardization exists, principally IBM but CDC and DEC standards
exist in limited areas. Peripherals market competitors must conform
to these standards or expect a minimal market share. Competitors
must often wait for IBM product announcements to ensure new
products conform, thus putting at risk their technology or performance
advantages. The prices charged by system suppliers cover their back-up
capability, even when apparently unbundled. Production costs are
typically about 25 per cent of a system sales price. Peripherals represent about half of the value. Where back-up is especially good the ratio
is higher. These high prices cannot be commanded by an independent
peripherals supplier unless he has a captive market.

To be successful, therefore, a typical European peripherals manufacturer needs to drive production costs down well below that of
a systems supplier. As the major systems manufacturers, such as IBM,
Burroughs, and CDC are also the biggest manufacturers of peripherals,
this necessitates very high production volumes for selected products,
to be competitive, or specialist products not covered by the major
suppliers.[8]

I.2. *Mainframe computers in Europe*

In the mainframe computer market, IBM creates and shapes the environment. IBM has first place in every European EDP (electronic data processing) market and in some cases well over half the total.

An integrated company, IBM manufactures almost its entire product range. The purchase of outside products, for example Qume Daisy Wheel printers, is normally an interim measure provoked by development delays or failures. IBM is not in the OEM business (original equipment manufacturer),[9] although IBM purchases photocopiers from Minolta, which it distributes under the IBM name, and subassemblies from Toshiba for a recently-launched large facsimile machine.

IBM is also involved in detailed discussions with Japan's largest electronics manufacturer Matsushita Electric, on a possible joint venture in Japan. Matsushita has been developing a range of office automation equipment handling graphics and a variety of facsimile machines. The joint venture may produce terminals, office automation equipment, and small business computers.[10]

The major member states have national champions, each strong and comfortable on home markets, but weak outside, even in European markets. Once they are exposed to the cold winds of the real world, Japanese and American products demonstrate, all too frequently, their greater competitivity.

With the exception of Olivetti in France, no European firm is in the top three outside its home country.[11] In addition, ICL, Olivetti and Siemens use Japanese technology and import Japanese mainframe computers.[12]

West Germany has failed to develop a strong computer industry in spite of $1.6 billion in government support during the years 1967 to 1982. The eight main German-owned computer manufacturers accounted for less than 40 per cent of domestic production in 1980. More than half of the $5.96 billion total was produced by IBM.[13] Most of the support funds were given to Siemens hoping it would turn into a viable rival to IBM. But its annual computer business is less than 3 per cent of IBM's revenues and is still losing money. Ironically Nixdorf, which received only $40 million of support, has grown faster and more profitably. Nixdorf specializes in small computers where IBM is less of a threat.

Dr Thomas Sommarlatte of Arthur D. Little, rhetorically asks why there is not an impressive number of profitable German EDP companies, and answers:

Most of them come from traditional electro-mechanical industries. They have had difficulty understanding computers and they put in the wrong people. Too often they tried to reinvent the wheel.[14]

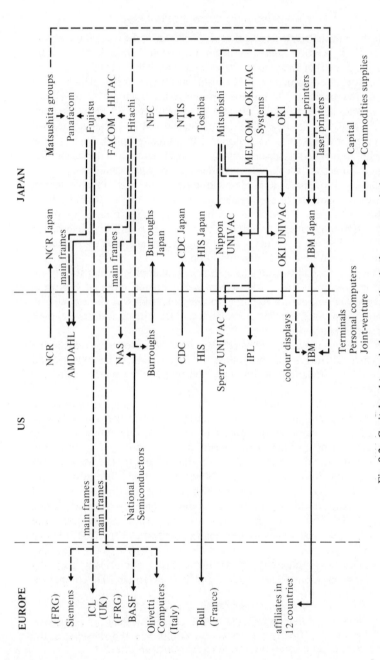

Fig. 9.2: Capital and technical co-operation in the computer industry.

Source: Economisuto, 13 July 1982.

In France; CII-Honeywell Bull—the heavy loss making, State-controlled computer group—has said it will remain in the red until 1986 at least. Squeezed by huge cash requirements to run ambitious investment programmes and cover current losses, the firm has pushed for more government finance, $372-425 million in 1983. French authorities are providing $212-83 million, an amount described by Francis Lortentz as insufficient to build up CII-HB's activities as the government desires. The group is believed to have lost well over $142 million in 1982. Doubling sales in recent years has been financed by a $1 billion debt.[15]

Supercomputers With a market approximately 50 per cent larger than West Germany's, Japan has two companies, Fujitsu and Hitachi, that were accepting supercomputer orders for autumn 1983 deliveries. They expect to sell about thirty systems over the next four years.[16] The Japanese hardware is the world's fastest, and thought to be about equal to the US's top two computers: CRAY ONE and Control Data Corporation's Cyber 205. Moreover, Japan may be far ahead in developing the next generation of supercomputers.[17] NEC (Nippon Electric Corporation) is also building a giant 'state of the art' computer as part of their fifth generation programme. There is nothing equivalent being done in Europe, unless one counts Dr Amdhal's Triology venture.

Europe has no independent supercomputer capability. France has launched a feasibility study for '*un grand ordinateur scientifique et culturel*', as there is great concern in military, scientific, and political circles with respect to undue dependence on Washington attitudes. The Euro-Siberian pipeline affair provoked political pressures taking the form of incredibly long and exceptional delays in the obligatory American government authorizations required before delivery could be made of two CRAY ONE supercomputers for French scientific research.[18] Similar reasons led General de Gaulle to introduce the first 'Plan Calcul', when in 1964 the Americans placed an embargo on a Control Data machine required by France to simulate H-bomb tests.[19]

The costs of the research and development required to build a supercomputer are estimated, perhaps optimistically, at Fr. 300 million and are not considered exorbitant. There would be important benefits, it is claimed, and production of the machines would not cost more than several million francs each when built on an individual basis.

The cost of developing and building a supercomputer may, however, be much more expensive than the above estimates. Last year, official French estimates suggested a supercomputer programme would cost as much as Fr. 800 million.[20] Whether the estimated cost is Fr. 300 or Fr. 800 million, there clearly could be a case for a joint European venture. Evidently the larger the resources required, the more powerful the case for co-operation. Such co-operation could be organized along Airbus lines, and involve co-operation on a bilateral or Community level. Strategic embargo risks would be significantly reduced, the cost to any one country reduced, and the technology developed of benefit to the entire European IT industry.

However, there is a question which must be resolved. Can we be certain a supercomputer effort is a necessary, rather than a prestige, contribution to the development of the European IT industry and its competitivity? Or would it wastefully misdirect scientific resources? It is worth remarking here that Japan has decided such an effort is important.

II. Industrial requirements

II.1. NC machine tools

The European machine tool industry is the world's leading exporter. Hence, its very survival depends on its ability to compete internationally.[21] The European industry employs 210,000, against the US's 96,500 and Japan's 34,000. The value of each employee's output is $23,000, $27,000, and $54,000 respectively.[22] The EC industry's net exports, $2.4 billion in 1982, are such that to insulate it from international competition would be catastrophic.[23] Yet in 1980, with the exception of the Netherlands, all EC countries were net volume importers of NC (numerical control) systems.[24]

The introduction of microprocessors has led to a brand new concept in machine tools. Recent trends demonstrate European machine tool manufacturers' declining ability to overcome external competition. Important advanced sectors involving numerical control are vulnerable.[25] In 1980 Japan produced more than three times the number of NC units as Europe, and 50 per cent more than the US and EC combined.[26] In 1981 Japanese exports of numerically-controlled lathes rose 15 per cent in value, while exports of machining centres rose by almost 60 per cent.[27] CECIMO (European Committee for Co-operation of the Machine Tool Industry) estimated Japanese penetration (by unit) of the Community market in 1980 at 36 per cent for machining centres, and 30 per cent for NC lathes, compared to 4.2 per cent and 17.9 per cent in 1976.

The Commission considers the European machine tool industry (comprised of more than 2,800 enterprises), and even more the robot industry, as strategic sectors in which a Community position of dependence must be ruled out.[28] But the European machine tool industry must be able to count on a domestic supply of standardized numeric controls matching its requirements. In a few years the

	Mainframe	DDP[1]	Storage periphs	Printers incl. T/printers	WP	FAX[2]	Data comms.	Private switching	Public switching	Telecomms. (general)
AEG/Olympia	–	e	–	e	Ew	Ew	–	–	–	–
Cable & Wireless	–	–	–	–	√	–	(W)	(W)	(W)	(W)
CII-HB	E	E	E	E	–	–	–	–	–	–
CIT-Alcatel	–	De	–	e	–	√	De	D	W	W
GEC	–	d	–	–	W	–	–	D	D	W
ICL	Ew	Dw	–	–	–	–	–	(√)	–	–
ITT (Europe)	–	(e)	–	De	–	(e)	E	E	E	W
Mannesman-Tally/Kienzle	–	E	√	W	d	–	–	–	–	–
Matra	–	Dw	–	–	–	–	–	–	–	D
Nixdorf	√	W	–	e	d	–	–	d	–	–
Olivetti	(e)	W	W	W	W	–	W	d	W	W
Philips	–	W	–	W	W	√	W	W	D	w
Plessey	–	–	–	–	√	(D)	W	D	–	w
Racal	–	–	–	–	–	–	W	–	–	W
Siemens	E	e	D	W	d	E	W	W	W	W
STC	–	–	–	D	√	(d)	D	D	w	W
Thomson-CSF	–	Ew	–	–	–	w	W	W	W	W
Triumph-Adler	–	Ew	w	–	w	–	–	–	–	–

Key Upper case – Strong
Lower case – Some strength
D, d – Domestic
E, e – Europe
W, w – Rest of world

√ – Has some product capability and market presence but no real strength
( ) – Bought-in product(s)

[1] DDP = Digital Data Processing
[2] FAX = code word for facsimile

Figure 9.3: Market strengths of major EC-IT companies.

Source: Dr Ian Galbraith, Mackintosh Consultants, December 1982.

TABLE 9.2

Development of the NC machine tool market in
the EC, US, and Japan (by value)

	Production %		Consumption %	
	1976	1980	1976	1980
EC	41	35	25	30
US	38	24	32	28
Japan	13	30	20	15
Others	8	11	23	27
Total	100	100	100	100

Source: Consultronique, 1981.

European market will be an estimated 100,000 units a year compared with 12,000 at present.

Close co-operation between EC machine tool manufacturers and producers of numeric controls is lacking. It is required to ensure that necessary investments can be made, and standardization agreements reached for interfaces, machines, control systems and operators. The consultation and co-ordination exercise for interface standardization has started. The Commission has also called upon machine tool and electronics manufacturers to submit joint proposals to ESPRIT (the European Strategic Programme of Research in Information Technologies).[29]

The European electronics sector is weak (see Figure 9.4) and is unable to satisfy on competitive terms the special needs arising from the use of electronically controlled machinery.[30] Further, it is difficult to find long-term finance and high-risk capital for a sector with low profits composed of small- and medium-sized enterprises.[31] A measure of the Japanese advantages over Europe are that its average product prices are 30–40 per cent lower.[32] In February 1983 Japan agreed to exercise some restraint over prices and exports of NC machining centres and lathes[33]—but one can wonder if the principal effect will be to damage European user industries' productivity and increase user-industry costs.

II.2. Robots

The European robot market was over $100 million in 1982, representing about 25 per cent of the world market.[34] Westinghouse expects the American robot market to grow from $150 million in 1981 to $2 billion in 1990, with another billion in sales of peripheral equipment—and America accounts for only a third of the world market for robots.[35]

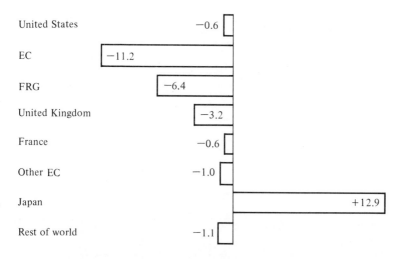

Fig. 9.4: Per cent change in share of world machine tool exports, 1981 *vs* 1970.

Source: American Machinist.

Japanese production growing at 38 per cent and 20 per cent in 1981 and 1982 respectively,[36] and General Motors' plans to install 30,000 robots on its production lines by 1990[37] illustrate the market's potential, and that giant companies are moving in on the robotics market.[38]

There will be a bruising battle for the huge robots markets between the Japanese robotics industry (led by FANUC), established robot manufacturers (like Westinghouse's Unimation, Cincinnati Milacron, and the Swedish firm ASEA), and affluent American latecomers (like General Motors, IBM, and Bendix).[39] As Unimation's founder and president, Joe Engelberger said, it is inevitable that the industry, consisting of many small manufacturers and a few big ones would undergo severe rationalization in the next years.[40] Further, MITI has chosen robotics as a targeted strategic sector.[41] So far Japanese exports of industrial robots have been very small, 3 per cent of production; but, growth in sales could be especially rapid.[42] Structurally, more than 60 per cent of Japanese machine tool exports in 1980 were NC machines compared with 16.2 per cent for the EC and 17.3 per cent for the US.[43]

Britain is making a serious attempt to establish itself as a major robot supplier by encouraging Japanese and American firms to build robots in the UK. For example, the National Research and Development Corporation is providing a $3.2 million loan against future sales and the Department of Industry a $1.6 million grant in order to

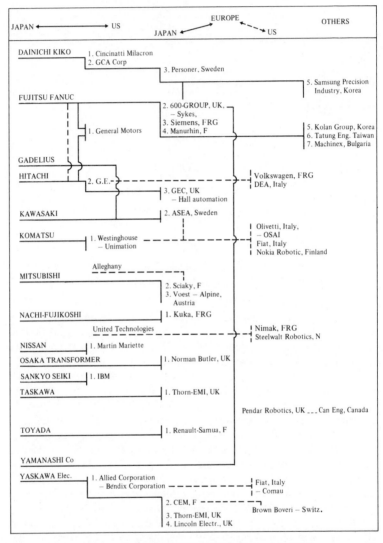

Fig. 9.5: Robots: Cross relationships—technology agreements, OEM arrangements, etc. among Japanese, American, and European firms.

support a $10 million investment by Unimation's UK subsidiary in a 250-job expansion project. The local parts content is now about 90 per cent, higher than the 75 per cent minimum within the three years stipulated by the Department of Industry. And UK-produced robots cost 30 per cent less than an American import.[44]

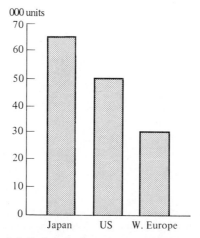

Fig. 9.6: Projected robot usage world-wide, 1985.

Source: Predicasts

Fig. 9.7: Estimate of robot population.

Source: Robot Institute of America.

In West Germany the situation is probably worse than in the UK. Even the huge West German company Siemens has an OEM (original equipment manufacturer) agreement with Fujitsu FANUC.

The French Economic and Social Committee estimates that the work of 4.6 million individuals in France will be affected by robotics.[45] Cie Electro-Méchanique now has an agreement with Yaskawa. This follows requests made through government and private channels for Japanese co-operation in developing and introducing robots.

— Yaskawa Electric will provide CEM with large assembly-carrier robots on an original equipment manufacturer (OEM) basis for marketing in France.

— Yaskawa & Co., Yaskawa Electric's trading division, will import small assembly robots from CEM's robot division, SCEMI (Société de Construction et d'Exploitation de Matériels Industriels) for sales in Japan.

— Yaskawa Electric will extend full co-operation to CEM to help produce large robots in France.

CEM, a wholly-owned subsidiary of Switzerland's Brown Boveri & Cie, will thus emerge as a 'specialized robot builder', designated by the French government and capable of handling both large and small robots.[46]

In general terms, the independent Community robot production and sales levels are lamentable. Things could get worse: IBM is reported to be planning to enter the robot field.[47] European prospects are at present poor (see Figure 9.8).

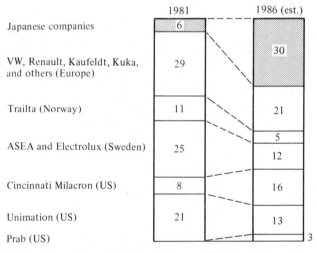

Fig. 9.8: Percentage share of Western European robot installations by suppliers, 1981–6.

Source: Western European Robotics, *Creative Strategies*, March 1982.

III. European robot technology

High marks are given by both European and American firms to Japanese robot-making technology. Together with growing recognition by US and European governments that factory robotization is a prerequisite for economic revitalization, this has led to American and European companies entering into a great variety of arrangements with Japanese firms while seeking Japanese technology and machines. According to Mr Imabe, President of FANUC, the leading Japanese robot firm:

Both Japanese and Western manufacturers are anxious to have an edge over competitors in promising robot markets, but we lay behind in basic research. US and European firms keep ahead of us in the field of high efficiency robots capable of walking around factories and offices on their own feet, and more sophisticated robots connected with CAD/CAM systems.[48]

Europe is not without success, for example Pendar Robotics' electro-pneumatic robot sells in Japan, the US, and Canada.[49]

III.1. The essential components

The European electronics industry in this strategically critical area is basically extremely weak, particularly in the mass markets vital for many applications and electronics products. The United States and Japan together control about 90 per cent of the world IC (integrated circuit) production.[50] A first task of any European IT policy must be to reconquer the internal market and master the essential production know-how and technological knowledge required to successfully develop IT products and applications.

European companies have had to invest heavily in US semiconductor companies to gain access to technology and leading-edge customers,[51] as shown below:

European investor	US company	Per cent ownership
Adolf Schindling	Solid State Scientific	25
Bosch	American Microsystems	25
CIT-Alcatel	Semi Process Inc.	25
Ferranti	Interdesign	100
GEC	Circuit Technology	100
Lucas	Siliconix	25
National Enterprise Board	INMOS	100
Philips	Signetics	100
Schlumberger	Fairchild	100
Siemens	Advanced Micro Devices	20
Siemens	Dickson Associates	100
Siemens	FMC	100
Siemens	Microwave Semiconductor	100
Siemens	Threshold Technology	23.5
Siemens	Litronix	100

The only vacuum-valve manufacturer in the world to make the transition via transistors to semiconductors reasonably successfully was

Philips. Similarly, no slide-rule company made a successful transition to electronic calculators. In Europe many of these relatively unsuccessful valve companies continue to dominate their home nation's electronics industry—they are Europe's 'national champions', the best we have.

'Japanese firms are now among the leaders in production of semi-conductors and components. Normura Securities estimated that in 1980 the sales of Nippon Electric in this product area were about equal to those of Motorola, with Texas Instruments still the leader. Hitachi, Toshiba, and National Semiconductor are closely grouped together behind the three leaders in sales. These statistics, however, under-estimate the US position, since they take no account of IBM and ATT, which produce only for internal consumption, but must be among the leaders in the field. Note, too, that *no European firms are seriously in this competition*. Micro-electronics seems to represent the future, but the drama is being played out between Japan and America, *with Europe out of it*', writes Akio Etori—award-winning, highly respected science and technology writer, and managing editor of the science magazine *Saiensu*.[52]

This is not only a Japanese viewpoint. A study prepared for the Joint Economic Committee of the US Congress, published in February 1983, stated, 'The case of integrated circuits should be seen as para-digmatic of competition in advanced technology industries where

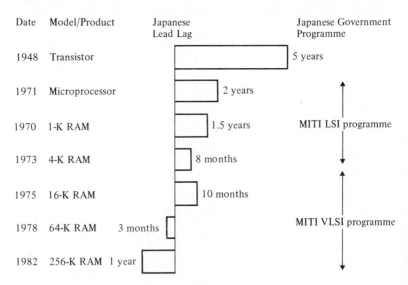

Fig. 9.9: Lead time of various IC producers *vs* Japan.

Source: Commission of the EC.

government support and private collaboration can serve to create real competitive advantage. *The competitive battle for leadership in this industry has become a fight between American and Japanese producers fought out in American and European markets.'*[53] In contrast, six major Japanese manufacturers are set to manufacture 64-K static RAM. Toshiba, Hitachi, and Fujitsu have already shipped 64-K RAMs to home and overseas markets. The others, NEC, Mitsubishi, and OKI, expect to start shipment shortly. These 64-K SRAMs are likely to become standard computer memory chips as they become available. They are similar in complexity to the 256-K DRAMs which are the current state of the art in the Japanese and American semiconductor industry and which are already supplied by Japanese manufacturers. NEC and OKI are now ready to take orders for megabit memories. Further NEC labs are working with four-megabit design.[54] In 1982 Japan produced an estimated 80 per cent of world 64-K RAMs.[55]

Despite 64-K RAM production by Siemens and INMOS, we should have no illusions. Europe's production levels are miniscule and far behind the learning curve, which foresees a 30 per cent reduction in

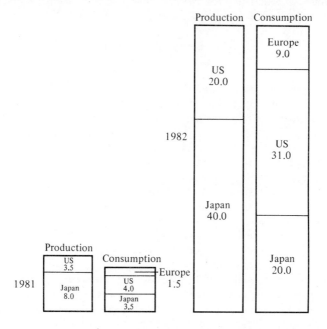

Fig. 9.10: Production and consumption of 64-K dynamic RAMS (millions of units).

Source: SIA, Dataquest.

production costs for each doubling of production. In addition the technologies are well behind the 'state of the art' in an industry which loses 25 per cent of its sales value for each year of technology lag. With government support Siemens, Europe's largest semiconductor manufacturer, has invested heavily to catch up in semiconductors. Industry experts are impressed by its efforts and agree their latest 64-K RAM compares well with those of its Japanese and American rivals.[56]

INMOS is the UK government-backed microchip manufacturer. More than $160 million of government funds has been invested. The flagship product, a 64-K dynamic RAM, started being manufactured in Wales, February 1983, four months ahead of schedule. The major shareholder is the British Technology Group. The Department of Industry and INMOS considered the 64-K DRAM will have a better chance of success than expanding production of 16-K static RAMs where main applications are in defence.[57]

Ferranti produces fifty versions of gate arrays. Launched in 1981, the company is reported to have the largest share of the world market (30 per cent). Customers are supplied with an intelligent CAD terminal, $75,000, for the basic 10,000 gate array design work. The Sinclair ZX81 uses Ferranti gate arrays.

IV. Consumer electronics

IV.1. The European TV market

The importance of common norms and standards is well illustrated in Europe's fragmented TV market. Philips has to supply over 100 different types of television sets to meet differing European standards.[58] In colour TV, Germany and the United Kingdom adopted slightly different versions of PAL, and France SECAM. Despite protracted negotiations a stereo TV standard has not yet been set, but Germany has already unilaterally adopted its own.[59]

Sometimes it is argued that setting standards early, as in colour TV in the United States, can result in sub-optimal decisions. Nevertheless, the Japanese conquered the US colour TV market by adopting America's own standard—not by creating a better one.[60] MITI, the Japanese Ministry of International Trade and Industry, succeeded in influencing the Japanese industry to adopt US colour TV standards in 1960, six years before Europe could agree on any standard whatsoever and consumer demand was stimulated by a special reduced VAT rate.[61]

The Japanese dominate the production of TV tubes. AEG-Telefunken's experiment demonstrates the validity of Mr Grundig's views regarding the need to organize and allocate component manufacture and specialization on a joint basis at the European level in order

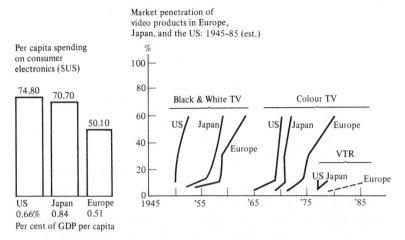

Fig. 9.11: Comparison of consumer electronics markets in EC, US, and Japan.

* UK, France, and FRG only. GDP based on purchasing power parity method.
Sources: Macintosh; *Electronics Weekly*; IMF; McKinsey analysis; OECD.

to produce price-competitive IT products. Especially in the case of television sets, tubes, and videotape recorders, Grundig states that the scale of production of Community firms and factories is too small to meet the Japanese high-volume production costs. In his opinion this was the main disadvantage European industry experienced when facing Japanese competition.[62] Heinz Dürr, the AEG group's chief executive said:

There is no way we can survive in home goods in the medium term with our volumes of production. The group's modern television plant at Celle operated at only 77 per cent of its 800,000 capacity last year.[63]

In February 1983 Japan agreed to limit TV-tube exports to the EC for three years, under the weather forecast formula. The upper limit for medium- and large-screen tubes in 1983 was 900,000 units.[64]

In the UK, employment is being increased from 90 to 190 in half an old Pye television plant purchased by Sanyo. They will be the first Japanese video firm manufacturing VTRs (videotape recorders) in the UK. Sanyo states it started television production to get round voluntary import restrictions agreed between the UK–Japanese authorities four years ago. Sanyo's own contribution was 250,000 units. *Perhaps the most marked effect is that Sanyo's ninety workers make 1,200 TVs a week, while Pye's workforce of 1,100 made only three times as many.*

Sanyo followed Sony, Hitachi, Toshiba, and Mitsubishi in making televisions in Britain. Sanyo claims it is not easy to get British components for its sets. They say they have to rely on Japan, as its UK plant was set up very rapidly and has only been producing for four months. The factory manager claimed just over half of the components were British.

The collapse of the indigenous UK TV industry in the 1970s certainly damaged component suppliers. Even so, Japanese manufacturers have a clear preference for Japanese parts even when a UK firm could supply. Not surprisingly therefore, Sanyo VTRs will be made almost entirely with parts from the Far East. Production is to start at 5,000 and rise to 10,000 a month over a couple of years. By then Thorn-EMI and Mitsubishi will also be manufacturing in the UK. The latter intended to assemble VTRs, initially at 1,000 sets a month in autumn 1983, a level which 'may ultimately' be doubled. All this occurs in a factory which is rent free for the first two years.[65]

IV.2. European VTR production

TDK indicates world VTR growth estimates of 63 per cent, 30 per cent, and 22 per cent in 1981, 1982, and 1983 respectively.[66] European makers sold an estimated 800–900 thousand units in 1982 in the EC.[67] The only two indigenous manufacturers—Philips and Grundig, linked by Philips' 24.5 per cent equity stake in Grundig—produce between 5 and 10 per cent of world production. Their 2000 system is not compatible with the Japanese VHS or Beta systems.[68]

Grundig, the leading West German consumer electronics group, is hoping to double the production of the European video-recorder 2000 system that claims 30 per cent of the West German, and 20 per cent of the European, market. In contrast *Telefunken* markets the VHS system developed by Japan Victor Co. (JVC), which claims overall about 55 per cent of the West German market, and Sony's Beta system, accounting for the remaining 15 per cent market share. To ensure economies of scale in production, Telefunken entered a joint venture with JVC and Thorn-EMI (UK), one third each, to produce video-recorders in Berlin. Thomson-Brandt has an option to join this venture later.[69]

Japan's ten exporters have 90 per cent of the EC's VTR market.[70] The EC imported about 5 million VTR units in 1983, up from 2.8 million in 1982.[71] Sales in 1982 included about 125,000 semi-finished units and kits, but these were expected to increase in 1983 to 500,000.[72] As a result of quickly completed mass-production VTR systems in Japan, Japanese manufacturers competed with each other for shares of the European market, pushing aside other nation's VTR manufacturers.[73] To ease mounting trade frictions and reduce the impacts of import curbs Japanese manufacturers, with Japanese government support, are promoting production ventures in Europe.[74]

The big three manufacturers—Matsushita, JVC, and Sony—have already started video cassette recorder (VCR) production in Britain or West Germany. Hitachi, Sanyo, and Mitsubishi Electric are also pushing similar production plans. Hitachi has established a new subsidiary in West Germany, Hitachi Consumer Products (Europe), to start production of 60,000 units a year in January 1984. 'In two years, the plant will double the production capacity and have about 400 local workers on its payroll', according to an Hitachi spokesman.

Matsushita Electric Industrial Co. is the latest Japanese company to jump on the European VTR bandwagon. The West German plans of MB Video, a joint venture of Matsushita and Robert Bosch, have gone into operation with an annual production target of 30,000 units a year. 'The MB video plant went on-stream on January 25, as scheduled', said a Matsushita spokesman. 'Sales of the products initially will be limited to West Germany, but we are hoping to increase production and expand the marketing area to all of Europe eventually'. The venture is still a small-scale operation that has about fifty Germans as production workers. Most of the parts and components are being shipped from Japan by Matsushita. This is Matsushita's first VCR plant outside Japan.

Sony and JVC have been building VTRs in Europe since 1982. Sony's West German subsidiary, WEGA, is making VTRs at the rate of 60,000 units a year. JVC's subsidiaries in West Germany and Britain —J2T Video (Berlin) and J2T Video (Newhaven) are turning out 240,000 and 120,000 units a year respectively.

Mitsubishi Electric planned to launch VCR production at the existing TV plant of its British subsidiary in summer 1983 at the rate of 60,000 units a year. An independent VCR plant, opening in the summer in 1984, is to double the production capacity.

Sanyo Electric meanwhile, planned to start VCR production at its British subsidiary's existing TV plant in September 1983.[75] Pressure to manufacture videos in Europe increased as restrictions on imports became imminent. In 1982, *two-million video machines were sold in Britain, 90 per cent of them from Japan.*[76]

Production scale will be similar to that of Hitachi's West German operation—60,000 units initially and double that figure in a few years.[77]

Japanese production of VTR sets was 13,129,000 in 1982—up 38.2 per cent over 1981 and up 44 per cent over 1980. Exports increased 2.06 and 2.13 fold in 1980 and 1981 respectively.[78] Major export markets in 1982 are shown in Table 9.3

Ironically, Britain is the largest market in the world for video recorders. In 1982 2.4 million units were imported.[79] *At present, the only production of VTR's in the UK is Thorn-EMI's. Further, all*

TABLE 9.3
Japanese VTR exports, 1982[80]

Country	Units	Percentage increase 82/1
US	2,504,000	5.5
UK	2,381,000	104.1
West Germany	1,469,000	29.4
France	753,000	198.2
Australia	416,000	108.3

Source: *Japan Times.*

Thorn-EMI's VTRs are assembled under licence from Japan Victor Company, and all components are imported.[81] Thorn-EMI hopes to source some components locally, but admits initially it is likely to be only cabinets and metal casings.

The combined UK production of Sanyo, Mitsubishi and Thorn-EMI, on the basis of present plans, would represent only 15 per cent of last year's import figure. But, almost all components will still be imported.[82]

Japan—EC trade accords   In autumn 1982 France required customs clearance for all VTRs to be made in Poitiers, with documentation in French. With only one extra customs officer assigned, a backlog of an estimated 200,000 recorders built up, and imports were reduced by 90 per cent in November 1982.[83] All these actions were taken despite there being no French manufacturer known to be manufacturing VTRs in France; all VTRs sold were imports, and almost all Japanese.[84]

In February 1983 Japan agreed to limit exports of VTRs for three years under the weather forecast formula. Following negotiations with EC Vice-Presidents Etienne Davignon and Wilhelm Haferkamp, Japan agreed to:

— establish a floor price under the Export and Import Transactions Law to limit 'schuchu gouteki yushutsu' or 'torrential' and 'laser-beam' Japanese VTR exports, and avoid disruption of European markets,
— so treat the European manufacturers, Philips and Grundig, that they will be able to manufacture and market at least 1.2 million VTRs in 1983, and
— limit VTR exports to a maximum of 4.55 million units (including chassis kits) in 1983.

An embarrassing aspect from the EC Commission's point of view is that it will depend largely on Japanese statistics to monitor the agreement. These are produced much more swiftly than import returns from Community member states. The Commission is now urging national capitals to speed up the counting and transmission to Brussels of their import figures.[85]

In 1984 and 1985 adjustments are to be made in a mutually agreeable manner. The EC undertook to normalize French 'Poitiers' procedures, to terminate the Philips and Grundig anti-dumping suit as soon as possible, and to halt the invocation of the GATT Article 23, Paragraph 2.[86] Thanks to this agreement almost all Common Market consumers have now acquired the dubious privilege of being able to pay more for these products, stated *Mainichi.*[87] But in an editorial *Sankei* recalled the development stage of television, when Japan limited the import of colour TV sets by tariffs in order to give the Japanese industry time to grow.[88]

Nevertheless, the agreement has great significance as it showed that even a new industry which was virtually a Japanese monopoly could be subjected to 'voluntary' export restraint.[89]

The February 1983 Japan–EC agreement does not include the next generation of 8 mm VTR systems.[90] In view of the conventional VTR export restraints manufacturers are expected to ensure they have the technology required to market the 8 mm system. The so-called 8 mm video discussion group (formed in March 1983, on the initiative of five VTR manufacturers including Hitachi) proposed outline specifications standardizing:

(i) the recording system,
(ii) 8 mm size tapes,
(iii) cassette size,
(iv) recording duration,
(v) drum diameter, and
(vi) recording methods of audio and visual signals.

Previously many manufacturers were inclined to delay 8 mm sales because of the high VTR demands in and outside Japan, and the incessantly developing videotape-production technologies. Now that increased conventional VTR sales are more difficult some manufacturers may place 8 mm videotape recorders on the market as early as autumn 1983.[91]

IV.3. Videotape

In videotape Japan is again the leader. TDK, the leading videotape manufacturer, indicates estimated world demand for VHS format T-120 videotape as 105, 150, and 207 million rolls in 1981, 1982, and 1983 respectively. TDK tape is up 54 per cent in 1983 and average videotape annual growth rate is 38 per cent.[92]

Japan accounts for about 80 per cent of the world's videotape output. The 1982 production was worth about $2 billion.[93] Magnetic tape manufacturers—such as TDK Electronics, Fuji Photo Film Co., and Hitachi–Maxell Ltd.—have expanded their production capacity by 50–100 per cent.[94]

Plans are afoot to start European video-cassette production in order to ease growing trade frictions, and increase European employment. Sony (France) plans to start production of 12 million video-cassettes a year (summer 1984). Among other companies, Hitachi–Maxell was building a video-cassette plant in Britain to start operation in January 1984, and JVC planned the same in West Germany for spring 1983.[95]

IV.4. Digital audio discs

For digital audio disc (DAD) systems—the very promising, futuristic audio discs and players—three DAD formats had been proposed. But so far only one format is available on Japanese and Hong Kong markets: the Compact Disc (CD) system. This disc and player system was originally developed by Philips, which later sought and received collaboration from Japanese manufacturers in making the CD system the sole global standard system.

Philips of the Netherlands and Sony of Japan have jointly developed the DAD player, which reproduces high quality sounds by reading digitalized sound signals on a disc through a laser device. The player carries about 150 basic patents. Philips owns about 100 of them and Sony about 50. In Japan, more than ten manufacturers have been turning out DAD players since autumn 1982 under licence agreements with Philips and Sony. The Japanese makers started shipping the players to Europe on 1 March 1982, according to the MITI officials. Philips started producing DAD players in Europe in Belgium, during March 1983.[96]

While Japanese manufacturers have been marketing CD players since October 1982, the original developer Philips, for reasons undisclosed, is not yet able to mass-produce its own creation. Not only that, Philips asked Japanese makers to delay marketing CD players in the Common Market until March 1983. Japanese manufacturers have already shipped players to EC countries for marketing. Thomson-Brandt has entered into a contract with a Japanese CD player manufacturer for the supply of Japanese players for marketing under the French firm's brand for six months.[97]

The EC has doubled the import tariff on CD players to 19 per cent. 'For the record, the spokesman of the EC Commission confirmed that it proposed to the Council to set the common external tariff on compact-disc players at 19 per cent for the next five years . . . By proposing this tariff, the Commission intends to give European industry the possibility of establishing itself in this new market before it is overwhelmed by Japanese industry, which has already conquered 75 per cent of the European market for hi-fi equipment.'[98] This is EC discrimination against Japanese products, when effectively no European maker other than Philips is believed to be able to mass-produce CD players. Under the terms of the February 1983 Japan–EC accord on Japanese export curbs for these items, almost all consumers in the Common Market have now acquired the dubious privilege of being able to pay more for products at present otherwise unavailable in Europe.[99]

V. Telecommunications and broadcasting

In today's increasingly competitive world markets, many established positions are being challenged. European markets in 1979 dollars are expected to grow from $12.5 to $17.2 billion from 1982 to 1987, i.e. 6.7 per cent a year. This compares with $19.9 to $29.1 billion in North America and $11.8 to $19.1 billion in Japan for annual growth rates of 7.8 per cent and 10.1 per cent respectively. Other markets are relatively small: Latin America $1.4 and $2 billion, Oceania $0.9 and $1.2 billion, and Africa $0.4 and $0.7 billion in 1982 and 1987, respectively, for annual growth rates of 7.7 per cent, 6.6 per cent, and 8.2 per cent. System markets are growing rapidly, particularly in some of the more advanced forms as Table 9.4 shows.

TABLE 9.4
System markets for telecommunications equipment
($ = 1979)[100]

	1982	1987	Per cent growth p.a.
Telephone	38.1	55.7	7.9
Record and data communications	4.8	7.6	9.6
Mobile radio	3.1	4.4	7.3
Satellite communications	0.5	0.9	12.8
Cable TV	0.3	0.4	5.7
Radio paging	0.1	0.3	12.2
Total	46.9	69.3	8.1

Source: Arthur D. Little.

European PTTs (Post Telephone and Telegraph administrations) have neither aggressively stimulated IT technology and applications nor served as demanding leading-edge customers of European IT

companies. Rather than contributing to the development of a competitive European telecommunications industry, the policies have
generally slowed progress and fragmented the European market.
The trends towards deregulation in the US and Japan will probably
accelerate the erosion of the European suppliers' positions already
under way.[101]

Most European PTTs are well behind the United States in introducing new technology in their networks. The UK and Germany have
only recently started using fully electronic switching in their networks. In the US this type of equipment was first installed in the
mid-1960s. Until recently Germany was far behind the US and Japan
in the use of optical-fibre trunk networks.[102] Instead of pushing
suppliers for innovation, European PTTs have tended to use them as
subcontractors.

The French PTT remains tightly in control of network services.
Recent nationalization of Thomson, CIT–Alcatel, and ITT France
enables the French PTT and industry departments to co-operate in
satisfying the French telecommunications market with French products.
Superficially, the French PTT has encouraged private competition at
the subscriber end by inviting foreign companies into the market. The
effect will be to stimulate greater use of the PTT's own network
services and assist French efforts to achieve a world-wide position in
terminal equipment.[103]

Louis Mexandeau, Minister of France's PTT, has recently signed an
order with TRT, Philips' associated French telecommunications company, for the delivery of 90,000 black and white terminals and 10,000
colour terminals for the French electronic directory service. The
contract amounting to Dfl 50 million, is the result of four years of
joint co-operation and research by TRT and La Radiotechnique.
Manufacture of the equipment ordered will be completed by La Radiotechnique. The terminals consist of a display screen and keyboard and
are provided free to customers by the French PTT.

In 1980 the French PTT started a trial service at Saint Malo: thirty-
five subscribers and twenty private companies were connected to
a videotex network. In May 1981 this trial was extended to include
another 1,400 subscribers in the Rennes district; today 4,500 subscribers are connected. This is well below original estimates, and one
wonders what happened to all the other terminals that have been
reported as 'ordered' over the past two years. It is not known when the
'electronic directories' are to be delivered.[104]

European PTTs have expanded their activities to try and avoid
deregulation and protect themselves against reduction of their monopoly powers.

In Germany the subscriber-equipment market is already theoretically open. The type-approval process is, however, sufficiently rigorous to discourage all but the most diligent West German suppliers. Despite cosmetic changes in the Deutsche Bundespost's (DBP) type-approval activity, it is continuing a strongly selective process favouring only a few approved national suppliers. The DBP has expanded its telephone range to reduce criticisms. To ensure a modern digital-transport network the DBP has announced its own plans for BIGFON, a national optical-fibre network reaching down to the domestic subscriber. The move is designed to deter private networks intending to enter the potentially lucrative market.[105]

In Britain Mercury Communications was licensed to build and operate as a second telecommunications carrier in the UK and overseas, following city dissatisfaction with monopoly GPO services. Mercury is to operate a digital communications system using microwave links and opto-electronic trunk lines. This was to provide a reliable, competitive service for transmitting 64-K and 2M bit/second information flows—first in London, by autumn 1983, and then nationally. An Intelsat link to North America is planned using an earth station in the London area for early 1984, offering faster, better quality and more secure service than now available through switched analogue network. Mercury now has an interswitching agreement with British Telecom. Unilever Computer Services has been licensed to operate a valve-added network service including electronic mail and protocol conversion. This move marks the deregulation of telecommunications services.[106]

V.1. Switching equipment

Switching equipment, increasingly related to computer and microelectronics technologies, is important to European telecommunications companies. The $3.4 billion a year German telecommunications equipment industry, long a force on world markets, failed to keep up with the latest technology. In 1978 Siemens and the Bundespost abandoned a twelve-year $400 million project to develop a new generation of analogue electro-mechanical switches, outdated by more advanced Ericsson and CIT-Alcatel electronic digital technology.[107]

Siemens suddenly found itself in the position of a 19th-century lighting manufacturer which had designed a superb gas mantle when electricity was invented.[108]

With a crash programme Siemens did well to develop a digital exchange, which is expected to sell when certified by the Bundespost in 1984.[109]

In the United Kingdom the PTT is still buying old-fashioned equipment. Far from demanding advanced equipment from its suppliers, the British PTT ordered cross-bar equipment—TXE-4 exchanges worth

$1.36 billion. This ensures that some of Britain's telecommunications networks will use 1960s technology in the twenty-first century.[110] Hardly stimulating productivity, most large contracts in the UK were awarded on a cost-plus basis.[111] In addition, domestic suppliers were protected from foreign competition by procurement policies and standards requirements differing from those established elsewhere in Europe.[112]

In 1971 the PTT long-range planners determined on the basic *System X format.* But shortage of finance delayed development contracts until 1976. Throughout the 1970s investment varied greatly, manpower was cut, new engineers not trained. All this slowed System X development, consequently it did not enter service until 1982. Four years earlier CIT-Alcatel and Ericsson were offering digital exchanges.[113]

Deregulation trends in telecommunications are important for Europe. Typically, deregulation results in new competitors and a flood of new products. After the US PBX market was deregulated, AT&T lost 30 market-share points from 1972 to 1978. Competitors increased from twelve to thirty-eight and newcomers introduced PBXs with better features and/or at lower cost. Rolm introduced fully digital PBXs, featuring message detail recording, call forwarding, conferencing, and automated least-cost routing—an unmatched combination of features, other than price.

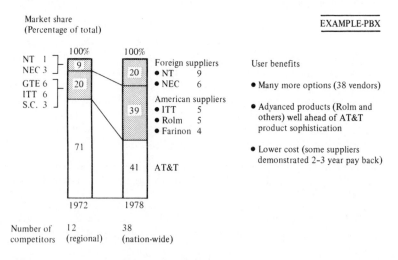

Fig. 9.12: Impact of US telecom deregulation.

Source: McKinsey & Company.

Deregulation of telecommunications services also gave low-cost, long-distance transmission (MCI, SPC), packet-switched data networks (Tymnet, Telenet), and satellite services (American Satellite, Satellite Business Systems).[114]

Deregulation in the UK, the intended opening of the telecommunications market, has put intense pressure on British Telecom to obtain modern products quickly. Thus *British Telecom* has sought overseas products, often collaborating with UK suppliers acting as agents and local manufacturers.[115] The rapid changes in technology and the slow rate of innovation by UK firms operating in a protected environment has forced British Telecom to buy PBXs from Mitel of Canada and IBM to enhance TXE4-A.[116] This parallels recent deals by Philips.

Individual national markets are not large enough to cover the development costs of a number of telecommunications products. The cost of new lines of digital switches, including software development and maintenance costs, ranges from $700 million to $1 billion. *At the normal 7 per cent of sales devoted to research, the sales required to justify the research and development are about $16 billion.* That is well over the size of the largest European market.[117] These figures emphasize the importance of creating an effective 'European' market for these products, particularly if they are to be price-competitive on international markets (see Figure 9.13).

Total extra-EC telecommunications exports are 50 per cent of the world total. But new extra-EC equipment exports are really only

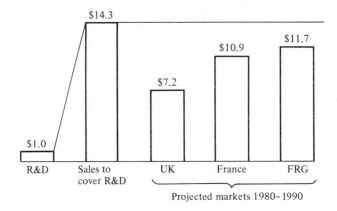

Fig. 9.13: European market fragmentation: next generation digital exchange ($ billions).

Sources: Interviews, Mackintosh, *Telephone Engineer and Management*, McKinsey analysis.

Japan
US
Rest of Europe
EC
9
8
29
54
16
11
23
50
1975
1980
True equipment exports
Philips Saudi Arabian contract
RøW(1) equipment
17
7
10
-Intra-EC
16
RøW(1) parts + spare parts

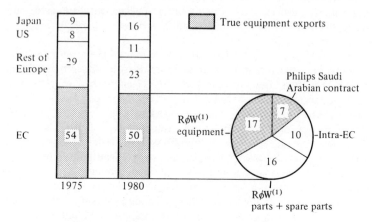

Fig. 9.14: Share of world telecom exports (% of total).

[1] Rest of world.

Sources: DOC, *Japan Electronics Almanack*; Eurostat.

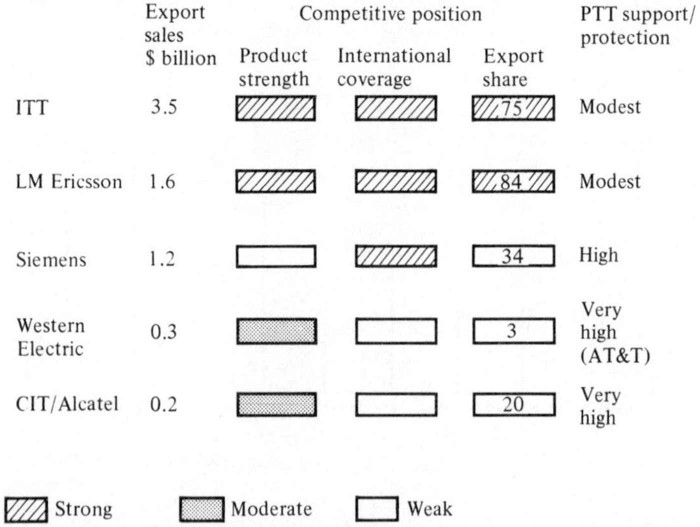

Export sales $ billion
Competitive position
Product strength
International coverage
Export share
PTT support/ protection
ITT
3.5
75
Modest
LM Ericsson
1.6
84
Modest
Siemens
1.2
34
High
Western Electric
0.3
3
Very high (AT&T)
CIT/Alcatel
0.2
20
Very high
Strong
Moderate
Weak

Fig. 9.15: European telecommunications companies and PTT support.

Source: McKinsey analysis.

17 per cent; of the rest 7 represent a signal contract with Saudi Arabia, 10 intra-EC trade, and 16 spare parts for equipment sold years ago[118] (see Figure 9.14).

Fundamentally, the most competitive telecommunication companies in Europe appear to be those which have received the least support and protection from their home base's PTT (see Figure 9.15). Plessey is attempting to reduce its dependance on the limited but very profitable UK telecommunications market, which accounted for 4.5 per cent of turnover and 54.5 per cent of company profits. Although growing rapidly and presently representing 6 per cent of the world market, the UK market will account for only 3 per cent by 1990. Plessey is therefore particularly pleased to have gained a vital toe-hold in the United States by the purchase of loss-making Stromberg-Carlson from United Technologies. The latter has agreed to sell only the public switch-making business; while Stromberg-Carlson will continue to make private exchanges for United Technologies, distribute, and sell service.

Stromberg-Carlson, employing 2,000, is one of the three main suppliers of digital exchange equipment to the independent telephone companies in the US. It has made losses for several years, in part due to the $80 million cost of developing its new digital exchange. The basic exchange has up to 16,000 lines (now being extended up to 32,000 lines) and is the first to obtain full approval from the US Rural Electrification Administration (REA), where it has or is installing 400 digital systems. Plessey pointed out that the market for public exchanges would double in the US as ATT's seven operating companies gained independence.

Plessey obviously hopes it will be able to make and sell System X in the US. System X, developed in the UK, is used in very large exchanges. Plessey will use its strengths in transmission equipment, integrated circuits, optical-fibre systems, connectors, and private systems like Monarch.[119] Nevertheless an important result of this deal is the larger market for digital exchanges within effective reach of Plessey.

Ferranti and the US-based General Telephone and Electronics Corporation have set up a joint venture to manufacture and sell subscriber telephone equipment. They aim to secure 15 per cent of the UK market within three years, taking advantage of the privatization of the UK telecommunications industry. Ferranti held about 2 per cent of the market in 1982.[120]

V.2. Mobile systems

Racal Electronics has extended its interest in marine and navigation systems by purchasing a US manufacturer of transmitters and receivers, Mega Pulse, for about $20 million. Sir Ernest Harrison, Racal's chairman, said the acquisition would bring expertise in advanced technologies, high-energy lasers, controlled fusion and electron-beam techniques.[121] Racal operates the Decca Navigator network, while Mega Pulse, according to Racal, is the leading supplier of the Loran-C navigation system and has sold systems to Canada, Saudi Arabia, and France.

A UK licence has been granted to operate a second mobile radio service in competition with British Telecom and Securicor. There was concern expressed about the particular forms of cellular radio technology they would support. Cellular radio is seen as the way to break out of restrictions now limiting the number of mobile radiophone subscribers. The situation was so bad in London that there was a thriving black market for radio-phone subscriptions. Cellular radio will dramatically increase the volume of simultaneous users and create new business. Sales in Europe are projected to be worth $3 billion by 1980.

Three major versions of cellular radio technology were involved:

– AMPS: a system designed as having the least channel capacity of the three, but the advantage of being operational in Washington DC.
– NMT: a Scandinavian system, also now operational and with greater channel capacity, but believed to be better suited to rural than urban environments.
– MATS-E: developed by Philips and CIT-Alcatel, this is considered to be the best system on paper, but has yet to be built.

Philips and CIT-Alcatel, together with Ferranti (the leader of the consortium proposing to use the MATS-E format) wanted to wait for superior European technology for a mobile telephone system able to last to the end of the century, rather than buy American technology to meet short-term demand. However, the UK licensing decision did not support this view, and gave the franchise to a consortium of Racal, Millicom (a US manufacturer of radio phones), and Hambros, which is proposing to use the AMPS technology.

With the German and Dutch governments also having rejected MATS-E, AMPS could have become the *de facto* standard for European mobile telephony, with obvious implications for European manufacturers. Motorola, who built the Dynatac equipment used in the Washington trial of AMPS, announced plans to build a $17 million manufacturing plant in the UK. The UK manufacturer Plessey is reported to be having discussion with AT&T to manufacture AMPS equipment, and Philips, despite their involvement with MATS-E, announced their willingness to produce AMPS equipment. By comparison, Thorn-Ericsson, the main backer of NMT through their manufacturing subsidiary SRA signed a potential deal to supply United Technologies in the US with cellular radio equipment in the event of their winning some of the thirty licences currently available in the US. The equipment would be an improved version of NMT called CMS8800. It should be noted, though, that SRA offers AMPS equipment in addition to NMT. Although there is some way to go before Europe is covered by a comprehensive cellular radio network, it appeared that European manufacturers lost on the first round. The delay in introducing an acknowledged superior system was not acceptable to telecommunications-planning authorities, already under pressure to provide improved services.[122] But in spring 1984 the French and West German governments agreed to adopt a third European standard, the MATS-E, for implementation in 1987.

V.3. Optical-fibre and conventional cable systems

Europe is about to make major investments in wide-based interactive cable systems. The intentions of France, West Germany, and the United Kingdom are to make wide use of optical-fibre systems. The technology acquired for these systems, while requiring continuing improvement, is in hand. France's first large-scale cable plan is geared resolutely to the new fibre optics. But PTT exports expect to work with classical coaxial cables for two years until French industry develops production capacity in optical fibres.[123] *The UK has 3,500 kilometres of optical-fibre cable already in operation.*

European research is scattered among member states with constant duplication, wasted resources, lack of critical research mass, and increased attendant risks of diverging standards and norms.

In the United Kingdom an estimated $4.8 billion is required to cable half the country. The decision has been made to introduce cable over the next two years. Private funds are to finance this cable investment, Kenneth Baker, Minister for Information and Technology has said:

It goes without saying the terms and the regime for this investment would have to be sufficiently attractive for that money to be forthcoming.[124]

In the US cable is financed privately. Boston's new cable television network will be laid at a cost of $94 million. Westinghouse Electric paid $646 million for a cable television company, Teleprompter, which operates 112 systems in thirty-two states. But, even in the US, where cable penetration is over 50 per cent, the initial return on capital is low.

A research study by CIT (Compagnie Industrielle de Telecommunications) based on a sample of UK, German, and French and Benelux households, concluded that the European subscriber is extremely price sensitive, at about $12.80 to $16 a month, most subscribers being in the C2 social grouping with a disposable income of $11,200 a year. A low cable penetration would make quality programming untenable without substantial advertising revenues. A BBC or ITV programme costs about $48,000 an hour.[125] A Eurogrid approach, with free connection to the cable system, in these circumstances would maximize the penetration and distribute benefits widely at an earlier date.

Despite government pressure for speed, the UK White Paper on cable will not be law before summer 1984. Franchise arrangements could take eighteen months, and it would be 1987 before any franchise could provide a service. It could take five years to bring cable within reach of a quarter of the British households. Professor James Ring, a member of the Hunt Committee, thought that only half might choose to subscribe. That would make 2.4 million homes by 1991/2 said Mr Townsin, Deputy Chairman of Young & Rubicam.[126] Other estimates put the cable take-up as 4–10 million homes by the mid-1990s.

Under French plans 1.4 million homes are to be linked to cable, partially optical fibres, by 1986–8, at a cost of $850 million.[127] This triples the present 500,000 or 2 per cent of French homes with television connected to cable systems, stated Philippe Wade, technical counsellor to the French Communications Minister.[128] One in every two French families will be connected to an optical-fibre network by 1995. Completion of the plan in 1985 is timed to coincide with the advent of satellite television, including the two channels planned by France. France is opting for a combination of local receiving stations linked to home networks. How else, officials ask, can they save the country from being submerged by individually received axials? How else—equally to the point—can they exercise any control over programmes?

'Political reasons came first' a post office expert said. The socialists, after long experience on the wrong side of the monopoly, have boosted local broadcasting, admitted non-commercial private radio, and re-opened the dossier on pay-television. The new Broadcasting Act, which came into force in summer 1983, lifted the monopoly on programmes. A political choice has to be made on the cable networks. Either the post office can set them up itself, or it can do so jointly with private interests.[129]

West Germany has under consideration the BIGFON optical-fibre network project. The BIGFON plan calls for 100,000 km/yr over 1985–96.[130] In carrying out such projects European PTTs could become leading-edge customers and provide a base load for suppliers. Such projects will stimulate IT awareness and help reduce business and consumer lags.[131]

Generally European and British companies are considered to be reasonably good at the research level in this field. But Japanese companies have done the development work required to produce quality products which can and are delivered on time.

Despite the AEG group's financial difficulties, AEG-Kabels' technological future in optical-fibre/glass-fibre cables equals that of its main West German competitors (Siemens, SEL, and Philips); but it does not do optical-fibre cable system development. This is carried out by ATN.[132] AEG-Telefunken's cable and systems division was one of the most profitable parts of AEG and included complete earth stations, satellite transponders, management and systems for communications satellites, optical-fibre cable systems, and stationary and mobile radio systems. Joint ventures were used to cover the enormous development costs required to ensure future presence in electronics market growth.[133]

Five of West Germany's electrical companies plan to build a factory in West Berlin to produce 100,000 kilometres of optical fibre a year by the end of 1984.[134] The companies—AEG-Telefunken, Siemens, Philips, Kabelmetal Electro, and Standard Elektrik Lorenz—have formed a joint venture to meet the requirements of the Bundespost's BIGFON plan.[135]

Fujitsu is possibly the world leader in the technology, and would have won a major contract in the United States if the Federal authorities had not intervened for defence considerations.

V.4. Satellites

Optical fibres will not eliminate the need for direct-broadcasting satellites (DBS). Satellites are here to stay, as they have unique advantages. The optical fibre means undersea-cable carrying television, something which was not possible before. It also enables satellite wideband capability to be extended via a local earth station to the individual factory, bank, or home. This can strengthen the role of satellites as a means of linking users of the telecommunications service into a multi-element wide-band system, whether user requirements are to receive television from almost any source, exchange high-speed data between computers, take part in conferences with people on the other side of the world, or place simple telephone calls. We must ensure the fascination of telecommunications will not inhibit the free flow of information messages, which satellites and other media are capable of carrying, now and in future programmes throughout Europe.[136] Surely it would be wasteful to force Europeans to access programmes of their choice by illicit individual dish antenna listening in on DBS.

DBS involve political, social, and economic factors affecting the development of space communication and commercial markets for associated products and services. In Europe, introduction of DBS revealed some significant developments. The International Tele-communications Union (ITU) assumed that such services would be provided on a national basis. ITU went to some lengths to ensure that the plans would result in minimum interference between services of adjacent territories. Inevitably this means programme reception intended for neighbouring countries is made technically difficult, except in border regions. Even there, reception will often require duplication of receiving equipment. There is a strong lobby against this, particularly within the advertising industry, which would welcome a more cross-national approach. The former view seeks to protect national cultural integrity. This is seen most strongly in Canadian and French views. An opposite view is seen in UN resolutions promoting the free exchange of information across national borders.

At the national level DBS can be seen as a threat to existing systems 'broadcasting' information, particularly cable distribution systems. But there is also a strongly held view that DBS will act as a stimulus to these operations, providing both new material to distributors and a means of escape from the relatively severe constraint of existing and future national regulations.

The imperatives vary from country to country. The Netherlands and Belgium, for example, are extensively wired and the cable systems will be able to receive and distribute programmes originating from domestic and foreign terrestrial sources, as well as from all direct-broadcast satellites in the arc of orbit visible from those countries. In such cases it is unlikely that individual dishes will be economically attractive to many people. In France and West Germany the terrestrial infrastructure is less well developed and direct-broadcast satellites offer a means for extending programme coverage and introducing new channels. Here we may expect the growth of cable systems and the introduction of individual dishes to proceed in parallel. In the UK terrestrial coverage is excellent but cable systems are neither modern nor extensive. A difficult decision now faces UK cable companies—whether to install 'second-generation' coaxial cables and risk not recouping the invest-ment before optical fibres become widespread, or await the availability of optical fibres and risk seeing the market split between individual dishes and British Telecom-supplied all-service wideband fibres. The lack of a widespread means of disseminating programmes will also delay the time by which the broadcaster(s) will cover the costs of renting satellite channels.

Space communication developments are not likely to be limited by technology availability. The principal choice lies between a mainly DBS system offering rapid expansion in available channels and a poten-tially slower cable system growth. The cable potentially offers many more channels, and other services involving, for example, two-way communication that cannot be offered via satellite. The enormous markets implied by the rapid spread in international, regional, and domestic systems, and by the advent of direct-broadcast satellites, provide a substantial potential business opportunity for countries with the developed technical and industrial capability to supply systems. Owing to the size of investment many nations will insist on supplying the major part of domestic needs in order to improve export prospects. It is difficult to imagine any significant penetration of US, Canadian, European, Soviet, or Japanese markets by foreign suppliers. Even Australia and India are currently planning to build up their space industries.

Growth in the world market for space hardware and earth stations has increased the number of potential suppliers, often supported by their governments. Consequently, competition is increasing to supply the needs of countries with no indigenous space industry, but able to pay.[137]

Satellite telecommunications is providing us with a prime example of space commercialization. Over the past two decades, the technology, the institutions, and the world-wide markets have matured to a considerable degree. We have seen that traffic growth has outstripped forecasts: today demand for space and associated terrestrial hardware is probably approaching $14 billion per year, without any sign of abating. One has only to look at the increase in value of each successive Intelsat procurement, at the enormous projections for direct-broadcast satellites, at falling costs per unit used, and at the markets for maritime, domestic, and regional satellites, to appreciate that a significant momentum has already been built up. This is indicative of an industry well past its days of pioneering, which needs to demonstrate its serious potential.

The markets are not all open to free competition, nor have the industries of all countries reached the same level of technological and price competitiveness. This rich promise of space telecommunications has led to the investment of public funds in the nurturing and building of national industrial and technological capabilities in countries which wish to protect their own ability to supply domestic needs or to maintain the possibility of supplying those of other countries. Europe does not have long-term competitors to the US Space Shuttle, which enjoys significant advantages for heavier vehicles. The world could be divided into segments, with some markets protected and available only to indigenous industry, and others where 'free competition' plays a greater role.

The success of Japan in the supply of earth stations may lead one to wonder whether they will achieve a similar world position in satellites. Japan has embarked on a programme of developments which includes the local manufacture of satellites, associated ground stations, and terminals, as well as the capability to orbit all but the larger satellites using Japanese launch vehicles. In short, a well-proven formula for Japanese success is now being applied to the potentially enormous space telecommunications market. The TV broadcast sector with the space and home dish-receiver segments are particularly attractive to Japanese industry.[138]

Satellite telecommunications and space development in Western Europe has been pursued with emphasis on building up an industrial and technological capability. Space investment came from national government departments, charged with this aspect of R&D policy, believing in the long-term future for space applications and not wanting competition from other countries to become insurmountable. Thus the European space capability, that in the early 1970s caused the member states of the European Space Research Organization (ESRO—later restructured into ESA) to initiate a change in the character of the organization from a space science-research body to one in which major emphasis was placed on space applications.

In Western Europe user interest has generally been low, despite pressure from space proponents to reorientate thinking and planning towards satellite-based systems. The development of telecommunications satellites had a late start. Western Europe PTT organizations finally provided grudging support in formulating requirements and agreeing to carry out a programme of in-orbit tests, but space systems did not feature strongly. In providing communications to platforms in the North Sea, the British, for example, adopted a tropospheric scatter solution, while the Norwegians elected to use part of an Intelsat IV transponder to link dishes on their platforms with land stations.

Following the development and in-orbit test phase of the European Orbital Test Satellite (OTS launched in 1978), the organization of European PTTs, Eutelsat, remain unconvinced that satellites economized, so it was necessary to provide the first two satellites of the operational ECS system at no cost in order to persuade that body to procure the remainder of the series.

Support given to industry should be aimed at developing competitivity rather than building up a technological capability. Government departments responsible for industrial advance are working more closely with potential users: PTTs and broadcasting authorities. They are attempting to create, by means of political persuasion, changes in financing satellite development, and ensuring satellite solutions receive more favourable consideration. Response from genuine users has, however, not been uniformly enthusiastic. Thus the French and West German broadcasters do not bear the R&D cost of the TDF1 and TV-SAT direct broadcast satellites now being developed.

In the UK this process has led to the creation of a joint industry–PTT company, which plans to use the funds of its founders plus those of merchant banks to provide satellite channels to UK broadcasters, and to employ space capacity to permit a business communications package to link small dishes located on the premises of firms using the service.

In addition to providing their national bodies with the capability to implement a direct broadcast service by satellite, the aerospace industry of various Western European nations has a product to sell in the emerging world markets and is provided with a 'shop-window' in which to display its expertise.

Although in the US—and Canada to a lesser extent—it is user demand which has now brought about the creation of a major industry, in Western Europe industry was built up to establish a technological capability, and attempts to influence users towards a space solution for some telecommunications needs.[139] Nevertheless, it is prudent to remember that economic or technological breakthroughs in space technology, very large satellites or space stations in the next ten to twenty years could force major versions of local, national and international communications plans and could change systems and equipment design—cable, waveguide, and radionets would then have modified roles in the digital world of tommorrow.[140]

V.5. Cable television

With the exception of the Netherlands and Belgium (which has more cable TV than telephone subscribers) *Europe is incredibly backward* compared with North America in the installation of cable TV systems. In contrast, despite the high distances involved, Canada has connected over 80 per cent of its homes. As early as 1973 Vancouver had a 44-channel cable system. The problem is not even restricted to cable TV. While South Korea has five broadcast TV programmes, the UK is installing a fourth and France is proposing a fourth and considering, like the UK, a fifth.

The problems are political not technical. Typically, even the European leader Belgium, with 15–16 Brussels cable channels, only received UK programmes in late 1983, despite having installed the physical plant required long before. Most member states have prevented private or PTT cable developments for reasons varying from government capital expenditure cut-backs to a deliberate policy of restricting viewer choice and controlling the programmes available. All too often European governments seek to control not only the advertising, and the violence and crime broadcasts, but also the local character and content, and the political content of news programming. Again, a leader in the field, Belgium has long had a pilot small-area TV programme. West Germany has two pilot multichannel cable systems to study consumer reactions. But there is no technical or economic reason why in most of Europe there should not be the electronic equivalent to the small town newspaper. There is no theoretical or economic reason why Italians in London should not have RAI-TV and other Italian programmes available. At the beginning of the 1970s Canada's British Columbia with a negligible francophone population, had French TV programmes which came from far greater distances.

TABLE 9.5
*Comparative assessment of the strengths in
information technology*

	Japan	US	W. Europe
Computer technology			
Fifth-generation computers	A	B	B
Super computers	A	A	C
Mainframes	A	A	C
Mini-computers	B	A	C
Personal computers	A	A	C
Software	C	A	A
Semiconductor technology			
VLSI	A	B	C
Microprocessors	B	A	C
Production and testing equipment	B	A	C
Next-generation devices	A	A	C
Communications technology			
Optical fibres	A	B	C
Optical public communications network	B	A	C
Semiconductor lasers	A	A	C
Digital electronic exchanges	B	B	A

In ascending order of strength: C B A

Source: Published by Ostasien Institut B.V. in 'Implications of the Industrial Strategy for the Community Office Automation Industry', 1983.

The market consequences of these political and social obstacles is that EC products are inappropriate for American markets shaped by city administrators insisting on the installation of 48-, 60- or even 100-channel interaction, or two-way cable systems, with special channels provided free of cost for city government, educational, legal, and medical institutions, and—at extra cost—insurance, shopping, fire, and burglar protection services.[141] European industry in these circumstances is simply unable to build up an export potential funded on large home markets for advanced equipment and services. Worse, Europeans remain IT-illiterate, and unaware of IT's ability to serve their individual needs at home and work.

VI. European Co-operation

The European Community approved the 1.5 billion ECU ESPRIT programme for co-operative precompetitive research (50 per cent financed by industry) in February 1984. Previously Philips and Siemens —Europe's two largest electronics groups—announced plans for close co-operation in long-lead research and development.[142] Similarly ICL, Machines Bull, and Siemens, established a joint institute in Bavaria to undertake precompetitive research in advanced computer systems.[143] Industrial co-operation at the EC level by the twelve companies involved in ESPRIT also seems possible for standards. In March 1984 they agreed to start designing their equipment from 1985 to meet existing and planned international standards, and pressed EC authorities to adopt these standards for future public procurement.[144] However, success in this area will require considerable support from national authorities. The difficulties involved are well illustrated by the Grundig–Telefunken–Philips saga.

By January 1983, Grundig had postponed its proposed takeover of Telefunken, the heavy loss making subsidiary of AEG-Telefunken. Negotiations awaited the outcome of the offer by French State-owned Thomson-Brandt for a 75.5 per cent share in Grundig. This ran into considerable political and industrial opposition[145] and was subject to the final decision of the FRG Economics Minister, who could overrule a Cartel Office veto.

Philips has a 24.5 per cent share of Grundig. The latter ran into serious financial problems, the result of fierce Far Eastern competition, particularly in the video-recorder market where severe price cuts had to be made. Grundig sought salvation in a wider reorganization of the European consumer electronics industry through a series of co-operation ventures which could ultimately bring together these interests of Thomson-Brandt, Philips, Grundig and, ultimately, Telefunken.

In a January 1983 joint statement, Grundig and Telefunken said, 'It is still the goal of both companies to co-operate closely in the field of consumer electronics in order to use the advantages of greater production volumes against competition from the Far East.'[146] Both companies called for a more sympathetic handling of their co-operation plans from the cartel authorities, national governments, and the European Commission. Dr Grundig dismissed talks of an alternative 'German solution' involving Siemens and Bosch.[147]

In March 1983 the Cartel Office decided against the Thomson-Brandt offer,[148] but subsequently allowed Thomson to take up a 75 per cent share of Telefunken, the consumer electronics subsidiary of limping AEG.[149] A difficulty could have been the State-ownership of Thomson-Brandt, which has been chosen by the French government as an instrument to recapture the domestic market, create exports, and secure jobs in consumer electronics, components, and telecommunications. Thus, Thomson-Brandt may not be steered by profit motives when deciding the location of production centres and sources. Indeed, it is not easy to refute suspicions that government backing enabled the French company to offer a price for Grundig that no German firm could sensibly match.[150] Effectively, nationalization of Thomson-Brandt complicates the development of French-based European international companies, unless it is clear that the merged company is now on commercial lines and not just a vehicle for French national interests.[151]

In December 1983 it was announced that Philips wanted to increase its holding in Grundig to just over 25 per cent—a blocking minority —from 1 April 1984.[152] The FRG Cartel Office indicated in March 1984 that its approval would be in doubt unless Philips sold its 15 per cent share in Löwe Opta, a West German television manufacturer, and Grundig sold its dictating-machines operation. The deal involved Philips operating with a consortium of banks in a complicated transaction which would permit the Philips' holding in Grundig to be increased indirectly to 31.6 per cent.[153] The equity directly held by Philips would in effect be reduced to 22.9 per cent, in a move to show the FRG Cartel Office that Philips is not acquiring a dominant hold over European electronics.[154]

These complications make it clear that the time has come for competition laws and regulations to be better adapted to the need for joint European ventures.

VII. Conclusions

This short overview of the European IT industry, despite its limitations, demonstrates that within Europe there is an urgent need to change attitudes and policies in government and industry. Entrepreneurial and aggressively competitive attitudes, leading-edge growth, development, and markets: all are required. Established comfortable relationships between member states, their PTTs, and national champions will not be sufficiently threatened and disrupted by truly competitive cost and technology considerations until significant steps are taken to create a genuine Community market in the interests of each and every member country.

Evidently if Europe is to survive and avoid becoming a backwater inhabited by the world's first subsistence-level industrialized peasants, it will be necessary to encourage growth of new enterprises and the decline of old at the European level. European survival requires ruthless support of the best and the strategically important, and elimination of the subsidized and outdated.

Market forces—powered by consumer demand and leading-edge procurement—must be liberated and reinforced. The Community must concern itself increasingly with the long-term technological perspectives that are beyond the realistic means of individual member states. To survive and prosper Europe must concern itself not with the survival of individual enterprises, but with the future. Europe must have economic policies and the effective use of resources allocated in the interest of European high-technology and, in particular, its IT sector.

For these reasons, and to ensure the critical mass required for efficient leading-edge research and development, the Commission proposed ESPRIT. But in itself this attempt to promote co-operative and precompetitive research efforts in the Community, if successful, can only represent one column of a Greek temple. Many complementary and indispensable policies must be implemented if Europe is to have a chance. These must involve finance, trade regulation, education, and strong policies encouraging competition, plus the effective creation of a European Common Market in the products and applications of IT. All are essential if the temple is to stand proud and there is to be realistic action on the scale required to precipitate the changes needed for success. European attitudes must be changed at the institutional and industrial levels.

Fortunately there are some indications that industry and member governments are beginning to realize the inadequacy and ineffectiveness of even the boldest national policies. It remains to be seen, however, whether Europe can effect the co-ordination and changes required. The needs are evident; the problem is to translate these requirements into political and industrial actions at the European level before it is too late.

Notes and Sources

[1] McKinsey & Company, *A Call to Action, The European Information Technology Industry*, January 1983, p. 20.

[2] Ibid.

[3] Dr Ian Mackintosh, Chairman, Mackintosh International, London, summer 1983.

[4] Mackintosh Consultants, *The European Computer Peripherals Industry*, vol. 2, 1980, p. 91.

[5] *Financial Times*, 13 April 1982.

[6] Mackintosh Consultants, op. cit., p. 30.

[7] Ibid.

[8] Ibid., p. 32.

[9] Ibid., p. 68.

[10] Paul Betts and Guy de Joncquières, *Financial Times*, 17 November 1982.

[11] McKinsey & Company, op. cit., p. 4:32.

[12] Gareth Locksley, 'The EEC Telecommunications Industry: Competition, Concentration, and Competitiveness', p. 190.

[13] Arthur D. Little study reported by Guy de Joncquières, *Financial Times*, 8 February 1983.

[14] Ibid.

[15] David March, *Financial Times*, 21 December 1982.

[16] *Japan Times*, 18 October 1982; see also Maurice English, 'Japanese and American Supercomputers', Memo 139-1, Commission of the EC, 26 November 1982.

[17] UPI, *Japan Times*, 10 November 1982; see also Maurice English, 'Japan ahead of U.S. in Supercomputers?', Memo 162-1, Commission of the EC, 29 December 1982.

[18] *Le Monde*, 22 January 1983.

[19] J. M. Q., *Le Monde*, 22 January 1983.

[20] Ibid.

[21] Commission of the EC, 'The European Machine Tool Industry, Situation and Prospects', SEC(83) 151 final, Brussels, 1983, p. 12.

[22] Ibid., p. 54.

[23] Ibid., p. 12.

[24] 'Develop Strategic Alternatives to Foster the Growth of a Strong European Numerical Control Industry', *Consultronique*, 18 December 1981, p. 44.

[25] Commission of the EC, 'The European Machine Tool Industry, Situation and Prospects', op. cit., p. 12.

[26] 'Develop Strategic Alternatives to Foster the Growth of a Strong European Industry', op. cit., p. 45.

[27] Commission of the EC, 'The European Machine Tool Industry, Situation and Prospects', op. cit., p. 25.

[28] Ibid., pp. 8 and 12.

[29] Ibid., pp. 10–11.

[30] Ibid., p. 27.

[31] Ibid., pp. 8–9.

[32] Ibid., p. 22.

[33] *Nihon Keizai*, 7 February 1983.

[34] *Financial Times*, 19 February 1983.

[35] *The Economist*, 11 December 1983.

[36] *The Japan Economic Journal*, 11 January 1983.

[37] Ibid., 24 July 1982.

[38] *Financial Times*, 8 December 1982.

[39] *The Economist*, 11 December 1982.

[40] 'Reports Peter Bruce', *Financial Times*, 15 January 1983.

[41] Commission of the EC, 'The European Machine Tool Industry, Situation and Prospects', op. cit., pp. 19–21, 25.

[42] Ibid., p. 27.

[43] Ibid., p. 24.

[44] *The Sunday Times*, 30 January 1983.

[45] Commission of the EC, 'The European Machine Tool Industry, Situation and Prospects', op. cit., p. 51.

[46] *Japan Economic Journal*, 11 January 1983.

[47] Interview with Tohio Kono, President of Dainichi Kiko, 26 July 1982.

[48] *Japan Ecnomic Journal*, 11 January 1983.

[49] *Financial Times*, 19 January 1983.

[50] McKinsey & Company, op. cit., appendices, p. 3:3.

[51] *A Profile of the European Semiconductor Industry*, Macintosh Publications Ltd., Luton, 1979, p. 2.

[52] Dr J. Abegglen and Mr Akio Etori, 'Japanese Technology Today', *Scientific American*, October 1982 (author's own emphasis).

[53] 'International Competition in Advanced Industrial Sectors: Trade and Development in the Semiconductor Industry', study prepared for the US Congressional Joint Economic Committee, 18 February, p. 145, (author's own emphasis).

[54] *The Economist*, 1 May 1982.

[55] Ibid., 15 January 1983.

[56] Guy de Joncquières, *Financial Times*, 8 February 1983.

[57] *Financial Times*, 18 January 1983.

[58] See Maurice English, 'IT European Markets—TV'. Memo 154, Commission of the EC, December 1982.

[59] McKinsey & Company, op. cit., p. 4:32.

[60] Ibid., p. 31:32.

[61] Ibid., p. 3:19.

[62] Kevin Done, *Financial Times*, 13 May 1983. See also Maurice English, 'Some Notes on the AEG-Telefunken Group'. Memo 140, Commission of the EC, 11 October 1982, p. 4.

[63] See Maurice English, ibid.

[64] *Mainichi*, 13 February 1983.

[65] *The Sunday Times*, 30 January 1983.

[66] *Japan Electronics Today*, 2 February 1983, p. 7.

[67] *Japan Times*, 15 February 1983.

[68] *Mainichi*, 14 February 1983; *Japan Times*, 4 February 1983.

[69] *Electronics*, 9 June 1977, p. 101, in Verner, Liipfert, Bernhard, and McPherson, *The Effect of Government Targeting on World Semiconductor Competition; A Case History of Japanese Industrial Strategy and its Costs for America*, 1982/3, p. 21.

[70] *Japan Times*, 14 February 1983.

[71] *Mainichi*, 14 February 1983.

[72] *Asahi Evening News*, 9 February 1983.

[73] *Sankei*, 14 February 1983.

[74] *Japan Times*, 14 January 1983.

[75] Ibid., 14 February 1983.

[76] *The Sunday Times*, 30 January 1983.

[77] *Japan Times*, 14 February 1983.;

[78] Ibid., 18 February 1983.

[79] *Financial Times*, 25 January 1983.

[80] *Japan Times*, 18 February 1983.

[81] *The Sunday Times*, 30 January 1983.

[82] *Financial Times*, 25 January 1983.

[83] *Japan Times*, 14 February 1983.

[84] *Mainichi*, 14 February 1983.

[85] John Wyles, *Financial Times*, 4 March 1983.

[86] *Mainichi*, 18 February 1983, and *Japan Times*, 15 February 1983.

[87] *Mainichi*, 14 February 1983.

[88] *Sankei*, 14 February 1983.

[89] *Nihon Keizai*, 14 February 1983.

[90] *Mainichi*, 18 February 1983.

[91] *Sankei*, 15 February, 1983.

[92] *Japan Electronics Today News*, 2 February 1983, p. 15.

[93] Ibid., p. 16.

[94] Ibid., p. 7.

[95] *Japan Times*, 14 February 1983.

[96] Ibid., 11 March 1983, p.9.

[97] *Mainichi*, 14 February 1983.

[98] 'States EC Flash', 24 January 1983, published in *Mainichi*, 14 February 1983.

[99] *Mainichi*, 14 February 1983.

[100] Arthur D. Little, Inc., 'World Telecommunications Information Program', in Arthur D. Little, *The Changing Basis of Competition in the 1980s*, October 1982, p. 21.

[101] McKinsey & Company, op. cit., p. 4:15.

[102] Ibid.

[103] Roger J. Camrass, 'Competition in Europe—Opportunities and Threats', in Arthur D. Little, *The Changing Basis of Competition in the 1980s*, October 1982, pp. 53–4.

[104] *Europa Report*, 19 February 1983, p. 5.

[105] Roger J. Camrass, op. cit., p. 53.

[106] Economist Intelligence Unit, *Review of Information Technology, Telecoms, Value Added Services*, January 1983, p. 1.

[107] Guy de Joncquières, *Financial Times*, 8 February 1983.

[108] *Financial Times*, 11 February 1983; see also Gareth Locksley, 'The EEC Telecommunications Industry: Competition, Concentrations and Competitiveness', op. cit., p. 100.

[109] Guy de Joncquières, *Financial Times*, 8 February 1983.

[110] Gareth Locksley, 'The EEC Telecommunications Industry: Competition, Concentration and Competitiveness', op. cit., p. 101.

[111] McKinsey & Company, op. cit., p. 4:16.

[112] Ibid., p. 4:16 and 4:17.

[113] Gareth Locksley, op. cit., p. 101.

[114] McKinsey & Company, op. cit., p. 4:19.

[115] Roger J. Camrass, op. cit., p. 54.

[116] Gareth Locksley, op. cit., p. 103.

[117] McKinsey & Company, op. cit., p. 4:17.

[118] Ibid.

[119] Jason Crisp, *Financial Times*, autumn 1982.

[120] Nick Garneth, *Financial Times*, 9 December 1982.

[121] Guy de Joncquierès, *Financial Times*, 15 January 1983.

[122] Economist Intelligence Unit, *Review of Information Technology, Telecoms, Value Added Services*, January 1983, Section 4.

[123] *Financial Times*, 14 October 1982.

[124] Bill Johnston, *Financial Times*, 16 September 1982.

[125] Ibid.

[126] At the Financial Times Cable Television and Satellite Broadcasting Conference, 27 January 1983, see Lynton McCain, ibid., 28 February 1983.

[127] Ibid., 14 October 1982.

[128] Lynton McCain, ibid., 28 February 1983.

[129] Ibid., 14 October 1982.

[130] Economist Intelligence Unit, op. cit., p. 1.

[131] McKinsey & Company, op. cit., p. 4:20.

[132] Kevin Done, *Financial Times*, 14 September 1982; see also Maurice English, 'Some notes on the AEG-Telefunken Group', op. cit., p. 5.

[133] Kevin Done, *Financial Times*, 4 December 1982; see also Maurice English, ibid.

[134] *Financial Times*, 14 December 1982.

[135] Economist Intelligence Unit, op. cit., p. 1.

[136] Peter Brunt and Alan Naylor, 'Telecommunications and Space', *Futures*, October 1982, pp. 433-4.

[137] Ibid., pp. 431-2.

[138] Ibid., pp. 432-3.

[139] Ibid., pp. 425-6.

[140] Robert S. Gordon, 'The Emerging Digital World—Survival in the Information Age', in Arthur D. Little, *The Changing Basis of Competition in the 1980s*, October 1982, p. 115.

[141] See Maurice English, 'IT European Markets—TV', op. cit.

[142] *Financial Times*, 20 December 1982.

[143] Ibid., 28 March 1982.

[144] Guy de Joncquières, *Financial Times*, 16 March 1984.

[145] Kevin Done, *Financial Times*, 25 January 1983.

[146] Ibid.

[147] *Financial Times*, 25 January 1983.

[148] *Wirtschaftswoche*, 11 March 1983.

[149] *The Economist*, 24 December 1983.

[150] *Financial Times*, 25 January 1983.

[151] Ibid.

[152] *The Economist*, 24 December 1983.

[153] John Davies, *Financial Times*, 14 March 1983.

[154] Walter Elis and Jonathon Carr, *Financial Times*, March 1983.

274-92

X
French Industrial Strategy in Sunrise Sectors

CHRISTIAN STOFFAËS*

I. The debate about positive industrial policies

The continuous, increasing economic crisis of the past ten years has confronted governments of industrialized nations with the need for an adequate economic policy to face it. Various techniques have been used in succession to fight stagflation, from Keynesian reflation to radical monetarism. So far, none of them seem to have met unchallenged success. Keynesianism has led to more inflation and more trade deficit, with only a moderate success in growth and employment. Monetarism seems to have reduced inflation, but has led simultaneously to economic stagnation or depression, and to more unemployment. Contemplating these economic failures, analyses are concluding more and more often that the real nature of the current economic crisis is that of industrial adjustment. The meaning of adjustment is that the existing industrial structure has to be adapted to the new conditions prevailing in world economic competition, as well as to the new technologies, the new demands of markets, and new tastes of consumers. If they are not adapted, these structures react to Keynesianism only by producing inflation, and to monetarism only by bankruptcies and industrial purge.

If that analysis is correct, another question then arises: how to develop new industries and diffuse new technologies while the general depression discourages risk-taking, and overcapacities and financial losses prohibit new productive investments? The debate about industrial policy has stemmed from that central question. Should the governments of free-market countries adopt a more interventionist attitude, in order to foster the development of new technologies and the growth of sunrise industries? Or should they stick instead to their traditional economic policies of *laissez-faire* and global regulation only at the macro-economic level?

* Deputy Assistant Secretary for Electronics and Information Technology in the French Ministry of Industry and Research and Professor at the Institut d'Etudes Politiques.

The responses to that question by the various governments of the western world vary widely. During the past ten years the degree of public intervention in industrial structures has generally increased in all countries. In particular, some governments have been massively involved in the rescue of so-called lame ducks—i.e. bankrupt industrial firms or entire depressed sectors, such as steel, chemicals, textiles, shipbuilding, etc. These interventions have generally been conducted under strong political and social pressures to sustain full employment, especially in depressed areas. Many West European governments, such as the United Kingdom, Sweden, Italy, and France have been led to develop that kind of industrial policy. These rescue policies took the form of nationalizations, financial loans and subsidies, or organized cartels and sometimes offered protection from foreign competition, as in the case of the EC Steel Plan or the Multifibre Agreement. These policies have been criticized as inefficiently defensive and aggravating the obsolescence of the industrial structure as a whole by preventing the reallocation of factors.

Most West European countries, as well as the United States, have been reluctant, however, to engage in a more positive kind of industrial policy. Contrary to the defensive industrial policies described above, positive industrial interventionism would involve a government in selecting new industries with a promising future, picking winners among existing firms or creating new companies to develop them, and backing the winners with public funds or various other protective measures in order to have them develop the desired manufacturing activities.

Harsh debates have subsequently centred around questions like these: Does a democratic government have the legitimacy to make such arbitrary choices as picking the winners? Would it not mean hidden protectionism and unfair competition, and profoundly distort the market mechanisms at the domestic as well as the international level? How could politicians or government bureaucrats possibly make more efficient investment decisions than professional bankers and entrepreneurs?, etc.

Still, some countries have successfully taken the approach of a positive industrial policy such as that described above—especially those that already had a long tradition of industrial *dirigisme* and administrative guidance. Among these, Japan has been the focus of general attention in the past few years, particularly because Japanese industry has been very successful and has challenged established US and European firms in traditional industries, such as automobiles or consumer electronics, and now threatens to challenge sunrise industries and advanced technologies, such as robots, computers, integrated circuits, etc.

The example of France also deserves attention. Among West European countries, France possesses the distinct peculiarity of having pursued positive industrial policies for a long time. In recent years, like all Western Europe, French industrial structure has suffered a lot from the economic crisis, especially in its traditional sectors, such as steel, textiles, and the like. But, at the same time, French firms were able to achieve great technological and commercial success in sunrise industries, such as electronics, telecommunications, aerospace, advanced armaments, nuclear engineering, etc. In many of these advanced industries, France has increased its exports on world markets and has even challenged the until-then unchallenged leadership of US firms. That is why, inside a collective work devoted to a global analysis of West European industrial policies and recommendations for the future, the case of France is worth studying. The institutional framework of French industrial policy will be examined first. Then the recent achievements and present orientations of sectoral industrial policies will be briefly reviewed.

II. Institutional framework

Economists have never been successful in drawing up a clear-cut theory of industrial policy. Industrial policy is by definition a highly pragmatic matter, dependent upon the current state of existing technologies, the period of economic history, and, above all, the political, sociological, and even cultural features of the country under examination. Industrial policy cannot be easily modelled, nor put into economic equations. Each country has its own way of handling industry. Some have a weak central government and a decentralized administration; some, on the contrary, have a strong central State. Some have a long trading experience, and a dynamic and innovative entrepreneurial class; some, on the contrary, are inward looking and have capitalists and conservative banks averse to risk.

For most western countries the best way to make industry efficient is to have no industrial policy at all and just let the market play. The truth, in fact, is that market mechanisms or government intervention are over-simplistic intellectual concepts which do not have the same meaning in Japan, the United States, the Federal Republic of Germany, Italy, or France. Analysis of industrial policies requires deep and interdisciplinary examination.

All this means that French industrial strategy can be described and understood only by reference to its historical tradition and its institutional framework, which have no counterpart in Anglo-Saxon nations or in other West European countries.

II.1 Historical tradition

The French government has experienced a long tradition of intervention to foster the growth and development of new industries and advanced technologies. Two main factors are at the heart of that tradition.

France was one of the first nations in Europe to achieve unity and centralization. Absolute centralization was continued and reinforced after the Revolution by the Jacobin Republic and other regimes that succeeded it. A centralized and powerful administration was thus built up as early as the eighteenth century and continuously developed thereafter. So economic intervention and industrial policy have always been, and still are, inseparable from national objectives such as national security, war and defence, and a balanced trade. France can thus be considered as a case-book example of mercantilism, having used the control of international trade and development of new industries as instruments of economic war and national prestige and wealth.

Being a Latin and Catholic nation, dominated by aristocratic landowners, France lacked the trading and capitalist tradition which existed in other European countries, such as the UK, Germany, and the Netherlands. The banks and entrepreneurs were more averse to risks and less dynamic in their ventures than their foreign counterparts. The French government expelled the Protestant merchant class in the eighteenth century. The wealthy preferred investing their capital in land or goverment bonds rather than industry and trade. These handicaps are demonstrated by the relative backwardness of French industrial development compared to the rest of Western Europe, especially in the nineteenth and early twentieth centuries. Thus government initiatives have been necessary to substitute for deficient private ventures, especially to develop capital-intensive or high-technology industries.

Colbertism (named after Jean Baptise Colbert, the minister of Louis XIV) can be identified with the first overall consistent national industrial strategy. Colbert's administration combined protection from foreign competition with various incentives—such as granted monopolies and patents, financial subsidies, and training programmes—in order to develop modern industries and complex technologies on French soil. The most favoured industries were those linked to armaments, e.g. gun foundries or battleship-yards. Import substitution industries for civilian needs, like linen, clothes, glass, tapestry, furniture, and chinaware, were also encouraged. Well-known enterprises—some still in existence, such as Les Gobelins, the Manufacture de Sevres, and Saint-Gobain—were funded as State manufacturers.

These traditions were pursued all through the eighteenth century. New administrations were created to encourage industrial development, as well as government technical schools to provide the various corps of State engineers with high-level specialists. During the nineteenth century, the Saint-Simonian movement developed the idea of a close association between the more dynamic entrepreneurs and bankers and the government administrations to foster the development of that century's sunrise industries: coal-mines, pig-iron furnaces, steel mills, waterways, steamships, railroads, etc. Following these ideas, the Second Empire enjoyed a particularly high rate of growth and productive investment from 1850 to 1870. Still, France went back to Malthusianism and protectionism during the Third Republic, until World War II. In 1940 France still had more than one-third of its working population in agriculture. In spite of some technological leadership, French industrial structure was scattered into small- and medium-sized firms, conservative and Malthusianistic. The Vichy government period introduced some change and developed the idea of a mixed economy, with a combination of liberalism and *dirigisme*. A new technocracy emerged in the ministerial departments and helped organize the economy for the constraints of war-time scarcity.

Following World War II France enjoyed a true economic miracle. Government planning and nationalized enterprises were key instruments for channelling funds and allocating capital investment in selected sectors such as transportation, energy, and other basic industries, e.g. highways, coal, hydroelectricity, steel, cement, chemicals, etc. Standing upon that strong industrial base, the French economy was then able to face European and world-wide competition when the Common Market's Treaty of Rome was signed. During the subsequent Gaullist period of the 1960s, new government-backed ventures were undertaken in high-technology industries as a response to the American challenge. The so-called *grands projets* were designed to give France national independence in technologies such as aircraft, space, nuclear weapons, nuclear energy, oil drilling and refining, computers, and electronics. In the 1970s the French high-technology industries already built developed their exports and achieved noticeable success on world markets, even challenging American leadership in military and civil aeronautics, helicopters, nuclear engineering, etc. At the same time, the government undertook new projects—especially in the fields of nuclear electricity, telecommunications, and electronics—in order to adapt French industry to the new technologies.

II.2. Policy tools and instruments: government technocracy

The national institutions of French industrial policy are no less distinctive than the country's historical tradition. Some are a century old, such as the *grandes écoles*; some are more recent, such as the government high-technology laboratories. But most of these institutions have no counterparts in other developed countries.

The technical ministries and their professional staff play an important part in the shaping and implementation of industrial strategy. The degree of influence exerted by a ministry depends upon the nature of its links with the industrial sectors dependent on it. For example, the links between the Ministry of Defence and the armaments industries, or between the Ministry of Post and Telecommunications and the telecommunications and electronic industries, are very close. Through public procurement, the ministries are able to shape the key industrial decisions, such as the technical standards of the equipment purchased, the prices, the structure of the industry, the export strategy, etc. The Ministries of Industry and Transportation have responsibility for the nationalized enterprises in the manufacturing, energy, and transportation sectors. Through this tutorship they are able to influence the strategies of these industries.

Public procurement, which guaranteed long-term orders and adequate research and development funds, appears to have been a key element in the technological success of such industries as electronics, aerospace, electrical engineering, railroad equipment, etc.

The Ministry of Research and Technology designs the budgets of the government laboratories and research centres, and makes sure that public spending for R&D is not sacrificed to short-term fiscal cuts. The financial Ministries, such as Treasury, Budget, and Foreign Trade, also play an important part in many aspects of industrial policy. The financial markets are closely regulated by the Treasury and the nationalized banks. The Treasury also monitors the debt strategy of the major public enterprises and distributes long-term public loans or capital endowments to industry, whether public or private. The Budget and Foreign Trade Departments monitor the various subsidies and export promotion loans to industry.

The ministries are staffed by professional civil servants, who enjoy a high degree of stability and run their careers in a corps attached to a ministry. The number of political appointments within the administration is thus very limited, especially in the technical ministries. The professional staff of the various corps are supplied by specialized higher-education establishments: the *grandes écoles*. These schools are run by the ministries and not by the University system. Their recruitment is through highly valued competitive examinations which attract the best students.

Among the *grand écoles* is the Ecole Nationale d'Administration, which supplies the administrative and diplomatic corps. More singificant for industrial policy are the scientific and engineering schools. Ecole Polytechnique, founded in 1974, and its *écoles d'application* provide specialized, high-level technical training for the various corps of State engineers. The Ecole des Mines and the Corps des Mines supply the staff of the Ministry of Industry and the energy and basic industry sectors. The Ecole and the Corps des Ponts et Chaussées play the same role for the Ministries of Public Works, Urban Development, and Transportation; the Ecole and the Corps de l'Armement for Defence, the Ecole and the Corps des Telecommunications for the PTT, etc.

II.3. Policy tools and instruments: public enterprises and laboratories

The key actors of industrial policy are of course the firms themselves, especially the large corporations who operate in high-technology sectors. The structure of the strategic industries is shaped by the Administration. This is true in the nationalized as well as the private sector. For a long time the concept of national champion meant that public benefits such as R&D grants, public procurement, etc., should be concentrated upon one single company to maximize the economies of scale effects. During recent years a more pragmatic approach has been used in order to maintain some competition where it was practicable. For example, in military aircraft there was one national champion, Dassault, which was a private firm until recently; the same holds for civil aircraft with Aerospatiale; for nuclear engineering with Framatome; for computers with CII-Honeywell Bull; or heavy electrical equipment with Alsthom. But in the oil industry there were two national champions, Total-Compagnie Française des Pétroles and Elf-Acquitaine, and in the telecommunications industry CIT-Alcatel and Thomson-CSF (merged in 1983).

The size of the nationalized sector in France is particularly high in comparison with other western countries. A first wave of nationalizations occurred just before and after World War II: transportation, energy, the main commercial banks, and insurance companies, as well as several manufacturing firms such as Renault, then went under government control. The purpose of those nationalizations was political, but the nationalized enterprises subsequently became important instruments of the reconstruction and of capital accumulation in basic sectors, as described above.

Another extension of the public sector occurred during the Gaullist period of the 1960s. New public enterprises were created or considerably developed to become instruments of the *grands projets* industrial policy: Elf-Aquitaine in the oil industry, Société Nationale Industrielle Aérospatiale in the aircraft and space industry, Compagnie Internationale pour l'Informatique in information technology, Cogema in nuclear materials, etc.

In 1981, following the political shift to the left, another wave of nationalizations extended the public sector to about 25 per cent of manufacturing industry, and within it to about 50 per cent of concentrated industry. Twelve major industrial companies and the remaining private banking sector went under government control. Thus most of the basic industries (steel, metals, chemicals, materials, etc.) and most of the high-technology equipment industries (aircraft, electronics, telecommunications, heavy engineering, etc.) are now run by nationalized enterprises.

The nationalized firms, although managed autonomously in their day-to-day decisions, operate in close co-operation and under the guidance of the ministries. Their long-term strategies are negotiated with the state within the framework of planning contracts. They receive public loans and capital endowments to sustain their investment and research strategies. A key which guides the planning agreements is that public enterprises should be able to invest counter-cyclically and to take long-term risks, with the support of government-supplied capital. Nationalized firms should thus be the major instruments used to fight against the effects of the industrial crisis, to conduct the restructuring and modernizations of traditional sectors that have run into financial trouble (such as steel and chemicals), and to develop new risk-taking industries (such as electronics, information technology, new energy sources, biochemicals, etc.).

Government laboratories and research centres in applied sciences are also important instruments of industrial policy. Most of them were created or considerably extended during the 1960s, when de Gaulle's government decided to increase the amount of public spending going to R&D for purposes of national independence. Significant among these laboratories are the Commissariat à l'Energie Atomique, which develops nuclear engineering and materials; the Centre National d'Etudes Spatiales, which develops space launchers and satellites; the Centre National d'Etudes des Télécommunications, which develops advanced telecommunications; and several others that operate in oceanology, information technology, biology, etc.

Most of the public enterprises and government research centres are staffed at the decision-making level by former technical civil servants and graduates of the *grandes écoles*. But it has to be noted that the large private firms have also been looking for former civil servants to staff their high positions for a long period of time. That close interpenetration of administrative and industrial technocracies has no equivalent in the western world, not even in Japan. More than any other factor, that interconnection helps to explain the close co-ordination and mutual trust which exists between administrative and industrial strategies in key sectors.

It is often argued that a major difficulty of industrial policy is the difference between political objectives and industrial objectives in time horizons. Politicians, it is said, operate in the short-term because politics are fluctuating and volatile; efficient industrial choices need a long-term approach.

Political stability, such as that provided by the Constitution of the Fifth Republic since 1958, is certainly a factor in explaining the long-range industrial strategy which has been a key element of success in many sectors. Nevertheless, it can be observed that during the Fourth

Republic, when governments suffered chronic instability, administrative stability substituted for political stability. Major industrial and technological government projects can thus be identified with the personality of a key professional civil servant—a high-level state engineer who occupied a senior position in his corps and at the same time had the full trust of the political authorities.

Such individuals as Pierre Guillaumat, who founded Elf-Aquitaine in the 1960s, André Giraud, who reorientated the strategy of the Commissariat à l'Energie Atomique in the early 1970s, Gerard Théry, who reorganized the Telecommunications Administration in the late 1970s, etc., can thus be described as administrative entrepreneurs, whose role was as decisive as that played by legendary capitalist entrepreneurs in other countries.

Having described these three specificities of French industrial policy—its historical tradition and cultural environment; its technocratic establishment, and its administrative institutions—it is now time to review the most recent strategic orientations in key sectors.

III. Sectoral policies: recent achievements and present orientations

During the past ten years, following a quarter of a century of fast growth, the French industrial structure has experienced depression and redeployments of an unusual magnitude, like most other West European nations. While traditional industries with obsolete technologies have met stagnation, harsh foreign competition, bankruptcies, and job lay-offs, some new industries have emerged and have developed their investment, employment, and exports. Electronic industries already employ 300,000 workers, nuclear-electricity engineering 150,000, aerospace 100,000, etc. The rapid development of these industries is, in great part, the result of ambitious government industrial strategies. These strategies, in general, were pursued with a long-run objective for several decades before reaching the stage of maturity.

The recent achievements and present orientation of industrial strategy will be explored in detail in three sectors: energy, aerospace, and electronics. In these three sectors French industry has been able to reach an advanced technological level and an internationally competitive position. This does not mean that there were no industrial policies in other sunrise sectors not belonging to these three categories. Pharmaceuticals, advanced shipbuilding, railroad equipment, and some other industries have also been the focus of industrial policy.

Nor does this mean that France has reached excellence in all the sunrise industries that will shape the whole industrial structure by the year 2000. French industry is not as advanced in sophisticated machinery, coal liquefaction, bio- and fine chemistry, precision instruments, robots, and very large scale integrated (VLSI) electronic components as it is, for instance, in helicopters, space launchers, high-speed trains, electronic telecommunications, missiles, nuclear reprocessing, and fast breeders. Why is this so and why have these three sectors been selected for review?

A common characteristic of the sectors where French industry has reached a strong technological and commercial position is high dependence on government procurement policy and state intervention. In advanced technologies, France seems to be good in sectors where government administrations are the main customer, and not so good in sectors producing for mass consumption or for general industrial equipment. Still more significant, as will become apparent, is that the main objective of these government industrial strategies seems to have been national security. The quest for national independence motivated the government when it decided to build a national military aircraft industry, a national nuclear industry, and a national computer industry. The quest for safety in key supplies also motivated the national oil policy and the nuclear electricity programme. Even if these industrial policies subsequently produced applications in non-military areas, their origins can almost always be traced to national independence objectives.

III.1. Energy

Energy has been an area with a marked degree of government involvement for a long time:

- the heavy capital requirements and the high degree of risk made it difficult to attract risk-averse private investment;
- it is a key strategic sector, energy being essential to all kinds of manufacturing activities;
- French soil is relatively poor in natural energy resources, whether coal, gas, or oil, so that France has always been obliged to import a significant part of its energy needs from abroad. Thus it has always been highly concerned with questions like security of supply and trade dependence.

Since the nationalizations of 1946, the energy sector has been run by State monopolies in coal, gas, and electricity: Charbonnages de France, Gaz de France, and Electricité de France. The energy policy is co-ordinated by the Ministry of Industry and the Ministry of Finance, which set the prices and direct the investment and financial strategies of the public enterprises.

Oil and gas imports have also been monitored and regulated by the State since a law passed in 1928. The oil industry is run jointly by the subsidiaries of three international majors (BP, Shell, and Exxon) and by two government-controlled French companies: Total-Compagnie Française des Pétroles (established in 1923 to exploit Iraq's oil reserves partly allocated to France by the post World War I treaties) and Elf-Aquitaine (created in 1966 from the merger of smaller, state-owned companies exploiting the reserves of the French domestic territory and the former colonial empire).

The two main recent achievements of energy policy in sunrise sectors have been oil technologies and nuclear electricity technologies.

During the 1960s, when oil's share of the national energy market rose from 20 per cent to 60 per cent, the main objective of energy policy was to build up an independent French oil industry. Using oil import regulations, the French administration helped Total and Elf boost their share of the national oil market to 50 per cent with the companies using the resources they owned in the Middle East, Sahara, or West Africa to meet the increased demand. With their profits, as well as with the aid of government subsidies and tax credits, the French oil companies were able to develop exploration domestically and abroad in order to find a substitute for the Saharan oil reserves that Algeria nationalized in 1970.

Thus Elf or Total have been (or still are) active in Iran, Iraq, the Gulf Emirates, the Gulf of Guinea, Indonesia, Canada, and the North Sea. They have also built an important national refining and petro-chemical capacity. Under government monitoring the two companies have also helped to develop a technologically advanced industry in various oil-related services. The Institut Français du Pétrole is an advanced fundamental research centre that also provides training for all kinds of petroleum engineers. Technip is an advanced refinery and petrochemical engineering firm. Successful firms have also been developed in other sophisticated technologies, such as geophysic exploration, off-shore drilling, oil- and gas-tanker building, etc. All these service firms are internationally competitive and are now able to sell on foreign markets.

France now has the third largest national oil industry in the western world, after the US and the UK. This achievement is all the more remarkable since at the beginning France did not possess the oil expertise of Anglo-Saxon nations or important national resources to exploit.

In nuclear engineering France started to accumulate technological expertise by creating the Commissariat à l'Energie Atomique (CEA) in 1945. That research centre was devoted initially to fundamental research, in which French scientists, such as Becquerel and Curie, were well advanced before World War II. The CEA also developed research for military applications.

These orientations were strongly developed when de Gaulle decided, in the 1960s, to build up a French national nuclear force. In the same decade the CEA acquired or exploited uranium mines in France and Africa and built a uranium high-enrichment plant for military uses at Pierrelatte, in South-east France. The CEA also tried to develop an electricity generation reactor using natural uranium, the graphite-carbon dioxide process (or *filière graphite-gaz*). That technology met some problems, so in the early 1970s the government decided to acquire the pressured-water-reactor licence (PWR) from Westinghouse and to build a giant uranium low-enrichment plant, Eurodif, at Tricastin, also in south-east France, in co-operation with Italian, Spanish, and a few other foreign partners.

In 1973 France was ready to react to the first oil shock, which had a strong impact on the French economy. At that time France imported 75 per cent of its energy needs; oil alone, representing 60 per cent of French energy consumption, was almost entirely imported. The French government decided in a few weeks to start a very ambitious nuclear electricity programme that had no counterpart elsewhere. Electricité de France (EDF) was encouraged to launch the construction of six electric nuclear PWR plants per year, each having 900 MW production capacity. The nuclear engineering industry was simultaneously reorganized.

The contractor for the nuclear boiler is Framatome, a subsidiary of both the Commissariat à l'Energie Atomique (CEA) and the French private engineering group Schneider, and a licensee of Westinghouse. The agreement with Westinghouse provided that the licensee would recover its full independence by 1980. EDF gave the electric generator contracts to Alsthom, a subsidiary of the now-nationalized group Compagnie Générale d'Electricité (CGE). Simultaneously, decisions were taken for the CEA to extend the enrichment plant Eurodif, to build a reprocessing plant for used nuclear fuels in La Hague in west France, and to develop research for building a commercial fast breeder reactor, Superphenix, which would make the uranium supply problem virtually non-existent.

After a decade of rapid development, the French nuclear engineering industry now employs 150,000 workers and has reached a world leadership position, because over the same period most western countries chose to reduce their nuclear programmes, mainly for safety or ecological reasons. French industry now fully masters all nuclear technologies and controls all the production steps, from mining to enrichment, electricity generation, reprocessing, and fast breeding. Safety problems are also carefully watched by a special administration, independent from both EDF and CEA.

The nuclear electricity equipment programme, which amounts to about 25 billion 1983 francs per year, was slightly reduced in 1981.

Instead of launching six 900 MW plants per year, only two or three 1,300 MW plants will now be built every year. Nuclear generation has already totalled or partially replaced fuel and coal generation within EDF plants: nuclear generated electricity now represents about 50 per cent of total electricity consumed in France. The objective is that by 1990 nuclear electricity will represent 75 per cent of total electricity used in France (the rest being mainly hydroelectricity), and 30 per cent of the total energy needs of the nation. By then the share of oil will have been reduced to 33 per cent, down from 60 per cent in 1973. This means that electricity will have to penetrate a variety of final uses, such as industrial heating or domestic heating, as a substitute for fuel-oil, gas, and coal. The development of electric equipment at the utilization stage will thus be fostered.

With the national equipment programme now stagnant, the French nuclear engineering and electric engineering industries are trying to reorientate their production towards exports. Some contracts have already been captured abroad.

Besides nuclear electricity, it has to be noted that important government programmes have also been launched to develop energy conservation and new energy sources, such as solar photovoltaic cells, geothermy, and biomass. These programmes are monitored by the Ministry of Industry and Research and its affiliate, the Agence Française pour la Maitrise de l'Energie.

The magnitude of the energy-transition programme undertaken in France is by far the most ambitious in the world. This programme will alleviate the hard burden of imported oil on the French economy, and has already developed fast-growing new industry, employing highly trained workers and engineers. Sunrise energy industries also promise to be a powerful locomotive in future for the whole French industrial structure and its exports.

III.2. Aerospace

French engineers contributed highly to the birth and development of aircraft technologies at the beginning of the twentieth century. The army also rapidly understood the rising importance of these new technologies for warfare purposes.

From both these factors stem traditions of French excellence in aeronautics and active industrial policies in all sectors of the aerospace industry. France now holds second place in the world in this industry. It is admittedly still far behind the United States, but ahead of many other advanced industrial powers, such as the UK, Germany, and Japan.

After several waves of restructuring and concentration in the past decades, the French aerospace industry is now organized into three main companies, all under government control: Sociéte Nationale Industrielle Aerospatiale or SNIAS (civil aircraft carriers, helicopters, missiles, space launchers, and satellites); Dassault-Breguet (military aircraft); and SNECMA (aircraft engines). There are also several smaller companies and many subcontractors, such as Matra (missiles), Turbomeca (helicopter engines), Messier-Hispano (landing equipment), etc.

The main instruments of industrial policy in aeronautics have been public procurement, research subsidies, export credits, and industrial diplomacy. The central objective of aerospace policy was at first national independence in military aircraft. The French aeronautic firms have thus received long-term research and production contracts from the Ministry of Defence in order to develop a national aircraft industry. These orientations cannot be isolated from de Gaulle's decision to leave the NATO defence organization in the early 1960s. Unlike most West European nations, France chose not to rely upon US aircraft builders for its defence needs. A very successful generation of military aeroplanes then developed: Mystère 20, Mirage III, Mirage IV, etc.

In order to extend the scale of operations and to reduce average production costs, the national policy was then completed by an export promotion policy, which was particularly active during the 1970s. Thanks to export credits and the effort of government diplomacy, the French aircraft industry was able to develop its sales in the Middle East (Saudi Arabia, Iraq, etc.) as well as in Latin American, Asian, and African countries. Successful generations of missiles (Roland, Exocet, etc.) and helicopters (Alouette) were developed for national needs and then exported by the same means.

It is well known that defence is by far the largest market for the aeronautics industry. France used the technological strengths it built up thanks to military procurement in order to develop civilian applications. For this French firms receive financial support from the Ministry of Transportation, and public procurement backing from the national airline company, Air France.

The short-range civilian carrier Caravelle, developed in the 1950s, was not as commercially successful as it could have been. Then, in the 1960s, the first supersonic commercial carrier was developed, in cooperation with the British Aerospace Company. Concorde was a costly technological success, but a commercial failure, as is well known. Following the Concorde undertaking, SNIAS and the French government chose in the 1970s to develop a new medium-range civilian carrier in co-operation with a German firm. The commercial niche was well chosen and gave the Airbus project the chance to capture a large world market at the expense of the hitherto unchallenged aircraft companies. Airbus is now giving birth to a whole generation of derived projects, with other European firms coming to join the association.

Airbus is a truly European venture, but French industry was clearly the co-ordinator of the project.

SNECMA has simultaneously developed a jet engine project for Airbus, using the technological strength it accumulated in the past with military jet engines. The CFM-56 engine project is undertaken with the co-operation of the American firm General Electric. Civil helicopters, as well as business and leisure planes, have also been developed by the French aeronautic firms.

In space technologies, which France first entered two decades ago, the era of technological and commercial success is now coming after many years of research efforts. The Centre National d'Etudes Spatiales (CNES) was funded as one of the Gaullist *grands projets* to be the co-ordinating body of the national space policy. CNES built a launching base at Kourou, in French Guyana, and developed several projects for military and civil purposes in co-operation with the French aeronautics firms SNIAS and Matra: ballistic missiles for the French strategic nuclear force; space launchers; telecommunications, broadcasting, and scientific observation satellites, etc.

The civilian space launcher and satellite programme have been conducted in co-operation with other European firms, within the framework of the consortium Arianespace. The launcher Ariane reached the stage of the commercial applications in 1983, and has already captured a large share of the highly promising telecommunications satellite-launching market.

By all standards, aerospace has been one of the undisputed successes of French industrial strategy in sunrise sectors. French firms are profitable, technologically competitive, and able to export a large share of their production. Again the national security objective was central in the policy, and in its implementation.

III.3. Electronics

During the past four decades—from the discovery of the transistor to the development of VLSI—electronics has undertaken a series of technological revolutions which have contributed to a massive extension of its uses. Initially confined to the area of wireless radio communications, electronics has subsequently been applied to radar and guidance systems, scientific calculators, and office computers.

Now a new wave of micro-electronic applications is spreading into the entire economy with the diffusion of personal computers and new generations of electronic consumer goods, the application of robots to automated manufacturing, and the combination of information technology and telecommunications.

The electronics revolution promises to be as important in its economic consequences and as pervasive in its effects as was the industrial revolution founded on the machine. Its effects will be felt through the new products and services it offers, as well as through the improved productivity it gives production processes. The full mastering of electronic technologies and the growth of electronic industries thus appear to be key priorities for any industrial policy.

The French government has given electronics top priority since 1981. Industrial policy now adopts a global approach towards electronic industries, illustrated by the concept of *filière électronique*. This concept stresses the technological interdependence between the various industrial sectors incorporating electronic techniques.

The analysis of the strengths and weaknesses of French industry in the *filière électronique* reveals a contrasted situation, with strong points in professional electronic equipment and telecommunications, average positions in computers and electronic components, and rather weak points in electronic consumer goods, electronic office equipment, robots, scientific instruments, etc. The key idea of the new industrial strategy is to develop the weak points by taking advantage of the strong ones which already exist.

The emphasis is thus being put upon integrated circuits, computers, electronic consumer goods, and robots. The objective of the *Plan Filière Electronique* is a programme of investment and R&D amounting to 140 billion 1982 francs over the five-year period 1983-7—in order to reach a growth rate of 9 per cent per year and a trade surplus of 20 billion FFr by 1987 (against a 3 per cent growth and a 10 billion FFr trade deficit in 1981). This programme is to be financed by the firms themselves, with government support coming from the Ministries of Defence, PTT, and Industry and Research. The policy will be implemented by the now nationalized four major French electronics firms: Thomson-CSF, CIT-Alcatel, Matra, and Bull, who have been recently restructured and reorganized to rationalize the specializations between them.

French industry shows strong positions in two sectors where industrial policy has been active and dynamic for many years: heavy electronic equipment for professional uses (such as military and broadcasting) and electronic telecommunications. In both sectors the trade balance is positive and French firms have a technological leadership. The strength in professional electronic equipment has been developed through the administration's public procurement policy. The main firms involved in professional electronic equipment are Thomson-CSF, a subsidiary of the Thomson conglomerate, and Matra; in telecommunications they are CIT-Alcatel, a subsidiary of the Group Compagnie Générale d'Electricité (CGE) and Thomson Telecom.

The Ministry if Defence and the National Broadcasting Authority (TDF) have developed a national independence approach for their electronic equipment since the beginning of the 1950s. Research and development have been encouraged in radar, aircraft equipment, missiles, etc., with research contracts granted by the Ministry of Defence to French firms. Production was also encouraged by long-term purchasing contracts. Once technological maturity was reached, exports were encouraged by special loans and promoted through the efforts of industrial diplomacy in order to increase the scale of production and thus amortize research and development spending. Exports to the Middle East were particularly successful in the 1970s, even challenging US companies' leading positions.

In the telecommunications industry France has been dependent on the multi-national giants, such as ITT and Ericson, for a long time. In the late 1960s the research centre of the Ministry of PTT, the Centre National d'Etudes des Telecommunications (CNET), developed investigations into electronic commutation. The technology was then transferred to the French company CIT-Alcatel. In the early 1970s the French government decided to increase massively the amount of public investment in telecommunications equipment, which was relatively backward until then. The decision was taken to merge Ericson-France and ITT-France into Thomson-CSF, with the agreement of their foreign parent companies. The total amount of investment in telecommunications equipment has been around 30 billion 1983 francs per year during the past ten years. Thanks to these public purchases, and thanks to the research subsidies associated with public procurement, the French telecommunications industry has been able to develop the most advanced technologies and to start production on a mass scale. Active R&D programmes have been developed in fibre-optic networks, computers, and domestic terminals. Simultaneously, exports have been promoted where commercial positions are still open, especially on the new markets of Third World countries.

In two other sectors of the *filière électronique*, electronic components and computers, French industry competitiveness remains uncertain, in spite of industrial policies pursued in the past.

The Plan Calcul started in 1966, as one of the Gaullist *grands projets*, and was designed to make France independent in scientific calculators. The French private computer company, Bull, had been purchased by the US's General Electric a few years before. A semi-public company, CII, was funded with the co-operation of Thomson and CGE in order to develop national computers with the support of government research grants and public procurement, all monitored by the Ministry of Industry. In 1975 CII was merged with Bull, which had by then been repurchased by the US group Honeywell, in order to form CII-Honeywell Bull (CII-HB).

CII-HB is now the largest European computer company. France also has a leading position in software services, with a number of medium-sized service firms highly competitive and technologically advanced. But in spite of public subsidies and public procurement support, CII-HB still loses money and carries a heavy debit (as do most computer firms, except IBM). In 1982 the government decided to increase financial support to CII-HB and to rationalize the structure of the French information industry: SEMS and Transac, both in mini-computers and peripheral equipment, have been merged with CII-HB to form the group Bull, whose strategy is reorientated towards the new generation of computers.

The plan for integrated circuits was initiated in 1976. Five French companies received public research subsidies from the Ministry of Industry and Public Procurement or from the Ministries of Defence and PTT in order to develop the production of LSI (large scale integrated) circuits. They were also encouraged to sign agreements with leading US firms, such as Harris, National-Semi-Conductors, Intel, etc., in order to transfer LSI technology from Silicon Valley. The plan was confirmed and the amount of public support was increased in 1982. The French electronic components industry was then restructured around two companies, Thomson and Matra.

Industrial policy plans have also been launched recently in two weak sectors of the *filière électronique*, which until then had remained outside the scope of government interventionism. In consumer electronics, Thomson (which still holds some good industrial and commercial positions in colour TV sets) has been encouraged to extend its operations on the European market. Thomson has acquired several smaller firms in Germany in order to extend its scale of operations, the most recent acquisition being AEG-Telefunken. Thomson has also been encouraged to sign an agreement with the Japanese group Matsushita-JVC, in order to develop production of videotape recorders under the VHS standard.

In robotics an ambitious plan was launched in 1981 to restructure and modernize the French machine tool industry. The smaller firms will be encouraged to merge and to develop numerically-controlled machines and automats with the support of public research grants, procurement from nationalized firms, and government training programmes, again monitored by the Ministry of Industry.

IV. Concluding remarks

Can the French experience in industrial policy in sunrise sectors be transplanted to other countries? Is it applicable for industrial strategies at the European level? These questions are particularly important in the present decade.

European industry as a whole is in effect confronted by the same kind of problems as French industry alone. These problems are adjustment to the new economic and social conditions prevailing in the world, the conversion of sunset industries, and the development of sunrise industries.

French culture and industrial organization are probably much closer to those of other West European nations than Japan's, so more usable lessons can possibly be derived for Europe from the French experience. Still, as shown above, the French tradition of interventionism as well as its policy tools and institutions are very specific and distinctive, and probably have no counterpart elsewhere. Moreover, industrial strategies in sunrise sectors have in the past found their main inspiration in nationalistic purposes, such as national defence and security.

If the EC as a whole desired to reach the same results as France did, this may mean that it should adopt a more independent approach for its defence and a common armaments policy, as well as a more protective stand in its trade and energy policies. This, of course, raises important political problems, since it is obvious that the European Community members do not share the same views about these questions. Germany, Italy, and Benelux mainly rely on the US for their defence and armaments; the Netherlands, Germany, and the UK are strongly committed to free trade and are reluctant to have any kind of *dirigisme*, while Italy has a rather weak central administration; the UK is more open to multinational US and Japanese firms than the others; etc.

At the same time a European approach to the development of sunrise high-technology industries is being felt more and more necessary. The solidarity between European industry is not well established: Europe needs more co-ordinated industrial standards, more open public procurement, more co-operative ventures and mergers between its firms, etc. The European market is used more efficiently by American and Japanese multinational firms than by the European firms themselves. In order to compete successfully with Japanese and US firms on world markets, the European scale of production and co-ordinated national policies will increasingly appear as strategic factors to amortize the costs of research and development and of mass production.

This need has already been felt in the past decade in such industries as civil and military aircraft, space launchers and satellites, nuclear enrichment, etc. Co-operative projects like Airbus, Tornado, Jaguar, Ariane, and Eurodif could then probably be considered as models for future European co-operations. Still, a clear lesson of past experiences is that European industrial co-operation should be guided by pragmatism and modesty. It is probably more efficient to look for bi- or trilateral co-operations, developed step-by-step, involving firms and national administrations sharing common views and objectives, instead of trying ambitious projects that involve all European countries simultaneously.

PART III

CORPORATE STRATEGY AND THE FUTURE OF EUROPEAN INDUSTRIAL POLICIES

XI
The Micro-Foundations of Industrial Policies 6160
6110

GUNNAR ELIASSON*

I. The problem

The theory of industrial policy making is a natural part of a more general theory of market regulations (or market imperfections) covering its institutions and what link them together in the market process. We have to understand the policy maker, his motives, and the body of interests that he represents. We also have to understand the recipient of policy—the firm—and how its behaviour can be modified to suit the policy maker. This paper is concerned with the latter aspect, although it recognizes—as a matter of realistic convenience—that policy bodies operate according to their own utility functions and should not automatically be associated with the public interest.

It is a fairly well-established fact that the long-term rate of return determines the value growth of a firm, if currently generated resources can be reinvested at the same rate of return. This chapter recognizes a firm that is solely concerned with pursuing such long-run profit objectives of its own.

Maximum value growth of a firm is not synonymous with maximum output or employment growth of the same firm or industry. Since output and employment are typical targets of national policy makers, a conflict between business objectives and national policy targets may exist.

This chapter investigates—as a *first* area of policy concern—under what circumstances a micro–macro targeting conflict does exist.

We may think of socially desirable target modifications, like keeping unemployment low, or nationalistic target modifications, like maintaining a viable defence industry or beating the Americans in sophisticated electronics. Whatever the reason for the micro–macro targeting conflict, it manifests itself as modifications of those targets the firms would be aiming at if left on their own. Lack of competence, lack of resources,

* President, the Industrial Institute for Economic and Social Research (IUI), Stockholm.

or pure profit motives have been cited as reasons in the debate on why business targets have to be modified. These have also been the most frequently voiced reasons for *industrial policy action.*

Most business organizations are complex structures that are guided by a group of people (owners and managers) more or less devoted to the profitability target and supported by an information-enforcement system through which the business organization is run. This system connects the group of decision makers *outwards* with an uncertain external environment and *inwards* with an (also) uncertain or incompletely known internal organization. The information system determines the efficiency by which the organization can be influenced (guided), and the efficiency of business target fulfilment.

The *second* area of policy concern that we discuss, hence, has to do with the means whereby and the places wherein the business organization can be influenced by policy makers to achieve a modification of business targets to meet national policy targets.

Industrial policy making has always been a loosely defined concept. It is concerned with affecting the structural adjustment process, and as such conventionally contrasts with stabilization policies that takes structure more or less for granted. By such a standard, industrial policy makers appear to be engaged in most kinds of economic policy except the traditional fiscal and monetary repertoire.[1] This somehow means that industrial policy making is concerned with getting the economic system and its prices and quantities in a nice balance that is compatible with a long-term stable growth rate and with what is politically desired.

For the time being we will leave the term loosely defined as that. Part of our problem in what follows will be to narrow it down, make it more concrete, and relate it to the decision machinery of a business organization.

II. The target dichotomy

Maximum value growth of the firm is conventionally defined as the first priority of business management. Maximum value growth means the maximum rate of creation of economic resources. For a whole industry this tends to be associated with maximum economic growth and employment in the longer term. Hence, *industrial policy makers* would not appear to be inclined to interfere with the market process of business management to correct business targets at the expense of long-term profitability, except for three reasons.

First, that there are other, feasible, organizational solutions that achieve at least the same profit performance and an improved perform-ance in other socially or politically desired dimensions.

(i) *between* firms as improvements in market performance (*market* approach)

(ii) *within* firms as improvements in management performance (*positive* approach).

Second, that there is another *micro-allocation* or another *timing* of value growth that achieves at least the same long-term growth in the value of business resources and an improved performance in other dimensions.

Can profits be sacrificed now to the benefit of social targets without diminishing the present value of the firm to its owners? For government industrial policy makers to achieve such ends they have to possess a superior overview of the entire industry situation. We call this the *planning* approach.

The first policy option is concerned with improving either the ways by which the economy is organized and run (anti-trust policies belong here) or the ways in which firms operate. The latter was, in fact, an explicitly stated objective for forming the Swedish State-operated business conglomerate.[2] To be successful the necessary industrial competence needs to reside within the policy-forming body and/or have access to it. Such 'static', one-shot, efficiency improvements, if feasible, shift the production possibility frontier—of the economy of the firm—outwards, all other things being equal.

The second policy option has to do with improving the dynamic efficiency of business operations or with the time preference of the nation. For instance, it is possible that a cost incurred now (e.g. higher unemployment due to a reallocation of labour) may result in a larger output gain in the longer term and the disappearance of the unemployment problem.

One has to recognize that internal 'structure-improving' operations, defined as above, belong to the normal operating repertoire of firms, conglomerate business organizations, or industrial groups. Continuous internal restructuring is the normal means to increase productivity and to attain profitability targets. So the new aspect brought in here is that new solutions can be attained that cater for variables which business management tends to neglect, but without violating the basic business targets.

The third reason for policy interference is different and has become a focal point for policy concern during the stagflation experience of the 1970s. Due to exogenous environmental changes a firm may suddenly face a factor and product price combination that

(i) it cannot cope with in terms of maintaining its rate of return target, and/or

(ii) makes it opt for a factor output combination that means less output growth and less employment.

If so, the government may want to change the adjustment process of the firm by slowing it down and/or correcting its development path to be more compatible with policy objectives. This may be at the expense of the owners, or they may be compensated for the additional costs incurred in adopting a modified set of targets, so that the firm's value growth or profit objective will not be impaired. We call this the *subsidy* approach to industrial policy making. In the post-1973 economic crisis among industrial nations, such policy ambitions have become widespread to hold down unemployment.

This chapter discusses and identifies the means by which such alternative solutions can be achieved.

Many principal discussions of this problem have already been published. On this score we offer very little that is new to the existing literature. The contribution of this chapter lies on the empirical side, in that it responds to the question *How* to carry out policies.

This means that we have to identify where exactly the business information and decision systems 'open up' for policy influence. To do so we first have to describe the nature of the modern manufacturing firm, which differs considerably from the concept used in economic theory, and then proceed to identify its administrative guidance systems. After that we can discuss the options open to policy makers. Finally, we return to the original question, namely, are there alternative environmental, management, and/or policy regimes that are capable of performing better than the systems implemented today? We discuss options and experience under the headings: the *positive*, the *subsidy*, the *planning*, and the *market* approach to industrial policy making.

III. The modern firm[3]

This chapter is mainly directed towards the large firm. There are three reasons for this. Sheer numbers keep policy bodies from interacting with more than a small, select group of large firms. The large firms wield financial power. They can honour industrial policy contracts with the government.

This little group often dominates industrial output and employment and the opinion is frequently voiced[4] that government industrial policies should be run through these large firms and their networks of subcontractors. We shall return to this problem and also to the small firm, or the new entrant, in the capacity of being a guardian of the competitive vitality of the market environment of large firms.

The modern manufacturing corporation more or less internalizes the following six activities: namely those of

(i) an innovator, including the management of R&D activities;
(ii) an investment and long-term financing institution;

(iii) a bank;
(iv) an insurance company;
(v) one or more production entities;
(vi) a marketing and sales institution (a trading house);
(vii) an educational institution.

A list of other functions can also be added, like purchasing, tax analysis, public relations, and the function that is perhaps most important, and growing, in the context of policy making: the government-relations function.

In the small 'one plant, one firm' business unit (the classical concept of a firm in economic theory), physical hardware production normally dominates in terms of using up resources. Other functions increase in relation to size, and in the large western corporations they together probably use up more, or much more, than 50 per cent of currently applied resources within the company. I know large, internationally known firms where the figure is just about 10 per cent. The point I want to make here is that the 'service content' of value added in manufacturing is increasing rapidly across the business population in an advanced industrial economy, and that it is already a dominating feature in sophisticated technological and/or large firms.[5] In fact, the twenty-five largest Swedish manufacturing firms should be characterized as large international marketing institutions rather than production organizations. Such a factor input structure carries strong and new implications for the effects of policy making.

The seven administrative functions listed above differ enormously in character. They are vested with different management groups within the firm. They are normally not well co-ordinated, either in time or in 'function'. The practical reason for this is the sheer difficulty of combining and co-ordinating activities that are extremely diverse in nature and talent requirements. Contrary to popular opinion in business administration literature a decade or so ago, there is no corporate model available for this purpose except in the minds of a few high-level executives. Their talent in this respect defines their management competence.

These seven administrative functions are hierarchically layered. Figure 11.1 gives a rough idea of their ranking. The existence of these different activities within the firm defines the nature and behaviour of the modern manufacturing corporation as something very much beyond a well-structured production process. In large western firms (like Siemens, Philips, or Electrolux) the various financial functions isolate the interior firm activities, like production and investment, from environmental disturbances, including policy making on the part of governments. The effects of industrial policy making that we will be

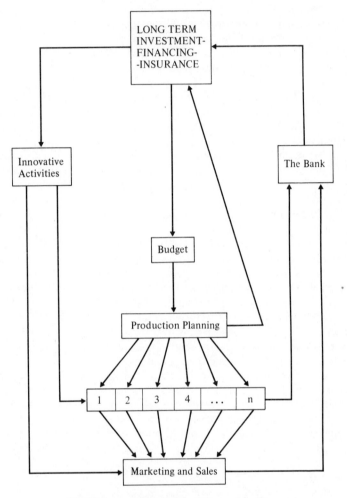

Fig. 11.1: Activity structure of a modern firm.

discussing also differ significantly, depending upon that policy's objectives and through which management channels they are implemented.

We have so far regarded the modern firm as if it were a given entity, composed of a fixed set of organizational units and functions. In the long run this is also a clear misrepresentation of a firm, and especially of a successful firm, the inner life of which is extremely 'dynamic'. Long-term growth and survival of a business organization is always accompanied by continuous restructuring of the nature of productive activities within the firm. Part of this shows up as a consequence of the relative growth of the various activities shown in Figure 11.1, and part of it shows up in the form of exit and entry of production entities from and to the firm. Most of this structural change simply alters the nature of the activities, and hence does not appear explicitly in this classification scheme.

IV. The administrative system of a modern firm

The large western business unit can be very much seen as a bundle of production plants held together by an investment institute, a bank, an insurance company, and a marketing organization. In fact, all activities except the physical production process are administrative devices that allow the firm's organization to beat the market in terms of efficiency and to expand in size.[6]

Without the superiority of these administrative co-ordination systems, one would expect each production plant to be on its own in the market, producing and selling. The rationale for the large western firm rests on the efficiency of such management information and enforcement systems relative to the market. We have to pass some judgement in this chapter on the extent to which the existence of some business organizations (like large conglomerates or international firms) depends on efficient management systems or inefficient market regimes. If the profitability of atomistic action at places within the organization is higher than co-ordinated action, this would mark the limit of the business organization and signal that these marginal operations are ripe for exit—and vice versa. Hence, at those boundaries the co-ordinated group will start to leak funds or to have difficulties in attracting funds. In fact, the financial boundary defined and determined as such is the proper foundation of a theory of the size and growth of the firm.[7] However, if the capital markets are highly regulated and/or undeveloped and a below-market interest rate is artificially maintained (which frequently seems to be the case)[8] and if large financial units are favoured in their ability to get access to long-term external sources of funds, then one could easily envision the growth of colossal and profitable financial conglomerates which are internally inefficient.

Similarly speaking, large economies of scale in distribution and marketing can often support an inefficient or obsolete production system. A few highly profitable products can cover internal loss operations and less successful endeavours in other areas for a long time. Having said this, one has to recognize that the interior of a large firm often hides major inefficiencies of the kind we expect to follow from some forms of industrial policy making. The reasons may be the same as those for policies: not to reduce unemployment too fast. For many large companies the image of being a good employer is a perfectly rational part of its long-term profit oriented strategies.

Any industrial policy action on the part of a government has to be empirically informed about these matters to be successful. In fact, policies have to be implemented either by affecting the business environment or through direct incentive or enforcement measures applied to the firm's management system.

Before discussing policy instrumentation, I shall briefly outline some features of the various administrative systems of a modern firm. First, some general comments about the management system typically in use are relevant. With growth, with size, and with long-run survival of the firm, successful, innovative activity and a constant restructuring of the internal life of the firm seem to be a must.[9] These are badly defined activities which are difficult to predict and do not lend themselves to routine operating management. The larger the business operation, the more important that such activities do not drown in day-to-day routine management.

Two features appear to be important ingredients in the design of successful planning and control systems:[10]

(i) an efficient procedure to delegate management of routine operations downwards in the organization in order to free top management for strategic decisions;

(ii) an efficient way to set reasonable and enforceable targets from the top down on the basis of incomplete and unreliable information.

The organization is often streamlined accordingly: there are as few targets as possible, responsibilities are geared to negotiated agreements around those targets, and targets represent systematic breakdowns of the dominant profitability objective.

However, the normal state of affairs, even in large companies, witnesses top management heavily involved in day-to-day operations, strategic thinking often being delegated to staff 'strategic planners' who are typically academic and non-communicative with operations. That arrangement works as long as nothing unexpected occurs in the environment of the firm.

Well-designed management systems separate process from innovative management and place the former on a grid of administrative routines that respond with 'flashing red lights' if something is off routine. The annual budget process is the most important administrative routine in this context. It generates a reference set of measures or targets with which current performance can be compared. Most large western companies, and most typically the large American companies, have instituted automatic 'flashing' routines when the company is 'off budget' in some significant way. Of course, these targets and the whole budget are made up solely on the objective function or the value system of the firm and its owners. The value system of a typical, well-run business organization is monolithically concerned with profitability. It is supreme in its disregard for, say, the employment consequences of its action. As few inputs as possible should be used for the production of one unit of output. This has to be recognized when we discuss the potential of industrial policy action. It is important to ask to what extent interference with these objectives impairs the overall efficiency of business management and profitability.

The larger the organization, the more distant management is from the physical action going on, and the more important the quality of the measurement system used to learn about what is going on and to enforce corporate objectives from a distance.

In terms of Figure 11.1 only the long-term innovative activities are not subjected to routine management, except in the sense that a 'cost-frame' has been allocated to them. The rest is routine management controlled by the short-term budgeting process.

However, even if top management time has been successfully freed from routine day-to-day operations, whether there is enough talent at the top for the entire business organization to be successful on the innovative side and in long-term strategic decisions is an entirely different question.

The key to successful delegation is an efficient target and enforcement system in which top management can have confidence. This, in turn, requires that targets are simple and monolithic, that measurements are reliable and interpretable, and that targets can be placed very close to what is feasible, perhaps with an extra effort. We note again a potential conflict when industrial policy making is aimed at attending to social variables, i.e. when new targets are added and the guidance system is made more complex.

Simplicity in goal formulation (to avoid a complex analytical and unreliable planning apparatus that would lack significant information inputs of sufficient quality and precision when they are needed) is a key notion in large-scale management systems. The solution is delegation and lower level autonomy down to the limit where simple goals (targets) can be enforced.

The necessity to simplify means that firms' administrative systems differ considerably in 'philosophy'. One extreme version is not to place any restrictions on what the various profit centres do as long as minimum profit standards are passed. The other extreme is the top–down/bottom–up agreement on a detailed plan, with corporate headquarters monitoring much of the detail through efficient reporting against the plan system. Firms occupy much of the range between these extremes. Electrolux, for instance, is run by the less-detailed, profit-oriented, decentralized method of the first type. The latter bureaucratic system has often been typical of large US corporations.[11]

It appears that the less detailed but more flexible administrative system proved most successful during the messy market conditions of the 1970s. On the same grounds, the bureaucratic US systems have been criticized for being rigid and unresponsive to needs for structural adjustment, etc.[12] For our purpose we take note of the different opportunities to influence the business organization, depending on which system it operates. The bureaucratic system is more amenable to industrial policy action than its opposite for the simple reason that the latter is not even set up to allow its own management to guide it on to paths that take it away from the profit target. It is perhaps natural that industrial policy bodies and unions often favour organizations equipped with a bureaucratic management order.

V. Target setting and efficiency

Target setting on the basis of insufficient knowledge is the key 'art' of large-scale management. The interior structure of a large firm is unknown to those who manage the firm, to the extent that they cannot participate in, guide, or *directly* monitor the 'how to do things' process.[13] Rather, rules of thumb or proxies are resorted to in more or less sophisticated ways.[14] By this I mean that one abstraction applied throughout the theory of planning,[15] namely that the necessary information for an informed decision can be gathered through a sequence of top–down/bottom–up exchanges of information, is principally wrong. The abstraction is wrong in the sense that it leads to the wrong policy conclusions on business behaviour if used as presented in the literature. There are two reasons for this. First, lower-level management by definition always possesses superior and more detailed process knowledge than higher-level management. Hence, there is always a vertical bargaining relationship in a firm and information will normally be withheld locally because this leaves more autonomy there.

Second, at some limit the capacity to co-ordinate, analyse, and use information ceases to be efficient because of sheer complexity and required time. Hence, a reference and most efficient solution cannot be determined in principle and no top firm management operates on the premise that such a state is attainable. I argue on the basis of several empirical inquiries—my own in particular—that this limit occurs at quite an early stage and that business organizations as a rule are fraught with pockets of considerable slack. The existence of this slack, as well as its extent, is known to top management, but not its exact location within the organization.[16] There is no central knowledge from which one can calculate a reference to measure potential efficiency improvement. Hence, both static efficiency and the idea that firms minimize costs by searching across a well-known interior structure have to give way to some more pragmatic way of relating actual performance to something that is 'better'.

The solution is to set tough but reasonable targets on the basis of previously achieved performance. I have called this 'Maintain or Improve Profit' (MIP) targeting.[17] Targets that are too high or impossible to achieve are not taken seriously. If targets are below what is feasible, performance soon adjusts downwards. The art is to be just right without knowing why. A good reference for a minimum target is what has been achieved before. This and a little bit more should be reasonable to exhort slack in an organization, if slack of some magnitude exists within it. *How* to achieve it is left with the lower-level management. If a simple, distant enforcement system can be organized within a firm, then top-level management will be relieved of much nittygritty control work and worrying. Systematic use of comprehensive budgeting, targeting, and control devices is the key tool in this part of the management process. I would argue that most large western firms adopted central management systems of more or less this kind during the 1970s. US firms were leading the way already in the 1960s.[18]

There is one way to salvage intellectually the classical concept of a planned system as an information-exchange device (as developed on the basis of Léon Walras' general equilibrium concept by Lange, Marglin, Weitzman, Malinvaud, and many others).[19] This possibility should be mentioned here, but then be rejected, since the authors mentioned conceptualize a central fully informed decision as possible in principle. Use of such arguments would lead to misconceived policy conclusions.

In an abstract way the MIP type of target-setting device that we discuss could be seen as a *time-consuming*, iterative exchange of information. Top management imposes a rate of return requirement. Lower-level management responds 'in action'. 'Central planners' learn from actual performance and adjust targets and so on. If time stops and nothing else changes, this process would 'eventually' lead to an optimum solution. In practice this is normally an annual procedure. In some large American companies it is partially repeated every quarter. The classical planning cycle, on the other hand, is a hypothetical, static (timeless) device. Central planners offer a price vector and lower-level management come up with hypothetical, but true, performance data on their (known) production functions. Central planners change the price vector, etc. until markets have been cleared or a solution has been reached.

In the real firms that we are discussing, such a negotiating sequence hardly even approaches a solid foundation of fixed facts to be fed into the super master plan at the top. Rather, it is likely that if top management pushes too far in being knowledgeable about lower-level affairs, lower-level responses and/or higher-level deficiencies in using the information lead to a lowering of overall corporate performance.

Hence, improving the general level of knowledge in a (business) organization means a marginal improvement up to a point, and that point strikes the optimum combination of delegation and centralization of decision making.

VI. Efficiency and productivity in a modern firm

A great controversy exists over the question of why productivity growth slowed down during the 1970s. Practically all debate and empirical analysis has been carried out in terms of aggregate growth accounting, which leaves few openings for explicit policy discussion.

Growth accounting is static in nature. It relies on stable aggregate functions which require all requisites to be of a static equilibrium. Within such a framework, efficiency concepts will be in terms of departures from static efficiency.

Using a different viewpoint—a dynamic micro-to-macro economy with interacting price and quantity structures—very different results appear on the nature of productivity change. Essentially one can demonstrate a very large organizational factor behind total factor productivity growth.[20] The technological factor fades into insignificance as the measurement grid is made finer and finer.[21] Restated somewhat, new investment and new technologies do not yield productivity increments *per se*. Only if entered into the production process in the right way do productivity increases occur. In the right way always means being accompanied by organizational change between sectors, between firms, and within firms.

Within firms 'in the right way' is synonymous with management competence. If the necessary organizational adjustment does not occur, new investment and new technologies do not yield productivity improvements. At the sector level this is nicely illustrated by comparing the manufacturing sectors in the Netherlands and Sweden during the 1970s. In the Netherlands manufacturing investment ratios declined and employment declined greatly after 1973. In Swedish manufacturing, investment ratios increased considerably for several years and employment decreased only moderately. Despite this, Dutch manufacturing output grew at a rate of 1.4 per cent per year from 1973 to 1980, while output declined in Swedish manufacturing. One reason (among others) for the relatively good industrial performance in the Netherlands was a reduction in investment in heavy, basic industries, notably heavy chemicals. On the other hand, the increases in the

Swedish investment ratio were in basic industries, notably government-operated, that later turned into crisis industries.[22]

At the shop-floor level several case investigations reveal how new, sophisticated machinery was installed at the wrong place or at the wrong time in the production flow, with no productivity increases. At the same time significant productivity increases have often been achieved simply by changing the production flow patterns and using the same equipment.[23]

If this is correct, which is our maintained hypothesis, the ways in which industrial policies are enacted—not the expenses incurred—become crucial for the policy results.

VII. The innovative function

The innovative function of a company is the most problematic one when it comes to management. This activity is there, by definition, to change the business organization in ways that cannot easily be planned ahead. All short-run functions in Figure 11.1 are operated according to well-structured targets and rules of thumb to maximize short-run (static) efficiency in each period within current capacity constraints. The investment function is similarly organized to move capacity constraints outwards on the basis of perceived market growth rates in prices and quantities. The innovative function is fundamentally different. It aims at changing the rules and roles of other functions if need be, i.e. creating a larger and more complex body of targets and decision rules that incorporates the routine set of rules, but also allows top management to see how to leave the current operating domain of the firm.

R&D activities are normally subject to a cost budget, but organized in many different ways and at different levels in large companies. It appears that most of the internal R&D activities either search for external technological information or routine development activities (like designing a new automobile) or are close to the commercial stage, e.g. getting from the first prototype into commercially viable volume production.[24] Much of such 'innovative activity' can be incorporated in fairly tightly run management systems.

A second innovative activity has to do with the combined talent exercised in restructuring existing activities, finding new organizational solutions to old problems, and buying and selling parts to and from the firm. Success here requires both talent in seeing the solutions and capacity to enforce change. This is almost always a top-management task with little formalized management attached. This is the typical activity top management should have both talent and time to pursue, and it appears, as mentioned earlier, that efficiently run management systems are designed to achieve just that.[25]

A third innovative function that typically belongs to the top-executive echelons has to do with the current reshaping of the firm's organization. Part of this involves restructuring management systems as such. Part of it means changing the content and limits (size) of the organization. Mergers and divestment of parts of the firm into a new and commercially more viable entity have been characteristic activities of many successful firms during the 1970s. Electrolux Corporation, the world's largest producer of vacuum cleaners, is a case in point. It has acquired Facit (office equipment) and Husqvarna (stoves and other kitchen equipment, sewing machines, motor bikes, motor saws, etc.) partly to obtain additional production capacity and partly to achieve market dominance (e.g. kitchen equipment). Its negotiations with West Germany's ailing AEG group in 1982 further illustrates this strategy. Co-operation arrangements in technology is another example; e.g. between Renault, Peugeot, and Volvo in 1971 to develop and build an automobile engine, between Lancia and Saab-Scania to develop a new automobile, and between Ericsson and Philips to install a new digitally based telephone system in Saudi Arabia. Such co-operative deals that involve legislation and transnational contracts are always open to national policy designs, especially when it comes to preventing agreements. The US–European 'conflict' over the Soviet pipeline is a case in point. It appears that companies are seldom well prepared to cope with such 'unexpected' interventions on the part of national authorities, etc.[26]

Finally, the main top executive job is concerned with shaping the right corporate culture. It appears again that the increasing extent of direct involvement by government in firms affects this function in many ways. It may be difficult, for instance, to push hard for strict profitability achievements and tough internal reorganizations in ailing companies when employees know that generous government sub-sidizers are watching on the sidelines.[27]

VIII. The investment decision

The investment decision within an existing production activity is a well-structured procedure subject to a trail of formal administrative routines. Investments in hardware climb to the top for approval, in order of size and financial demands. A screening of financial demands takes place at the corporate top. The principles behind that screening are top-level priorities. This is illustrated by the fact that major investment decisions and mergers are always prepared outside the strategic planners' department and enter formal plans as a fact.[28] An important fact to consider in the context of industrial policy making is that major projects seldom become public before being decided. Neither central policy makers nor other policy bodies will ever have a chance to argue with firms for target changes on the basis of explicit corporate plans. This is not the way plans are drawn up or used in well-run companies. The literature and the management education process, however, abound with formal rules for monitoring the investment and growth decisions within a firm through a formal planning procedure. The message is that criteria are there to stem a steady flow of ideas from below and to constrain spending on capital account within a financial frame—the investment budget. Thus (and this has been a basis for government policy making throughout the industrialized world) if that financial frame could somehow be expanded, more investment and faster economic growth would follow. Means to achieve this have been accelerated fiscal depreciation, investment fund systems, regulated access to capital markets, or low interest rate policies.

IX. Industrial policy making

IX.1. Industrial policies in a European perspective

The 1950s and 1960s were characterized both by high and increasing growth rates among western industrial countries and by a gradual dismantling of restrictions to free international and domestic trade. A slow development in the opposite direction has prevailed since the beginning of the 1970s. It is undoubtedly true that fast, aggregate economic growth eases the social burden associated with the fast structural change that always accompanies growth. Hence, goes the argument, fast structural change cannot be accommodated as easily when growth is down, since there are no job openings for all those people who lose their jobs. The argument appears compelling, but it misses the simultaneity of the economic process. Growth makes it politically easy to accept structural change and to dismantle regulations and restrictions to trade. But the causality also runs the other way: increasing trade stimulates economic growth. Hence, the very fact that a reversal of the positive process of the 1960s has been initiated is very unlucky for the industrialized world. It is reinforcing; so once started, the international co-operation needed to stop it may take decades to organize. It is very difficult to argue or demonstrate convincingly that concerted economic policy action will produce the desired end-result because it will not do so immediately. There is a considerable time lag, as there was to reverse the growth momentum.

In this dynamic process of the 1970s some countries appear to have been more exposed than others: those with a large proportion of basic industries or old, outmoded capital, and those with short, employment-oriented political horizons. The two political handicaps seem to come together with extra force on the European scene, where the structural adjustment needed in the wake of the so-called 'oil crisis' has been large, and the political ability to do something, or allow the markets to work, is smaller than appears to be the case in the US and probably Japan.

Deindustrialization has been a catchword in the policy debate, the implication being that industries representing the public conception of industry ('smoke-stack industries') are contracting or closing down. New industries, on the other hand, tend to go undetected for a long time (barring spectacular activities within the information industry), and many do not belong to the popular concept of a real manufacturing industry. *Multinationals* are another industrial phenomenon; they pose a threat to the national State and its policy makers through their ability to choose locations and activities from a global, rather than a national, menu.

If policy makers have a nationally confined objective function and a severely restricted, or incomplete, knowledge of the ongoing industrial transformation process, 'fear of the markets' and an inclination to preserve past industrial structures will be the typical traits of political ambitions. The first nationalistic factor is there by definition. The second conservative tendency follows logically from the nature of industrial action, being typically a massive ongoing search process for new combinations and solutions with a high failure rate as a normal characteristic. Being well informed will be a very unusual state in a game where structural change mostly consists of exit and entry of institutions or parts of institutions. Being uninformed and unaware will be typical of those not directly involved in the action. There is very little that can be done to improve the situation for central policy makers in this respect. This circumstance perhaps explains the strategic orientation of most industrial policies enacted in most countries so far: slowing down change and attempting reconstruction of institutions from within, rather than creating new activities and scrapping old ones.

European industrial policies also originated in attempts to save the old basic industries that were first to suffer from new competition from other parts of the world and from the wage-driving (cost-driving) effects of new, rapidly growing industries that were able to absorb higher factor costs. There is no mention of an 'industrial policy' in the Treaty of Rome; the term was not invented at the time. But structural policies directed towards agriculture and competition, in particular, are presented. In Scandinavia we find a parallel discussion of so-called 'selective policies'. Even more important, perhaps, was the creation of a common business strategy, or a supranational management body, in the coal and steel sectors as early as the 1950s.[29]

A parallel and also typical evolution of European industrial policies was the encouragement, stimulation, or subsidization of industrial research, and even the operation of detached industrial research centres. The European Atomic Energy Commission is an instance of this. The main ambition here was to promote industrial innovation and competitiveness.

IX.2. Policy approaches

Industrial policy making in the various industrial countries has followed four widely differing paths. One positive approach has been concerned with supporting and stimulating new technological industrial activities by direct involvement in the *How* process in companies. A second policy path trodden is the *subsidy* way. It has been directed towards either reorganizing commercially failing businesses or simply (perhaps unintentionally) prolonging their lives in order to attend to certain social variables, like employment.

A third industrial policy path is the classical *planning* approach. The central policy agency may see itself as possessing a superior overview of the business environment and, hence, believe it should interact with all firms to achieve an orderly and efficient group action. The theory behind this is that improved information and overview make possible an analytically explicit optimal solution. This is the way French planning has often been presented.[30] In Japan the Ministry of International Trade and Industry (MITI) has been regarded as combining the third planning task with the first positive one of stimulating innovative activities.

The fourth and final industrial policy approach is that of non-interference in the internal management process of firms. Using different terminology we would call the first three kinds of policy mentioned *selective*, and the fourth *general* or *market* oriented. Policy action this time is only through the business environment of the firms, either by making it more competitive (free trade, anti-trust, etc.), by building the right infrastructure (schooling, transport), or by providing the right cultural climate and political preference structure (stimulating entrepreneurial attitudes, honouring property rights, etc.).

Swiss, US, and Danish industrial policy making may be roughly said to belong to this latter category.[31] Swedish industrial policy also followed this path to the end of the 1960s, then changed on to an interference track.

The most convenient way to discuss and evaluate industrial policy action is to deal with each of the four types of policy in turn, relating the policy specification back to the business management system described above. When evaluating the efficiency of policy action we will emphasize the view stated above: that productivity change at all levels of aggregation, down to our finest measurement grid, is a matter of structural or organizational change within the aggregate. Without the accompanying structural change, there will be little (total factor) productivity growth—regardless of the state of technical knowledge or hardware installed.

IX.3. Positive policies[32]

A key mercantilistic notion, particularly among European policy makers, has been direct governmental technological support of industry to improve, for instance, international competitiveness. Practically all countries have instituted government committees to investigate and propose remedial action on the perceived 'electronics gap' vis-à-vis the US. The Japanese government's support programme to leap-frog the US in certain areas (e.g. a new generation of computers) is a case in point.

The computer, electronics, nuclear, and aircraft industries have the highest priority in French industrial policy. The main reason for a domestic computer industry seems to be national independence in the field. France uses direct subsidies and government research as means, and the government is pushing both to establish a viable micro-electronics hardware industry and educate the population to be capable and willing to enter the new technological world. The electronic telephone directory is an illustration of this ambition. However, the expected spin-offs from this venture have so far not materialized.[33]

Similarly, the UK government is supporting British firms developing their own 'very large scale integration (VLSI)' capabilities. It is also supporting the use of micro-electronics in industry.

The FRG has also poured vast amounts of money into a select group of companies, notably Siemens, to achieve a catch-up effect in micro-electronics hardware production. In one important field—telecommunications—the government purchasing agency has been laying down domestic specifications that virtually exclude foreign competitors. Similar stories could be told of nuclear programmes (especially breeder reactor) and aircraft industry programmes.

What are the possibilities of success? Not so good. There are three basic reasons.

(i) Government-supported technological ventures, where government agencies specify what to do and how to do it, tend to leap beyond what the market is prepared to absorb. Projects tend to be technologically ambitious but economically unviable. Government-supported nuclear programmes, Concorde, and some other more or less grandiose commercial failures are cases in point. Such ventures, if ever designed, would soon have been stopped by the internal targeting and control procedures of a normal, profit oriented, commercial company.

(ii) Government support tends to introduce slack, or commercial sloppiness, in the internal operating procedures of firms. Development departments grow into academic institutions. If there is sufficient funding, technically 'interesting' projects are not terminated on commercial grounds, etc.

Government protection from outside competition does similar harm to efficiency. It also diverts attention away from foreign markets. It is impossible to market sophisticated systems products that do not adhere to international standards. It is costly to maintain double product designs. Ericsson, a Swedish firm, openly argues that FRG post office specifications on telecommunications equipment have efficiently kept an otherwise formidable competitor out of their markets.

(iii) Government intervention and guidance of industrial technological development in an advanced industrial economy may be a policy trail towards obsolescence.

The argument is that central government agencies will never be as informed about the commercial and technological frontiers as the advanced companies actively operating in the field. Furthermore, our introductory presentation of the modern firm tells us that success and sophistication may have as much or more to do with non-technical matters, like marketing. In this field, no competence at all resides in government bodies. The AXE digital telephone exchange, developed by Ericsson (in fact, in co-operation with the Swedish Telecommunications agency) was a technological design ('a concept') breakthrough that captured a large part of the world market. Ericsson's new venture to enter the 'information market' is very much a marketing investment.

The Boston Consulting Group was hired jointly by the Swedish government, Volvo, and some other bodies to carry out a 'crisis study on Swedish industry'.[34] On the basis of the perceived Japanese success in supporting so-called 'feeder industries', like steel and shipbuilding, that fed cheap industrial inputs (steel and transport) into Japanese engineering industries, the Boston Group argued for concerted government action to close down basic crisis industries and push firms into new, technologically advanced sectors.

There is, however, a tremendous difference in planning to mimic and speed-up an industrialization process that other countries had already been through—as was the policy situation for Japan in the 1950s—and pushing already industrialized countries into new, unknown commercial and technological terrain. The upper crust of Swedish, German, Dutch, British, and French industries are already on the frontier. If such industries have abstained from going in one particular direction, there may be a good reason for staying out. A government push to get domestic firms into very large-scale, very sophisticated, heavy-investment hardware production in micro-electronics (as for instance in France, the UK, and the FRG), with a considerable time lag compared to US and Japanese manufacturers, may easily get its industries stuck with producing the previous generation of technology products.

It is interesting to note that in the 'Grand Project' carried out for the Swedish government by the Swedish Academy of Engineering Sciences,[35] engineers, economists, business leaders, and politicians had great difficulties in achieving a consensus on exactly how the government should get involved in stimulating a structural adjustment path out of the economic crisis. Agreement was easy to reach on the need for a steadily improving infrastructure (e.g., education and basic research) and—barring all social problems—the need to allow crisis industries to die. Besides that, an extensive survey of the literature and world experience demonstrated that risk-sharing between the government and firms in sophisticated new product developments was one of the few industrial policy activities that were agreeable to most participants. In fact, the existence of *competent and curious public and private buyers* was considered important for technological progress in general. Defence contracting, however, was not generally recommended as an industrial policy by the majority. Strict commercial control of development projects was a key phrase that often appeared in the proceedings and in the publications.

It is interesting to note in this context Vogel's argument,[36] that a key reason for Japanese industrial development success is that they have not had a large part of human and other industrial resources tied up in non-commercial defence and space R&D work. In Japan almost all industrial R&D spending has to pass the market test.

IX.4. The subsidy approach

The bulk of industrial policy action—unintentionally or deliberately —has been directed towards supporting the losers.[37] Steel and ship-building are the recipients of enormous government support throughout Western Europe and, indirectly through defence spending, in the US. These basic industries and other supported industries as a rule do not engage in sophisticated forms of production by present western standards. Product design and marketing are small parts of total value added. In general, crisis industries appear to draw relatively little on human capital inputs and hence are subjected to early competition from developing countries, where the most important human capital input—industrial competence, experience, and skilled workers— is extremely scarce.

It seems that the bulk of State-operated companies in European countries exist as a result of governments having to bail out ailing industrial firms to support employment.[38] Such policies also seem to be extremely costly in terms of misallocated resources and lost growth in output.[39] I would argue that Sweden's extremely costly industrial subsidy programme—up from one of the lowest rates in the industrial world in the early 1970s to a record breaking 16 per cent of value added in manufacturing in 1982, and in practice all structure conserving —is the major explanation of the complete collapse of manufacturing output growth in Sweden since 1973.

With few exceptions, the stated ambitions of these rescue operations have been expressed in terms of positive reconstruction of companies from within, indicating that business units once in trouble can be reorganized where they happen to be located, using the same human resources and causing a minimum of intermediate unemployment. We have already indicated above why the odds are heavily weighed against success in such ventures. Entry and exit is the normal vehicle for rejuvenation of industries; for those business units that have succeeded in doing it from within, as a rule a major change of human resources has been the key to success.

One particular instance of industrial subsidizing should, however, be mentioned. If the government is solely concerned with dampening the unavoidable unemployment consequences of a crisis situation, it would be rational to attempt to minimize costs associated with the rescue operation. One solution is to put the operation on the market and give the job to the 'lowest bidder'. More or less explicit arrangements of this type have been tried in Sweden. Electrolux has been involved in several rescue operations (Facit, Gränges, etc.). Contracts to do just that have, in fact, been signed between the Swedish government and its own 'State Operated Company'.[40]

IX.5. The planning approach:
picking the winners or bailing out the losers

The classical approach to industrial policy making is that of the government planner. His central position gives him an overview. By communicating back and forth with the producers, his 'visible hand' directs the economy at large to an optimal solution that can incorporate desired aspects of the social welfare function.

As mentioned in the theoretical overview above, this requires three things: that the necessary information can be obtained, that it can be interpreted in terms of a policy, and that the economy adjusts when the informed policy hand waves.

Much justification for government interference in business decisions has been argued on the basis of this overview potential, an argument that has also been associated with the forming of large conglomerate manufacturing firms or with the more continental forming of groups of firms loosely knit around an 'industrial bank'.

One quoted aspect is the overview ability to spot and pick the winners. Another is to spot a tendency in time to prevent over-investment in one particular area. The classical and often cited example of the latter is the boom and over-extension in forest industries in the early 1960s. Global steel investment and allocation is an even better example today. The Swedish State-operated company was instituted on this premise, and the overview argument has been the basic one for 'branch type planning' or 'guidance' tried in some western economies.

As mentioned above, even though ambitions have been high, the end result has usually been that of bailing out losers. The main political reason for the bail-out has been to avoid local unemployment, but the positive employment effects have been at best temporary. An important side effect has been to bail out the associated owners as well, covering at least some of their capital losses.[41]

Overview is seldom the main reason for success in business companies, except in simple product markets. As argued above, the whole idea of picking well-defined ventures from a given population, the characteristics of which we can learn by simply allocating time and money, is wrong from the start. The main reason for success among the not so many conglomerate successes has been the ability to direct cash flows away from mediocre and ailing production, forcing them eventually to exit. 'Scrapping' has never been the typical trait of State-operated companies.[42]

IX.6. *The invisible hand: the market*

During the last few years the *market solution* has become a catchword in the debate on the structural problem of western economies; it is an alternative to direct central involvement in business operations. At a high level of abstraction, the current discussion echoes the more than 40-year-old debate of Lange and von Hayek.[43] At lower levels of abstraction it is, however, much more difficult to come to grips with a meaningful definition of what a market solution to industrial policy really is. For one thing, one needs a well-developed, micro-based, and dynamic theory to discuss such distinctions at all. In the absence of this theory one has to make do either with looser language, or listings of policy measures of a more general nature that are arbitrarily labelled general! One criterion for generality is that the measure leaves choices to the micro-decision units (firms). Examples are variously designed and calibrated tax incentives to move investments, e.g. to stimulate R&D investments. Had subsidies been a 'generally available right' for all firms beyond a minimum, well-defined state of distress, subsidies would also belong here.

Capital market policies securing a low, long-term interest rate level would also be a general policy, were it not for the fact that the low market interest rate means excess demand for such credits, and regulation has to be imposed to take care of the lines of unsatisfied potential borrowers. Administrative selection procedures will always be arbitrary and selective.

As we go through the list of policy 'candidates', we find that they mostly work through affecting the price system, albeit leaving a choice at the micro level to adjust activities to the manipulated price system.

In a sense then, we are back full circle to our original problem. Industrial policies by definition, we agreed, are enacted to correct long-term structural problems in the economy. Structural problems, in turn, depend on and originate in a malfunctioning of the price system. Then industrial policies concerned with getting the economy on a long-term, stable, maximum growth track should be concerned with getting the price structure of the economy right, i.e compatible with that long-run 'equilibrium' (if I may use that word) growth trajectory. Part of this problem is to enforce the corresponding quantity adjustment in the economy. To do this one has to know roughly which long-term price, quantity, and growth spectrum to aim for.

Theoretically this requires that we have a full-fledged, dynamic, micro–macro theory of the economy within which technical change is either explained or imposed exogenously in a consistent manner.[44] I believe that research in economic theory should be directed towards accomplishing something of that kind, if economic theory is to be useful in understanding the growth process of an economy. But so far we have to make do with an irrelevant body of static theory for this problem.

There are, however, indications that the choice of market regime may have an enormous effect on the long-run growth performance of the economy;[45] and the choice of industrial policy action is certainly the important part of the choice of market regime.

We cannot even determine on theoretical grounds whether or not a market-oriented industrial policy is compatible with the *subsidy* approach above, although I am inclined to argue that it is, in the sense of determining a political or social discount rate of the country. If high, one trades in less short-term adjustment for less long-term growth. Sweden clearly made that kind of a choice during the 1970s. If one believes in the long-term positive supply effects of Mrs Thatcher's policies in the UK, then one can say that the UK has chosen the policy track just opposite to that of Sweden. The sad thing is that professional economics currently provides no means of assessing the ultimate outcome of either policy. What should we say today, as policy makers, if we knew for sure that the current UK policy programme, enacted through the 1980s with continued consequences, would create an industrial success story by the middle of the 1990s?

On the *positive* industrial policy side there is no real compatibility. Either central policy bodies know the operating technologies and skills better than actual business performers at the micro-level, or they do not. This is an empirical question.

In the overview *planning* case the central government body tries to beat the market. The answer as to whether it can is 100 per cent empirical. It is partly an institutional problem. Is the economy organized in an institutionally efficient manner? Does it have the right size of firms, the right degree of specialization, the right labour and capital mobility, etc? Partly, however, existing institutional structures are dependent upon the kind and extent of central interference in the market. According to our earlier arguments, we think we have found that such interferences have not benefitted market efficiency.

A particular kind of market-conforming, general industrial policy aims at supplying low-cost basic services to the entire economy, or building an *infrastructure*. The most important examples are schooling at all levels, health care, transport systems, and retirement schemes. One key characteristic of these schemes is that there exist both private market and collective (non-market) solutions to such infrastructure investment activities. On the retirement side, private and public insurance schemes run parallel in most western countries. Schooling and health services are predominantly run by public bodies in most European countries, but almost everywhere private alternatives exist, notably in the US. If we look back into the past, we observe that—excluding the military side—the 'industrial policy' of supplying educated, healthy, and confident workers to industry and supplying a low-cost transportation and communication system to firms was *the main public activity* well into the 1960s.

X. Large and small

One particular practical problem associated with the 'overview' possibilities in industrial policy making concerns the number of business units that can be monitored. A few decision units pose only small problems of communication; a few hundred create a difficult management situation (Electrolux Corporation is composed of about 400 subsidiary operations); several thousand units make life impossible for the industrial policy maker. The practical solution has been a heavy orientation towards the large corporations (some even argue that this is the most efficient approach[46]) with more scattered attention to the multitude, represented by many 'small business programmes' in most industrialized countries.

It is educational to recall in this context Schumpeter's dismal prediction that a small group of large firms, by virtue of their superior technologies, would eventually dominate all markets.[47] Identification with the central government would then become natural, and basic democratic values would be jeopardized.

The rationale for running policies through a small set of large firms is the presumed pull effect on the rest of the economy through vertical purchasing and subcontracting. The importance for the entire industry of a few large firms can certainly be demonstrated for the small industrial economies. The dangers associated with running industrial policies through the large firms are, however, apparent. Besides the threat to democratic principles posed by a close co-operation of industrial and political power centres, large firms tend to operate in mature markets with mature products, perhaps, a dominant market position.

A typical problem of top management in such firms is to find new, profitable activities in which to invest the cash proceeds from the mature product range to create a new base for long-run survival. The mature product range is often managed quite efficiently on the short-term production side, with a view to maximizing the cash flow as long as the product is viable.

Hence, policy interference based on the presumption of strong backward links to the production and delivery side is very likely to be *structure preserving* all the way down—especially if it has been initiated by early problems of the mature product range. The effect may be worse if management attention is also turned away from concern about profit and efficient production, towards concern with added policy objectives as available subsidies. A new 'government market' is, so to speak, created.

If size should matter at all, the case for being concerned with the small firms appears better founded. There is evidence indicating that truly innovative and efficient industrial R&D occurs in very small, newly founded business units, despite the fact that large corporations do the bulk of industrial R&D spending. Small business units certainly do not possess the large-scale and risk-spreading potential in the financial dimension that is associated with big business. It is, hence, quite easy to present a logically coherent case for financial support to small business ventures, and such programmes abound in industrial countries. The problem again is deciding how to choose among the large number of small firms: do you pick those who 'apply'? do you look for candidates? etc. Looked at from that end, we are reformulating the well-known problem of how to manage innovative activities within large corporations.[48] The case often heard for government involvement is that industry is not doing a good job in its own specialities, or that since we have the resources, it does not hurt to do more of a good thing.

The logical sequel to such an argument, however, would be for policy makers also to do all they can to facilitate the institutionalization of efficient equity or venture capital markets for small businesses. This has, in fact, been done in some countries, but it has not been a typical trait of industrial policies directed towards small businesses.

In mentioning venture capital, the argument leads naturally to a vaguely defined distinction popularly referred to in discussing the industrial finance systems of the west: the *industrial bank* system usually associated with continental Europe, and the *market* system of the City of London and the US. The industrial bank integrates industrial and banking competence. In the market system the two skills are more specialized and separated. If size is of any consequence at all, there would be an indication in favour of arrangements of the industrial bank type, within which three different functions would become more efficient.

First, the financial economies of scale associated with the banking function would reduce the overall financial risk of the industrial activities brought together. Second, industrial decision makers and suppliers of finance are very differently endowed with information. Joining them would certainly reduce the overall risk associated with the industrial activities for the suppliers of funds, and hence lower the cost of finance. In this particular context long-term funding of risky investments with very long gestation periods can be arranged 'internally' and, in situations where the small firm might be reluctant to take on external finance at market interest rates. The third reason is the enhanced potential for 'internal' reshuffling of funds, taking resources out of stagnating activities and ploughing them into prospective new ventures.

In the market finance system, on the other hand, the market would so to speak impose too high rate-of-return requirements and force an unduly short planning horizon on investment. Small firms would encounter difficulties in carrying out large ventures which take a long time to generate a cash flow. Indirect evidence of this might be that the 'market systems', particularly in the US are also populated by the really large corporations of the world, of a size comparable to the banking groups of Europe. These large, often conglomerate, business units typically internalize the banking and investment institute functions within the same corporate body.

All of this appears to suggest that government-supported financing arrangements to small- and medium-sized industrial firms should be beneficial. But this would not be a correct inference. The rationale for both the industrial banking and market systems of industrial finance is to make exercising the profit motive more efficient, both in the short- and the long-term, through internal risk reduction and more efficient channelling of funds *out of* loss-making activities and into profit-generating investments, speeding up structural change and scrapping obsolete capital in the process. Only if these were the primary objectives—and not the provision of funds as such—would government policies directed towards small firms be beneficial to their growth.

XI. Concluding remarks

Classical macro-economic theory endows the central policy-making authority with the supreme power of pulling the economy along by simply manipulating demand. There is little place in such an intellectual scheme for micro-level skills to influence the supply process. No distinction is made between differential qualities associated with factor inputs being dependent upon where they happen to be allocated. Once these aspects are introduced, our policy discussion has tended to come down with a negative verdict on selective policies interfering with internal operating rules of firms. The reason for this conclusion can be summarized as *insufficient information or skill endowments* in the policy bodies.

Part of this has to do with lack of business skills and experience. Part of it has to do with the ability to obtain, digest, and transform into informed decisions the mass of complex data that resides in the business sector. This argument or fact contradicts the classical planning approach in selective industrial policy making and covers all dimensions: within firms, across business units, and over time. One way of bypassing this problem has been to concentrate policy ambitions on a select group of very large companies that can be monitored, where personal contacts can be established and so forth.

If a few large business organizations make up a large share of manufacturing value added and employment, and if they tend to connect backwards through extensive subcontracting arrangements to a large number of small firms, the information requirements are thought to be smaller. Technically, a semi-aggregate approach to planning thus appears feasible. But a viable firm is never managed as a production scheduling problem, and large firms tend to represent mature industries. Hence, such organization of industrial policies is likely to be structure-conserving. It will not stimulate innovative behaviour and it will direct high-level attention away from markets towards government coffers. These cannot be desired effects of industrial policies.

A high concentration of value added by a small number of firms and a heavy subcontracting pull effect is characteristic of the small, but highly advanced industrial nations like the Netherlands and Sweden, where an advanced stage of specialization has been achieved. Simultaneously, however, the large firms of these countries have also become sophisticated and highly specialized by growing international. So the heavy pull effect also has to do with the large firms being—in a significant way—large, international, marketing, and trading firms. Such firms are, of course, difficult or impossible to influence through direct industrial policy action of the positive or visible-hand type that we have discussed.

In the large industrial countries where the mass of industrial activity is domestic, a bureaucratic symbiosis between policy makers and business may perhaps work. In the small industrial country, where the large groups are more internationally established than domestically, this symbiosis ceases to be operational. There the only workable scheme for industrial policy action seems to be the 'old Swedish policy model'[49] which means milking the business sector of value added to finance public sector growth and egalitarian schemes to the maximum extent possible, leaving all technical and commercial decisions to business leaders and managers and (*nota bene*) industrial ownership in private hands. The old Swedish policy model developed over several decades as a joint, and partially documented understanding among the unions, businesses, and a durable social democratic government. In this policy model no action was allowed to help firms in distress or to support regional problem areas. No political concern was voiced about labour that did not want to move or adjust. This is an almost 100 per cent market policy solution. The important question is why its abandonment towards the end of the 1960s ran parallel with an extreme stagnation of the Swedish economy—much beyond what can be explained by the parallel world recession. Was this the result of the abandonment of the market policy solution and/or the destruction of incentives that came with it?[50] My personal answer would be yes.

Gigantism in the business world appears to be the result of economies of scale in a broad sense, production not being the most important instance.[51] Being large financially and diversified in many markets means protection from both the erratic behaviour of capital markets and monetary policies from an insurance point of view. However, extensive exploitation of the 'insurance' potential tends to generate inefficiencies, as we have argued.

Hence, our proposition would be that the mixing of public policies and business management is an extremely dangerous scheme in the longer term. The empirical evidence suggests that large business firms managing to reach large size and protection from the vagaries of outside markets tend to experience a gradual collapse of efficiency from within. They become bureaucratic and organizationally rigid. Business instincts never breed in such a climate. Symbiosis with a government bureaucracy and indirect access to the finance system of the public sector multiply the same dangers.

Not only does pressure to perform diminish as the ability to measure and monitor internal performance do. Attention also tends to be diverted away from commercial activities if a growing part of income comes directly from public coffers. The problems tend to become more and more similar to those associated with public bodies, which have been discussed extensively in the literature.

It appears that the major vehicle for successful industrial transformation in a world characterized by dynamic and intense international competition is a sufficient flow of new entrants to guarantee a sufficient number of technological and commercial successes, and an exit of industrial activities of a large enough magnitude to free resources for commercially viable activities. If industrial policy makers were involved in this process, they would have a natural task in providing a good infrastructure for the creation of the entry flow (efficient education, good basic research, and especially a positive political climate for entrepreneurship). There is a lot of work to be done here throughout the industrialized world.

If, nevertheless, central industrial policy makers want to get involved in the real business activities, there is a suitably demanding task that has been badly managed in the recent past; namely, to create an efficient and orderly 'scrapping' or exit function of the economy. This task does not require particular industrial skills that can only come after a long, personal experience in the market. Exits can be planned, and it is extremely important for the macro-behaviour of the economy that they in fact occur.

This exit function was once termed 'creative destruction' by Joseph Schumpeter. It was the key ingredient of the old Swedish (industrial) policy model, applied for some twenty years during a period of prosperous industrial growth).

Notes and Sources

[1] Of course no short-term policy or activity is 100 per cent neutral *vis-à-vis* long-term development.

[2] G. Eliasson and B. C. Ysander, *Picking Winners or Bailing Out Losers*, Industrial Institute for Economic and Social Research (IUI) Working Paper, No. 37, Stockholm, 1981.

[3] Many of the empirical results reported in what follows draws on current micro-econometric research at my institute. This includes a large project on 'Information Technology, Productivity and the Management of Large Business Organizations' in progress and my earlier interview study on *Business Economic Planning*, 1976. I have tried to keep references to our own research down to a minimum, but several conclusions require explicit references to back up evidence.

[4] See, for example, J. Bray, *Production Purpose and Structure*, Frances Pinter, London, 1982.

[5] G. Eliasson, 'Electronics, Economic Growth and Employment—Revolution

or Evolution', in H. Giersch, ed., *Emerging Technologies: Consequences for Economic Growth, Structural Change, and Employment*, J. C. B. Mohr (Paul Siebeck), Tübingen, 1982(a).
[6] R. H. Coase, 'The Nature of the Firm', *Economica*, 1937, and K. Arrow, *The Limits of Organization*, North Holland, Amsterdam, 1974. See also Sels Lectures on Public Policy Analysis, 1970-1.
[7] G. Eliasson, *Business Economic Planning—Theory, Practice and Comparison*, John Wiley & Sons, 1976, pp. 231 ff.
[8] R. Teigen, 'Financial Development and Stabilization Policy: A Study of the Scandinavian Economies', *Economic Research Report*, No. 19, Federation of Swedish Industries, Stockholm, 1976.
[9] G. Eliasson, 'Företag, marknader och ekonomisk utveckling', in *Industriell utveckling i Sverige*, IUI, Stockholm, 1980.
[10] G. Eliasson, 1976, op. cit.
[11] Ibid., ch. 10. See also J. Dearden, 'MIS is a Mirage', *Harvard Business Review*, January–February 1982.
[12] R. H. Hayes and W. J. Abernathy, 'Managing our Way to Economic Decline', *Harvard Business Review*, July–August 1980.
[13] G. Eliasson, 1976, op. cit.
[14] R. M. Cyert and J. G. March, *A Behavioral Theory of the Firm*, Englewood Cliffs (N.J.), 1963; S. G. Winter, 'Economic National Selection and the Theory of the Firm', *Yale Economic Essays*, Spring 1964; H. A. Simon, 'Theories of Decision Making in Economic and Behavioral Science', *AER*, June 1959, and 'Rational Decision Making in Business Organizations', *AER*, September 1979.
[15] G. M. Heal, *The Theory of Economic Planning*, North Holland, Amsterdam-London, 1973.
[16] G. Eliasson, 1976, op. cit.
[17] Ibid., pp. 236 ff.
[18] Ibid. It is already obvious here that these are very delicately balanced systems. Explicit, quantified trade-offs between target variables are not possible if top-level management has to be involved—not even trade-offs in timing. Hence, *targeting* is restricted to short-term operating management. Long-term decisions are organizationally separated.

If new target variables are added, the targeting system breaks down for the same reason. For instance, if government industrial-policy people want to raise or pay for the attainment of higher employment targets at the expense of profitability, and if this policy is fed through the central monitoring system, it invariably impairs the efficiency of the targeting system, and hence lowers the global 'static efficiency' of the entire firm.

Similarly, if other support to ailing businesses—such as subsidies—is fed through the central monitor, it softens up the targeting function. Reasonable profit targets can be achieved anyway because of subsidies. Top–down pressure diminishes and bottom–up willingness to comply diminishes if it is known that generous crisis relief will nevertheless be administered.
[19] O. Lange, 'On the Economic Theory of Socialism', *Review of Economic Studies*, 1936-7; S. A. Marglin, 'Information in Price and Command Systems of Planning', in Guitton-Margoliz (eds), *Public Economics, Public Production and Consumption and Their Relations to the Private Sector*, proceedings of International Economics Association Conference, Biarritz, 1966; M. Weitzman, 'Iterative Multi Level Planning with Production Targets', *Econometrica*, vol. 38, 1970; E. Malinvaud, 'Decentralized Procedure for Planning', in Malinvaud-Bacharach (eds), *Activity Analysis in the Theory of Growth and Planning*, Macmillan, London, 1967.
[20] B. Carlsson, 'The Content of Productivity Growth in Swedish Manufactur-

ing', in *The Firm in the Market Economy, IUI 40 Years, IUI Yearbook, 1979-80*, Stockholm, 1981.

[21] G. Eliasson, 1982(a), op. cit.

[22] This investment boom in Sweden, stimulated by the government, was praised by the OECD at the time. See H. Fries, 'Structural Change and Industry Performance in Four Western European Countries', 1982, in Eliasson-Sharefkin-Ysander (eds), *Policy Making in a Disorderly World Economy*, IUI Research Report, No. 1, 1983.

[23] G. Eliasson, *Elektronik, teknisk förändring och ekonomisk utveckling*, IUI Booklet No. 110, 1981(a); S. Nilsson, *Förändrad tillverkningsorganisation och dess återverkningar på kapitalbindningen. En studie vid ASEA*, IUI Booklet No. 115, 1981.

[24] G. Eliasson and O. Granstrand, *The Financing of New Technological Investments*, IUI Booklet No. 121, 1981 and *Venture Capital and Management*, forthcoming IUI Working Paper, 1982.

[25] G. Eliasson, 1976, op. cit., ch. 11.

[26] L. Jagrén and T. Pousette, *Industriföretagets sårbarhet*, IUI Research Report No. 15, 1982.

[27] G. Eliasson and B. C. Ysander, op. cit.

[28] G. Eliasson, 1976, op. cit.

[29] A. P. Jacquemin, 'European Industrial Policies and Competition', in Coffey (ed.), *Economic Policies of the Common Market*, Macmillan, London, 1979, p. 35.

[30] E. Malinvaud, 1967, op. cit.

[31] G. Eliasson and B. C. Ysander, op. cit.

[32] This section draws on a report by the Swedish Computers and Electronics Commission that surveys computer technology and industrial policy making among the industrialized countries. *Datateknik och industripolitik*, Statens Offentliga Utredningar (SOU), No. 17, Stockholm, 1980.

[33] *Business Week*, 4 July 1983, pp. 32 ff.

[34] Boston Consulting Group, *A Framework for Swedish Industrial Policy*, Boston and Stockholm, 1978.

[35] Swedish Academy of Engineering Sciences, *Kunskap och konkurrenskraft* (Knowledge and Competitiveness), Stockholm, 1979.

[36] E. F. Vogel, *Japan as Number One—Lessons for America*, Harvard University Press, Cambridge (Mass.), 1979.

[37] B. Carlsson, *Industrial Subsidies in Sweden: Macro-economic Effects and an International Comparison*, IUI Working Paper No. 58, 1982, estimates that the subsidies for direct 'rescue' operations in manufacturing in the UK, Italy, Norway, Sweden, and West Germany amounted to 1.3, 3.5, 3.6, 6.9, and 0.6 per cent of value added in manufacturing, respectively. Including general subsidies, these figures increase to 3.6, 7.1, 7.6, 16.0, and 4.0 per cent of value added, respectively. It turned out to be impossible, despite considerable effort, to obtain similar figures of comparable quality and known content on French manufacturing.

[38] B. Hindley, *State Investment Companies in Western Europe*, Macmillan, London, 1983.

[39] B. Carlsson, op. cit.

[40] G. Eliasson and B. C. Ysander, op. cit.

[41] Ibid.

[42] See the various country essays in B. Hindley, op. cit.

[43] O. Lange and F. A. von Hayek, 'Socialist Calculation', *Economica*, new series vol. VII, May 1940, pp. 124-49.

[44] G. Eliasson, 'On the Optimal Rate of Structural Adjustment', in Eliasson-Sharefkin-Ysander (eds), *Policy Making in a Disorderly World Economy*, IUI Conference Report No. 1, 1983.

[45] Ibid., and F. A. von Hayek, 'The Use of Knowledge in Society', *American Economic Review*, vol. 39, September 1945, pp. 519-30.

[46] J. Bray, op. cit.

[47] J. Schumpeter, *Capitalism, Socialism and Democracy*, George Allen & Unwin, London, 1942.

[48] G. Eliasson and O. Granstrand, op. cit.

[49] G. Eliasson, 'The Firms in the Market Economy—40 Years of Research at IUI', in *The Firm in the Market Economy, IUI 40 Years, IUI Yearbook, 1979–80*, Stockholm, 1981.

[50] G. Eliasson, 1982, op. cit., and E. Schwartz, *Trouble in Eden, A Comparison of the British and Swedish Economies*, Praeson, New York, 1980.

[51] C. Pratten (*A Comparison of the Performance of Swedish and U.K. Companies*, Cambridge University Press, 1976) observes that while Swedish firms are small compared to British firms by financial standards, they are large on an establishment basis, much more productive, and generally enjoy relatively more economies of scale because they are operating in 'small' international markets that they dominante.

XII

Corporate Strategies in Transition

HENRY ERGAS*

I. Adjustment: an ongoing process

What are we to make of the call for 'adjustment'? What should we understand by the terms 'high technology', 'up-market', 'high value-added', 'knowledge-intensification', 'sunrise (or 'sunset') industries'? And how do these terms relate to what firms actually do?

Adjustment is, of course, the bread and butter of what firms in a market economy do. In striving to acquire and defend competitive positions, firms continuously seek to adjust to changing patterns of demand, of technology, and of input cost and availability—some succeeding to a greater extent than others.

Greater competitive challenge   The specific feature of our present situation lies not in the ongoing fact of adjustment, but in its magnitude—in the extent of the environmental challenge which firms face, and of the restructuring which firms will have to undertake. Factors underlying this situation include:

- a sustained deterioration in the macro-economic climate, involving lower, more erratic growth and considerably greater exchange and interest rate instability;
- continued pressure on prices and profit margins as a result of adverse distribution shifts and of movements in raw material prices;
- the entry of important new producers, in particular from Japan and the newly industrialized countries (NICs), or European and North American markets;
- approaching saturation in a number of previously rapidly-growing product markets, aggravating cyclical reductions in demand;
- the accelerated development and horizontal and vertical diffusion of new technologies, particularly electronics and information processing, altering entry barriers and technological strategies in a broad range of industries.

Uneven impact on industries   Not all industries have been equally affected by these factors. Some industries—for example pharmaceuticals

* Principal Administrator, Planning and Evaluation Unit, OECD, Paris.

or branded foods continue to benefit from the favourable impact of demographic and social trends on demand. Other industries—particularly those based on information technology—have enjoyed extremely high rates of growth of output, as advances in technology create new products and improve existing ones; but competitive pressures in these industries are rapidly increasing, as R&D costs rise and as more firms and countries try to capture a share of the pie. Finally, a broad range of established industries—including among others, chemicals, textiles and clothing, aluminium, steel, shipbuilding, automobiles, white goods, and machine tools—have had to deal simultaneously with all the factors raised above.

The net result in the more highly concentrated industries has been to destabilize existing oligopolies. Slow growth in demand has transformed competition into a struggle for market share, aggravated in some cases by continuing increases in capacity as investments decided upon in more prosperous periods come on stream. At the same time, the growth of fringe producers, combined with vast differences in strategic objectives between firms (in particular, between private and public sector firms), has made it increasingly difficult to maintain strict pricing discipline. A forthcoming OECD study documents the consequent change in price behaviour: throughout the post-war period, prices in highly concentrated industries responded less to cyclical variations in demand than prices in fragmented industries, and the behavioural disparity between these sets of industries was progressively widening. But the recession subsequent to the second oil shock reversed this pattern, with sharply greater downward price flexibility in the traditional oligopolies.

The strategic response   How will corporate strategies adapt to these changes? The answer will clearly depend on the markets and industries studied and on the size, structure, and management philosophy of the firms involved. However, it is important to attempt to discern, out of the mass of varying responses, common trends and elements, since these set the framework within which public policy must be defined.

One corporate response, of course, is to *diversify out* of industries facing substantial adjustment pressures. A deteriorating market position is often the major motive for diversification. That this response is widespread is suggested both by sectoral experience (for example, tyres, steel, glass, and automobile components) and by management research.[1] However, research also shows that successful diversification out of weak market positions and into completely new businesses is extremely rare, for at least three reasons:

— successful diversification requires large volumes of cash;

- the weaker firms in an industry rarely have any firm-specific strategic assets they can transfer out to other industries;
- it is extremely difficult for firms in one industry to correctly appraise strategic options in a completely different industry.

Barring this escape route, firms must, by and large, respond to the specific challenges of the major markets in which they operate. The precise nature of this response will depend on a number of factors. Some of these are industry-specific—e.g. capital-intensity, the extent to which the product can be differentiated, and the importance of technology as a competitive weapon. Others are more firm-specific— namely, the firm's market share, the extent of its vertical integration and diversification, and its management history and philosophy. However, despite this diversity, recent management research suggests that:

- even in industries where competitive pressures are greatest (from the NICs, from Japan, or from excess capacity), viable corporate strategies exist which yield successful firms rates of return *no lower* (and in many cases higher) than those earned by firms in superficially more attractive industries;[2]
- these strategies share a number of common elements, though the *balance* between these elements varies with industry and firm characteristics.[3]

In effect, in the industries where competitive pressures are greatest, the corporate strategies of successful firms seem to centre on three interrelated objectives: (a) to reduce *market vulnerability*, i.e. the risk of the firm losing market share to lower cost or technically superior competitors; (b) to increase *manufacturing flexibility*, i.e. the speed with which the firm can adapt to changes in customer requirements, demand levels, and technical possibilities; and (c) to minimize *capital risk*, i.e. the firm's vulnerability to reductions in the overall level of demand.

These objectives have major implications for the way in which firms' main functional activities are organized. In particular, firms are seeking:

- to strengthen and integrate their technology base;
- to use this base to achieve greater product differentiation and customization;
- to co-ordinate this product policy more closely with manufacturing, especially through 'focused' manufacturing strategies;
- and to specialize their operations in their areas of greatest strength, through greater recourse to subcontracting and joint ventures on the one hand, and to centralized procurement and purchasing procedures on the other.

II. Strengthening the technology base

Technology is increasingly viewed by management theorists and practitioners as central to the definition of successful corporate strategies.[4] Underlining this perception is the admission that, as has been argued for the US but is equally valid for Western Europe, 'The edge that US companies have long enjoyed in mass production technology and in the resulting economies of scale—an edge long believed essential to competitive success—no longer obtains. Most of the standard US technology is either already widely diffused or easily transferable.'[5]

At the same time, management faces an increasing range and pace of technical advances, which by altering entry barriers, changing industry boundaries, and creating new substitute products, can undermine even the most carefully thought out corporate strategy.

The response to this challenge takes two basic forms. First, greater resources are being devoted to technological development, both for in-house R&D and for access to external technology sources. Thus, despite unfavourable macro-economic circumstances and some reduction in public-financed support, business enterprise expenditure on R&D in the OECD area has continued to grow throughout the last decade, with indications, particularly in the United States, of an accelerating increase towards the decade's end.[6] Equally, the available evidence, though limited, is consistent with sectoral information suggesting a sharp rise in firms' access to external technology sources.[7]

Secondly, firms are paying increasing attention to the effectiveness of their technology strategy through improved R&D management and infrastructure and by rationalizing their product range around their areas of greatest technological strength.[8]

In effect, though the post-war period has seen a substantial expansion in the activities of conglomerates, management research in the 1970s has increasingly stressed the advantages of greater technological integration within firms. Thus, Rumelt examined the financial performance of *Fortune's* 500 firms over the period 1950–70; he found that in terms of price/earnings ratios, return on investment, and return on equity, firms pursuing strategies of *closely related diversification* (that is, operating in products using a similar technology base) significantly out-performed firms pursuing strategies either of vertical integration or of unrelated, conglomerate-type expansion.[9] Similar results for the United States have been reported more recently by Salter and Weinhold,[10] and by a number of studies of Western European economies.[11]

Considerable research remains to be done in this area, but it seems likely that the principal advantage of related diversification to firms lies in the more effective transfer of functional skills within these firms, particularly as regards the co-ordination of R&D with manufacturing and marketing. Given greater emphasis on technological competition, the importance of achieving such co-ordination has increased; and, partly under the influence of strategic planning methods, a growing number of firms have sought to integrate their product portfolio around a common technological base.[12]

Though numerous examples of this can be cited—e.g. ITT, GE, RCA, Bendix, United Technologies, TRW—relatively little is known about the overall extent and direction of this process. However, there is evidence of an increase in the number of divestments, which may be seen as a form of 'de-diversification'.

Thus, Chiplin and Wright found that while divested subsidiaries accounted on average for 12.6 per cent of the value of acquired UK companies over the period 1959–74, this share increased to 17.9 per cent over the period 1975–9, with horizontal divestitures accounting for only one-third of the total.[13] Equally, Vernon and Davidson,[14] examining the European subsidiaries of several hundred US multinationals, found that the number of subsidiaries divested or withdrawn increased from some 3 per cent of the total number of subsidiaries in the early 1960s to nearly 10 per cent in the first half of the 1970s. Similar results with regard to US multinationals were reported by Hood and Young.[15]

III. Product differentiation

By strengthening and integrating their technology base, firms primarily seek to increase the extent of their *product differentiation* and *market segmentation*. In practice, this means:

- using improved technology to upgrade overall product quality;
- tailoring or customizing product features more closely to the requirements of specific customer groups;
- increasing the value of the products to customers by providing greater after-sales services, engineering and technical assistance, and improved credit and delivery terms.

This strategy is generally presumed to have three major benefits for the supplying firm. First, it increases customers' 'switching costs'[16] and reduces their price elasticity of demand, so that the supplying firm becomes less vulnerable to the development of substitute products, to the activities of lower-cost competitors, or to adverse movements in exchange rates. Second, to the extent to which the firm can transform its product into an 'essential input' for customers, it can more easily reduce the cyclical variability of the product's demand, for example by expanding its portfolio of long-term contracts. Third, in a slowly growing or declining market, it is generally easier to increase sales to existing customers by product upgrading than to expand the customer base.

Extensive empirical research on competitive strategy in hostile environments bears these presumptions out.[17] The main results of this research can be summarized as follows:

— successful firms in highly competitive industries devote considerable efforts to market segmentation by concentrating sales on growth segments, being selective about distribution channels, and developing close links with clients and distributors;
— these firms make market segmentation effective by developing and improving differentiated products: that is, high quality, innovative products responding to specific customer requirements and requiring focused (rather than large-scale) R&D and marketing;[18]
— at the same time, successful firms defend their relative cost position, primarily through the careful co-ordination of manufacturing with product policy.

IV. Focused manufacturing

Though considered effective from a marketing point of view, the segmentation strategies recommended above have frequently been criticized on two grounds:

— that firms implementing such strategies are particularly vulnerable to changes in product specifications or customer requirements, and hence need high levels of manufacturing flexibility;
— that this flexibility, combined with the inevitably small volume achievable on any particular market segment, prevents them from using large-scale production techniques, undermining their relative cost position and hence their profitability.

However, a better conceptual understanding of manufacturing management, combined with advances in manufacturing technology, have drastically altered this perspective, increasing both the attractiveness and viability of niche strategies.

Central to analytical developments in this area are the concepts of 'focused manufacturing' and of 'postponed product differentiation'.[19] These can be summarized as follows:

— an increase in product differentiation and customization is inevitable, given greater competitive pressures;
— however, to maintain cost discipline, reduce inventories, and reap economies of scale (both in manufacturing and design) differentiation should be concentrated in the final stages of production or

distribution, i.e. 'postponed'; operational research techniques have been developed for determining the optimal stage at which differentiation should occur;
— a particularly effective way of postponing differentiation is to utilize modular design: this allows economies of scale in the production and distribution of components while facilitating the design engineer's task in product development;
— given modular design and determination of the optimal stage for differentiation, manufacturing operations should be 'focused': that is, large-scale, high-volume operations should take place in one set of plants, while small-scale, low-volume operations take place in another.

While these approaches offer powerful operational research tools for minimizing the cost of product differentiation in terms of economies of scale, inventory, and design, new computer-based manufacturing technologies are changing the cost relativities associated with manufacturing volume.

In effect, the primary strategic significance of the technologies associated with Computer Aided Design (CAD)/Computer Aided Manufacture (CAM) lies in their 'potential for reversing the trend toward more cost-efficient but inflexible production units. This potential stems from their ability to loosen the ever-tighter integration of product with process.'[20]

Three features of these technologies are particularly important here.[21] To begin with, Computer Aided Design permits significant reductions in the time and skills required for designing, engineering, and testing complex products, hence reducing the fixed costs associated with product customization and flexibility strategies.

Secondly, the integration of Computer Aided Design with Computer Aided Manufacturing is cutting the lead times and costs involved in going from product design to tooling, while the use of 'group technology' algorithms for optimizing process layout and scheduling has significantly reduced the number of work stations, machining units, and internal transport mechanisms needed for any given level of manufacturing flexibility.

Finally, the development of increasingly sophisticated, programmable, general purpose machines and assembly devices (such as computer numerically controlled machine tools, robots, and flexible manufacturing systems), and the growing user-friendliness and standardization of their software have led to greater flexibility in several key dimensions of the manufacturing process:

— mix flexibility: the processing at any one time of a mix of different parts loosely related to each other;

- parts flexibility: the addition of parts to the mix and the removal of parts from the mix over time;
- routing flexibility: the dynamic assignment of parts to machines— for example, the re-routing of a given part if a machine used in its production is incapacitated;
- design-change flexibility: the fast implementation of engineering design changes for a particular part;
- volume flexibility: the accommodation of shifts in volume for a particular part.[22]

The highly successful use by Japanese firms of all kinds of advanced manufacturing technologies as part of broader market segmentation/ product flexibility strategies has been widely documented.[23] Equally, there is evidence of intensive use of these technologies by a number of Scandinavian producers—primarily oriented to high-quality, or niche markets—and by small- and medium-sized Italian firms operating in markets characterized by rapid changes in fashion, e.g., furniture, textiles and clothing, footwear.[24] However, recent data on sales of automated manufacturing equipment suggest that its use is now becoming widespread throughout the advanced industrial economies, though major international disparities in penetration levels are likely to persist, reflecting both macro-economic and industrial-structure differences between countries.

V. Industrial specialization

Finally, the shift towards more technologically integrated companies —operating in differentiated product markets, and supporting these markets through flexible manufacturing strategies—has implications for the *degree of firm specialization*, particularly as regards:

- the relations between firms and their suppliers, i.e. the organization of the purchasing function;
- the degree of vertical integration, i.e. the balance between activities carried on in-house and out-house;
- the distribution of the risks associated with capacity expansion and new product development.

V.1. Purchasing

Traditionally, purchasing has had the lowest prestige among the main functional areas associated with the management of manufacturing firms, and has typically been decentralized to the plant level. Over the last decade, however, there has been a drastic change in the importance and organization of the purchasing function, largely as a result of four factors:

- temporary shortages of critical new materials and growing concern about their long-term availability;
- declining margins on output markets, leading firms to seek reductions in input costs;
- the rising cost and risk associated with holding inventories of inputs, leading firms to demand shorter delivery delays and more rapid response times from suppliers;
- greater emphasis on the technological level and quality of purchased inputs, reflecting the growing importance of technological competition.

One common response in companies to this situation has been to establish a strong central procurement function, both for purchasing those supply items in common use among decentralized divisions, and for setting mandatory standards for purchasing operations at division and plant level.[25] This yields three major benefits to the firm.

First, it permits the development of specialized competence in the purchasing area. The fixed costs associated with developing this competence, and with systematizing and updating information on sources of supply and terms of availability, are generally regarded to be high —too high for duplication to be acceptable even within large firms. As companies seek to widen their search for purchased inputs—for example, by extending it to foreign markets—the importance of properly organizing this search function rises.

Second, centralized purchasing increases the firm's bargaining power relative to suppliers and permits it to *reap economies of scale*. This is particularly important given the increase in concentration and in supplier organization which has occurred in certain raw-materials markets. Equally, the greater dependence of firms pursuing product market segmentation strategies on the quality and cost of purchased items may—in the absence of strong centralized procurement— make them vulnerable to 'vertical squeeze'.

Finally, it is widely recognized that centralized procurement changes the *nature of buyer/supplier relations*. To begin with, by centralizing purchases at the corporate level, the company will often command attention of higher management levels in supplier organizations that are themselves large and decentralized. This leads to greater recognition of longer-term commitments on both sides, facilitating long-term contracts, capacity expansion, or product development by the supplier, and joint efforts to design customized or particularly advanced inputs.[26]

Advances in information technology have also played a major role in this regard. Thus, the development of on-line data banks containing information on the availability and cost of standard industrial inputs in a broad range of countries and markets has encouraged firms to expand the horizons and sophistication of their search process. At the same time, the use of computer systems to schedule centrally the flow of inputs from multiple sites to decentralized plants has increased the potential for 'un-bundling' the purchase, storage, and use functions, and for removing the bulk of procurement from plant locations.[27]

V.2. Vertical integration

The greater efficiency of the purchasing function in and of itself alters the optimal degree of vertical integration—that is, the balance between in-house and out-house activity. By changing the relative costs associated with producing an intermediate input in-house as against sourcing it from an independent supplier, improved purchasing should lead to greater reliance on outside supply. In practice, centralized purchasing has played an important role in implementing policies of 'de-verticalization', but the primary stimulus for these policies has come from:

- the increased pace of technological change in a broad range of component industries;
- the greater risks associated with capacity expansion.

The impact of accelerated technological change on vertical integration, though uneven across industries, seems generally to be the result of two conflicting pressures. In effect, accelerating technological change raises the costs and risks associated with vertical integration, but makes it increasingly important for downstream firms to have 'a tap' on upstream technology.

Thus, accelerated technological change is usually associated with considerable uncertainty about which technology, design, and features will ultimately prove successful. Responding to this uncertainty involves diversifying the technology portfolio by expanding the range of products on which R&D is carried out and experimenting with alternative product variants and sources of supply.

In these circumstances, vertical integration can be extremely risky, since:

- high minimum R&D commitments may be required for competitively producing the product in-house;
- vertical integration can involve heavy cost absorption, detracting funds from the firm's principal product lines;
- the integrated firm risks being locked-in to an inefficient in-house supply source, reducing the attractiveness of its product;
- integrated firms can cut themselves off from the research, know-how, and engineering support of their suppliers—without having the resources required to duplicate these internally.

Though these are potent factors making for 'de-verticalization'—
especially in a period of deteriorating margins and of frequent appeals
to balance-sheet discipline—accelerating technical change also increases
the importance for firms of having 'a tap' into component technology.
This is true for three major reasons:

- there are often substantial design interdependences between the
  component and the final product, so a firm which waits for new
  components to come on market before redesigning its products
  may find it difficult to retain technological leadership;
- given strong design interdependences, a unique component technology may be required to achieve product differentiation in the final
  market; conversely, firms relying on standard components may not
  be able to differentiate their product fully;
- if, as a result of technological change, the component is an increasingly important part of the final product, unintegrated firms can be
  liable to 'vertical squeeze': i.e. supplying firms may exploit their
  bargaining power to secure more favourable terms, or extensive
  vertical integration by the firm's competitors or by component
  suppliers may foreclose the firm from the components market.

The response to these conflicting factors depends to a large extent
on the size of the firm and on its market position. However, sectoral
information suggests that, on balance, firms are adopting a much
more selective attitude to vertical integration than in the past, in
particular by:

- limiting vertical integration to critical components which are unavailable on the open market and are central to the firm's product
  strategy;
- finding contractual alternatives to vertical integration for the bulk
  of their input requirements.

In general, the contractual alternatives to vertical integration involve
types of 'quasi-integration', long-term contracts, joint development
projects, or horizontal joint ventures for the development and supply
of components. Unfortunately, few empirical studies are available on
the use of these co-ordination mechanisms, though they seem particularly widespread in the sourcing of innovative capital goods.

V.3. Capacity expansion

Even abstracting from the impact of accelerating technological change,
pressures for a redefinition of firms' specialization also come from the
growing risks associated with *capacity expansion*.[28] Basic factors here
include:

— *slow and erratic demand growth*, which makes it difficult to absorb
capacity overshoots and reduces the disposal value of surplus assets;
— *entry by new producers*, especially state-owned enterprises and
heavily subsidized firms (particularly, but not only, in the NICs);
in a number of industries these new producers are expanding capacity
independently of demand, increasing the risk to their commercially-
minded competitors;
— *higher capital costs*, making it increasingly important to avoid excess
capacity.

Under these conditions, any firm considering capacity expansion—
horizontal or vertical—must carefully examine the balance-sheet
implications, especially as regards operating leverage and the share of
fixed costs in the firm's total cost structure. Given cautious, risk-
averse behaviour, it becomes extremely attractive to transfer capacity
expansion risks on to third parties.[29]

This transfer basically involves two parameters: the distribution of
balance-sheet risk on the one hand, and the distribution of control over
capacity on the other. Three strategic alternatives can be identified in
this regard:

— transferring both risk and control;
— pooling risk but retaining (some part of) control;
— transferring risk while retaining control.

The first of these options is, of course, that associated with pure
arm's length transactions between customer and supplier. In these
transactions, the customer firm retains control only to the extent of
its market power. The customer firm may, however, seek some insurance against changes in availability by using a mix of long-term contracts
and spot purchases for the item.

The second of these options is typically associated (a) with horizontal joint ventures between firms purchasing common inputs (where the
firms jointly finance the capacity used to produce the inputs and share
the risks and control over the operation)[30] and (b) with joint ventures
between supplier and customer firms (which, by permitting better
information transmission, may reduce risks to both parties).

The third option involves using the firms' strategic assets to obtain
control over an operation the firm does not own. For example, multinational mining corporations[31] increasingly focus on supplying technology, management, and access to distribution and marketing while the
host countries, particularly developing ones, assume ownership
(frequently by borrowing from international financial markets) and
most of the financial risk. Similarly, firms in manufacturing activity
markets can, by carefully identifying their strategic assets, 'unbundle'

these assets from those involving the greater balance-sheet risk and increase the leverage these assets provide.

Summarizing, greater attention to purchasing, to technological co-operation, and to risk-avoidance are likely to lead to a replacement of internal co-ordination mechanisms *within* firms by contractual relations between firms. These relations will exploit inter-firm technology, production, and marketing complementarities—so that they may well be associated with a major unbundling of these functions at a corporate level.

VI. Summary and concluding remarks

We have therefore tried to identify some components of successful corporate strategies in a deteriorating macro-economic climate. Clearly, these strategies will not be uniformly appropriate for *all* industrial markets, but we think that, subject to suitable modifications, they can serve in a broad range of cases. Equally, even where they are appropriate, not all firms will apply them. But it seems reasonable to suppose that those which do will grow more rapidly and set the framework within which public policy will have to act. Four central features will characterize these firms' strategies:

- *technological integration*: though diversified, they will have integrated their products and processes around a central technological base, and will centre their R&D effects on this base;
- *market segmentation*: they will use this technology base to supply products and services which meet specific, possibly customized, requirements;
- *manufacturing focus*: to maintain their relative cost position, they will seek the maximum scale economies, but reconcile this with product strategies through 'postponed product differentiation' and the use of advanced manufacturing technologies;
- *industrial specialization*: through greater reliance on centralized procurement and vertical and horizontal contractual relations, they will more narrowly focus their in-house activities, thus reducing their exposure to risk.

These changes certainly do not exhaust the adjustments underway in corporate behaviour. In effect, the industrial firm is a complex administrative system involving an interaction of four basic levels: the firm's relation to the financial and capital markets; to the (internal and external) labour markets; to the product markets; and to the state. In this chapter we have focused on the firm's relation to product markets; but important changes at any one level, if they are to be sustained, require matching changes both in the other levels of the firm's relation to the environment and in the firm's administrative structure. The intellectual challenge today is to integrate what we know about each of these levels in a comprehensive picture of the industrial response to prolonged economic crisis.

Notes and Sources

[1] See, for example, N. Gavioli, 'La fabbrica dell' Alternativa', *Mondo Economico*, June 1982.

[2] See, for example, D. K. Clifford, 'Thriving in a Recession', *Harvard Business Review*, July–August 1977; W. Hall, 'Survival Strategies in a Hostile Environment', *Harvard Business Review*, 1980.

[3] Compare, for instance, W. Hall, who deals mainly with assembly-oriented manufacturing firms, ibid; Boston Consulting Group, who deal with 'commodity-like' markets in *Les Impasses Concurrentielles*, 1982; and J. P. Ponssard and B. Collomb on competitive strategies in the cement industry in 'Creative Management in Mature Capital Intensive Industries', paper presented at the Creative and Innovative Management Conference, Austin (Texas), 1982.

[4] See, for example, A. Kantrow, 'The Technology–Strategy Connection', *Harvard Business Review*, 1980; R. H. Hayes and W. J. Abernathy, 'Managing Our Way to Economic Decline', *Harvard Business Review*, July–August 1980; W. J. Abernathy, K. B. Clark, and A. M. Kantrow, 'The New Industrial Competition', *Harvard Business Review*, September–October 1981; C. Antonelli, *Cambiamento Technologico e Teoria dell' Impresa*, Loescher, Torino, 1981; D. Bitondo and A. Frohman, 'Linking Technological and Business Planning', *Research Management*, November 1981; and M. Porter, 'The Technological Dimension of Competitive Strategy', working paper, Harvard Graduate School of Business Administration, 1982.

[5] W. J. Abernathy, K. B. Clark, and A. M. Kantrow, op. cit., p. 70.

[6] OECD, *Trends in Science and Technology in the OECD Area During the 1970s: Resources Devoted to R&D*, September 1982, and *The Economist*, 6 November 1982.

[7] P. Mariti and R. Smiley, 'Joint Ventures', paper presented to the 1981 Conference of EARIE, Milan, 1981.

[8] See D. Bitondo and A. Frohman, op. cit., and R. N. Foster, 'Boosting the Payoff from R&D', *Research Management*, January 1982.

[9] R. Rummelt, 'Strategy, Structure and Financial Performance of the Fortune "500"', unpublished DBA dissertation, Harvard Business School, 1982, and B. R. Scott, 'The Industrial State: Old Myths and New Realities', *Harvard Business Review*, March–April 1973.

[10] M. S. Salter and W. A. Weinhold, *Diversification through Acquisition*, The Free Press, New York, 1979.

[11] For example, D. Channon, 'Strategy and Structure of British Enterprise', unpublished DBA dissertation, Harvard Business School, 1971; H. Thanheiser 'Strategy and Structure of German Enterprise', unpublished DBA dissertation, Harvard Business School, 1971; R. J. Pavan, 'Strategy and Structure of Italian Enterprise', unpublished dissertation, Harvard Business School, 1972; and C. F. Pratten, *A Comparison of the Performance of Swedish and UK Companies*, Cambridge University Press, 1976.

[12] As early as 1972 Hayes noted that ' "Synergy", the buzz-word of the Decade of Acquisitions, is now used, more often than not, with a rather derisive connotation. Executives today talk instead of "focus", "organisational competence" and "technical expertise".'; R. H. Hayes, 'New Emphasis on Divestment

HENRY ERGAS 341

Opportunities', *Harvard Business Review*, July–August 1980; on the impact of strategic planning methods see P. Haspeslagh, 'Portfolio Planning—Use and Limits', *Harvard Business Review*, January–February 1982.

[13] D. Chiplin and M. Wright, 'Divestment and Structural Change in UK Industry', *National Westminster Bank Quarterly Review*, February 1980.

[14] R. Vernon and W. Davidson, 'Foreign Production of Technology-Intensive Products by US-based Multinational Enterprises', working paper No. 79-5, Harvard Business School, 1979.

[15] N. Hood and S. Young, *Multinationals in Retreat*, Edinburgh University Press, 1982.

[16] 'Switching costs' are the fixed costs buyers face in changing suppliers, distinct from the relative price/performance of alternative suppliers' products. See M. Porter, *Competitive Strategy*, The Free Press, New York, 1980, chs. 1 and 6.

[17] See D. K. Clifford, op. cit.; R. Hamermesh, M. Anderson, and J. Harris, 'Strategies for Low Market Share Businesses', *Harvard Business Review*, May–June 1978; R. Hamermesh and S. Silk, 'How to Compete in Stagnant Businesses', *Harvard Business Review*, September–October 1979; W. Hall, 'Survival Strategies in a Hostile Environment', op. cit.; R. Buzzell and F. Wieseman, 'Successful Share-Building Strategies', *Harvard Business Review*, January–February 1981.

[18] Thus Hamermesh and Silk found that while there was little statistical relation between product quality, R&D intensity, and return on investment in high-growth industries, the marginal pay-off to higher product quality and R&D intensity in low-growth industries were very significant. Confirming this result, Buzzell and Wieseman found high pay-offs to improved marketing, particularly in industrial markets.

[19] See W. Skinner, 'The Focused Factory', *Harvard Business Review*, May–June 1974, and *Manufacturing in the Corporate Strategy*, Wiley, 1978; J. L. Haskett, 'Sweeping Changes in Distribution', *Harvard Business Review*, March–April 1983; and J. C. Tarondeau, *Produits et Technologies*, Dalloz, Paris, 1982.

[20] D. Gerwin, 'Do's and Don'ts of Computerised Manufacturing', *Harvard Business Review*, March–April 1982, p. 113.

[21] There is a very extensive technical literature on CAD/CAM. However, the economic significance of these technologies is particularly well highlighted in R. Gonenç, 'L'electronisation industrielle au Japon', *Sci. Soc. du Japon Contemporain*, No. 2, October 1982.

[22] D. Gerwin, op. cit., p. 114.

[23] See especially R. Gonenç, op. cit.; Y. Leclerc, 'Les PME Japonaises face à l'introduction des biens d'équipement automatisés', *Sci. Soc. du Japon Contemporain*, No. 2, October 1982; and JETRO (Japanese External Trade Research Organization), *Productivity and Quality Control*, New York, 1982.

[24] See Computer and Electronics Commission, *The Promotion of Robotics and CAD/CAM in Sweden*, Ministry of Industry (Sweden), 1981; and CESPE, *Innovazione e Ristrutturazione Nel Settore Delle Macchine Utensile*, Franco Angeli, Rome, 1981.

[25] See H. L. Davis, G. D. Eppem, and L. G. Mattsson, 'Critical Factors in Worldwide Purchasing', *Harvard Business Review*, November–December 1974; E. R. Corey, 'Should Companies Centralise Procurement?', *Harvard Business Review*, November–December 1978; and J. C. Tarondeau, *L'Acte d'Achat et la Politique d'Approvisionnement*, Editions d'Organisation, Paris, 1979.

[26] Another factor here is that automated processes typically require higher quality, more uniform inputs, produced to narrow manufacturing tolerances. To secure these inputs, customer firms almost invariably need to develop closer, more harmonious relations with their suppliers. It appears that the greater ease

with which Japanese manufacturers have been able to develop such relationships has been an important factor in their more widespread use of advanced manufacturing techniques.

[27] A well-known expert on industrial purchasing, E. R. Corey, considers this to be the most important factor in determining the future evolution of the procurement functional. See E. R. Corey, 'Should Companies Centralise Procurement?', op. cit., p. 110.

[28] See M. Porter, *Competitive Strategy*, op. cit., ch. 15; Leone and Mayer, 'Capacity Expansion Strategies', *Harvard Business Review*, 1980; and C. Oman, *New Forms of Foreign Direct Investment*, OECD, Paris, 1983.

[29] C. Oman, ibid.

[30] These ventures may be attractive when they facilitate oligopolistic coordination between firms, *independently* of their impact on capacity risks.

[31] See C. F. Bergsten, *American Multinationals and American Interests*, Brookings Institution, Washington DC, 1978; R. Mikesell, *New Patterns of World Mineral Development*, British North American Committee, New York, 1979; and especially C. Oman, op. cit.

XIII

Large Firms in the European Corporate Economy and Industrial Policy in the 1980s

PAUL A. GEROSKI AND ALEXIS JACQUEMIN*

I. Introduction

The current crisis in the advanced Western economies and the renewed emphasis on market discipline and viability in the policy thinking of many governments have reinforced the urgency felt by many for a carefully constructed and coherent industrial policy within the Community. In this context, large firms are controversial institutions. They have grown with the Common Market and helped to shape it. Today they are socially and politically important because of the number of people they influence, directly or indirectly, as employees, suppliers, and customers. Severely affected by the current crisis and having met with great difficulties in their adaptation to it, large firms are now embroiled in industrial policy discussions. On the one hand, as large centres of economic power whose actions have a large social impact, they are natural targets for policy implementation; on the other hand, their size *per se* may be the subject of policy action.

That large firms will be subject to attention from the viewpoint of implementation seems reasonable to us. The administrative costs of directing attention towards (and monitoring the subsequent response of) the several hundred largest firms in the Community are clearly much lower than the costs of a much broader-based policy aimed at many thousands of decision makers, despite the fact that strategic behaviour between administrators and large-firm managers may somewhat deflect the basic policy.[1] Much more important is the fact that the largest firms are directly responsible for a large share of output, investment, employment, and exports in the Community, and indirectly responsible for a good deal more, because of the vertical links between them and smaller firms from whom they subcontract or to whom they

* Paul Geroski, Lecturer, University of Southampton and Visiting Professor, Catholic University of Louvain. Alexis Jacquemin, Professor of Economics at the University of Louvain-la-Neuve and Senior Fellow, Centre for European Policy Studies.

supply other services. As a result, any policy which alters the output, investment, or employment decisions of these firms will have large multiplicative repercussions throughout the Community; and any policy relating to the conduct of firms that is co-operatively agreed upon and implemented with these several hundred largest firms will effectively apply to several thousand more.[2] For these reasons we shall assume that attention is to be focused on large firms for purposes of implementation and shall not concern ourselves with this topic in this chapter.

Rather, we shall address ourselves to the crucial industrial-policy question of elaborating a framework to evaluate the economic performance, internal structure, and corporate management of these large industrial enterprises in light of the present crisis. The framework we develop will be applied to the particular question of identifying policy actions within the limits of the Common Market, which could improve the efficiency of large-sized firms.

In Section II we first briefly review the argument relating firm-size to the responses called forth by the challenge of large markets perceived in the late 1950s and 1960s, and discuss the available evidence on these issues. We then show in what sense the current crisis presents a different challenge than the one which led to the emergence and growth of many of Europe's corporate giants. In Section III we discuss the appropriate current direction and implementation of industrial policy with respect to large corporations, identify the main internal and external constraints faced by these firms, and make policy proposals.

II. Large European corporate size: old and new issues

Even before Servan Schreiber's well-known book,[3] Europeans were obsessed with the small size of their firms compared to US and (latterly) Japanese rivals, and with the differences in performance widely thought to be associated with that size difference. The 'crisis' of the 1950s and 1960s was generally perceived to be that of meeting the challenge of large markets and fully exploiting economies of scale and other advantages of size:

. . . the creation of the European Common Market, with its open boundaries, has meant a profound change. Within the short period of ten years, barriers to free competition, whether consisting of customs duties, import quotas, the right of establishment, and so on, were largely torn down . . . Uncertainty increased because the environment was no longer stable.[4]

European firms were thought to have the incentive to become more competitive because of increasing competitive pressure from the US, Japan, and various Third World countries, as well as the newly enlarged 'home' market which opened up before them. In the realm of policy, the need was strongly felt to set up:

. . . a framework allowing European undertakings to acquire the size and means to confront . . . industrial dinosaurs. . . .[5]

. . . the aim to be achieved is to make the EC into an oligopolistic market. This is because it is concentration [which] . . . result[s] in the advantages that are to be expected from the restructuring of European industry. . . .[6]

Indeed, the challenge of such scale economies was felt to be so strong that many were willing to sacrifice potential diversity of products by encouraging the concentration of production on a relatively small range of goods.

The response to this mutation was a sustained period of intense merger activity, starting in the late 1950s throughout the advanced Western economies, and reaching historic peaks in the middle and late 1960s.[7] The principal result was that the largest firms' share in overall Community economic activity increased quite substantially. In Britain for example, the share of net output of the largest 100 firms rose from 27 per cent to slightly over 40 per cent from 1953 to 1970. By 1965 the 50 largest European firms had 15 per cent of Community gross output; by 1979 this had doubled to 30 per cent.[8] In countries like West Germany and the UK, during this period, the increased concentration of activity in markets (however narrowly defined) was mainly due to merger activity.[9] Widespread increases in market concentration appear to have occurred elsewhere in Europe as well.

This private-sector activity was evidently prompted by a number of factors, including the increased competitive challenge facing the Community and the enhanced opportunity that the EC's formation gave for exploiting scale economies. However, whatever the details of private-sector motivation, the 1960s also saw a happy congruence between private and public goals. Weak anti-merger laws, their even weaker implementation,[10] and the occasional enthusiastic government promotion of particular mergers fuelled the merger boom and hastened the transformation of the European economy.

The arguments concerning the advantages of size, which can and were used to justify such policy actions directed at increasing firm size, are well known.

The clearest and least ambiguous advantage of size is that it is necessary to exploit various scale economies, allowing production to occur at lower real input cost per unit of output. Such economies arise from advantages to division of labour, overcoming indivisibility, and so on. However, it is worth recalling that these economies are more restricted in scope than is thought in popular discussions, for purely pecuniary economies can decrease average costs with size. That is, lower input prices could be based not on the economies of bulk transactions, but rather on enhanced bargaining power which does not lower real input costs, but merely redistributes profit between firms. Along with advantages in large-scale production of a single product, 'economies of scope' or cost complementarities in producing different goods may give rise to multi-product economies of scale, encouraging the production of a broad range of goods in greater or less depth (depending on the interaction between product-specific scale economies and such economies of scope). Aside from obvious examples like joint products, such complementarities may be created by shared indivisible inputs, or inputs with a public good character.[11]

A second advantage of size is a little less well known. Quite clearly there are costs to making transactions in a market, and, in certain situations, it is reasonable to replace a market by an institution which co-ordinates such transactions internally.[12] The necessity to bargain in bilateral monopoly situations (with the specialist behind and in front), the uncertainty generated about final demand, the excessive inventories that need to be held, and so on, can easily overwhelm whatever division of labour advantages there are. Hence, situations which are characterized by a great deal of uncertainty, bilateral monopoly or oligopoly, information asymmetries, incentive problems, high monitoring costs, sunk costs, etc., are all liable to be situations in which use of a market to make transactions will be too costly, and in which it may prove more efficient to internalize these transactions within an institution, such as a privately owned firm. Appreciable firm size may thus be a response to market failure, and quite independent of scale economies.[13]

Of course, to exploit such advantages, the 'internal market' must be designed in a manner capable of dealing with the market failure which brought it into existence. The appropriate structure of a firm depends upon its strategy, broadly conceived to encompass product range, scale, growth method, geographical spread, and so on.[14] One of the simplest structural distinctions that can be made is between functionally organized and divisionalized firms: i.e. between firms whose activities are organized on the basis of functional divisions, like marketing, production, and so on, and firms whose activities are organized on the basis of products. The advantages of the former are that the division of labour can be exploited within functional groups. However, in larger, more diverse firms such advantages are generally outweighed by the disadvantages of overlong communication lines and overloading of top executives, who are forced to neglect strategic thinking in order to monitor and administer the organization. In this case, divisionalization and the creation of independent profit centres will facilitate the control which the top can exert over the entire organization, thus freeing top management from the bulk of administrative tasks without sacrifice. It has been noted in several empirical studies that divisionalization (when it is the appropriate strategy for a firm to pursue) is an organizational response which can increase a firm's efficiency and profit.[15] Indeed, one of the extreme manifestations of this view argues that '. . . the modern corporation is mainly to be understood as a product of a series of organizational innovations that have had the purpose and effect of economizing on transaction costs . . .'.[16]

Contrasting with the previous arguments, it must be recalled that, well before the onset of the 1970s crisis, numerous econometric studies put into question the view that higher profitability, faster growth, and more intensive research activity could be expected from larger European firms.[17] Most authors find no (or a negative) relationship between firm size and profitability. Very similar results have been obtained by looking at the consequence of mergers, which usually appear to result in lower profits and sometimes even in lower growth for the acquiring firm.[18] Since these effects have been observed for as long as seven years after a merger, it is hard to argue that they reflect transitional costs. Certainly more direct studies of the productivity effects of mergers confirm that the efficiency claims in favour of most mergers are either imaginary or else vastly inflated.[19] Direct estimation and measurement of single and multi-product scale economies similarly confirms that few of the larger plants of more heavily concentrated industries can be justified by scale economies.[20] The growth rate of sales seems to be more or less independent of firm size, which suggests that no comparative dynamic efficiencies exist. More direct study of this in the voluminous literature on the relation between firm size and research and development[21] has produced a large amount of evidence '. . . against the hypothesis that a necessary condition for technological change and progressiveness is that firms should be large scale and dominate the market in which they operate . . .'.[22]

Whatever the advantages of large firms in terms of productive efficiency or dynamic efficiency, it is also fairly clear that those with large plants have far more than their share of industrial relations trouble. They also face subtle and difficult problems in the designing of jobs which are sufficiently enriching and stimulating to bring forth maximum effort on the part of the work-force without the need to pay enormous wage premiums.[23] Finally, little evidence has emerged to contradict the view that large firms simply aim to stabilize their returns, and that they use their positions of market power to cushion, reduce, or transfer risk.[24] This suggests that large firms frequently can be very slow to make a decision, and very averse to risk in outlook.[25] Perhaps the best examples of this are to be found in the all-important areas of technical dynamism. It is common to find that corporate research projects are unduly conservative, that basic breakthroughs occur in university or government laboratories, or via private individuals,[26] and that large firms can be slower to adapt to new technology than medium-sized firms.[27]

Whether or not one wishes to characterize the events of the late 1950s and 1960s as a crisis, there is no disputing that it was widely felt that competitiveness of European industry needed to be raised. The events of the 1970s are a different story. The characteristics of the current crisis are, at base, supply shocks:

. . . it is not the policy choices but rather the policy options that have worsened in the 1970s, with supply shocks driving the stagflationary process. . . .[28]

These shocks seem to be several in variety. One is clearly the large rise in raw material prices, with oil only the most obvious example. Apparently linked with this is a sharp slowdown in total factor productivity growth, and the growing incursion of various Third World or newly industrialized countries into traditional Western industries, such as steel or shipbuilding. In partial response to the lengthening stagflation, there have also been a series of quite radical changes or reversals in government policy (including, latterly, rises in interest rates to quite stupendous levels and sharp cutbacks in government spending) which can only have added to the confusion.[29] More generally, rapid and variable rates of inflation linked with a larger variability of relative prices, more erratic growth, and greater instability of exchange and interest rates, have generated a higher degree of uncertainty.

The policy and private sector response required to meet such shocks is fundamentally different from the 1960s. Important supply shocks require the ability to adapt to a new environment, to create and rapidly implement new techniques or methods of operation, and to shift resources into new fields and away from traditional areas of activity. It is less a question of minimizing costs, given known techniques and fairly stable factor prices and product demand, but more one of finding and developing new techniques and products appropriate for very different factor price constellations and of shifting grounds of comparative advantage.[30] Indeed, in such cases, the need for flexible and reasonably rapid adjustment to new circumstances is liable to require some sacrifice of static efficiency; and the need to do things fairly rapidly impedes the intensive study and perfection needed to do them well.

Thus, the challenge of the 1970s requires a different response from that of the 1960s. What is more, it requires a response conditional on the response made to the earlier crisis, which led to the creation of the current giants of European industry. Indeed, today the European economy is dominated by a group of very large firms responsible for a very large share of aggregate activity however measured. In this respect, Europe is not different from the US and Japan: i.e both the relative and absolute size of European firms now compares with US firms, while in absolute size they are much larger than Japanese rivals. Also, like the US and Japan, European industry is dominated by fairly stable groups of large firms, except that they vary in national origins. But despite these similarities, performance of large European firms, and especially their rates of return, is definitely inferior to either of their sets of rivals. (See the Appendix for preliminary information at the overall and industrial levels.)

These results suggest that size is not sufficient for greater efficiency in large firms. The poor performance of European firms would not, it appears, be ameliorated by direct policy action on size, encouraging the growth of large firms. In view of the crisis it is liable to be more productive to concentrate attention on how a firm's structure and business-mix spread risks; on whether its internal organization favours flexibility and encourages the taking of important strategic choices; on the appropriateness of its non-price as well as price policies in the face of world competition; on whether its social, political, and legal environment offers an incentive scheme and not a paralyzing constraint; and so on.[31]

III. Corporate structure and new industrial policy

Large corporate size is neither a 'necessary' condition for efficient adaptation to large changes in the economic environment, nor a 'sufficient' condition for efficient adaptation to a more static environment in which competitive efficiency in the usual sense is important. It therefore follows that while large firms are important from the point of view of implementation, size is not a major focus of policy action from the point of view of policy goals. Clearly, a large multi-unit business enterprise must replace small traditional enterprises where scale economies and efficiencies due to learning are important. This is also true where administrative co-ordination permits better achievement of lower costs and higher profits through internal allocation mechanisms than co-ordination by the invisible hands of market mechanisms. In industries and activities which use capital intensive, technologically advanced, high-volume processes of production, which require specialized skills, and other services and facilities lowering the cost of transacting business, and which demand a careful co-ordination of output flows to meet the demands of national and world markets, a predominance of large industrial groups may well be a necessary condition for static and dynamic efficiency.[32] But this necessary condition must be supplemented by others ensuring the realization of the potential for high-quality decision making within such large multi-unit enterprises. Given that large size is not a prerequisite in many industries, there is also a clear need for policy intervention which allows small firms to overcome external barriers to their dynamism. This may involve restraining or rationalizing their large rivals; it may also involve eliminating certain forms of conduct (such as entry-deterring tactics) on the part of larger firms. For reasons of efficient policy implementation, this policy for small firms should often operate via the large firms. Such a policy would operate towards encouraging limited joint ventures and subcontracting, with appropriate access to research facilities. It may also contain a strong countercyclical element, since small firms generally bear much of the brunt of crises and suffer from a high degree of asymmetry in risk bearing.

Returning to large firms, we feel that the first important step in developing industrial policy is the definiton of general rules or presumptions for policy, rather than determining policy on a 'case-by-case', 'firm-by-firm' basis. The need for such an orientation is fairly clear. Case-by-case or firm-by-firm policies are generally neither coherent nor successful, and only leave policy makers the option of reacting to events (frequently when it is too late) rather than acting in anticipation. One positive virtue of general policy rules which sould be stressed is that their adoption defines a clear policy intervention strategy. This is good for private decision makers, whatever its details, since it eliminates a major source of uncertainty from their decision-making environment.

Further, it seems to us that the design of general policy rules can interact more fully with the basic concerns of corporate strategy. Today firms face and try to overcome a hostile environment by selecting appropriate strategies, and several large corporations are indeed demonstrating their ability to survive and even to prosper when industry trends change from favourable to unfavourable. Corporations like Daimler-Benz, Michelin, Caterpillar, and General Motors, by coupling low-cost position and high-quality feature-differentiated products, have enjoyed relatively good performance.[33] A broad range of currently fashionable business 'success formulas' have been replaced by a narrower range of strategic choices involving aggressive reinvestment in their base business, use of incremental capital for meaningful resegmentation and limited diversification moves, and the creation of new internal administrative structures and mechanisms to recognize and effectively manage such repositioning.[34] But, simultaneous with such successes, many qualified observers have observed that the past several years have seen corporate managers show a marked deterioration in competitive dynamism. The most vigorous criticisms have come from US specialists in management. In a recent publication, a selection of articles published in the *Harvard Business Review*,[35] various authors argued that managers have been guided by a too-myopic concern with the quarterly profit statement and have ignored long-term investment in technological and manufacturing excellence. According to R. Hayes and W. Abernathy[36] '. . . it is not adequate to attribute the current difficulties of American business to such factors as the rapacity of OPEC, deficiencies in government tax and monetary policies, and the proliferation of regulations'. A more basic explanation is 'a failure of management'. They observe, especially in large organizations, an increase in management behaviour that could be regarded as excessively cautious, even passive. Maximum short-run financial returns have become the overriding criteria, coupled with a search for reducing total corporate risk by parcelling it out among a sufficiently large number of separate product lines, businesses, or technologies.

Several implications follow from this view. One cause for concern is the tendency of managers to integrate backward because of apparent short-term rewards, with the danger of paralysing the long-term ability of the company to keep on top of technological change. 'Long-term contracts and long-term relationships with suppliers can achieve many of the same cost benefits as backward integration without calling into question a company's ability to innovate or respond to innovation.'[37] An example is the contrast between US and European strategies in automobile manufactures. It has been argued that the American auto industry's huge investment in automating the manufacture of cast-iron brake drums probably delayed by more than five years its transition to disc brakes. Similarly, American managers seem to restrict investment in process development to only those items likely to reduce costs in the short run, while European managers have a strong commitment to increasing market share through internal development of advanced process technology. Top American management has also increasingly allocated time and energy to the process of corporate acquisitions and mergers. 'The great bulk of this merger activity appears to have been absolutely wasted in terms of generating economic benefits for stock-holders.'[38]

This recent research, based on a vast amount of case studies, underlines the limits of the 'spontaneous' answers which corporate strategy can be expected to give to the current crisis. The large European corporations do not necessarily share all of the previously mentioned problems of the US giants; on the other hand, they are affected by supplementary difficulties. It therefore seems appropriate that a broad line of policy outlook ought to be drawn according to the specific constraints large European firms face. Here we shall distinguish between internal and external constraints.

III.1. Internal problems

We have stressed that in industrial activities where large multi-unit enterprises are 'necessary', size is not 'sufficient' to guarantee reasonable performance. Indeed, many large European industrial groups, although often in the right sectors, are unable to exploit their position for several reasons originating within these firms themselves.

First, until recently, corporate control in Europe appears to have been held in the hands of holding companies, banks, and families who have supplied generation after generation of managers for European business enterprises.[39] Thus, the concept of 'managerial capitalism' does not fit the European experience as closely as it does the American. An implication of this is that large diversified groups are often not organized according to a recognizable 'industrial logic' with strong complementarities or close substitution between the many activities of the firm. Instead many are organized along a 'financial' or 'personal' logic, based upon the intra- and inter-sectoral control linkages created by the owners of capital rather than by professional managers. For example, recent case studies[40] have shown a noticeable weakness of European financial groups whose managers show too great a dependence on short-term financial measurements, like return on investment, and are led to exercise a control that extends well beyond the financial sphere which is their expertise. In this vein it is worthwhile noticing that to explain the current difficulties met by the American management, some authors[41] refer to a shift in functional background of newly appointed top executives of the largest corporations. Statistics show that since the mid-1950s there has been a rather substantial increase in the percentage of new company presidents whose primary interests and expertise lie in the financial and legal areas.

The difficult problem here is the reshaping of these large enterprises in order to give them a better internal coherence (a difficulty currently confronting the French nationalized groups, for example). This is related to the problem presented by the many state-owned (or highly regulated) enterprises among the largest European firms, such as British Petroleum, Renault, and Salzgitter. Neglecting oversimplified views like: 'public enterprises will do the best for the general economic welfare' or 'government is less efficient than private business because the profit motive is absent', the real policy problem with regard to these firms is how to combine the responsibility of public interest with the necessity of meeting the conditions of competition. The existing statistical evidence suggests that the large European public industrial enterprises which compete with privately owned rivals do not exhibit a comparable profitability. This is, of course, only part of the overall performance by which these firms must be judged.[42] But it does once again raise some of the problems which emerge from the separation of ownership and control. Clearly, owners divorced from immediate business decision-making, and lacking appropriate training (whether they be civil servants, bank officers, or grandmothers who own large blocks of shares) ought to be more thoroughly imbued with the demands and necessities of strategic competitive decision-making, including the tight interaction between the R&D, production, financial, and commercial functions within the corporation.

A second problem to be faced is the internal organization adopted by these large undertakings. According to recent studies,[43] by 1970 a multidivisional structure (in which a general office is responsible for measuring performance, planning and allocating resources, and co-ordinating and controlling the operating units) was adopted by 54 of the largest companies in France, by 50 in Germany, and by 57 in the UK, compared with 80 in the US. Once it is recognized that industrial efficiency and competitiveness rely to a great extent on the way in which people and resources are organized within the firm, it is clear that various historical delays and national characteristics, which have retarded industrial management in the area of internal structure, continue to impose constraints on the implantation of appropriate strategic policies.[44] From this point of view, the Japanese experience is rather interesting.

In contrast with familiar systems (in which labour allocation among the various productive activities in the economy is based mainly on a very imperfect labour mobility among firms and groups through hiring and firing), labour allocation in the Japanese economy occurs to a large extent within the internal labour market of the large multi-unit enterprises.[45] By assuring the employee stability of employment, the large Japanese firm has acquired, in compensation, the right to flexibly operate its internal labour market, organizing movement among various jobs and preventing each worker's skill and know-how from being limited and fixed to any simple type of job. This labour allocation appears to have a number of further advantages. For example, the resources needed to implement diversification plans required by a changing environment are usually not procured from outside, but come from accumulated technologies, know-how, and knowledge of the firm's resources.

The key to successful diversification depends on discovering the linkage of its main business to any prospective new one and planning to fully employ the firm's related management resources in its development.[46]

This diversification strategy contrasts with the usual 'product portfolio management model', which stresses purely financial (e.g. risk pooling) advantages and encourages conglomerate diversification too far away from a common technological base.

Indeed, what could be called 'human resource management' is one of the main explanations of the high adaptive capability of the large Japanese industrial groups. It contrasts sharply with the sluggish European adjustment, with the poor industrial relations records of many large European firms, and with the reluctance of many of them to invest heavily in training manpower. Such considerations lead to the argument that the current productivity problem will not be solved through monetary policy nor through more investment in research and development, but will be remedied only when firms learn how to manage people in such a way that they can work together more effectively.[47] This requires top management to communicate effectively, to share responsibility with employees, to invest in training them in new technical skills, to develop a sense of collective responsibility, and to explore new methods of reconciling industrial change with preservation of minimal security for the individual.

At the Community level, a corresponding industrial relations and social policy is clearly needed. It is not possible to restructure industry and redeploy workers without a programme for the creation of new jobs and the retraining of workers. Europe also needs an industrial relations charter, including flexibility of training and some form of worker–management communication and worker participation. The European charter should also make provisions for equity participation, profit-sharing, and contracts between employers and unions. Finally, a European industrial education policy is needed to stimulate more transnational co-operation, joint research projects, and exchange among universities, technical colleges, and industry. Despite the worst unemployment for forty years, there is an acute shortage of skilled people at critical levels.[48]

III.2. External constraints

As noted earlier, previous policy encouraged increases in market concentration. This has led to competition between large national firms, supported (in diverse ways) by their governments, and to fragmentation of the internal European market. Preferences for national production have been particularly strong, and have developed through discriminatory purchasing by public and semi-public sectors in the Community. By contrast, the firms organized on a European scale are often treated with suspicion by various governments, reluctant to allow them the benefits of their various industrial policy instruments, such as financing, R&D aid, public contracts, norms and standards, and so on. Furthermore, these firms are confronted by heterogeneous and sometimes conflicting national institutions, regulations, and policies, at the commercial, fiscal, social, and political level. As the European Commission noted,[49]

. . . for a company to organize itself on a European scale, which ought to be a considerable asset in the Common Market, in fact, turns out to be a handicap.

Various policy considerations can be advanced to deal with this situation. First, the EC authorities could offer better information on the Common Market as a whole, operating as a substitute for the information that would be provided by a fully competitive capital market, and reducing the uncertainties due to the diversity and the variability of national policies.

They must also provide existing large firms with organizational structures and corporate forms corresponding to transnational European enterprises, and give them sufficient advantages to compensate for the obstacles established by national governments' actions in their own narrow self-interest. It is within this perspective that one should view the proposals for directives on the harmonization of company law and those aiming to create new juridical forms, such as the European company, the European co-operation grouping, and the common enterprise. (The same applies to the directives relating to industrial property, fiscal law, and capital markets.) All these regulations must be conceived as presenting to potential trans-European firms the means to overcome some national discriminatory policies. One explanation of the difficulties met by the large European firms in trying to exploit the potential embodied in their size is the necessity to find indirect legal methods to achieve what could not be obtained straightforwardly. Such indirect means have spawned a number of multiple international holding companies, a structure which complicates and makes costly real economic, commercial, social, fiscal, and technical integration. It is therefore not surprising that the few efforts to create transnational European groups since the Treaty of Rome have failed (e.g. Dunlop-Pirelli, Fiat-Citroën, Agfa-Gevaert, Unidata, etc.) Similarly, it is necessary to develop a more positive common trade policy, as required by Article 113 of the Treaty, e.g. by setting common technical and quality norms for the whole of the Community. It is also necessary to see European preferences with regard to public procurement (most often linked with pace-making, high-technology industrial activities) as calling for the creation of a European public agency charged with the co-ordination and execution of an integrated supply policy.

A second external constraint often faced by European firms is illustrated by the recent agreement between the Dutch firm Philips and the US firm ATT. In common with its many predecessors, this appears to suggest that for many large European firms, the best partner for a joint venture is not a private or public firm belonging to one of the EC countries, but a foreign one—American or Japanese. This partly reflects the difficulties of trans-European co-operation and the lack of official encouragement given to intra-European co-ordination and development.

The corresponding policy response must be based not on European nationalism, but on willingness to provide positive fiscal, financial, commercial, and social conditions within the EC as a whole. Flexible, problem-oriented joint ventures can also be used as the means by which temporary structural alterations within industries can be made to meet specific challenges. The often-discussed Japanese government-sponsored co-operative R&D projects are a useful experience in this spirit. They substitute for what seems to be achieved in the United States as a by-product of well-functioning markets for experienced scientific and engineering manpower.[50] The Japanese joint research in very large-scale integration electronic chips, in flexible manufacturing systems, and in biogenetic engineering, while not totally satisfying, has still enhanced the diffusion of information on sophisticated technologies, so that more firms can compete with world-class technologies. However, such joint research has not been allowed to weaken strong competition among the participating firms in the product market, avoiding joint actions in manufacturing and markets.[51] Furthermore, the corresponding institutional mechanisms work through incentive rather than control.[52] The ESPRIT programme, financed on a fifty–fifty basis by the Community and industry, is the first EC effort along the same lines. The 1984 work plan covers ESPRIT's five main sectors: advanced microelectronics, software technology, information processing, office automation, and computer-integrated manufacturing.

A further and more disputable step in this line would be to co-ordinate various activities of large firms (such as large investment in production, in R&D, or in commercial strategies) at the European level in order to avoid duplication and the consequent emergence of excess capacity. As is well-known, the tendency towards overshooting in investment may be particularly strong when there is unexpected change in the trend of demand or the pattern of production, and when investments must be made in large indivisible chunks in order to exploit economies of scale. Furthermore, as shown by Scherer,[53] certain aspects of oligopolistic market structure and conduct appear to increase the observed instability of investment within industries. At the European level, characterized by a still poor circulation of information, the risks of capacity expansion are amplified, as illustrated by the situation in synthetic fibres, shipbuilding, and a number of other industries. The idea of a co-ordinating system was first mooted in the proposed 'Fourth Medium-Term Economic Programme' which stated that the Commission could require notification at regular intervals concerning main investment projects in certain capital-intensive sectors. This was suppressed in the Council decision of 14 March 1974, but ought to be the subject of further study.

The basic ideas behind these suggestions of how to deal with external constraints concern the relative merits of different degrees of decentralization and centralization in the interrelationships between the large multi-unit European enterprises, and the role of policy in the organization of specified high-technology industrial activities, such as chemicals, aerospace, computers, and advanced electronics. In a world characterized by large externalities and public goods, what is the optimal degree of co-ordination and co-operative behaviour between firms? How can one ensure that the co-operation for cost-saving contractual arrangements among competitors and for developing various capabilities will not degenerate into collusion in the product market? If the appropriate policy is to encourage co-ordination between isolated private decision makers in some dimensions, linkages between industrial and antitrust policies are clearly necessary to preserve competition and efficiency. This necessarily requires regular interaction between policy makers and decision makers which, in turn, requires the design of simple, relatively fast monitoring mechanisms. Regular transfers of information and a system in which policy makers must respond to proposals within relatively short periods of time are mandatory. The shortness of the time period clearly depends on the regularity of the transfers.

This leads to the fact that there is still a need for policies to achieve the integration of the Common Market as well as to reduce the market imperfections that impede the starting of new activities, especially by small businesses.[54] From that point of view, anti-trust legislation is a form of industrial policy. Contrary to what is sometimes argued, we think that a relaxation of the European competition policy would not strengthen the Community's industrial policy. The existing rules are already very flexible (especially through the distinction between 'good and bad cartels' in Article 85 §3 and the absence of any preventive control of mergers). Any change aimed at organizing more cartels and favouring more mergers will not help provide domestic restructuring, nor will it improve European competitiveness in exports or imports.[55] Furthermore, many business practices, briefly discussed earlier and adopted in reaction to the crisis, do not necessarily improve the overall welfare of the industry or the economy. Confusion between an effective individual industrial corporate strategy and a collectively efficient industrial policy is quite dangerous and is, unfortunately, quite frequently made. For example, product differentiation and market segmentation can lead to monopolistic competition and various forms of non-price competition whose welfare consequences are very doubtful.[56] 'Customization' of transactions, in the Okun's sense, could reduce dynamic adaptations to new techniques and innovation, and lead to dangerous biases in the range of choice open to consumers. Finding contractual alternatives to vertical integration can show a firm's will to use its market power to transfer risk (while retaining control) on to the shoulders of less powerful, but nevertheless efficient, partners. Centralized purchasing as well as centralized selling can allow bargaining processes that do not lead to an efficient allocation of resources.[57] More generally, the study of 'strategic behaviour' adopted by established firms to take up advanced positions and deter entry suggests that private and social valuation can widely differ.[58]

IV. Conclusion

We think that the European authorities, in designing general industrial policies, must certainly come to a better understanding of the prerequisites and mechanisms for creating resources, how companies and markets function, and which constraints affect European corporate strategies. But by the same token, these public authorities must not forget that theirs is the public interest and that it is incumbent on them to take a longer and broader view, making visible, when necessary, the invisible hand needed to guide the convergence of interests.

Appendix: The largest corporations in the EC

The 100 largest corporations in the EC occupy a central place in its economy, accounting for about 30 per cent of the output and employment of the manufacturing sector in 1976. (Taking into account the role of subcontracting subsidiaries, spillover effects, and so on, obviously magnifies this figure.) Moreover, there has been an increase in the overall concentration of sales, assets, and employment controlled by them since at least 1965. The 50 largest companies alone increased their share of manufacturing output from 15 per cent in 1965 to 30 per cent in 1979. Rough approximations for 1980 suggest that they account for about 20 per cent of EC industrial employment. Finally, it appears that about 30 per cent of EC exports are actually internal transactions carried out within these 100 firms.[59]

Furthermore, if we limit ourselves to these largest manufacturing companies in the EC, ranked in terms of sales, it is clear that the distribution of these firms by country of origin has remained very stable over time. Table 13.1 shows that since the early 1960s (at least) about 85 to 90 per cent of these firms have originated from only three of the nine EC countries: the United Kingdom, West Germany, and France, with roughly two-thirds in the top 100 coming from the

TABLE 13.1

Country location of the largest 100 firms in the EC:
the number of firms from the largest 100 originating from various EC countries

	1963		1971		1976		1980	
	Manu-facturing	Industrial	Manu-facturing	Industrial	Manu-facturing	Industrial	Manu-facturing	Industrial
United Kingdom	44/55	41	40	39/40	37	30/31	39	33/34
West Germany	25	27	26/27	26/27	28	30	27	30
France	18	17	18	18	21	24	20	20
Italy	6	7	5/6	6/7	6/7	7/8	5/6	5/6
Netherlands	4/5	5	5/6	5	5/6	5	5/6	5/6
Belgium	1	2	3/4	3/4	2	3	3	6
Luxembourg	1	1	1	1	0	0	0	0

Notes: The double entry indicates ambiguity; e.g. Royal Dutch Shell. The distinction between 'manufacturing' and 'industrial' is that the latter includes oil and mining activities.
Source: *Fortune*, August 1964, 1972, 1977, 1981.

first two. If oil is included and we consider the industrial sector as a whole, there is less inequality between the United Kingdom and West Germany.[60] The oil companies have recently been entering into these ranks more and more, with their numbers growing from seven to sixteen between 1971 and 1980. Of these sixteen, ten are US subsidiaries. This temporal stability can also be seen by noting that about 60 per cent of the top 100 European firms in 1963 were still on the list in 1980.

At the broadly defined industrial level, the distribution of these top 100 in 1980 shows some interesting variation when cross-classified by country. Table 13.2 shows that the large French firms are fairly evenly spread, while those of West Germany are concentrated in chemicals, iron and steel, automobiles, and metals, and those of the United Kingdom in petroleum, food, and tobacco. West Germany particularly shows a marked concentration: its 27 per cent of the largest EC firms are clustered into slightly more than 50 per cent of the thirteen broadly defined sectors or industries. What is more, the identity of the five largest EC firms in petroleum, electrical construction, and chemicals has not changed over the period 1974 to 1980.[61] Overall the changes noticed in other sectors are usually shifts within the ten top firms. It seems clear that the current patterns of national specialization, as reflected in the dominance of certain large firms, is broadly similar to that of the early 1960s.

To what extent is this picture of dominance unique to the European economy? Comparing these 100 largest European companies with the 100 largest in the US and Japan, it appears that the five largest US firms plus the ten largest European firms commanded sales approximately equal to that of the largest 100 Japanese firms in total. By contrast, the ratio of output to worker in these 100 Japanese firms is about 720.000 FF compared to 530.000 FF and 430.000 FF for the 100 largest US and European firms respectively. On the basis of the 1973 *Fortune* list, 19 (or approximately 38 per cent) of the world's 50 largest industrial companies were based in the EC, representing 27 per cent of the group's total sales and 22 per cent of its net income. By 1980, 19 EC firms were again on this list, but accounting for 35 per cent of total sales and 25 per cent of net income. In the same year the US had 23 firms on the list, accounting for 53 per cent of total sales and 61 per cent of net income. While there do not appear to be any major discrepancies in size between European and US firms, and while both sets of firms are much larger in size than the leading Japanese firms, the entire picture is changed if we look at their comparative performance.[62]

This latter observation can be confirmed in a second way. Among the world's fifty largest companies in 1980, those which were American had an average net income to sales ratio of 5.03 per cent. For Japanese

TABLE 13.2
Percentage of the top 100 EC firms in 1980 by industry and country

Industry	UK	FRG	France	Italy	Belgium	Netherlands	Luxembourg
Petroleum	.143	.096	.15	.18	.222	.083	—
Food	.206	—	.05	—	—	.083	—
Electronics	.063	.096	.15	—	—	.332	—
Steel and iron	.063	.128	.15	.18	.222	.166	1.00
Chemicals	.063	.288	.05	.18	.333	.332	—
Automobiles	.063	.160	.15	.18	—	—	—
Tobacco, paper, cosmetics	.127	—	—	—	—	—	—
Metals	.095	.128	.05	—	.222	—	—
Coal-mining	.063	.064	.05	—	—	—	—
Construction materials	—	—	.05	—	—	—	—
Rubber	.015	—	.05	.09	—	—	—
Office machinery, computers	.030	.032	.05	.18	—	—	—
Aircraft	.063	—	.05	—	—	—	—
Total	100%	100%	100%	100%	100%	100%	100%

Note: The classification of firms into industry is a little arbitrary for the more diversified firms; therefore, the table must be considered as qualitatively correct.
  Source: Fortune.

firms within that group the figure was 3.92 per cent, while European firms only achieved 3.15 per cent. Inspecting the 100 largest firms in each of the three geographical areas produces a very similar picture: 4.8 per cent, 2.7 per cent, and 1.4 per cent respectively for the US, Japan, and Europe. For European firms, a reduction in this ratio compared to previous years was evident, coming mainly from a deterioration in performance of British and French companies. On the other hand, the figures for European firms may be unduly high because of government subsidies.

Of course, the ratio of net incomes to sales is a performance measure of less than universal appeal, but these figures seem consistent with a wealth of anecdotes and casual observations concerning inferior European performance. What is important from our point of view is to emphasize that this observed poor relative performance by European firms appears not to be caused by unfavourable size differentials *vis-à-vis* the US, and cannot be due to lack of exploitation of the advantages of size *vis-à-vis* Japan.

The material discussed in the previous two paragraphs was derived from highly aggregated figures. From an analysis of the data published by *Fortune*, further information has been obtained for twelve broadly defined industries and the five leading firms within them for Europe, Japan, and the US (where available).[63] In general, the same results turn up at this more disaggregated level. On the one hand, European firms are of comparable size to the US (except in petroleum) and generally much larger than Japanese firms. Furthermore, the degree of size asymmetry (measured by the Herfindahl index) among the European leaders for nine comparable industries is not obviously and systematically different, it is lower among the US leaders in five cases, but higher in four cases. (From 1974 to 1980 there has been no marked increase in this index.)

On the other hand, European performance is inferior to that of Japanese and US firms (drink is one exception), although there is much more variation in performance than in size. Finally, it is worth remarking that, with a few exceptions—such as food and drink, the five largest European firms in each industry have different national origins. Thus, while the concentration within each sector is roughly comparable across the European countries, the cultural, legal, and policy differences within European industries must imply a significantly lower cohesiveness than implied by the concentration levels for US or Japanese industries.

Notes and Sources

[1] This problem of strategic interaction between regulator and regulated has been the subject of much attention in the US. One manifestation is the so-called

'Averch-Johnson' effect, in which firms regulated by rate of return inflate their capital base. For general discussions see W. Shepherd and C. Wilcox, *Public Policies towards Business*, R. Irwin, London, 1975, Part IV.

[2] As a slight digression, it is worth noting that much the same point applies to the implementation of macro-economic policy, since there is a close relationship between the decisions of these large firms and the movement of macroeconomic variables. It is clear that the short- and long-term supply decisions of these firms, as well as managerial preferences and their emphasis on research activity, affect macro-economic growth and development if only because most investment and research undertaken privately is undertaken by these firms. A 'micro-to-macro model' of the Swedish economy has been developed at the Industrial Institute for Economic and Social Research of Stockholm. For recent theoretical work in this area, see H. Odagiri, *The Theory of Growth in a Corporate Economy*, Cambridge University Press, 1981, and T. K. Ng. 'A micro–macroeconomic analysis based on a representative firm', *Economica*, No. 49, May 1981, pp. 121–39.

[3] J. J. Servan-Schreiber, *Le défi américain*, Denoël, Paris, 1976.

[4] A. Jacquemin and H. de Jong, *European Industrial Organization*, Macmillan and Wiley, London and New York, 1977, pp. 6 f.

[5] R. Lecourt, 'Concentrations et fusions, facteurs d'intégration', *Revue du Marché Commun*, January–February 1968.

[6] A. Marshal, 'Nécessité économique des concentrations et fusions', *Revue du Marché Commun*, January–February 1968.

[7] See the description in F. Scherer, *Industrial Market Structure and Economic Performance*, Rand McNally, Chicago, 1980, 2nd edition (pp. 118–41), or D. Mueller, *The Determinants and Effects of Mergers*, Oelgeschlagere, Gunn, Cambridge (Mass.), 1980.

[8] G. Locksley and T. Ward, 'Concentration in Manufacturing in the EEC', *Cambridge Journal of Economics*, No. 3, 1979.

[9] For example, see L. Hannah and J. Kay, *Concentration in Modern Industry*, Macmillan, London, 1977, for UK and J. Müller 'The impact of mergers concentration: study of eleven West German industries', *Journal of Industrial Economics*, December 1976, pp. 113–32, for West Germany.

[10] e.g., A. Jacquemin, 'Concentration and mergers in the EEC: towards a system of control', in K. Hopt (ed.), *European Merger and Control*, W. de Gruytere, Berlin, 1982. The comparison with the US is revealing here. See F. Scherer, *Industrial Market Structure and Economic Performance*, ch. 20, op. cit.

[11] For an outstanding discussion see F. Scherer, ibid., pp. 81–8. For empirical evidence on multiplant economies, see F. Scherer, A. Beckenstein, E. Kaufer, and R. Murphy, *The Economics of Multiplant Operation: An International Comparison Study*, Harvard University Press, Cambridge (Mass.), 1975. On a theoretical plane see W. Baumol, J. Panzar, and R. Willig, *Contestable Markets and the Theory of Industry Structure*, Harcourt, Brace and Jovanovich, New York, 1982.

[12] See O. Williamson, *Markets and Hierarchies*, The Free Press, New York, 1970, or O. Williamson, 'The modern corporation: origins, evolution, attitudes', *Journal of Economic Literature*, No. XIX, December 1981, pp. 1537–68. The classic discussions of R. Coase, 'The nature of the firm', *Economica*, No. 4, 1937, pp. 386–405, and F. Hayek, 'The use of knowledge in society', *American Economic Review*, No. 35, September (1945), pp. 519–30, are also worth consulting, as is K. Arrow, *The Limits of Organization*, W. W. Norton, New York, 1974.

[13] But see A. Jacquemin and M. Boyer, 'Organizational and industrial actions for efficiency and market power', *Département de Science Economique*, Université de Montréal, Cahier 8234, 1982.

[14] The material is drawn from A. Chandler, *Strategy and Structure*, MIT Press, Cambridge (Mass.), 1962, *The Visible Hand*, Belknap Press, Cambridge, 1977, and 'The M-form: Industrial group, American style', *European Economic Review*, Vol. 19, No. 1, 1982; O. Williamson, *Corporate Control and Business Behaviour*, Prentice Hall, Englewood Cliffs, 1970, *Markets and Hierarchies*, The Free Press, New York, 1975, and 'The modern corporation: origins, evolution, attitudes', *Journal of Economic Literature*, No. 19, December 1981, pp. 1537–68; and R. Caves, 'Corporate strategy and structure', *Journal of Economic Literature*, No. 18, March 1980, pp. 64–92.

[15] See J. Cable and P. Steer, 'Internal organization and profit: an empirical analysis of large US companies', *Journal of Industrial Economics*, No. 27, 1978, and H. Armour and D. Teece, 'Organizational structure and economic performance: a test of the multidivisional hypothesis', *Bell Journal of Economics*, No. 9, 1978.

[16] O. Williamson, 'The modern corporation: origins, evolution, attitudes', *Journal of Economic Literature*, No. 19, op. cit.

[17] F. Scherer, *Industrial Market Structure and Economic Performance*, op. cit., and A. Jacquemin and H. de Jong, *European Industrial Organization*, op. cit.

[18] G. Meeks, *Disappointing Marriage: a Study of the Gains from Merger*, Cambridge University Press, 1977, and D. Mueller, *The Determinants and Effects of Mergers*, op. cit.

[19] K. Cowling, P. Stoneman, J. Cubbins, S. Danberger, J. Cable, G. Hall, and P. Dutton, *Mergers and Economic Performance*, Cambridge University Press, 1981, and J. Cubbin and G. Hall, 'The use of real cost as an efficiency measure: an application to merging firms', *Journal of Industrial Economics*, No. 28, September 1979, pp. 73–88.

[20] F. Scherer, *Industrial Market Structure and Economic Performance*, op. cit., pp. 81–118.

[21] Also see F. Scherer, ibid., ch. 15, for a careful statement and summary, or M. Kamien and N. Schwartz, *Market Structure and Innovation*, Cambridge University Press, 1982, ch. 3.

[22] Ch. Kennedy and A. P. Thirlwall, 'Surveys in applied economics: technical progress', *The Economic Journal*, March 1972.

[23] S. Prais, 'The strike-proneness of large plants in Britain', *Journal of the Royal Statistical Society*, Series A, No. 14, Part 3, 1978, pp. 368–84; F. Scherer, 'Industrial structure, scale economies and worker alienation', in R. Masson and P. Qualls (eds), *Essays on Industrial Organization in Honor of J. S. Bain*, Ballinger, Cambridge (Mass.), 1976.

[24] R. Caves and B. Yamey, 'Risk and corporate rates of return: comment', *Quarterly Journal of Economics*, August 1971.

[25] In a poorly documented area, Y. Aharoni, *The foreign investment decision process*, Harvard Graduate School of Business Administration, Boston, 1966, is a classic study of how limited decisions about setting up foreign subsidiaries can be.

[26] e.g., K. Schott, 'Investment in private industrial research and development in Britain', *Journal of Industrial Economics*, No. 25, December 1976, pp. 81–99, or C. Freeman, 'The role of small firms in innovation in the UK since 1945', *Committee of Inquiry on Small Firms, Research Report No. 6*, London, 1971, and the classic study by J. Jewkes, D. Sawers, and R. Stillerman, *The Sources of Invention*, W. W. Norton, New York, 1969.

[27] e.g., the adoption of the oxygen furnace in the US steel industry. See, among others, W. Adams and J. Dirlam, 'Steel imports and vertical oligopoly power', *American Economic Review*, No. 54, September 1964; W. Adams and J. Dirlam, 'Big Steel, invention and innovation', *Quarterly Journal of Economics*,

No. 80, May 1966, pp. 167–89; G. Maddalz and P. Knight, 'International diffusion of technological change: a case study of the oxygen steel making process', *Economic Journal*, No. 77, September 1967, pp. 531–58; J. Sumrall, 'Diffusion of the basic oxygen furnace in the US steel industry', *Journal of Industrial Economics*, No. 30, June 1982, pp. 421–38; S. Oster, 'The diffusion of innovation among steel firms: the basic oxygen furnace', *Bell Journal of Economics*, No. 13, Spring 1982, pp. 45–6.

[28] J. Sachs, 'Stabilization in the world economy: scope and scepticism', *American Economic Review*, No. 2, May 1982, p. 57.

[29] That frequent and radical changes in government policy can be detrimental to investment is elegantly argued in S. Nickell, 'The influence of uncertainty on investment, *Economic Journal*, No. 87, March 1977, pp. 45–70.

[30] e.g., see R. Nelson, 'Assessing private enterprise: an exegesis of tangled doctrine', *Bell Journal of Economics*, No. 12, Spring 1981, pp. 93–111, who makes clear that the usual arguments in favour of free markets do not apply in the same way (or with such compulsion) when the economic system is undergoing fundamental change.

[31] An interesting recent illustration of the role played by the non-price variables in the competitiveness of European industry is given in the 1979 *Report* published by European Management Forum, Geneva. They argue that German and Swiss companies excel in terms of sales and marketing acumen, the quality of their products, their ability to deliver on time, and the dependability of their after-sales services and that Germany and Switzerland benefit from a financially dynamic environment, little political polarization, and a high degree of socio-political consensus and stability. On the contrary, France is rated highly on its industrial efficacy resulting from major restructuring efforts, but is perceived to lack commercial spirit and to have a too strong socio-political polarization.

[32] D. Encaoua and A. Jacquemin, in 'Organizational efficiency and monopoly power: the case of French industrial groups', *European Economic Review*, No. 19, 1982, have shown that the large French industrial groups operate in industries whose characteristics call for internal co-ordination and require an organizational type which these groups can provide.

[33] M. Porter, *Competitive Strategy: Techniques for Analyzing Industries and Competitors*, The Free Press, New York, 1980.

[34] W. Hall, 'Survival strategies in a hostile environment', in *Harvard Business Review, Survival Strategies for American Industry*, Wiley, New York, 1983. See also T. Peters and R. Waterman, *In Search of Excellence; Lessons from America's Best-Run Companies*, Harper and Row, New York, 1982.

[35] *Survival Strategies for American Industry*, ibid.

[36] R. Hayes and W. Abernathy, 'Managing our way to economic decline', in *Harvard Business Review, Survival Strategies for American Industry*, Wiley, New York, 1983. See also W. Abernathy, K. Clark, and A. Kantrow, 'The new industrial competition', ibid.

[37] R. Hayes and W. Abernathy, ibid.

[38] Ibid., p. 31. These authors use the expression 'merger mania', as do B. Bluestone and B. Harrison, *The De-industrialization of America*, Basic Books, New York, 1982. This last 'radical' analysis contains a whole chapter on 'conglomeration and the new managerialism'.

[39] A. Jacquemin and E. de Ghellinck, 'Familial control, size and performance in the largest French firms', *European Economic Review*, No. 17, January 1980.

[40] Ph. de Woot, *Recherches sur les groupes, premiers résultats*, Université Catholique de Louvain, July 1982.

[41] R. Hayes and W. Abernathy, 'Managing our way to economic decline', in *Harvard Business Review, Survival Strategies for American Industry*, op. cit.

[42] e.g., W. Adams and J. Dirlam, 'Private planning and social efficiency', in A. Jacquemin and H. de Jong (eds), *Markets, Corporate Behaviour and the State*, M. Nijhoff, The Hague, 1976.

[43] A. Chandler and H. Daems, *Managerial Hierarchies*, Harvard University Press, Cambridge (Mass.), 1981.

[44] Commission of the EC, *The competitiveness of European Community Industry*, III/387/82, Brussels, March 1982.

[45] e.g., M. Aoki, 'Managerialism revised', *International Journal of Industrial Organization*, No. 1, 1983. K. Imai and H. Itami, 'The Firm and Market in Japan', *Institute of Business Research*, Discussion Paper No. 104, Hitotsubashi University, Tokyo, 1982.

[46] See also Y. Hideki, A. Sakuma, H. Itami, and T. Kagono, *The Diversification Strategy of the Japanese Firms,* Nihon Keizai Shinibun, Tokyo, 1981.

[47] W. Ouchi, *Theory Z, How American Business can meet the Japanese Challenge*, Avon Books, New York, 1982. This author rightly underlines that the difficult objective is to separate the culturally specific principles from those universally applicable to economic organization. He concludes that some forms of the essential characteristics of Japanese companies must be transferable. It is indeed the case, as exemplified by the various US companies which have improved their performance after having been taken over by Japanese firms or after adopting Japanese practices, such as 'free flowing' assembly lines or quality control circles.

[48] D. Nicholson, 'Why Europe needs an industrial policy', *Chief Executive*, No. 13, Autumn 1980.

[49] Commission of the EC, *The competitiveness of European Community industry*, op. cit.

[50] G. Saxonhouse, 'Japanese high technology, government policy and evolving comparative advantage', mimeo, University of Michigan, Ann Arbor, 1982. Recently, however, ten US corporations (including Control Data, Advanced Micro Devices, Motorola, and Honeywell) have decided, with the agreement of the Department of Justice, to start a co-operative R&D project, called 'Microelectronics and computer technology', in the field of components. The aim is to safeguard the American pre-eminence in micro-electronics.

[51] It is interesting to note that the organizer of the VSLI Research Association was subsequently recruited as an executive by IBM.

[52] US General Accounting Office, Report to the Chairman, Joint Economic Committee, US Congress, *Industrial Policy: Japan's Flexible Approach*, GAO/ID-82-32, 25 June 1982.

[53] F. Scherer, *Industrial Market Structure and Economic Performance*, op. cit., pp. 370–4.

[54] Proportionately the US has four times as many small businesses as the EC; during the past years over 60 per cent of all new jobs in the US were provided by newly started, small businesses employing less than twenty people. D. Nicholson, 'Why Europe needs an industrial policy', op. cit.

[55] Theoretical and empirical research shows that domestic concentration is likely to yield a higher level of imports than a competitive industry. The case of exports is less straightforward. For a recent survey, see A. Jacquemin, 'Imperfect market structure and international trade', *Kyklos*, No. 1, Spring 1982.

[56] R. Marris and D. Mueller have strongly argued that 'the possibility arises that the total cost of investment in non-price competition exceeds the benefits. There is simply no analogue to the invisible theorem for non-price competition.'

See 'The corporation, competition and the invisible hand', *Journal of Economic Literature*, No. 18, March 1980, p. 57.

[57] L. Johansen, 'The bargaining society and the inefficiency of bargaining', *Kyklos*, No. 32, 1979, shows how direct bargaining has a tendency to dissipate the gains-from-trade through strategic behaviour.

[58] For a survey where the roles of credible threats pre-commitments, and reputation effects are examined, see P. Geroski, D. Encaoua, and A. Jacquemin, 'Strategic competition and the persistence of dominant firms: a survey', in J. Stiglitz and F. Mathewson (eds.), *New Developments in Market Structure*, MIT Press and Macmillan, Cambridge (Mass.) and London, 1984.

[59] These last figures are derived from the Commission of the European Communities, 1982.

[60] As already noted by G. Locksley and T. Ward, 'Concentration in manufacturing in the EEC', *Cambridge Journal of Economics*, No. 3, 1979, by extending the coverage from manufacturing to total industry, the companies which are displaced are disproportionately UK concerns.

[61] This persistence has been noted elsewhere. See F. Scherer, *Industrial Market Structure and Economic Performance*, op. cit., pp. 45–56, and D. Mueller, 'The persistence of profits above the norm', *Economica*, No. 44, November 1977, pp. 369–80, for the US; A. Jacquemin and W. Saez, 'A comparison of the performance of the largest European and Japanese industrial firms', *Oxford Economic Papers*, 1976, for Europe.

[62] A recent study by A. Rugman, 'The internal markets and economic performance of European multinational enterprises', comparing the performance of the 50 largest European multinational enterprises and those of the 50 largest US multinationals, shows that the latter have both higher returns and lower standard deviations. See also, P. Bucksley, J. Dunning, and R. Pearce, 'An analysis of the growth and profitability of the world's largest firms, 1967 to 1977'. Both papers were presented at the Conference on 'The impact of Large Firms on the Performance of the European Economy', Brussels, June 1981. For an earlier international comparison, see W. Adams, 'International differences in corporate profitability', *Economica*, No. 43, November 1976, pp. 367–79.

[63] The precise details are easily obtained from various issues of *Fortune*. In the interest of space, the relevant tables are not presented here.

XIV

Towards Concerted Industrial Policies in the EC

PIERRE DEFRAIGNE*

The European Commission has every reason to view the proliferation of national industrial policies in the Community with concern: not only are they failing in their objectives, but they are also liable to result in a reversion to nationally divided markets within Europe. Thus they may not halt the slide of European industry, they may precipitate it by breaking up the Common Market.

I. EC measures inadequate

The EC is partly to blame for the present state of affairs. Ever since the Common Customs Tariff was established in 1958, the Community has been whittling it down through the Kennedy and Tokyo Rounds. This had the doubtless admirable purpose of opening up new markets to the EC exports in return, but it did not always take into account the need for tariff protection for the spearhead industries (a need which has become more marked with technological progress) and it particularly did not get to grips with non-tariff barriers at Community level.

Inadequate harmonization of laws and regulations (company law, taxation, and various consumer protection and environmental conservation arrangements), and lack of progress in opening up public-sector purchases, creating European standards in place of national ones, and unifying export credits has left the whole armoury of non-tariff trade barriers in the hands of the member states.

Not only has this slowed the growth of intra-Community trade in a number of major sectors (capital goods, telecommunications, construction, etc.), but the member states are now—in this period of crisis—using non-tariff barriers on occasions as the second line of defence (after the Common Customs Tariff and the Community's quantitative arrangements) against imports from third countries and from their Community partners. The need for this defence is now

---

* Chef de Cabinet to Viscount Davignon, Commission of the EC.

felt all the more keenly since the process of convergence of national economies in the EC has ground to a halt, mainly as a result of insufficiently vigorous and consistent macro-economic policies.

Twenty-five years after the inception of the Common Market there are still no European transnational groups, other than those that were already there (Shell, Unilever, and Philips). Those which tried to organize themselves at European level—Dunlop-Pirelli, Fiat-Citroën, Agfa-Gevaert, Unidata, MBB-Fokker, Estel—gave it up as a bad job.[1]

Thus, 'national champions' and the subsidiaries of American, Japanese, and Swiss multinationals hold the field today. Incidentally, some of the multinationals' subsidiaries have settled very nicely in the EC—e.g. Ford Europe, IBM Europe, ITT, Canon, and Sony[2]—which does not make it any easier to make a simple distinction between 'European' and 'non-European' companies.

This situation has come about mainly because the links between governments and the big firms are so close that the firms will think twice before cutting the umbilical cord and launching out on 'denationalized' trans-European schemes. A one-off joint venture with a Japanese or American competitor is a more attractive proposition: that way you make up your technological lag without foregoing the protectionist umbrella and/or the privileges (public-sector purchasing, R&D, major export contracts, tax relief, financial link-ups, etc.) accorded by the state. Consequently, as long as Europe fails to grant trans-European groups *de facto* preference at least equivalent to what the individual states accord their major industries, there will be no European groups.

II. National industrial policies

The individual countries' national industrial policies, though based on sometimes opposing doctrinal approaches, are much of a muchness. However, France's policy, which involves the nationalization of one-third of industrial value added and 90 per cent of bank credit, raises problems of a specific kind. The temptation to 'think national' is, a priori, stronger in the nationalized sector than in the private sector, even though it cannot be denied that even before nationalization Colbertism was in evidence in several sectors in France.

National industrial policies can be justified in the usual ways: external economies, increased returns to scale, the role of government (defence, transport, etc.), or the short-sightedness of the market (energy investment, environmental protection, fundamental research and development). But in practice industrial policies are usually either concessions extracted from governments by lobbies or last-ditch attempts to offset the failure of macro-economic policies (excessive interest rates and/or real wages, adverse exchange rates, etc.) or an environment disadvantageous to operators, where the apparent successes may hide unaccounted costs.

Instead of aiming at maximizing value added, these policies often give precedence to preserving jobs at any cost or creating jobs at the risk of impairing the firm's or the sector's competitiveness.

Where economies of scale would require going beyond the national market, national policies usually underpin 'national leaders' which, although they absorb public funds at the expense of smaller companies in the same sector, still fail to reach the size required by their real relevant market, which is European or world-wide. Since national policies are unable to use the combination of demand-pull and domestic competition (because the national markets are too small), they have to rely on 'technology-push' and 'pick-the-winners' operations, which are much more risky and often fail because they are incomplete.

Industrial policies based on extending public-sector industry further increases the risk of returning to national markets. There is a great temptation to try to kill two birds with one stone by earmarking public-sector purchasing (and even purchasing by state-aided private concerns), R&D funds, export subsidies, and so on for the nationalized corporations, even where these are supposedly 'competitive'. The combined position of principal shareholder and public authority affords opportunities for arbitrary state intervention which are extraordinarily hard to forego when the 'national leader' is not doing as well as expected. The brunt of such intervention falls on other domestic firms, which do not receive such support, as well as on foreign competitors.

Another risk of national policy is to give too much weight to maintaining *all* stages in a particular process within the country, rather than in the Community as a whole. In practice it is impossible for an average-sized national industry to excel in all stages of production. Attempting to do so may well prove to be very costly in terms of public resources. Furthermore, national attempts to create and sustain vertically integrated industries makes it impossible to find foreign partners, because they are afraid of being dominated by the nationalized partner.

What can and should the Community do in the face of these disturbing developments?

'Repressive' action   Although the Treaty of Rome skated lightly over the problems nationalization[3] could pose to the unity of the Common Market, the existing rules on obstacles to free movement (Article 30), abuses of dominant positions (Article 85 *et seq.*), public corporations (Article 90), and state aid (Article 92) do provide the Commission

with a battery of weapons for dealing with protectionism. Moreover, the Commission is constantly endeavouring to improve its instruments and working methods in all these areas. In this way it strengthens its bargaining power *vis-à-vis* the member states. However, there are limits to this approach. A government wishing to stimulate industrial investment, or to promote R&D and job creation, cannot be dissuaded simply by arguing that this is against the rules of the Treaty.

III. Promotion of a European strategy

The Commission has evolved an approach to negotiating with governments and industry to work out constructive alternatives. Some examples are given below.

III.1. Commodities sectors

Steel The Commission has pushed through a comprehensive, integrated policy focused on the progressive restructuring of the industry, using its powers under the European Coal and Steel Community (ECSC) Treaty. The measures comprise:

- external trade: voluntary export restraint by third countries;
- internal market organization: a system of production quotas and guidance prices in a still highly fluid European market;
- state aids: a code authorizing national aids in return for cutbacks in overcapacity and a return to profitability;
- steel investment loans:
- tide-over and retraining assistance for redundant steelworkers;
- low-interest loans for the redevelopment of steel-producing areas.

The steel industry's workforce has been reduced by over one-third in the past six years, so it is clear that restructuring is a hard practical fact. Further efforts in this direction are still required, however, because of falling demand and technological progress.

Oil refining As a result of the overcapacity in this sector, the Commission has recommended that companies should organize themselves in such a way as to reduce their capacities and that governments should not grant any further aid for the creation of new capacity.

Textiles Protection under the Multifibres Agreement is now coupled with a strict policy on national aids, which are only authorized if structural reorganization and profitability are the result.

Man-made fibres Anti-dumping measures *vis-à-vis* American fibres, on grounds of the two-tier pricing of natural gas in the United States, have given the industry a breathing-space in which to restructure. This it will definitely have to do, the Commission having banned all aid for new capacity. Overcapacity is a problem in the commodities sector generally (aluminium, zinc, petrochemicals, etc.), and a particularly critical one in capital-intensive undertakings. To deal with it companies may have to form crisis cartels, on which the Commission is now more open-minded than it used to be.

Shipbuilding   Shipyard subsidies were authorized by the Commission when European restructuring targets were set for the shipbuilding industry in 1977. However, as the EC is the world's biggest trading area and 90 per cent of EC trade with the rest of the world is seaborne, we have to preserve a basic strategic shipbuilding capacity.

III.2. Growth sectors

Information technology   A comprehensive growth strategy is being prepared with the companies and governments. Several operations are already in hand:

- *of the 'technology-push' kind*: the ESPRIT programme (European Strategic Programme for Research in Information Technology) for 'pre-competitive' technology has been mounted with the twelve largest European companies, but it is also open to small- and medium-sized firms, universities, and research institutes;
- *of the 'demand-pull' kind*: promoting European standards; deregulating and progressively opening-up public-sector telecommunications purchasing; installing prototype integrated digital networks for the European Institutions; promoting data banks and on-line networks (Euronet and Diane, Caddia);
- *Community funding*: the New Community Instrument (NCI) along with the European Investment Bank will fund major infra-structure and energy projects, innovation projects, and make loans to small- and medium-sized firms.

Videos   Voluntary-restraint agreements with Japan seem pointless if European producers are not able to supply European consumers with a product they want at a competitive price, which could be done through economies of scale and using the right technology.

Compact audio-discs   When a European producer brings out an entirely new product perfected by its own technology, the Community should give it adequate protection during the launching period—as it has now done for Philips.

Aircraft industry   Airbus-Industrie was set up at the initiative of industrialists and governments. It forms the basis for a European industry with a promising future in the field of civil aircraft construction. The Community as such is not directly involved, but its support for the venture is whole-hearted. The fact that only a few member states are involved in the project does not make it any less 'European'. European joint ventures do not necessarily have to involve all ten countries. It is perfectly conceivable that only three, four, or five countries and possibly (as in the case of Airbus) non-Community partners should be involved. It is important that the efforts of certain countries to make progress should not be blocked by others which have not yet attained a similar level of technology or do not wish to make the effort involved.

After a long battle with the Council, the Commission decided not to commit funds from the Community Budget to a helicopter research programme because the manufacturers were not willing to contribute matching amounts to prove their interest in the programme.

Motor vehicles Producers are anxious for effective Community protection against Japanese imports, given the limited success of the bilateral understandings. The Commission is making this conditional on the unification of the internal market being completed by the time that provisions for Community type-approval of vehicles from third countries are adopted. These provisions will be implemented, of course, in line with the commercial policy agreed on jointly. The Commission is also encouraging co-operation on components (engines, transmission, and accessories). Lastly, it is mindful that Community rules concerning the environment, consumer protection, and energy conservation need to be framed and implemented in such a way as to strengthen the position of Community industry.

Machine tools Japan has made its home market impenetrable for foreign competitors and simultaneously launched a fierce offensive concentrating on the numerically-controlled machine sector. In the face of this mounting Japanese competition the Community machine tool industry has turned to the Commission for help with its endeavour to strengthen its industrial base.

The Commission has decided to support the industry's efforts through measures designed:

— *on the supply side* to encourage structural adjustment (state aid and co-operation) and the spread of advanced technology in this sector (standardization, repercussions of ESPRIT), to help finance innovation through the NCI and the European Investment Bank (EIB), and to improve vocational training facilities;

— *on the demand side* to provide support in connection with market exploration, to encourage productive investment and the harmonization of user demand, and to help restore the balance of trade with Japan.

These selected examples from different sectors have several features in common: they are indicative of the efforts to achieve a single internal market, promote competitive structures and effective Community-wide competition, and secure the necessary minimum protection to allow national operations to be progressively integrated into a common approach.

For make no mistake, the choice today is not an abstract one between free trade and Community-level protectionism *per se*. It is one between national protectionism in all its forms—serving to buttress enterprises which are in danger of becoming dwarfed or obsolescent, and Community preference—which would provide European industry with the preconditions for an integrated market where competition can do its job of stimulation and selection. Admittedly, any form of protectionism can go too far and be counter-productive, but these risks can reasonably be expected to be much reduced in the case of Community preference because as long as there is competition *within* the Community this will mitigate the ill-effects. Thus Community preference can be more easily restrained and dismantled than national protectionism.

IV. New aspects of European industrial policy

The EC Treaty expected industrial integration to come about through market forces. The Treaty is rather helpless in the face of the national industrial policies and the mixed economies which most member states have developed in order to seek an answer to the economic crisis.

The process is further complicated by alternating governments in France and the UK which are doctrinally poles apart: reprivatization and deregulation here, nationalization and a voluntaristic industrial policy there. On the face of it, this does not leave much scope for Community measures requiring consensus, or even unanimity, as is the case under Article 235 of the Treaty of Rome.

However, it is the Community's job to identify the pre-conditions for successful national measures which may differ widely in both their means and their ends. There are three such pre-conditions:

(i) major restructuring and stimulation schemes must proceed via the Community, since they necessarily involve commercial policy, national aids, and concentration or co-operation relating to at least the whole Community market ('relevant market');

(ii) co-operation between government-owned and private enterprises is necessary at European Community level. But such co-operation, based on widely differing starting-points (market requirements on the one hand, government expectations on the other) is easier in a Community context (e.g. ESPRIT provides us with a fruitful co-operation between Thomson, ICL, Siemens, Olivetti, Plessey, and others;

(iii) there must be no threat of domination by the partner in a position to call on the backing of the public authorities and funds from the national budget. Here, too, the Community framework provides guarantees (rules on aids, free movement, and public contracts).

The Community can help to meet these pre-conditions by basing its strategy on three elements:

— unification of the Common Market by doing away with non-tariff barriers (NTBs) between member states in the sector in question, and ensuring that the various forms of extra-Community protection introduced by individual member states are 'Communitized';
— Community preference for European industry (European NTBs, co-ordinated public-sector procurement, R&D, export credit, access to the Community's financial instruments) and, where appropriate, 'topping-up' of trade protection (unbinding Common Customs Tariff (CCT) and quantitative arrangements);
— defining new ground rules for mixed economies in the Community.

This last assignment goes beyond the sectoral aspects of these strategies and takes us on to the general business environment. Although rates of interest, levels of wage costs, the cost and financing of the welfare system, labour market rigidity, company taxation, reduction of red tape, and the like are all admittedly important, we are concerned here with industrial policy aspects proper.

The main questions in this respect do not have simple answers— that would be too easy. But they do raise issues which should be thought through to help guide future action.

Firstly, could we agree (e.g. on the basis of Article 90 of the Treaty of Rome) on a code of conduct for mixed economies whereby the sovereignty of states would be subject to certain rules with regard to

— the criteria and conditions for nationalization and de-nationalization,
— transparency in dealings between government and public corporations (funding, public-sector purchasing, aid of various kinds),
— non-discrimination between nationalized corporations and private enterprises,
— Community arbitration in the event of disagreements between public authorities and enterprises?

Secondly, how are the non-European multinationals to be incorporated in a Community approach? To what extent should they benefit from Community preference, given their location in the Community?

The issue is extremely complex because it is not just a matter of owner-ship and management. There are a number of objective and behavioural factors which determine whether an undertaking is 'European' or 'non-European'.

For example, there is a complex range of possible situations:

— from multinationals merely setting up showrooms or assembly lines in Europe to European subsidiaries responsible for the entire production process from R&D to marketing;
— from companies which are subject to government-imposed con-straints where strategic supplies are concerned to companies which are not subject to such constraints;
— from multinationals benefitting from the R&D programmes or public contracts of a non-European country which is not prepared to grant the same advantages to European companies, to companies based in non-EC countries which would accept a reciprocal arrangement.

Community preference should therefore involve an adequate amount of discretion to ensure that it can be implemented gradually and in such a way that it is mainly the European groups which benefit, without excluding foreign firms which make a significant contribution to the development of the Community.

Thirdly, there is the question of alliances between European firms and 'foreign firms'—the Trojan Horse syndrome!

This raises still another question. Is it not the case that relations between the US, the EC, and Japan are now so enmeshed where indus-trial matters are concerned that an excessively restrictive Community preference policy would inevitably cause discrimination and tension, and might entail quite significant costs in some cases in the short-term? Perhaps the solution lies in better access for 'European' firms to public contracts or R&D programmes in the US and Japan on reasonable terms?

V. Concluding remarks

These are highly political questions that cannot be answered with reference to industrial policy alone. The implications of transferring certain responsibilities for industrial policy from the member states to the Community are twofold.

Firstly, Community industrial strategy would no doubt be more liberal within the Common Market than the continued juxtaposition of several national industrial policies would be, even if individual countries were to backtrack on their liberal traditions.

Secondly, such an industrial policy would also be more discriminating *vis-à-vis* the outside world than present Community practice though this would involve some cost as against the unrestrained international division of labour. The alternative would be a greater co-operation with our industrialized partners, but negotiated on the basis of reciprocal access to their own set of national preferences (public procurements and R&D programmes).

To this end, Europeans need to have sufficient confidence in themselves, and in each other.

This can be achieved in a broader framework embracing political co-operation and defence; in other words, if Europe becomes a real power.

Notes and Sources

[1] URENCO and Airbus-Industries are exceptions here. But they are not, strictly speaking, industrial groups, mainly because the legal instrument—the European limited company—still does not exist.

[2] Some of these companies have as many staff members in Europe as at home. Thus ITT has 20 employees per million dollars' sales in Europe compared with 18 at home. For Canon the figures are 12:12, for IBM 10:15, and for Sony 6:9, As for Ford Europe, it is the strong component of the whole group.

[3] Article 222: 'The Treaty shall in no way prejudice the rules in member states governing the system of property ownership.'